Global Perspectives on Teacher Performance Improvement

Osama Al-Mahdi
Bahrain Teachers College, University of Bahrain, Bahrain

Ted Purinton
Bahrain Teachers College, University of Bahrain, Bahrain

A volume in the Advances in Higher Education and Professional Development (AHEPD) Book Series

Published in the United States of America by
IGI Global
Information Science Reference (an imprint of IGI Global)
701 E. Chocolate Avenue
Hershey PA, USA 17033
Tel: 717-533-8845
Fax: 717-533-8661
E-mail: cust@igi-global.com
Web site: http://www.igi-global.com

Copyright © 2022 by IGI Global. All rights reserved. No part of this publication may be reproduced, stored or distributed in any form or by any means, electronic or mechanical, including photocopying, without written permission from the publisher.
Product or company names used in this set are for identification purposes only. Inclusion of the names of the products or companies does not indicate a claim of ownership by IGI Global of the trademark or registered trademark.

Library of Congress Cataloging-in-Publication Data

Names: Al-Mahdi, Osama, 1974- editor. | Purinton, Ted, editor.
Title: Global perspectives on teacher performance improvement / Osama
   Al-Mahdi, and Ted Purinton, editor.
Description: Hershey, PA : Information Science Reference, [2021] | Includes
   bibliographical references and index. | Summary: "The contributed
   chapters in this book examine the implementation of proven, high quality
   teacher professional development practices in unique environments around
   the world covering a wide range of issues such as from professional
   learning communities to teacher coaching and teacher professional
   development"-- Provided by publisher.
Identifiers: LCCN 2021043031 (print) | LCCN 2021043032 (ebook) | ISBN
   9781799892786 (Hardcover) | ISBN 9781799892793 (Paperback) | ISBN
   9781799892809 (eBook)
Subjects: LCSH: Teachers--In-service training--Cross-cultural studies. |
   Teachers--Training of--Cross-cultural studies. | Teacher effectiveness.
   | Education--Cross-cultural studies.
Classification: LCC LB1731 .G57 2021 (print) | LCC LB1731 (ebook) | DDC
   370.71/1--dc23/eng/20211021
LC record available at https://lccn.loc.gov/2021043031
LC ebook record available at https://lccn.loc.gov/2021043032

This book is published in the IGI Global book series Advances in Higher Education and Professional Development (AHEPD) (ISSN: 2327-6983; eISSN: 2327-6991)

British Cataloguing in Publication Data
A Cataloguing in Publication record for this book is available from the British Library.

All work contributed to this book is new, previously-unpublished material.
The views expressed in this book are those of the authors, but not necessarily of the publisher.

For electronic access to this publication, please contact: eresources@igi-global.com.

Advances in Higher Education and Professional Development (AHEPD) Book Series

ISSN:2327-6983
EISSN:2327-6991

Editor-in-Chief: Jared Keengwe University of North Dakota, USA

MISSION

As world economies continue to shift and change in response to global financial situations, job markets have begun to demand a more highly-skilled workforce. In many industries a college degree is the minimum requirement and further educational development is expected to advance. With these current trends in mind, the **Advances in Higher Education & Professional Development (AHEPD) Book Series** provides an outlet for researchers and academics to publish their research in these areas and to distribute these works to practitioners and other researchers.

AHEPD encompasses all research dealing with higher education pedagogy, development, and curriculum design, as well as all areas of professional development, regardless of focus.

COVERAGE

- Adult Education
- Assessment in Higher Education
- Career Training
- Coaching and Mentoring
- Continuing Professional Development
- Governance in Higher Education
- Higher Education Policy
- Pedagogy of Teaching Higher Education
- Vocational Education

IGI Global is currently accepting manuscripts for publication within this series. To submit a proposal for a volume in this series, please contact our Acquisition Editors at Acquisitions@igi-global.com or visit: http://www.igi-global.com/publish/.

The Advances in Higher Education and Professional Development (AHEPD) Book Series (ISSN 2327-6983) is published by IGI Global, 701 E. Chocolate Avenue, Hershey, PA 17033-1240, USA, www.igi-global.com. This series is composed of titles available for purchase individually; each title is edited to be contextually exclusive from any other title within the series. For pricing and ordering information please visit http://www.igi-global.com/book-series/advances-higher-education-professional-development/73681. Postmaster: Send all address changes to above address. Copyright © 2022 IGI Global. All rights, including translation in other languages reserved by the publisher. No part of this series may be reproduced or used in any form or by any means – graphics, electronic, or mechanical, including photocopying, recording, taping, or information and retrieval systems – without written permission from the publisher, except for non commercial, educational use, including classroom teaching purposes. The views expressed in this series are those of the authors, but not necessarily of IGI Global.

Titles in this Series

For a list of additional titles in this series, please visit:
www.igi-global.com/book-series/advances-higher-education-professional-development/73681

Implementing a Virtual Coaching Model for Teacher Professional Development
Suzanne Myers (University of Kansas, USA) Amber Rowland (University of Kansas, USA) and Martha D. Elford (University of Kansas, USA)
Information Science Reference • © 2022 • 258pp • H/C (ISBN: 9781799875222) • US $195.00

Driving Innovation With For-Profit Adult Higher Education Online Institutions
David Stein (The Ohio State University, USA) Hilda Glazer (Capella University, USA) and Constance Wanstreet (Franklin University, USA)
Information Science Reference • © 2022 • 325pp • H/C (ISBN: 9781799890980) • US $195.00

Collaborative Approaches to Recruiting, Preparing, and Retaining Teachers for the Field
Maria Peterson-Ahmad (Texas Woman's University, USA) and Vicki L. Luther (Mercer University, USA)
Information Science Reference • © 2022 • 300pp • H/C (ISBN: 9781799890478) • US $195.00

Self-Directed Learning and the Academic Evolution From Pedagogy to Andragogy
Patrick Hughes (Texas Tech University, USA) and Jillian Yarbrough (West Texas A&M University, USA)
Information Science Reference • © 2022 • 276pp • H/C (ISBN: 9781799876618) • US $195.00

Strategies for the Creation and Maintenance of Entrepreneurial Universities
Colette Henry (Dundalk Institute of Technology, Ireland) Bárbara Filipa Casqueira Coelho Gabriel (University of Aveiro, Portugal) Klaus Sailer (Munich University of Applied Sciences, Germany) Ester Bernadó-Mansilla (TecnoCampus, Spain) and Katja Lahikainen (LUT University, Finland)

For an entire list of titles in this series, please visit:
www.igi-global.com/book-series/advances-higher-education-professional-development/73681

701 East Chocolate Avenue, Hershey, PA 17033, USA
Tel: 717-533-8845 x100 • Fax: 717-533-8661
E-Mail: cust@igi-global.com • www.igi-global.com

Table of Contents

Preface xv

Acknowledgment xxiii

Chapter 1
Technology-Enhanced Professional Development With a Situated
Community of Practice: Promoting Transformational Teaching 1
    Bridget K. Mulvey, Kent State University, USA

Chapter 2
Improving the Quality of the Early Childhood Care and Education Workforce
in Turkey 23
    Asil Ali Özdoğru, Üsküdar University, Turkey

Chapter 3
The Core of Professional Development for English Language Teachers: The
Case of Bahrain 39
    *Hasan Mohsen Al-Wadi, Bahrain Teachers College, University of
        Bahrain, Bahrain*

Chapter 4
Turkish Postdoctoral Scholar Teaching Experiences and Professional
Learning Opportunities From a Phenomenological Lens 52
    Saadet Kuru-Çetin, Mugla University, Turkey
    Nihan Demirkasımoğlu, Hacettepe University, Turkey

Chapter 5
Masters of Change? Reflections on the Use of an MA Programme to Upskill
the College Sector in Bangladesh 73
    Lucy Bailey, University of Bahrain, Bahrain

Chapter 6
Teacher Professional Development for Inclusion in England and Bahrain..........91
    Hanin Bukamal, University of Birmingham, UK

Chapter 7
The Triple Entente in Brazil: In-Service English Language Professional Development 108
    André Hedlund, Pontifical Catholic University of Paraná, Brazil

Chapter 8
School-Based In-Service Teacher Training and Peer-to-Peer Learning as an Element of Professionalization 123
    Wiltrud Weidinger, Zurich University of Teacher Education, Switzerland
    Rolf Gollob, Zurich University of Teacher Education, Switzerland

Chapter 9
Embedding Authentic and Effective Awareness About Mental Health in Pre-Service Teacher Training 149
    Frederic Fovet, Royal Roads University, Canada

Chapter 10
Quality Management Teacher Professional Development Model: For Quality Education as Internal Efficiency 177
    Cleophas Peter Chidakwa, University of Zimbabwe, Zimbabwe

Chapter 11
Professional Development for Educators in Singapore, South Africa, and Zimbabwe: Lessons to Learn From Each Other 204
    Tawanda Chinengundu, University of Pretoria, South Africa
    Jerald Hondonga, New Era College, Botswana
    John Chakamba, University of Zimbabwe, Zimbabwe
    Rumbidzayi Masina, University of Zimbabwe, Zimbabwe
    Abigirl Mawonedzo, University of Zimbabwe, Zimbabwe

Chapter 12
Using ICT and Digital Tools in Teacher Professional Development in the UAE 232
    Ghadah Hassan Al Murshidi, UAE University, UAE
    Elaine Wright, UAE University, UAE

Glossary 248

Compilation of References 253

About the Contributors 295

Index 300

Detailed Table of Contents

Preface xv

Acknowledgment xxiii

Chapter 1
Technology-Enhanced Professional Development With a Situated
Community of Practice: Promoting Transformational Teaching 1
    Bridget K. Mulvey, Kent State University, USA

The purpose of this chapter is to present an overview of a year-long professional development program on earth systems science and a related investigation into teachers' knowledge and skill development related to technology integration and what promoted transformational changes. Teachers progressed to recognize the spatial nature of science, use technology more for inquiry, and give students control over the technology more. Teachers identified as most helpful the program's cultivation of a community of practice, with teachers supporting each other in their learning and planning to teach. They also identified model lessons during program sessions as helpful, as they were aligned with required standards, focused on big ideas in science, and provided teachers with the time to explore technologies and experience technology-enhanced lessons as learners before developing and teaching their own lessons with their own students. The author then shares recommendations for similar professional development programs.

Chapter 2
Improving the Quality of the Early Childhood Care and Education Workforce
in Turkey 23
    Asil Ali Özdoğru, Üsküdar University, Turkey

Children's learning and development is shaped by their early experiences and environments. Early childhood care and education (ECCE) is a set of programs and services provided to children from birth to school years that supports their learning and development. Availability of quality ECCE programs is vital for the development of not only children and families but also communities and countries. High quality ECCE programs have certain structural and process characteristics. One of the most important determinants of quality in ECCE programs is the quality of professional workforce serving children and families. In order to increase quality, there should be systems and supports for the training and development of high quality ECCE professionals. This chapter takes a look into Turkey, outlines its preservice education for ECCE teachers, presents a national in-service training project, and offers implications for practice. There need to be effective policies and strategies to cultivate a high-quality workforce in early childhood education and development across the world.

Chapter 3
The Core of Professional Development for English Language Teachers: The Case of Bahrain..39
Hasan Mohsen Al-Wadi, Bahrain Teachers College, University of Bahrain, Bahrain

The lesson study strategy or what was called 'research lesson' has recently been a global mode in professional development programmes that can assist in filling the gap between what, how, and why teachers need to change and improve their teaching practices inside the classroom. This chapter provides a systematic review of the application of the lesson study strategy as an approach for seeking professional development on the part of the English language teachers in some Bahraini schools through a tailored school-based professional development programme. A comparison of the lesson study practice in Bahrain to the international practices will be made through determining the aims and procedures followed in this programme and the impact after its implementation. Lessons and consideration for future implementation of professional development programmes that are based on the lesson study strategy for ESL/EFL teachers in Bahrain will also be highlighted and discussed.

Chapter 4
Turkish Postdoctoral Scholar Teaching Experiences and Professional Learning Opportunities From a Phenomenological Lens....................................52
Saadet Kuru-Çetin, Mugla University, Turkey
Nihan Demirkasımoğlu, Hacettepe University, Turkey

The purpose of this study is to analyze the professional learning and development opportunities of postdoctoral researchers from the faculty of education with phenomenological design to discover the experiences of the Ph.D. research assistants and assistant professors working for a teaching university at non-tenure status. The data were gathered through semi-structured interviews and analyzed using content analysis. The findings revealed that postdoctoral scholars experienced difficulties such as material development, teaching methods, and classroom management skills.

Results suggested that postdoctoral scholars' teaching experiences mostly improved by their individual efforts and more university support is needed to to manage this stressful experience. The postgraduate's abroad experience is another factor that requires special attention in the role transition of academics since the cultural contexts of the studied and teaching may differ to a large extent. Universities should develop programs that are well-designed and include practice-based learning opportunities.

Chapter 5
Masters of Change? Reflections on the Use of an MA Programme to Upskill the College Sector in Bangladesh 73
Lucy Bailey, University of Bahrain, Bahrain

This chapter reflects on the author's experiences as Director of the Master Trainers strand of the Bangladesh College Education Development Project, a World Bank-funded programme to upskill pedagogical skills of Bangladeshi college teachers. The chapter contextualises the project in terms of educational and economic challenges in Bangladesh and discusses the challenges and opportunities afforded by the model of professional development adopted. Although the programme is still in process, which precludes detailed programme impact analysis, three dimensions of the project are identified as promoting effective change in college education: teacher ownership of the initiative, master trainers' engagement in their masters studies, and attention to means to maximise large-scale change. It is argued that cohort delivery of a Master's degree is more economic than sending individuals overseas for post-graduate study. In addition, although issues of teacher ownership are complex, the chapter describes how participants were given opportunities to evaluate and implement their own priorities for change.

Chapter 6
Teacher Professional Development for Inclusion in England and Bahrain..........91
Hanin Bukamal, University of Birmingham, UK

The global pursuit for inclusion officially started with the United Nations Salamanca Statement, which called for the integration of children with special educational needs (SEN) into mainstream schooling. This triggered a substantial universal restructure of education systems, which includes a major reconsideration of teacher education for inclusion in order to prepare teachers to teach their diverse learners. Through a comparative case study design, this study explores inclusive practices in primary education in England and Bahrain. More specifically, the study examines the way in which schools support teachers' in-service professional development (PD) which then aid in the implementation of inclusive education. The findings reveal PD practices for inclusion in England which focus on support for SEN and improving teacher attitudes towards inclusion as well as PD practices in Bahrain that emphasise the assimilation of new teachers and the promotion of a collaborative teaching environment.

Chapter 7
The Triple Entente in Brazil: In-Service English Language Professional
Development 108
  André Hedlund, Pontifical Catholic University of Paraná, Brazil

This chapter aims to discuss the current scenario of Brazilian English language professional development opportunities through the lens of two organizations: Brazil's English Language Teachers (BrELT), an online learning community, and the Brazilian Teachers of English to Speakers of Other Languages (BRAZ-TESOL). The third perspective of PD will be described through the role of an emerging trend in the last decade: bilingual education solutions and their ongoing mentoring programs. These three levels of PD are quite representative of what is done in Brazilian in-service training and can offer insightful lessons to other countries. BrELT symbolizes the more informal, free-adherence type of PD through an online community. BRAZ-TESOL requires a paid membership and offers more formal PD opportunities to teachers as well as the possibility of joining chapters and SIGs. Bilingual programs such as Edify make on-demand mentorship available to private school teachers who adopt the program.

Chapter 8
School-Based In-Service Teacher Training and Peer-to-Peer Learning as an
Element of Professionalization 123
  Wiltrud Weidinger, Zurich University of Teacher Education, Switzerland
  Rolf Gollob, Zurich University of Teacher Education, Switzerland

The IPE (International Projects in Education) Centre of the Zurich University of Teacher Education (PHZH) deals with questions of lifelong learning of teachers in many of its international collaborations. The chapter deals on the one hand with the question of how the continuing education of teachers is organized in Switzerland, what successful forms and approaches are, and on which learning theories they are based. Learning from colleagues in peer-mentoring programs as one element of school development is presented from various perspectives. The concept of school-based in-service teacher training (SITT) is presented and discussed for a successful implementation on school level. In addition, practical examples from various cooperation projects around the world are briefly presented to explain how experiences can be further developed thanks to careful cooperation and to learn from this that teachers around the world perhaps learn most effectively from their colleagues if there is a good concept behind this approach.

Chapter 9
Embedding Authentic and Effective Awareness About Mental Health in Pre-Service Teacher Training 149
    Frederic Fovet, Royal Roads University, Canada

The chapter examines the urgent need for pre-service teacher training programs to integrate content on mental health. In the current neo-liberal context, there is increasing pressure on universities to streamline and shorten these programs, when in fact there might be a need to add content to their existing structure. Developing pre-service teachers' awareness around student mental health is a pressing need but one campuses are usually reluctant to address when it may represent a widening of their scope. The chapter analyzes phenomenological data collected by the author around his lived experience of delivering a course on mental health within a Canadian pre-service teacher training program. It examines the complex, rich, and diverse outcomes that are achieved (1) on teacher candidates' approaches to inclusion, (2) on their ability to navigate their own mental health issues, and (3) more widely on their willingness to embrace social model approaches to disability. The chapter examines the repercussions of this reflection on the transformation of pre-service teacher programs.

Chapter 10
Quality Management Teacher Professional Development Model: For Quality Education as Internal Efficiency 177
    Cleophas Peter Chidakwa, University of Zimbabwe, Zimbabwe

The chapter presents the Quality Management: Teacher Professional Development model for quality education as internal efficiency in Zimbabwe's primary schools. The model is a product of a qualitative phenomenological doctoral study. The researcher analyzes quality management practices from three rural primary schools consistently awarded the Secretary's Merit Award for performance 'par excellence'. The model is cost effective and work embedded. Teachers get professionally developed daily as they work in schools. As a process quality management model, it involves planning, organizing, leading, monitoring, and controlling. Teachers participate in quality management by being members of school-based committees or teams. The QMTPD model develops teachers in some of these aspects: effective teaching; classroom management; setting, marking, and moderating tests; diagnosing and remedying weak learners. Effectiveness of the QMTPD model is manifested in the literacy rate of above 90% that Zimbabwe has attained.

Chapter 11
Professional Development for Educators in Singapore, South Africa, and
Zimbabwe: Lessons to Learn From Each Other 204
    Tawanda Chinengundu, University of Pretoria, South Africa
    Jerald Hondonga, New Era College, Botswana
    John Chakamba, University of Zimbabwe, Zimbabwe
    Rumbidzayi Masina, University of Zimbabwe, Zimbabwe
    Abigirl Mawonedzo, University of Zimbabwe, Zimbabwe

Teacher professional learning is an integral component to support the increasingly complex skills learners need in order to succeed in the 21st century. The purpose of this chapter is to compare teacher professional development in Singapore, South Africa, and Zimbabwe and identify gaps and share good practices between the countries to help teachers learn and refine instructional strategies. Continuous professional teacher development, which is managed by the South African Council of Educators, is a system that encourages educators to grow professionally. Zimbabwe has mainly relied on cascaded professional development workshops. However, critics of this model of professional development argue that this model often has no meaningful impact on classroom practice. In Singapore, most professional development is subject specific and provides teachers with opportunities for networked learning, collegial sharing, and collaboration. From the findings, the recommendation is that there is need for cooperation between countries to strengthen teacher professional development systems.

Chapter 12
Using ICT and Digital Tools in Teacher Professional Development in the
UAE 232
    Ghadah Hassan Al Murshidi, UAE University, UAE
    Elaine Wright, UAE University, UAE

The teaching profession is a constantly changing, diverse environment, striving to meet the needs of the youth of today. One aspect which has transformed teaching is information and communications technology. However, one area which has been slower to embrace this digital era is professional development. Even though continuous teacher professional development is seen as an important aspect of equipping teachers to be effective in the classroom leading to best practice, time constraints, budgets and timetabling difficulties can hinder teachers' access to high quality professional development programs. This chapter will aim to highlight ways the online learning environment has been maximized in order to enhance the professional practice of teachers within the country. The chapter will give a brief outline of other ways in which the UAE has sought to enhance education via online methods; how the visions and goals of the nation's leaders depend upon effective, efficient, and high-quality teachers; and an outline of various forms of online professional development.

Glossary 248

Compilation of References 253

About the Contributors 295

Index 300

Preface

In-service teacher professional development is central to most empirical conceptions of educational quality. It usually garners a significant share of school system budgets–both in terms of delivery and potential staff promotions or salary increases. Many reports and conferences have been devoted to outlining best practice in teacher professional development, and full academic journals and trade magazines are dedicated to its advancement. As the techniques and strategies for educational reform have spread rapidly throughout the world, teacher professional development practices have also been spread across borders, as well. Our aim in this book is to provide contextual understandings of how teacher professional development programs are implemented around the world so that we can better see similarities and differences in this important activity of educational development. Perhaps more importantly, we aim to demonstrate the effectiveness of the professional mechanisms in the field of education at reaching across borders, as well as appropriately contextualizing for local purposes.

The chapters in this volume present specific programs or approaches for in-service teacher professional development within the context of the countries in which they are based. These chapters illustrate the complexities of in-service teacher professional development through the local adaptations of generally globalized practices. As such, this volume is a survey of descriptive accounts, intended to provide readers with a rich understanding of in-service teacher professional development programs and policies, internationally. While many such programs are often tied to wider teacher development schemes that include pre-service teacher training, these chapters concentrate on the formalized learning that takes place within the span of a teacher's practice.

Many papers and studies have sought to quantify learning gains or other empirical outcomes from various types of professional development. Some of these studies have linked budgets to outcomes, demonstrating the impact of financial resources. Others have theorized on the frameworks for adult/professional learning and sought to validate specific styles. Our aim, however, is quite different. In these chapters, we seek no empirical answer to programs, budgets, or styles. Rather, the aim of these chapters is purely descriptive. The literature on in-service teacher professional development is filled with empirical studies of effectiveness. But for readers wishing for a survey of practices around the world, the existing literature falls short. As we planned this volume, we aspired to rich descriptive accounts of programs with a very simple goal: to reflect upon the similarities and differences of program implementation around the world.

The academic literature on teacher professional development demonstrates incredible consensus on practices. Professional development that is focused on content pedagogy, adapted to real contexts (e.g., through colleague-focused collaboration, peer-to-peer coaching, and cross-school networks), and sustained over time is perceived to be superior in terms of improving instructional performance and even student learning outcomes (Darling-Hammond, Hyler, & Gardner, 2017). Yet in practice, purposes for teacher professional development do not have full agreement (Villegas-Reimers, 2003). A review of studies in one journal, *Teaching and Teacher Education*, demonstrates a fairly unified assumption of purpose by researchers–learning of teaching strategies in a way that prompts change in instructional behavior–yet a fairly tenuous agreement of this by practitioners and policymakers. For example, many school systems and national governments use in-service teacher professional development for labor purposes, such as determining promotions and salary increases. Teacher professional development is frequently a tool for school systems to convey policy changes, introduce curriculum initiatives, streamline procedures, or ensure fidelity to curricula. The academic community would prefer to always think about in-service teacher professional development as a vehicle for student learning outcome gains. But the reality is that this academic consensus is wishful thinking.

Assuming that in-service teacher professional development is intended for student learning gains, what does the literature say? While there are plenty of optimistic studies and meta-analyses, the overall quality of causality is not definitive, principally due to the lack of large-scale experimental studies (Yoon, Duncan, Lee, Scarloss, & Shapley, 2007). One reason for this is methodological:

There are almost as many program types as there are programs, with variations in subject and pedagogical focus, hours spent, capacity of the trainers, and a host of other variables. Yet reporting on these often seeks to reduce them to a small handful of variables, and each scholar decides independently which variables are most relevant to report. (Popova, Evans, Breeding, & Arancibia, 2018, p. 27)

To address this, particularly for low and middle income countries, the World Bank commissioned a unifying instrument, the In-service Teacher Training Survey Instrument, to parse characteristics for more accurate comparisons (Papova, Evans,

Preface

Breeding, & Arancibia, 2018). The study found that enacting lessons within the professional development and focusing on subject-specific content are both fairly predictive of student learning gains. Tying salary increases, as well as other monetary incentives, has a positive correlation, as well.

Yet these features are fairly superficial. They do not tell us specifically how professional development is provided, nor do they explain the ways in which countries and school systems adopt and implement strategies. As is fairly common in the literature on international educational development, policy borrowing is understood widely to be the main vehicle for communicating and transferring professional knowledge in the field of education across borders and into practice (Phillips & Ochs, 2003). The concept of policy borrowing is premised on arguments about the neo-liberal globalization agenda, furthered by multilateral organisations, such as the OECD and the World Bank, and enhanced by more deeply connected global knowledge flows, often through academic and professional dissemination methods. Governments, seeking to improve social and economic outcomes, as well as to link budgets more closely with policy goals, look for policy solutions from "model" countries in target domains. For example, countries seeking to increase competitive employment in STEM subjects have looked to countries that perform well on these measures–and then they look for high-level policy constructs that can be "borrowed" and implemented at home. The effectiveness of this approach has been doubted, as fundamental knowledge may not be transferred as readily as high-level policy constructs; furthermore, in the field of education, many national successes are often combined with specific cultural or historic features that are not easily seen through a specific policy. Available mechanisms for knowledge transfer across borders are fairly week and predisposed to superficial features (Purinton & Skaggs, in press). Furthermore, unlike pre-service teacher education, which is mainly the domain of universities–whose missions and structures are relatively institutionalized–in-service teacher professional development is often operationalized as temporal initiatives by school system bureaucracies or quickly changing governments, or they are imported through short-term development projects or brand-name partnerships. Thus, they do not always aim for permanency.

We begin with Bridget K. Mulvey's description of a science teacher professional development program in the chapter, "Technology-Enhanced Professional Development With a Situated Community of Practice: Promoting Transformational Teaching." It offers an illustration of professional development design in the context of national curriculum policy changes. Situated in the continuing roll-out of national science standards in the United States, Mulvey's chapter portrays the ways in which science teachers used technology to increase their own understanding of science content and scientific inquiry. From this, we see firsthand how professional development is constructed so to impact not only knowledge but action within classrooms. Despite how simple this may seem, teacher in-service professional development has been plagued for decades by concerns that it does not impact practice, or worse yet, student learning outcomes. This chapter gives us a glimpse into how such change can be made possible.

Early childhood teacher preparation poses a unique challenge around the world, given the critical importance of this stage of learning yet the difficulties in attracting high quality educators to the field. Asil Ali Özdoğru presents the case of early childhood teacher in-service professional development in Chapter 2, "Improving the Quality of Early Childhood Care and Education Workforce in Turkey." This chapter offers a good illustration of how in-service teacher professional development can help to overcome larger policy challenges. In this case, when the national system is unable to produce ready-made high quality teachers for a sector, teacher professional development fills the gaps. This is particularly important for teacher labor shortages and disconnects between expected competencies and university production.

The now-famous lesson study method of teacher professional development has been adapted throughout the world. In Hasan Mohsen Al-Wadi's chapter, "The Core of Professional Development for English Language Teachers: The Case of Bahrain," we learn about how it has been utilized in the Middle East. This is provided within the context of a national strategy for improving the quality and outcomes of the teacher workforce. While the in-service teacher professional development strategy is just one subset of a larger set of reform initiatives in the country, it illustrates how reformers avidly take–and then adapt–international practices to improve outcomes on specific measures.

In an account of higher education teaching faculty in-service professional development, Saadet Kuru-Çetin and Nihan Demirkasımoğlu discuss the needs and opportunities for instructional professional development to people deemed experts in their subject areas in their chapter, "Turkish Postdoctoral Scholar Teaching Experiences and Professional Learning Opportunities From a Phenomenological Lens." This chapter illustrates the extent to which postdoctoral experts have practice-related concerns about their instructional strategies and performance. Often, institutions or school systems select professional development topics to direct educators into adopting certain traits or practices. It is often assumed to be a vehicle to direct educators into a pathway expected by a policy decision. In the case of this chapter, we see that the very fundamental aspects of academia are frequently underdeveloped in PhD programs, creating a distinct desire among academics to obtain on-the-job support to fill necessary gaps.

In Lucy Bailey's chapter, "Masters of Change? Reflections on the Use of an MA Programme to Upskill the College Sector in Bangladesh," we learn about a cohort-based postgraduate qualification delivered on-site by a foreign institution in Bangladesh as a way to scale up high-impact practices in university classrooms throughout the country. Train-the-trainer approaches are used throughout the world, but this specific instance differed in that the "master trainers" obtained masters degrees. This increased the buy-in among participants, and developed through them a richer body of knowledge with which to build capacity in others. In advanced economies around the world, we frequently see that graduate degrees are either prerequisites to employment as teachers or standardized pathways to promotion. This chapter illustrates the uniqueness of a graduate degree program to accomplish large scale change in a developing country.

As a comparative analysis, Hanin Bukamel examines teacher professional development for inclusion between the UK and Bahrain in her chapter, "Teacher Professional Development for Inclusion in England and Bahrain." Here we see the consistencies in practice between two dissimilar countries. Both are in different stages of development for inclusive education, yet they each demonstrate a high degree of international knowledge regarding the importance of teacher attitude toward inclusivity and the role that professional development plays in promoting that attitude. However, each country approaches teacher professional development through the cultural lenses used in the country to interpret inclusivity in educational and social settings.

André Hedlund's chapter, "The Triple Entente in Brazile: In-Service English Language Professional Development," characterizes teacher in-service professional development in Brazil by illustrating the approaches of two in-country providers. Comparative in nature, this chapter examines three programs within one country. Each of the three has unique characteristics that are likely reflected in other similar professional development provider organizations within Brazil or elsewhere. For example, one program is a social media-run digital environment, free to teachers; another is a centralized TESOL organization that offers a more refined set of professional development tools. Despite the rather generic approach considered by most researchers of in-service teacher professional development, whereby non-branded techniques are adapted to any school or professional learning context, this chapter offers a unique view of how those generic strategies get operationalized either through international organizations on one end of the continuum or leaderless digital environments on the other end.

Continuing with a detailed analysis of the structure of inservice teacher professional development programs, Wiltrud Weidinger and Rolf Gollob write about school-based professional learning and peer-focused mentorship in Swiss schools in their chapter, "School-Based In-Service Teacher Training and Peer-to-Peer Learning as an Element of Professionalization." Further, cases of application of the Swiss system to Bosnia-Herzegovina and Romania are provided. The chapter dissects the components of school-based professional development by analyzing the evidence-based ingredients and applying them to real contexts within schools. In the case of this chapter, the Zurich University of Teacher Education implemented a specific program in Swiss schools, adapted it in the process of delivery according to real-time identified needs, and then adapted it also to schools in Bosnia-Herzegovina and Romania. This chapter offers case studies that build confidence that the generic assumptions built into the scientific literature on in-service teacher professional development are indeed useful and applicable across borders.

Frederic Fovet's chapter, "Embedding Authentic and Effective Awareness About Mental Health in Pre-Service Teacher Training," describes efforts in Canada to increase teacher knowledge about mental health among students in schools. The chapter discusses the challenge that professional development programs have when they serve to modify the scope of teachers' work. In this case, teachers are given skills to address a issue that teachers in the past usually did not see as falling under their realm of responsibility. While the chapter mostly covers pre-service teacher professional development on this topic, we included it for this volume precisely because it illustrates a dynamic between teacher professional learning and scope of labor requirements and social demands. While teacher professional development can be considered as resulting from policy directives, this chapter demonstrates that it can often be the driver of modifications to expectations for teachers. Increasingly this has been seen around the world since 2020, in that teachers carry multiple social roles in addition to their educative role.

In Chapter 10, "Quality Management Teacher Professional Development Model: For Quality Education as Internal Efficiency," Cleophas Peter Chidakwa describes an award-winning project used in rural primary schools in Zimbabwe. It is based on a long-standing, internationally recognized philosophy for organizational performance improvement. In this chapter, we see its application and impact on schools in Zimbabwe.

Chapter 11 is a comparative analysis from Tawanda Chinengundu, Jerald Hondonga, John Chakamba, Rumbidzayi Masina, and Abigirl Mawonedzo, who examine national strategies for teacher professional development in "Professional Development for Educators in Singapore, South Africa and Zimbabwe: Lessons to Learn From Each Other." In this chapter, we learn that national strategies are only as good as their intent and the capacity of the educators tasked with carrying out the responsibilities. In particular, we learn about the necessity of close connection between educational institutions and local labor markets. In a globalized world, knowledge about teacher professional development–as we will see throughout this volume–travels quickly. Yet its relevancy is in doubt if it is not aligned to specific needs on the ground.

In the final chapter, Ghadah Hassan Al Murshidi and Elaine Wright describe teacher professional development for ICT in the United Arab Emirates in "Using ICT and Digital Tools in Teacher Professional Development in the UAE." Once again, we see clear national context in the strategy presented. With an increasing digitization focus on all sectors of the UAE, education is perceived as a piece in a larger puzzle. In other country contexts, ICT education may frequently be perceived as an instigator to prepare citizens for future work and means of work; ICT-based teacher professional development in this case can either be seen as providing teachers with the instructional tools to ensure that students are capable of navigating work in the digital world. In the case of the UAE, while this is still true, the chapter illustrates that the project fits within the national initiative and is thus conceptualized in parallel to many other digital reform efforts.

Taken together, these chapters demonstrate the power of the professions of education. Bolstered by evidence and disseminated through universities, school systems, multilaterals, for-profit providers, NGOs, social media platforms, and multilaterals–and everything in between–in-service teacher professional development around the world has converged on core principles, key strategies, and common delivery mechanisms. Our goal here was not to synthesize the evidence on any method but rather to portray the diversity of methods around the world–and at the same time, demonstrate the remarkable consistency. As avid supporters of the globally-connected professions of education, we hope that these chapters will inspire advocates of continuous professional learning to maintain their pursuits, knowing that they have professional colleagues in nearly every country who have the very same pursuits–and often very similar strategies–to provide practicing teachers with the latest knowledge and evidence.

REFERENCES

Avalos, B. (2011). Teacher professional development in Teaching and Teacher Education over ten years. *Teaching and Teacher Education, 27*(1), 10–20. doi:10.1016/j.tate.2010.08.007

Darling-Hammond, L., Hyler, M. E., & Gardner, M. (2017). *Effective teacher professional development.* Learning Policy Institute. doi:10.54300/122.311

Phillips, D., & Ochs, K. (2003). Processes of policy borrowing in education: Some explanatory and analytical devices. *Comparative Education, 39*(4), 451–461. doi:10.1080/03050060032000162020

Popova, A., Evans, D., Breeding, M. E., & Arancibia, V. (2018). *Teacher professional development around the world: The gap between evidence and practice.* World Bank Policy Research Working Paper (8572).

Purinton, T. & Skaggs, J. (in press). *Knowledge mobility is the new internationalization: Guiding educational globalization one educator at a time.* Lanham, MD: Lexington/Rowman & Littlefield.

Villegas-Reimers, E. (2003). *Teacher professional development: An international review of the literature.* UNESCO International Institute for Educational Planning.

Yoon, K. S., Duncan, T., Lee, S. W. Y., Scarloss, B., & Shapley, K. L. (2007). *Reviewing the evidence on how teacher professional development affects student achievement.* U.S. Department of Education, Institute of Education Sciences, National Center for Education Evaluation and Regional Assistance, Regional Educational Laboratory Southwest.

Acknowledgment

The editors would like to thank the peer reviewers for their effort and expertise they contributed to the double-blind review of the book chapters, without which it would be impossible to maintain the high standards of refereed scientific research.

Chapter 1
Technology-Enhanced Professional Development With a Situated Community of Practice:
Promoting Transformational Teaching

Bridget K. Mulvey
Kent State University, USA

ABSTRACT

The purpose of this chapter is to present an overview of a year-long professional development program on earth systems science and a related investigation into teachers' knowledge and skill development related to technology integration and what promoted transformational changes. Teachers progressed to recognize the spatial nature of science, use technology more for inquiry, and give students control over the technology more. Teachers identified as most helpful the program's cultivation of a community of practice, with teachers supporting each other in their learning and planning to teach. They also identified model lessons during program sessions as helpful, as they were aligned with required standards, focused on big ideas in science, and provided teachers with the time to explore technologies and experience technology-enhanced lessons as learners before developing and teaching their own lessons with their own students. The author then shares recommendations for similar professional development programs.

DOI: 10.4018/978-1-7998-9278-6.ch001

This chapter focuses on lessons learned about technology integration in instruction from a year-long teacher professional development program, Earth System Science, in the United States of America. The program focused on supporting science teachers from high-need school districts with a substantial percentage of students from families of low socioeconomic status. The chapter aims to:

- Describe the issues surrounding technology- and inquiry-based instruction in general and in context of the United States of America.
- Describe the professional development program and how it was evaluated.
- Share findings related to the program evaluation.
- Inform other professional development programs that involve technology and inquiry.

SCIENCE TEACHERS' INCORPORATION OF TECHNOLOGY AND INQUIRY

Mission and Context

The Earth System Science teacher professional development program was informed by research on technology-enhanced and inquiry-based instruction and related professional development programs. This chapter focuses on how to support transformational changes in teachers' technology-enhanced, inquiry-based science instruction via a situated community of practice (teachers working together to plan and reflect on their own instruction to improve).

Teachers need to be prepared to teach science in ways that are more closely aligned with the ways scientists work, represented by constructivist teaching practices such as inquiry. Inquiry instruction can support greater student learning gains compared to traditional instruction (e.g., Furtak et al., 2012). Science inquiry incorporates an important subset of the core science practices identified in the *NGSS*: development of questions, data analysis and interpretation, development of explanations, and evaluation and communication of information. The NGSS promote the integration of science practices within the context of science content knowledge. Yet teachers commonly mistake "hands-on" activities with little or no meaningful connection to scientific ideas as inquiry instruction (Gates, 2008), and many strong teachers struggle to teach by inquiry (e.g., Capps & Crawford, 2013; Vitalis Akuma & Callaghan, 2019). To address these issues, it is important for teacher professional development programs to focus on content knowledge and active learning opportunities (e.g., Wilson & Berne, 1999).

Research indicates that technology can support inquiry instruction (e.g. Lee, Linn, Varma, & Liu, 2010; Maeng, Mulvey, Smetana, & Bell, 2013). Technology that is easier and faster to learn to use also can "enhance" critical thinking (Patterson, 2007) and prepare learners for GIS training and use (Almquist et al., 2014). Maps and virtual globes such as Google Earth™ may offer helpful entry points for inquiry, balancing usability and analytic power (Curtis, 2019).

Despite its potential, using technology to facilitate inquiry instruction and student learning is complicated and difficult (Williams et al., 2004). A synthesis of technology-enhanced professional development research concluded that long-term support and a constructivist pedagogy orientation are crucial program components (Gerard, Varma, Corliss, & Linn 2011), helping to overcome the difficulties. Individualized support, local data and problems/issues use, and logistical support are important components of successful technology-focused professional development programs with a geospatial emphasis (e.g., Baker et al., 2009; Hammond et al., 2018; Moore et al., 2014; Trautmann & MaKinster, 2014). Hammond and colleagues (2018) recommend that "efforts must find the points of connection, entering into the existing curriculum by meshing with established expectations of content coverage and assessments that align to prescribed learning goals" (p. 281).

As noted by Blanchard et al. (2016), most teachers have not experienced professional development that promotes transformative ways of using technology to change their teaching and how their students learn (Hew & Brush, 2007). Earth System Science represents a program that aimed to promote such transformative technology use. Technology professional development does not ensure that teachers will understand and adopt the technology or use it in ways to promote student learning (e.g., Tyler-Wood et al. 2018). Technology-enhanced teacher professional development needs to be for an extended period of at least a year, with a constructivist orientation such as scientific inquiry (Gerard et al., 2011). Extended professional development programs, such as the three-year technology-enhanced inquiry professional development of Blanchard and colleagues (2016), can improve teachers' teaching beliefs and comfort using technologies as well as student achievement on standardized tests. Gerard and colleague's (2011) meta-analysis of teacher technology professional development indicated that university-supported programs tended to be more effective than school-based programs. The Earth System Science program was supported by Kent State University of Kent, Ohio, United States of America.

These evidence-based recommendations guided development and facilitation of the Earth System Science program. The program situated technology-enhanced and inquiry-based instruction in relevant earth and environmental science content.

Context: United States of America

Science teaching in the United States of America is largely informed by the national science education standards, the *Next Generation Science Standards* [NGSS] (NGSS Lead States, 2013). These standards have been adopted by 20 of 50 states as of 2021. Also, 24 additional states have standards that are informed by these national standards (https://ngss.nsta.org/about.aspx). The standards focus on a three-dimensional approach to teaching and learning that integrates disciplinary core knowledge, science and engineering practices, and crosscutting concepts. The practices situate inquiry in a scientific disciplinary context. The *NGSS* framework provides an evidentiary base for the standards. The standards aim to address problems in the country's teaching such as activity-focused teaching in the country, with content playing a less central role than higher-achieving countries on the Trends in International Mathematics and Science (TIMSS) video study (Roth & Garnier, 2007).

Earth System Science

The year-long teacher professional development program was funded by the United States of America's Ohio Improving Teacher Quality Program, providing five free graduate-credit hours at a large research university in the state of Ohio to 23 Ohio science teachers who taught in publicly funded middle school and high schools, teaching students of ages 11-18. This evaluation focused on 15 of the 18 general education teachers who volunteered to be participants. The remaining 5 participants were special education teachers, addressed in a separate study.

The program focused on the following goal: improve teachers' technology-enhanced, inquiry instruction in earth and environmental science content contexts. This instruction was modeled in science content associated with interactions between Earth's spheres (atmosphere, hydrosphere, cryosphere, geosphere), as recommended by Orion and Libarkin (2014). As Ohio did not adopt the national standards, the program was informed by the state science standards, which were informed in part by the national standards. Teachers worked in a situated community of practice during program sessions with substantial individualized coaching to promote transformational technology-enhanced, inquiry instruction.

Details of Implementation

Two instructors developed and facilitated the Earth System Science program. One instructor was a science teacher educator with a master's degree in geological sciences and the other instructor was a geographer with an emphasis on geospatial technology.

Table 1. Professional development program schedule

Session	Content	Scientific Practices	Technologies
1 (summer)	What is science Earth systems science	Asking questions	
2 (summer)	Minerals Periodic table Nature of science: empirical Rock cycle	Analyzing and interpreting data	Hand lens Rock hammer
3 (summer)	Rocks Fossils	Analyzing and interpreting data Constructing explanations	Smart phones: geotagging photos Google Earth™ Google Maps™
4 (summer)	Plate tectonics, volcanoes, earthquakes Disaster preparedness and mitigation	Developing and using models	Maps Google Maps™ Google Earth™ GPS units Seismographs Simulations
5 (summer)	Rivers Floods Algal blooms	Obtaining, evaluating, and communicating information	Google Earth™ GPS-enabled video cameras
6 (summer)	River field trip	Constructing explanations	Maps Google Maps™ Google Earth™ Smartphones GPS units GPS-enabled video cameras
7 (summer)	Weather Severe weather	Engaging in argument from evidence	Models Maps
8 (summer)	Grade level Inquiry Projects	Asking questions Planning and carrying out investigations	Maps Google Maps™ Google Earth™ Smartphones GPS units GPS-enabled video cameras
9 (academic year)	Groundwater Pollution	Using mathematics and computational thinking	Groundwater model (in person and simulation)
10 (academic year)	Human-nature interactions Sustainability	Analyzing and interpreting data Patterns	Agent-based participatory simulation
11 (academic year)	Glaciers Climate	Analyzing and interpreting data	Models
12 (academic year)	Age dating Geologic history	Using mathematics and computational thinking	Scanning electron microscope Petrographic microscope
13 (academic year)	Review Plan future instruction		

The year-long program involved an intensive 60-contact hour summer portion over eight days and 37.5-contact hours over five days spread out over the academic year. This followed recommendations from the meta-analysis of Gerard and colleagues (2011) for teacher professional development to include long-term support and a constructivist orientation to teaching. An overview of the topics addressed is provided in Table 1. Guest scientists supplemented instruction with focused investigations and question and answer sessions about the content, their careers, and how they do scientific inquiry.

Technology was introduced gradually, with an increasing emphasis on stronger analysis available with different tools. International Society for Technology in Education (2016) informed the technology instruction. The guidelines advise that technology should:

1. be introduced within science content contexts.
2. address meaningful science via appropriate pedagogy.
3. capitalize on the technology's unique features.
4. help to increase the accessibility of scientific views, and
5. cultivate students' conceptions of the association between science and technology.

Technology such as Google Earth™ extended inquiry beyond what data could be collected in the school or local environment, expanding investigations in time (historical, e.g. New Orleans' recovery from Hurricane Katrina) and place (global investigations possible, e.g. plate boundary inquiry, city sustainability assessment). The program integrated the identification and meaningful use of local and regional data through sites such as the National Aeronautics and Space Administration, National Oceanographic and Atmospheric Administration, United States Geological Survey, and readily available Google Earth™ layers.

Model lessons offered the teachers experiences as learners first, followed by unpacking the teacher perspective. For example, teachers used GPS units and Google Earth™ to find, collect, and analyze geographically oriented data to investigate problems such as flooding and post-disaster recovery. Then the teachers worked in small groups, considering how to modify the lesson and technology use for one of their courses to meet their students' needs.

Situated Community of Practice for Technology-Enhanced Inquiry Instruction

High quality teacher professional development programs involve active learning (Borko, 2004) and a community of practice, which involves teachers working and learning about teaching together, in the relevant context of their own classroom instruction (Ball & Cohen, 1999; Banilower & Shimkus, 2004; Borko et al., 2008; Putnam & Borko, 2000; Wilson & Berne, 1999). The meaningful context of teachers' own instruction represents a type of situated learning (Lave & Wegner, 1991), supported by a community of practice. In Earth System Science, teachers worked within small course-specific groups to plan and reflect on their own technology-enhanced, inquiry-based instruction.

As collaboration is an important component of effective professional development programs (e.g., Garet et al., 2001; Wilson & Berne, 1999), each academic year session began and ended with 30 minutes of teachers working in grade-level groups to apply and make sense of their own instruction and student learning in the context of the program. During this time, participants modified program lessons and strategies to address science content in their grade level, meet the needs of their students, and integrate relevant and available geospatial technology when appropriate. Additional grade-level group time supported further exploration of Google Maps™ and Google Earth™ and its possibilities, with instructors devoting much time to coaching these groups and those individuals who had expressed frustration that was limiting their potential to learn. Instructors actively promoted connection between teachers and cultivated a community of practice.

Participants then taught and video-recorded the lessons that they modified or developed in their own classrooms with their own students. Participants reviewed the video-recordings to reflect on the teaching and learning experiences and student learning outcomes. These recordings provided a relevant, situated context for the teachers' reflection and learning. Teachers' individual written reflections were submitted to the professional development course instructors for review and individualized feedback. In these ways, the situated community of practice groups provided differentiated support for the teachers.

Formative Assessment and Individualized Coaching

Instructors consistently monitored teachers' experiences and reactions to program lessons through formative assessments including in-class discussions and exit slips and written reflections. Instructors met after each session to informally analyze exit slips, written reflections, and what happened in that session. In this way, the instructors identified emergent themes and important outliers during and after the sessions, working together to align instruction with each other and with participants' identified needs.

Instructors also used more formal assignments to provide individualized coaching. Teachers completed a series of four assignments involving video-recording themselves teaching their own students. Feedback focused on lesson design, big ideas in science, students' role in the lessons, teacher questions, and student experiences/learning. As needed, the science education instructor sent follow-up emails to engage teachers in the application of feedback to future lesson and unit planning.

Overview of Program Impact

A qualitative case study design was used to characterize changes in the 15 teacher participants' use of maps, geospatial images, and mapping technologies. Data sources included: lesson artifacts; video-recorded lessons with participants' own students; written reflections on video-recorded lessons; exit slips for each program session; and observational notes of program sessions to improve internal validity via triangulation across data sources. During the academic year, lesson artifacts were collected (e.g., video-recorded lessons, lesson observational notes, lesson plans, assessments, student worksheets, teacher and student presentations, and student work examples). Data analysis followed the guidelines of Bogdan and Biklen (1992) for analytic induction to identify patterns in how the group of teachers' instruction changed over time with respect to technology and inquiry, as well as how teachers perceived the professional development program as informing those changes. The nature of science aspect of the professional development program was not examined for the present chapter.

Program evaluation identified three themes related to changes in teachers' science instruction over time: increased attention to spatial nature of science inquiry; shift from technology as visualization tool to science inquiry tool; and increased student responsibility. Below, the themes are presented with supporting evidence, followed by the aspects of the program that teachers identified as the most helpful.

INCREASED ATTENTION TO SPATIAL NATURE OF SCIENTIFIC INQUIRY

Initial Lack of Attention to Spatial Inquiry

At the beginning of the program, the teachers reported using maps and images to support their science instruction. They had not explicitly considered or drawn attention to the spatial nature of many science investigations, especially in earth and environmental science.

Summer Changes in Spatial Inquiry Understanding and Initial Planning

During the summer portion of the course, teachers increased their attention to the spatial nature of much scientific inquiry, surprised by the potential of spatial data and geospatial technology. Teachers recognized the power in having students consider the importance of place, looking for patterns in data represented in maps, Google Maps™, and Google Earth™. They began to develop spatial questions or to identify the tools they want to use for spatial investigations such as: "Using the polygon tool in Google Earth, I could outline and fill in the entire school district. … We could then identify the total amount of time needed for plates to move that same distance over time. … Not only will this activity help to develop their spatial awareness, but it will also give them some semblance of "deep geologic time" on our planet." (Sam, Summer Reflection 2).

Academic Year Attention to Spatial Inquiry

During the academic year, teachers recognized the power of maps and the spatial nature of much scientific inquiry. This attention to spatial components of inquiry extended to the application to their teaching practice. All teachers implemented partially-oriented inquiry in lesson and unit openers and one- to two-day lab activities. All integrated and/or had students collect/create authentic data, remotely sensed and place-based images, and/or maps to support students' spatial thinking. Teachers highlighted the power of using real data with students to make lessons more meaningful and student-centered. For example, Sara commented, "I am now trying to have students create, discuss, apply knowledge, and make connections using real world data. Since I have tweaked my teaching style, students have been asking great questions that show they are critically thinking." The teachers identified strong student engagement and academic outcomes.

Many teachers also integrated more extensive inquiry-based units. For example, Lori engaged in student-initiated exploration of earthquakes within tectonic plates, rather than near plate boundaries. Students found and analyzed maps, then sought out additional information about earthquakes in different regions of the United States of America. One group explored relationships between Oklahoma earthquakes and fracking (Lori, Video-recorded Lesson). In this way, inquiry focused on spatial patterns in inquiry-based units.

In another example, Kara taught a unit on erosion and deposition. She asked students to compare an aerial image of a shoreline at two different time points. She asked, "What part of the shoreline eroded most?" She then encouraged students to support their answers with evidence from the images. This initial activity was extended into a hands-on investigation of how water interacts with model shorelines comprised of different materials and with shorelines of different shapes. Kara asked students to draw the shoreline to create a map and mark changes over time to support a comparison across models. The spatial nature of this and other inquiries supported a shift to inquiry-based instruction, described more in the section below.

SHIFT FROM TECHNOLOGY AS VISUALIZATION TOOL TO SCIENCE INQUIRY TOOL

Initial Views of Technology as Visualization Tool

Regardless of teachers' familiarity with technology-enhanced instruction before the program, the teachers used technology only sporadically and, when used, technology was not being used in inquiry-based ways. Participants self-identified this issue in reflections on their past instruction. Ryan reflected:

I took my first technology course about 15 years ago. I was excited to begin using these new tools and couldn't wait to include them in my lessons. I soon found myself discouraged and confused that they were not as effective as I thought they would be. ... I realize that I was putting the cart before the horse. I wasn't using technology to enhance my lessons. I was using lessons to enhance technology.

Similarly, Kristy commented, "I have used Google Earth in the past as a visual to demonstrate what was being taught with water quality and eutrophication caused by farming runoff" and "I used spatial data as a visual tool but not as a starting point for inquiry." Thus, Ryan, Kristy, and others unpacked their past instruction, identifying specific limitations in the ways they used technology in their teaching before participating in the Earth System Science program.

Summer Changes in Technology for Inquiry Understanding and Initial Planning

Through the summer professional development sessions, most participants shifted their perceptions of technology as a visualization tool to technology as a support for inquiry investigations. For example, Sara commented, "I am hoping with increased use of technology in my classroom, the correct student support, and time that my students will learn to ask questions that will lead them to research the answers to their own questions." She continued, "The integration of Google Earth into my classroom teaching should challenge all my students to ask questions." During the summer, teachers recognized the transformational potential of technology to shift their instructional practice toward inquiry.

In small group and whole class discussions, teachers expressed desires to change their instruction to emphasize students' ideas, thinking, and questions. Tom called Google Earth™ a *game changer* for teaching earth system science. These general expressions of interest in changing instruction translated into some initial planning of specific student inquiry investigations during the summer sessions. For example, Tom began to plan a substantial GPS and Google Earth™-based inquiry project for his grade 8 students. Ryan created an initial draft of a long-term water quality investigation that incorporated GPS units and Google Maps™ in the areas surrounding his school.

Academic Year Instruction Using Technology for Inquiry

During the academic year, 14 of the 15 teacher participants used technology for inquiry in their video-recorded lessons; most teachers facilitated in-depth lessons/investigations that integrated technology such as Google Earth™ and GPS units. For example, three teachers implemented a multi-day plate tectonics inquiry investigation in Google Earth™ that they had experienced as learners in the program (Lori, Richard, Tom, In-person and Video-recorded Lessons). Students studied the broad and zoomed-in imagery of multiple examples of each type of plate boundary to infer general patterns in features associated with each boundary. For two participants' students, discrepant data sparked questions that then students investigated via Google Earth™.

In another example inquiry lesson, Kendra showed a class two Google Earth™ images of Joplin, Missouri, one from before and one from the month after a devastating 2011 tornado (Kendra, Lesson Artifacts). Students identified similarities and differences between the images labeled with the month and year they were taken, without an introduction to the place or disaster. Students made inferences about what created the damage, some suggesting a thunderstorm or tornado. One student referenced the narrow yet intense path of destruction as evidence to support a tornado over a thunderstorm as the cause of the destruction. Students then compared the two images for changes in the natural and built environments between the two images. Kendra then connected the images to primary and secondary succession in ecosystems. This illustrates participants' shift to inquiry instruction, with some continued teacher control of the technology. Many participants moved beyond this teacher control to encourage students to manage technology for data collection, analysis, and/or communication (see section below).

Overall, the teachers used technology such as Google Maps™, Google Earth™, and GPS units to support inquiry-based science teaching, moving well beyond their self-reported technology use prior to the course.

INCREASED STUDENT RESPONSIBILITY FOR TECHNOLOGY

Initial Teacher Control of Technology

Before the program, teachers largely controlled maps and mapping technologies during technology-enhanced lessons. When students used the technology, which was limited, they did so mostly for Internet research (web quests, read articles; 10 participants, as indicated by pretest).

Summer Changes in Who Should Be Responsible for Technology

During the summer program, teachers began to recognize how much control they had been holding onto in their classes. Participants critically reflected on their past science instruction and brainstormed ways to improve their instruction. A little over half of the participants began to envision students being in control of the technology. Kristy commented, "I feel like I usually do the mission planning but that is never related to students, the planning that scientists do before they do experiments and investigations. This would help students understand real science" (Kristy, Summer Reflection 8). She also shared, "I would love to get to the point where students can come up with their own research and use Google Earth just like scientists are today." She and other participants were aware that they had kept most of the control over technology in the past and expressed the desire and importance of changing this. Participants wanted students to be responsible for making decisions and thinking more within investigations, coming closer to the work that scientists do. Ryan similarly reflected:

Without fully understanding the tools and potential, I realize that my [past] attempts were rather clumsy and inefficient. I would use my computer and class projector to take my students to places around the world and show them examples of plate boundaries and the geologic features associated with them. The student's role was to sit in their seats and be amazed by my skill and the possibilities of Google Earth. I am now seeing how much better this could be. My activity was far from inquiry based. In the future, my students will be using this tool to answer questions, look for relationships, developing explanations, and drawing conclusions. I hope to be amazed by THEIR skill and use of this tool for real science (Ryan, Summer Reflection 8).

These changes were not without difficulty, however. Willa, Mike, and Sidney struggled with their own technology use throughout the summer sessions. Willa reflected, "I am feeling like I would not be able to spare the time required to plan such an investigation" (Willa, Summer Reflection 5). Mike and Sidney focused on their own perceived inadequacies in the facilitation of student-led investigations. The struggles limited these participants' vision of their academic year technology-enhanced instruction and the role of their students in these lessons. These issues midway through the summer sessions led the instructors to include extended times for supported planning for the remaining three summer sessions as well as during the academic year.

Academic Year Instruction with Student Control of Technology

During the academic year, all teachers moved beyond their technology struggles enough to envision and implement student-led inquiry investigations, 13 of which were maps / mapping technology-enhanced. Teachers shifted to give students much more control of the technology and even of the related inquiry investigations compared to past years In an example of an inquiry-based unit with students largely responsible for meaningful technology use, Tom fully operationalized his summer plans for an extended science inquiry project. The two professional development program instructors helped to plan and facilitate a data collection field trip for all eighth grade students in his school, along with technology and mathematics teachers at the school. Students were divided into teams to cover different portions of the field site, then used GPS units to mark locations of squirrel nests and record the waypoint number, type of tree, and where in the tree the nest was found in their science notebook. Students had hypothesized that there might be a correlation between tree type and quantity of nests. Back at school, the students imported their data into Google Earth™ to analyze it and look for patterns. Students did not reach a clear conclusion, but this presented an opportunity for students to develop questions that stemmed from their initial investigation. This participant's school had many technological issues, yet he fought past the problems to facilitate a substantial inquiry project with his students (Tom, In-person Lesson Observational Notes and AY Reflection 2). Both teachers and their students engaged in more intellectual risk taking, aligned with scientific inquiry.

Student responsibility for technology use also supported differentiated instruction. For example, in an alternative school that involved students taking different science classes together in the same classroom, Corinne gave students control over technology to do scientific inquiry investigations, with the teacher providing different levels of support to differentiate her instruction by content and difficulty. Students worked in small groups on laptops to conduct different Google Earth™-based inquiry investigations aligned with their particular science course. Corinne reflected:

Using Google Earth is also a great option for differentiation. I have to constantly differentiate between content areas but it can also be used to differentiate between ability levels. ... Google Earth is extremely flexible and can be utilized on so many different scales of difficulty as well as so many different data points. (Corinne, AY Reflection 4)

Overall, student control over technology supported meeting students' varied needs, even in a multi-course classroom setting. Student responsibility over technology was commonly accompanied by a similar teacher shift for student ideas to be central to the learning experiences.

MOST HELPFUL ASPECTS OF PROGRAM, AS IDENTIFIED BY TEACHERS

Based on analysis of observational notes of program sessions, written reflections after each in-person program session, and exit slips, five themes emerged associated with what participants found to most support technology-enhanced instruction: (1) experiencing many model lessons; (2) time to explore technologies; and (3) community of practice.

Experiencing Model Lessons

Teachers first experienced technology-enhanced inquiry lessons as students in the program. These model lessons provided participants with examples of how maps and technology such as Google Earth™ are more than great visualization tools—they are tools for inquiry. The model lessons were then unpacked from a teacher perspective, considering teaching strategies. Teachers identified seeing the supportive constructivist instructional strategies such as productive teacher questions, wait time, pre- and formative assessments, and cooperative learning roles embedded within lessons. Teachers considered the technology use in model lessons to reshape their understanding of technologies as transformational. Teachers expressed great thanks for purposeful and consistent times to debrief model lessons, and work together with each other to make sense of the session's implications for their instruction.

Time to Explore Technologies for Inquiry

Teachers identified having plenty of time to explore various technologies to be instrumental to changes in their beliefs and instruction related to technology. Particularly over the summer when the technologies such as hand-held GPS units and Google Earth™ were introduced, instructors gave participants time for open explorations of the tools after some initial engagement. For about three days after a technology's introduction, some participants expressed the need for additional time to explore and requested help with specific aspects of using the tools themselves or using the tools to support inquiry with students. Instructors responded with additional model lessons, instructional videos, and handouts to further support their efforts.

Community of Practice

Teachers identified support of fellow teachers and instructors with learning about and planning to incorporate technologies into inquiry-based instruction as instrumental to their growth. The community shared stories, ideas, and resources to support each other. Teachers also identified as important the purposeful and consistent times to debrief model lesson and work together with each other to make sense of the session's implications for their instruction. Responsiveness of instructors to participants' needs- written reflections, with open focus, after in-person sessions supported timely identification of participants' needs and instructors' steps to meet those needs. "I felt very valued as a student in the classroom. The instruction was tailored to our needs and our time was used as wisely as possible" (Kristy, Summer Reflection 8). Indeed, instructors read teachers' reflections nightly, after each summer session, to monitor then support adjustments in tentative plans for the next day and to individualize coaching. Exit slips revealed that the attention to individual participants' questions, concerns, frustrations and other emotional reactions, and successes strongly supported teachers' sense of safety and comfort in the class. The instructors learned more about the teachers and the teachers came to trust that the instructors very much were there to adapt to their need and support their efforts at the varied levels needed in the class. Cultivating this relationship led to great openness in class discussions and written reflections, allowing instructors to better anticipate participants' needs through time (Class Observation Notes, Exit Slips, Reflections).

Teachers supported each other during and between program sessions, including the sharing lesson resources with each other via a shared DropBox folder. The continued emphasis on community and a shared goal of supporting students in doing science in ways that more closely mirror the ways of scientists, were identified as essential program components.

The continued emphasis on community and a shared goal of supporting students in doing science more like scientists were identified as essential components. The support of peers also helped teachers to continue to strive to work around school and district philosophical and technological constraints, mitigating some of the potential negative impact on instruction.

SOLUTIONS AND RECOMMENDATIONS

This investigation of a professional development program found that focusing professional development programs on technologies that are easier to use for meaningful inquiry can promote changes in teachers' instruction, aligned with Curtis (2019). Perceptions and use of technology moved away from teacher show-and-tell toward technology as a game changer that supported student inquiry and differentiation. This aligns with the findings of Lee et al. (2010) that technology can support inquiry instruction. Differentiation of a program can support teachers—from those in both technology-poor and technology-rich environments, those with none to substantive inquiry and technology teaching experience—to feel empowered to enact effective technology-enhanced, inquiry-based science instruction. This may be particularly important when professional development program teachers range from novice to expert in technology, pedagogy, and science content knowledge, as was the case in the Earth System Science program described here.

These outcomes are aligned with previous research (e.g., Blanchard et al., 2016; Campbell et al., 2014; Trautmann & MaKinster, 2014). For example, Blanchard and colleagues (2016) concluded that a three-year technology-enhanced professional development program improved teachers' comfort using technologies. This was associated with improved student academic achievement, particularly for those with lower initial achievement, even when teachers implemented technology for more logistical purposes. Before a program, teachers focused on information transmission and held more teacher-centered beliefs (Campbell et al., 2014). After the program, teachers focused on more reforms-based teaching such as inquiry held more student-centered beliefs about teaching. Campbell and colleagues (2014) recommended considering how science teaching goals and purposes interact with other beliefs over time. Trautmann and MaKinster (2014) concluded that their secondary science teacher participants improved their perceptions of their own technology expertise and their ability to use geospatial technology in their instruction. Both Trautmann and MaKinster's study and the present investigation provide evidence to support the helpfulness of individualized and continued support of teachers. Teacher collaboration and relations and trust also supported teacher growth, aligned with Svendsen (2020).

Issues with time for planning and implementation aligned with previous research (e.g., Fitzgerald et al., 2019).

Overall, technologies have the potential to support inquiry, students' critical thinking, and differentiation. The present investigation provides evidence to support maps and mapping technologies as game changers. The middle and high school teachers developed substantially in their conceptions about and implementation of technology-enhanced inquiry instruction. All teachers taught by inquiry, integrating images (satellite, aerial, etc.), maps, and/or spatial data into their instruction more than the previous year. All but one teacher implemented technology-enhanced inquiry instruction. The development of a community of practice and model lessons seems to have been particularly important to the effectiveness of the program, potentially magnifying effects of the other program components.

Recommendations include considering alignment of technologies with specific science content, and incorporating technology into meaningful content-focused, inquiry-based model lessons such that technology is a means to an end rather than the point itself. The content and science practices are the main emphasis rather than the technologies. This is also why including simpler technologies with enough analytic power can be important. This allows easier access points for teachers to implement technology-enhanced inquiry instruction. To make selections of what technologies to integrate into a professional development program, consider to what extent a technology or its use is new to teachers when determining what support teachers may need.

Based on the Earth System Science program evaluation, teacher and student outcomes can be strengthened by cultivating a community of practice with teachers in a program. When teachers can reflect on model lessons with teachers in similar settings or teaching similar content, teachers support each other's growth. For teachers to work as a community, they need substantial time to explore new technologies, new uses of technologies, reflect on model lessons, adapt/develop lessons for their own classrooms, and reflect on their own and each others' lesson implementation with their own students and related outcomes.

It is recommended to consistently use formative assessment in a professional development program. This allows instructors to monitor and adjust the lessons, discussions, assignments, and type and extent of feedback to meet teachers' varied needs. The individualized coaching should be informed by each teacher's beliefs about teaching and learning. The coaching also should consider how to increase teachers' comfort with trying new things, in a safe and supportive community of practice in the program.

FUTURE RESEARCH DIRECTIONS

Despite the potential of technology, more needs to be done to promote all teachers and students to use them in transformational ways for inquiry. Harnessing the transformative power of technologies for K–12 inquiry involves engaging teacher in model lessons first as learners, then as teachers implementing lessons with their own students. Future research needs to address the development and evaluation of specific curricula, aligned with science standards. Teacher materials should support effective implementation yet offer flexibility for teachers to adapt to their local context and needs. A close-up examination of teachers' support of each other and individualized coaching in a community of practice setting also could inform professional development programs and grade-level teacher teams' work.

CONCLUSION

This chapter highlighted ways that a community of practice, time to explore technologies, and technology-enhanced model lessons can promote transformational changes in science teacher's instructional practice. A group of teachers, who become a supportive community, can be a catalyst for change. Teacher professional development instructors can magnify support for transformational change through the integration of a more bottom-up organization of a community of practice. Coupled with timely, sustained professional development instructor support, teachers can become agents of change.

ACKNOWLEDGMENT

This research was supported by the Ohio Board of Directors Improving Teacher Quality Grant Program in the United States of America.

REFERENCES

Ball, D. L., & Cohen, D. K. (1999). Developing practice, developing practitioners: Toward a practice based theory of professional education. In L. Darling-Hammond & G. Sykes (Eds.), *Teaching as a learning profession: Handbook for policy and practice* (pp. 3–31). Jossey-Bass.

Banilower, E., & Shimkus, E. (2004). *Professional development observation study*. Horizon Research.

Blanchard, M. R., LePrevost, C. E., Tolin, A. D., & Gutierrez, K. S. (2016). Investigating technology-enhanced teacher professional development in rural, high-poverty middle schools. *Educational Researcher, 45*(3), 207–220. doi:10.3102/0013189X16644602

Bogdan, R. C., & Biklen, S. K. (1992). *Qualitative research for education: An introduction to theory and methods*. Allyn and Bacon.

Borko, H. (2004). Professional development and teacher learning: Mapping the terrain. *Educational Researcher, 33*(8), 3–15. doi:10.3102/0013189X033008003

Borko, H., Jacobs, J., Eiteljorg, E., & Pittman, M. E. (2008). Video as a tool for fostering productive discussions in mathematics professional development. *Teaching and Teacher Education, 24*(2), 417–436. doi:10.1016/j.tate.2006.11.012

Campbell, T., Zuwallack, R., Longhurst, M., Shelton, B. E., & Wolf, P. G. (2014). An examination of the changes in science teaching orientations and technology-enhanced tools for student learning in the context of professional development. *International Journal of Science Education, 36*(11), 1–34. doi:10.1080/09500693.2013.879622

Capps, D. K., & Crawford, B. A. (2013). Inquiry-based instruction and teaching about nature of science: Are they happening? *Journal of Science Teacher Education, 24*(3), 497–526. doi:10.100710972-012-9314-z

Curtis, M. D. (2019). Professional technologies in schools: The role of pedagogical knowledge in teaching with geospatial technologies. *The Journal of Geography, 118*(3), 130–142. doi:10.1080/00221341.2018.1544267

Fitzgerald, M., Danaia, L., & McKinnon, D. H. (2019). Barrers inhibiting inquiry-based science teaching and potential solutions: Perceptions of positively inclined early adopters. *Research in Science Education, 49*(2), 543–566. doi:10.100711165-017-9623-5

Furtak, E. M., Seidel, T., Iverson, H., & Briggs, D. C. (2012). Experimental and quasi-experimental studies of inquiry-based science teaching: A meta-analysis. *Review of Educational Research, 82*(3), 300–329. doi:10.3102/0034654312457206

Garet, M. S., Porter, A. C., Desimone, L., Birman, B. F., & Yoon, K. S. (2001). What makes professional development effective? Results from a national sample of teachers. *American Educational Research Journal, 38*(4), 915–945. doi:10.3102/00028312038004915

Gates, H. A. (2008). *Middle school science teachers' perspectives and practices of teaching through inquiry* (Unpublished doctoral dissertation). University of South Carolina, Columbia, SC.

Gerard, L. F., Varma, K., Corliss, S. B., & Linn, M. C. (2011). Professional development for technologically enhanced inquiry science. *Review of Educational Research, 81*(3), 408–448. doi:10.3102/0034654311415121

Hammond, T. C., Bodzin, A., Anastasio, D., Holland, B., Popejoy, K., Sahagian, D., Rutzmoser, S., Carrigan, J., & Farina, W. (2018). "You know you can do this, right?": Developing geospatial technological pedagogical content knowledge and enhancing teachers' cartographic practices with socio-environmental science investigations. *Cartography and Geographic Information Science, 45*(4), 305–318. doi:10.1080/15230406.2017.1419440

International Society for Technology in Education. (2008). *National education technology standards.* Retrieved from: www.iste.org/standards.aspx

Lave, J., & Wenger, E. (1991). *Situated learning: Legitimate peripheral participation.* University of Cambridge Press. doi:10.1017/CBO9780511815355

Lee, H., Linn, M. C., Varma, K., & Liu, O. L. (2010). How do technology-enhanced inquiry science units impact classroom learning? *Journal of Research in Science Teaching, 47*(1), 71–90. doi:10.1002/tea.20304

Maeng, J. L., Mulvey, B. K., Smetana, L. K., & Bell, R. L. (2013). Preservice teachers' TPACK: Using technology to support inquiry instruction. *Journal of Science Education and Technology, 22*(6), 838–857. doi:10.100710956-013-9434-z

National Science Teaching Association. (2021). *About the Next Generation Science Standards.* Retrieved from https://ngss.nsta.org/about.aspx

Orion, N., & Libarkin, J. (2014). Earth systems science education. In N. G. Lederman & S. K. Abell (Eds.), *Handbook of research on science education* (Vol. 2, pp. 481–496). Routledge.

Putnam, R., & Borko, H. (2000). What do new views of knowledge and thinking have to say about research on teacher learning? *Educational Researcher, 29*(1), 4–15. doi:10.3102/0013189X029001004

Roth, K., & Garnier, H. (2007). What science teaching looks like: An international perspective. *Educational Leadership, 64*(4), 16–23.

Svendsen, B. (2020). Inquiries into teacher professional development—What really matters? *Education, 140*(3), 111–130.

Trautmann, N. M., & MaKinster, J. G. (2014). Meeting teachers where they are and helping them achieve their geospatial goals. In J. MaKinster, N. Trautmann, & M. Barnett (Eds.), *Teaching science and investigating environmental issues with geospatial technology* (pp. 51–64). Academic Press.

Tyler-Wood, T. L., Cockerham, D., & Johnson, K. R. (2018). Implementing new technologies in a middle school curriculum: A rural perspective. *Smart Learning Environments*, 5(1), 22. doi:10.118640561-018-0073-y

Vitalis Akuma, F., & Callaghan, R. (2019). Teaching practices linked to the implementation of inquiry-based practical work in certain science classrooms. *Journal of Research in Science Teaching*, 56(1), 64–90. doi:10.1002/tea.21469

Wilson, S. M., & Berne, J. (1999). Teacher learning and the acquisition of professional knowledge: An examination of research on contemporary professional development. *Review of Research in Education*, 24, 173–209. doi:10.2307/1167270

ADDITIONAL READING

Bodzin, A., Anastasio, D., Sahagian, D., & Henry, J. B. (2016). A curriculum-linked professional development approach to support teachers' adoption of Web GIS tectonics investigations. *Contemporary Issues in Technology & Teacher Education*, 16(3), 348–372.

Mulvey, B. (2012). A virtual tour of plate tectonics. *Science Teacher (Normal, Ill.)*, 79, 52–58.

Mulvey, B. K., & Curtis, J. W. (2018). Introduction to special content section "The power of mapping in primary and secondary science education.". *Cartography and Geographic Information Science*, 45(4), 289–291. doi:10.1080/15230406.2018.1429167

Orion, N. (2019). The future challenge of Earth science education research. *Disciplinary and Interdisciplinary Science Education Research, 1*.

Orion, N., & Libarkin, J. (2014). Earth systems science education. In N. G. Lederman & S. K. Abell (Eds.), *Handbook of research on science education* (Vol. 2, pp. 481–496). Routledge.

Wilkerson, M. S., Wilkerson, M. B., & Marshak, S. (2017). *Geotours workbook: A guide for exploring geology using Google Earth* (2nd ed.). W.W. Norton & Company.

KEY TERMS AND DEFINITIONS

Community of Practice: A group of people who work together on their own and broader group goals, usually with a shared emphasis.

Earth System Science: An integrated, system-based approach to teaching earth science.

Next Generation Science Standards: The national science standards of the United States of America with an emphasis on three-dimensional learning that involves the integration of disciplinary core ideas, science and engineering practices, and crosscutting concepts.

Scientific Inquiry: Both the ways scientists work to learn about the natural world and a constructivist model of instruction that emphasizes students doing science more like scientists do, focused on meaning making over memorization.

Scientific Practices: The actions scientists and science students do to learn about science, also considered to be science discipline-specific inquiry.

Situated Learning: Learning within contexts that are relevant and meaningful for the learner.

Transformation: In the context of technology-enhanced instruction, technology changes the role of teachers and students in teaching and learning, with students taking a more central role in the use of technology and related sense making.

Chapter 2
Improving the Quality of the Early Childhood Care and Education Workforce in Turkey

Asil Ali Özdoğru
https://orcid.org/0000-0002-4273-9394
Üsküdar University, Turkey

ABSTRACT

Children's learning and development is shaped by their early experiences and environments. Early childhood care and education (ECCE) is a set of programs and services provided to children from birth to school years that supports their learning and development. Availability of quality ECCE programs is vital for the development of not only children and families but also communities and countries. High quality ECCE programs have certain structural and process characteristics. One of the most important determinants of quality in ECCE programs is the quality of professional workforce serving children and families. In order to increase quality, there should be systems and supports for the training and development of high quality ECCE professionals. This chapter takes a look into Turkey, outlines its preservice education for ECCE teachers, presents a national in-service training project, and offers implications for practice. There need to be effective policies and strategies to cultivate a high-quality workforce in early childhood education and development across the world.

DOI: 10.4018/978-1-7998-9278-6.ch002

Care and education provided to children during early years of life has important outcomes for their lifespan development. High quality early care and education programs offer essential support in children's physical, cognitive, and social-emotional development. Program quality is closely related to characteristics and skills of the workforce providing care and education. Quality early education benefits not only individual children but also families and societies. In order to improve social and economic qualities of developing countries, investments need to be made in quality early education programs and workforce. This chapter takes a look at early childhood education in Turkey, reviews preservice and in-service education for the workforce, and offers implications for practice and policy.

Human development is a lifespan process from conception till death. Experiences in early life have long-term consequences in developing humans. Relationships and environments that children experience influence their development in adolescence and adulthood. Infants and children who experience quality family and school environments achieve better outcomes in physical, cognitive, and social-emotional domains of development across the lifespan (Pungello et al., 2010). Programs and policies that offer support at home and school contexts can have long lasting impact on the development of children and families.

Early childhood care and education (ECCE) is a set of programs and services provided to children and their families. ECCE programs involve infant and toddler care programs, early childhood education services, after-school care programs, and parenting programs (New & Cochran, 2007). Even though there are differences in definition and implementation across the world, infant-toddler care programs usually serve children from zero to three years of age, early education services serve children three to six, after-school care programs serve school-aged children, and parenting programs serve parents of children zero to eighteen.

There is a great diversity in the ECCE programs within and between countries. In the United States, there are both public and private programs that focus on children or parents with different sources of funding and procedures of regulation, licensing, and accountability (Gomez et. al., 2015). European countries also show a large variability in availability and funding of ECCE programs in relation to their respective welfare regimes (Aysan & Özdoğru, 2015). A UNESCO (2021) study that examined the ECCE programs in 193 countries found that only 63 countries (33%) had free and 51 countries (26%) had compulsory pre-primary education. Availability of high-quality ECCE programs play a significant role in the development of not only children and families but also communities and countries (Jenkins, 2014).

ECCE programs support the development of young children, school-age children, and their families. High quality programs help children develop linguistic and literacy skills, numeracy and other cognitive skills, self-regulation, and social-emotional skills. High quality programs share common elements of structure and process

(Cassidy et al., 2005). Structural quality is related to infrastructure, standards and regulations, staff education and training. Process quality involves interactions between children, staff, and parents. Quality infant-toddler care programs focus on supporting the development of secure attachment, sensitive parenting behaviors, responsive caregiving, and reflective curriculum planning (Lally, 2009). Development of high-quality programs require systematic planning, implementation, and monitoring that uses quality assessment and evaluation methods (Özdoğru, 2018). Quality of the ECCE programs depend to a large extend on the workforce including caregivers and teachers, administrators, and staff (Institute of Medicine and National Research Council, 2012). This chapter focuses on ECCE in Turkey and outlines preservice education of teachers, presents a national in-service training program, and offers implications for practice.

EARLY CHILDHOOD CARE AND EDUCATION IN TURKEY

Turkey is a demographically young and economically developing country located between Europe and Asia with a population of more than 83 million at the end of 2020. Children between the ages of 0 and 17 make up the 27% of the total population, which is higher than all European Union countries (Turkish Statistical Institute, 2021). More than 12.5 million children, which is 56% of the child population, were between the ages of zero and nine. As an emerging market economy and a newly industrialized country, Turkey stands as the world's 20th largest economy in terms of nominal gross domestic product (GDP). Since 2010s, the country is going through an economic stagnation known as the middle income trap. A high equity and quality education system is needed to train skilled human capital and move the country out of this trap (Yılmaz, 2014).

Turkey has a centralized national education system with 12 years of compulsory education free of charge in public schools for children 6 to 18. Even though the country made improvements in the system over the past years, there are many problems in the system in terms of financing, administration, access, equity, and quality. Turkey has increased its education spending relative to GDP in past years but still has a lower level of per-student spending and higher level of private spending in comparison to countries in the Organisation for Economic Cooperation and Development (OECD, 2020a). The national education system of Turkey is a large and highly centralized system in terms of administration and testing where teachers and schools report to have little autonomy. Turkey has low but increasing levels of participation in early childhood care and education among 0-6 population but there are wide regional differences in enrollment rates. The expansion of private schools and high-stakes placement exams seems to increase the inequity in access to quality education.

Early childhood care and education programs in Turkey essentially serve children under 6 years of age. Children 0-3 are served by care programs in crèches or daycare centers. Children 3-6 can attend education programs in preschools, practice classrooms, and nursery classrooms. There is no compulsory preschool education and ECCE programs are run by both public and private organizations. Different type of ECCE programs are also funded and supervised by various organizations such as Ministry of National Education (MoNE), Ministry of Family and Social Services, Directorate of Religious Affairs, municipalities, and nongovernmental organizations (Gol-Guven, 2017).

Participation in ECCE is increasing over the years in Turkey but there is still room for growth and concerns for equity. Rates of enrollment in ECCE programs increase by age but they are lower than many countries. Enrollment rates in 2017 were less than 5% for children 0-3 and 73% for 5-year-olds in comparison to OECD average of 26% and 95%, respectively (OECD, 2020a). There are also within country differences in enrollment rates. In 2016, enrollment for 3-5 year-olds was around 30% for children in İstanbul and Southeast Anatolia in comparison to up to 45% in the Mediterranean West and South Aegean (OECD, 2020a). Enrollment rates in pre-primary education for 3-5 year olds increased from 27% in 2009 to 42% in 2019 (MoNE, 2020). As shown in Table 1, 82% of 1.6 million students attend and 73% of 98 thousand teachers work in public pre-primary education programs as of 2020. Pre-primary education programs in Turkey have higher child-staff ratios and lower expenditure per child. In 2017, ratio of children to full-time teachers was 18 in Turkey and 14 in OECD countries, and annual total expenditure was $5,250 per child in Turkey and $9,079 across OECD countries (OECD, 2020b).

Table 1. Number and percentages of students, teachers, classrooms, and schools in pre-primary education in Turkey in 2019-2020

	Student n	Student %	Teacher n	Teacher %	Classroom n	Classroom %	School n	School %
Public MoNE	1,218,747	75%	62,004	63%	43,929	51%	22,582	69%
Public non-MoNE	121,760	7%	10,215	10%	7,886	9%	3,058	9%
Public total	1,340,507	82%	72,219	73%	51,815	60%	25,640	78%
Private MoNE	225,202	14%	17,704	18%	25,306	30%	5,141	16%
Private non-MoNE	64,011	4%	8,902	9%	8,407	10%	1,773	5%
Private total	289,213	18%	26,606	27%	33,713	40%	6,914	22%
Grand total	1,629,720	100%	98,825	100%	85,528	100%	32,554	100%

Source: (MoNE, 2020)

Early Childhood Preservice Education

One of the most important quality indicators in ECCE programs is teacher characteristics. Teachers' preservice and in-service education and training, working conditions and compensation, and psychological characteristics make a difference in the process quality of the programs. For example, in a recent study researchers found that preschool teachers' depressive symptoms influenced their students' early mathematical achievement in Head Start programs (Jeon et al., 2021). The study indicated that teachers' depressive symptoms were associated with the quality of their relationships with students' families, which in turn influenced children's approaches to learning in terms of their motivation, engagement, and persistence in learning. Several programs to support and improve ECCE teachers' work conditions were found to decrease staff turnover rates and increase quality of the programs (Child Care Services Association, 2021; Özdoğru & Widrick, 2011, Özdoğru & Wulfsohn, 2011).

Preservice teacher education in Turkey is usually a four-year undergraduate program. A small group of candidates from certain programs complete a one-year consecutive training program known as pedagogical formation. After graduating from high school, students take a national university entrance exam and centrally placed into programs based on their scores. Out of 203 universities in Turkey, 83 universities offer a Bachelor's degree in preschool education programs for a total of 5,065 available student slots in 2021. Preschool education programs are housed under faculties of education and offer a similar set of courses prescribed by the Council of Higher Education (CoHE). In the latest CoHE curriculum of 2018, there were 59 courses with a total of 240 European Credit Transfer and Accumulation System (ECTS) credits in three groups of courses as pedagogical content knowledge (PCK), pedagogical knowledge (PK), and general knowledge (GK) areas. PCK area courses make up 46% of the total credits including courses such as Introduction to Early Childhood Education and Music Education in Early Childhood, PK area courses make up 35% of the total credits including courses such as Educational Psychology and Classroom Management, and GK area courses make up 19% of the total credits including courses such as Digital Technologies and Community Service Practices. In the curriculum, there are two required teaching practice courses, which make up 11% of the total credits, and 16 elective courses that make up 25% of the total credits. In a research study on the new curriculum with university lecturer participants, the increase in the number of elective courses was evaluated positively but its inflexibility, reduced practicum, inadequacy of new courses, and lack of stakeholder participation in curriculum design were evaluated negatively (Tican-Başaran & Aykaç, 2020). In August 2020, instead of a central curriculum,

CoHE authorized universities to design their own teacher education curriculums by following earlier general guidelines.

Education and training requirements for ECCE teachers in Turkey show variation based on the supervising entity. ECCE teachers who work in public preschools and kindergarten classes that are supervised by the MoNE are required to have a minimum of a four-year bachelor's degree. On the other hand, teachers working in private childcare centers, preschools, and kindergarten classes need to have a minimum of a high school diploma. Teachers in public schools attend in-service trainings offered twice a year, while teachers in private schools may have more or less in-service training opportunities. In a study on Turkish preschool teachers' evaluation of their preservice and in-service education, more than half of the teachers (52%) thought their preservice education was adequate and more than half of the teachers (63%) reported not attending in-service trainings offered by MoNE (Öztürk et al., 2016). In another study, majority of preschool teachers reported that they need in-service programs about the characteristics of children with special needs such as giftedness and learning disability, early intervention programs, and techniques for national and international project preparation (Doğan & Tatık, 2014).

An Early Childhood In-Service Education Project

A recent national project in Turkey aimed to improve the knowledge and skills of teachers and the quality of early childhood education. The Inclusive Early Childhood Education for Children with Disabilities Project (IECEP) was a three-year project from 2017 to 2020 designed to support teachers' professional development in order to facilitate the access of 3- to 7-year-old children with disabilities to quality inclusive early education. IECEP was co-funded by the Republic of Turkey and European Union and implemented by MoNE Directorate General of Basic Education with technical assistance from UNICEF. Project stakeholders included MoNE Directorate General of Special Education and Guidance Services; MoNE Directorate General for Measurement, Evaluation and Examination Services; MoNE Directorate General for Teacher Training and Development; and Ministry of Family, Work, and Social Services (MoFSS).

IECEP aimed to improve access and quality of inclusive early education in Turkey. Access to quality pre-primary education among children with disabilities in Turkey is especially low (Diken et al., 2016; Sart et al., 2016). In 2019-2020 academic year, only one percent of all students in formal special education institutions (4,873 out of 425,774) were in the pre-primary education level (MoNE, 2020). Challenges of preschool education of students with special needs were found to relate to teachers' instructional practices, parents' involvement and support, and school's physical environments (Özdoğru, 2021). Preschool teachers were found to have low levels of knowledge, negative attitudes, and high need for in-service education about inclusive practices (Metin, 2018; Özaydın & Çolak, 2011; Sucuoğlu et al., 2014). In this context, IECEP was implemented in 90 pilot schools of six provinces from six different regions of Turkey. All the teachers in the pilot schools were involved in the project. Target population of the project was 180 children with disabilities, 1,180 children in overall, 1,180 family members or caregivers, and 1,000 educators including early childhood and first grade teachers, school counselors and administrators (MoNE, 2018).

IECEP provided knowledge and skills for teachers to use with children with disabilities to deliver quality inclusive education. Project materials were developed, distributed, and published online for teachers, families, and the community (Eğitimde Birlikteyiz, 2021). Materials included print and audio story and activity books for children, activity books for teachers, teacher education guidebook for trainers, family and community guidebooks, and conference booklets. Contents from the teacher guidebook were organized in ten chapters with a total of 132 pages. The chapters with most pages were Assessment of Development and Learning in Inclusive Learning Environments (40 pages), Supporting Learning in Inclusive Education Environment (28 pages), and Inclusive Education (16 pages). Contents of the activity books were analyzed in comparison to MoNE's national preschool education program (Türkoğlu, 2020).

IECEP activities produced a great deal of output and outcomes. The project used a training of trainers model, in which 142 teachers were trained and 1,250 teachers were trained by those trainers. Teacher portfolios were developed for the use of teachers trained in the project. Teacher education modules about inclusive teaching skills were uploaded into national Education Information Network. Thirty-eight set of children's books were distributed to 32 thousand students in 90 pilot schools. Children's festivals were organized in cities included in the project, Antalya, Bursa, Gaziantep, İzmir, Konya, and Samsun, with a total attendance of six thousand children. These festivals housed inclusive games developed for the project for children with and without disabilities to play together. Twelve family seminars were organized in those six cities with a total audience of 16 thousand participants (Kasap, 2020). In conjunction with the project opening ceremony in 2017 and the closing ceremony in 2020, two national conferences were organized where teachers and university professors came together and made presentations. Even though the formal project evaluation is not out yet, there have been many positive reviews and feedback about the project in local schools, directorates, and the media. The project, which was initially planned to conclude in May 2020, have been going through extensions due to the COVID-19 pandemic. The conference booklet for the closing ceremony and national conference as well as project reports are yet to be published.

IMPLICATIONS FOR PRACTICE

Quality of early care and education is important for children, families, and societies. The quality of workforce is particularly important in the implementation of ECCE programs. Caregivers, teachers, administrators, and staff with adequate education, training, and support can provide quality programming. Preservice and in-service education programs for ECCE workforce is essential in the improvement of program quality. The preservice and in-service education programs implemented in Turkey that were summarized before have implications for practice throughout the world.

The preservice education program for preschool education in Turkey has many strengths as well as areas of improvement. The program is designed with an international outlook following the European credit system as well as courses offering knowledge and skills based on the up-to-date scientific literature. It leaves room not only for content knowledge but also pedagogical and general knowledge. Elective courses enable students to develop in their chosen areas of interest. The recent decision by CoHE to move away from a centralized curriculum and allow universities to have more autonomy on their teacher education programs is democratic and empowering. On the other hand, different education requirements for early childhood professionals to work in different schools and varying levels of access to in-service training between public and private schools can be listed as some areas to be improved.

The in-service training project, Inclusive Early Childhood Education for Children with Disabilities Project (IECEP), that was implemented in Turkey is noteworthy for variety of reasons. Shared funding source and stakeholder participation of the project are good examples for other teacher professional development projects. Early childhood interventions and programs are known to be more successful when there are collaborative and participatory approaches among stakeholders from local and central government as well as public and private sectors of health, nutrition, education, child protection, and social protection (Britto et al., 2017; Neumann, 2010). Family and community involvement is also an essential aspect of quality ECCE programs and preservice and in-service teacher professional development programs need to improve teachers' skills to establish and maintain school, family, and community partnerships (Epstein, 2005).

IECEP addresses an essential area of ECCE service that teachers report to need more support. Children with special needs are an important group of students in ECCE programs and teachers are expected to provide them individualized and developmentally appropriate educational practices (Filler & Xu, 2006). Among the 3- to 9-year-old children in Turkey, 2.3% is known to have at least one disability (MoFSS, 2021) and early childhood teachers in inclusive classrooms report that they do not have adequate levels of knowledge on special education and need more support on early intervention and inclusive education (Doğaroğlu & Bapoğlu Dümenci, 2015). ECCE teachers who even report high level of knowledge on inclusive education are found to have low levels of self-efficacy perceptions about providing education to students with special needs and need in-service education on disability types and characteristics, program development, activity planning, classroom management, social acceptance, and skill building (Sönmez et al., 2018).

The adoption of training of trainers model and online learning environments in IECEP improve the projects outreach and sustainability. Training of trainers model in teacher professional development, also known as the cascade model, has the potential to improve delivery and outcomes of teacher in-service education programs, if the program is focused on knowledge in practice (Turner et al., 2017) and administered in a contextual, collaborative, and reflexive manner (Hayes, 2000). Distance and online models of teacher professional development can also be used effectively in early childhood teachers' in-service education programs. Online teacher in-service programs that promote a sense of presence produce better outcomes in satisfaction and learning (Holmes et al., 2010). In a study with preservice early childhood professionals, videoconferencing technology provided teachers and caregivers a much richer and effective classroom observation method (Pickering & Walsh, 2011).

The organization of two national conferences as part of opening and closing ceremonies of IECEP was a rewarding opportunity for teachers and academics to come together as a shared learning experience. Teachers in the field may find academic work impractical and inaccessible (Gore & Gitlin, 2004). School-university collaborations bring together teachers and academics providing valuable opportunities for teacher professional development (Cozza, 2010; Emstad & Sandvik, 2020). Scientific conferences, congresses, and other meetings of professional associations and teachers' unions enable teachers to share knowledge and experience with other teachers and academics (National Research Council, 2000). In a study with 200 Turkish preschool and primary school teachers, most commonly reported professional development activities were attending conferences and seminars, taking courses and workshops, and reading the academic literature (Özdemir, 2016).

CONCLUSION

Quality early childhood care and education programs are important in the development of infants and young children. High quality ECCE programs need a high quality workforce. Caregivers, teachers, and administrators who are well-trained through preservice and in-service training programs can provide quality care and education. Teacher education and professional development among ECCE workforce can be improved through strategies that build on existing capacities and link different sources. Effective professional development programs for ECCE teachers utilize needs assessment and analysis, engage in collaborative design and implementation, and include sound practices of program evaluation.

REFERENCES

Aysan, M. F., & Özdoğru, A. A. (2015). Comparative analysis of early childhood care and education in Europe. *Turkish Journal of Sociology, 30,* 167–194. doi:10.16917/IU/tjs.12775

Britto, P. R., Lye, S. J., Proulx, K., Yousafzai, A. K., Matthews, S. G., Vaivada, T., Perez-Escamilla, R., Rao, N., Ip, P., Fernald, L. C. H., MacMillan, H., Hanson, M., Wachs, T. D., Yao, H., Yoshikawa, H., Cerezo, A., Leckman, J. F., & Bhutta, Z. A.Lancet Early Childhood Development Series Steering Committee. (2017). Nurturing care: Promoting early childhood development. *Lancet, 389*(10064), 91–102. doi:10.1016/S0140-6736(16)31390-3 PMID:27717615

Cassidy, D. J., Hestenes, L. L., Hansen, J. K., Hegde, A., Shim, J., & Hestenes, S. (2005). Revisiting the two faces of child care quality: Structure and process. *Early Education and Development, 16*(4), 505–520. doi:10.120715566935eed1604_10

Child Care Services Association. (2021, June). *Retaining educated early childhood educators* [Policy Brief]. https://www.childcareservices.org/wp-content/uploads/Policy-Brief-Retaining-Educated-Early-Childhood-Educators.pdf

Council of Higher Education (CoHE). (2018). *Okul Öncesi Öğretmenliği Lisans Programı.* https://www.yok.gov.tr/Documents/Kurumsal/egitim_ogretim_dairesi/Yeni-Ogretmen-Yetistirme-Lisans-Programlari/Okul_Oncesi_Ogretmenligi_Lisans_Programi.pdf

Cozza, B. (2010). Transforming teaching into a collaborative culture: An attempt to create a professional development school-university partnership. *The Educational Forum, 74*(3), 227–241. doi:10.1080/00131725.2010.483906

Diken, I. H., Rakap, S., Diken, O., Tomris, G., & Celik, S. (2016). Early Childhood Inclusion in Turkey. *Infants and Young Children, 29*(3), 231–238. doi:10.1097/IYC.0000000000000065

Doğan, B., & Tatık, R. Ş. (2014). Okul öncesi öğretmenlerinin hizmet içi eğitim ihtiyaçlarının belirlenmesi. *The Journal of Academic Social Science Studies, 27*(27), 521–539. doi:10.9761/JASSS2418

Doğaroğlu, T., & Bapoğlu Dümenci, S. (2015). Sınıflarında kaynaştırma öğrencisi bulunan okul öncesi öğretmenlerin kaynaştırma eğitimi ve erken müdahale hakkındaki görüşlerinin incelenmesi. *Hacettepe University Faculty of Health Sciences Journal, 1*(Supp. 2), 460-473. https://dergipark.org.tr/en/pub/husbfd/issue/7893/103909

Eğitimde Birlikteyiz. (2021). *Eğitimde Birlikteyiz: Engeli Olan Çocuklar İçin Kapsayıcı Erken Çocukluk Eğitimi Projesi.* http://www.egitimdebirlikteyiz.org

Emstad, A. B., & Sandvik, L. V. (2020). School–university collaboration for facilitating in-service teacher training as a part of school-based professional development. *Acta Didactica Norden, 14*(2), 1–20. doi:10.5617/adno.7934

Epstein, J. L. (2005). Links in a professional development chain: Preservice and inservice education for effective programs of school, family, and community partnerships. *New Educator, 1*(2), 125–141. doi:10.1080/15476880590932201

Filler, J., & Xu, Y. (2006). Including children with disabilities in early childhood education programs: Individualizing developmentally appropriate practices. *Childhood Education, 83*(2), 92–98. doi:10.1080/00094056.2007.10522887

Gol-Guven, M. (2017). Ensuring quality in early childhood education and care: The case of Turkey. *Early Child Development and Care, 188*(3), 1–14. doi:10.1080/03004430.2017.1412957

Gomez, R. E., Kagan, S. L., & Fox, E. A. (2015). Professional development of the early childhood education teaching workforce in the United States: An overview. *Professional Development in Education, 41*(2), 169–186. doi:10.1080/19415257.2014.986820

Gore, J. M., & Gitlin, A. D. (2004). [RE]Visioning the academic–teacher divide: Power and knowledge in the educational community. *Teachers and Teaching, 10*(1), 35–58. doi:10.1080/13540600320000170918

Hayes, D. (2000). Cascade training and teachers' professional development. *ELT Journal, 54*(2), 135–145. doi:10.1093/elt/54.2.135

Holmes, A., Signer, B., & MacLeod, A. (2010). Professional development at a distance: A mixed-method study exploring inservice teachers' views on presence online. *Journal of Digital Learning in Teacher Education, 27*(2), 76–85. doi:10.1080/21532974.2010.10784660

Institute of Medicine and National Research Council. (2012). *The early childhood care and education workforce: Challenges and opportunities: A workshop report.* The National Academies Press., doi:10.17226/13238

Jenkins, J. M. (2014). Early childhood development as economic development: Considerations for state-level policy innovation and experimentation. *Economic Development Quarterly*, *28*(2), 147–165. doi:10.1177/0891242413513791

Jeon, S., Jeon, L., Lang, S., & Newell, K. (2021). Teacher depressive symptoms and child math achievement in Head Start: The roles of family–teacher relationships and approaches to learning. *Child Development*, *92*(6), 2478–2495. Advance online publication. doi:10.1111/cdev.13601 PMID:34131906

Kasap, S. (2020, March 4). 'Eğitimde Birlikteyiz' hareketiyle 32 bin çocuk kapsayıcı eğitime katıldı. *Anadolu Ajansı*. https://www.aa.com.tr/tr/egitim/egitimde-birlikteyiz-hareketiyle-32-bin-cocuk-kapsayici-egitime-katildi/1754490

Lally, J. R. (2009). The science and psychology of infant-toddler care: How an understanding of early learning has transformed child care. *Zero to Three*, *30*(2), 47–53.

Metin, N. (2018). Okul öncesi kaynaştırma sınıfında öğretmen. *Erken Çocukluk Çalışmaları Dergisi*, *2*(2), 428–439. doi:10.24130/eccd-jecs.196720182279

Ministry of Family and Social Services (MoFSS). (2021). *Engelli ve yaşlı istatistik bülteni Mayıs 2021*. https://www.aile.gov.tr/media/81779/eyhgm_istatistik_bulteni_mayis_2021.pdf

Ministry of National Education (MoNE). (2018). *Engeli Olan Çocuklar İçin Kapsayıcı Erken Çocukluk Eğitimi Projesi*. https://tegm.meb.gov.tr/www/engeli-olan-cocuklar-icin-kapsayici-erken-cocukluk-egitimi-projesi/icerik/537

Ministry of National Education (MoNE). (2020). *National education statistics: Formal education 2019/'20*. https://sgb.meb.gov.tr/meb_iys_dosyalar/2020_09/04144812_meb_istatistikleri_orgun_egitim_2019_2020.pdf

National Research Council. (2000). *How people learn: Brain, mind, experience, and school (Expanded Edition)*. Washington, DC: The National Academies Press. doi:10.17226/9853

Neuman, M. J. (2005). Governance of early childhood education and care: Recent developments in OECD countries. *Early Years*, *25*(2), 129–141. doi:10.1080/09575140500130992

New, R. S., & Cochran, M. (Eds.). (2007). *Early childhood education: An international encyclopedia* (Vol. 1). Praeger.

Organisation for Economic Cooperation and Development (OECD). (2020a). *Education policy outlook: Turkey.* https://www.oecd.org/education/policy-outlook/country-profile-Turkey-2020.pdf

Organisation for Economic Cooperation and Development (OECD). (2020b). Turkey. In *Education at a Glance 2020: OECD Indicators.* OECD Publishing. doi:10.1787/1701b91e-

Özaydın, L., & Çolak, A. (2011). Okul öncesi öğretmenlerinin kaynaştırma eğitimine ve okul öncesi eğitimde kaynaştırma eğitimi hizmet içi eğitim programına ilişkin görüşleri. *Kalem Eğitim ve İnsan Bilimleri Dergisi, 1*(1), 189–226.

Özdemir, S. M. (2016, October 27-30). *Temel eğitim öğretmenlerinin mesleki gelişim etkinliklerine katılım durumları ve öğrenme-öğretme sürecine etkisi* [Conference paper]. IV. Uluslararası Eğitim Programları ve Öğretim Kongresi, Antalya, Turkey.

Özdoğru, A. A. (2018). Program development, assessment, and evaluation in early childhood care and education. In V. C. X. Wang (Ed.), *Handbook of research on program development and assessment methodologies in K-20 education* (pp. 109–127). IGI Global. doi:10.4018/978-1-5225-3132-6.ch006

Özdoğru, A. A., & Widrick, R. (2011). *New York State Infant and Toddler Resource Network 2011 evaluation report.* Early Care & Learning Council.

Özdoğru, A. A., & Wulfsohn, S. (2011). *Social-Emotional Consultation in Infant and Toddler Child Care Programs: Final evaluation report.* Early Care & Learning Council.

Özdoğru, M. (2021). Özel gereksinimli çocukların okul öncesi eğitiminde karşılaşılan sorunlar. *Temel Eğitim, 11*(11), 6–16. doi:10.52105/temelegitim.11.1

Öztürk, T., Zayimoğlu Öztürk, F., & Kaya, N. (2016). Okul öncesi öğretmenlerinin hizmet öncesi eğitimlerine ilişkin görüşleri ve hizmet içi eğitim durumları. *Erzincan Üniversitesi Eğitim Fakültesi Dergisi, 18*(1), 92–114. doi:10.17556/jef.67571

Pickering, L. E., & Walsh, E. J. (2011). Using videoconferencing technology to enhance classroom observation methodology for the instruction of preservice early childhood professionals. *Journal of Digital Learning in Teacher Education, 27*(3), 99–108. doi:10.1080/21532974.2011.10784664

Pungello, E. P., Kainz, K., Burchinal, M., Wasik, B. H., Sparling, J. J., Ramey, C. T., & Campbell, F. A. (2010). Early educational intervention, early cumulative risk, and the early home environment as predictors of young adult outcomes within a high-risk sample. *Child Development, 81*(1), 410–426. doi:10.1111/j.1467-8624.2009.01403.x PMID:20331676

Sart, Z. H., Barış, S., Sarışık, Y., & Düşkün, Y. (2016). *The right of children with disabilities to education: Situation analysis and recommendations for turkey.* Education Reform Initiative. http://en.egitimreformugirisimi.org/wp-content/uploads/2017/03/UnicefOzelGereksinimliRaporENG.08.06.16.web_.pdf

Sönmez, N., Alptekin, S., & Bıçak, B. (2018). Okul öncesi eğitim öğretmenlerinin kaynaştırma eğitiminde öz-yeterlik algıları ve hizmetiçi eğitim gereksinimleri: Bir karma yöntem çalışması. *Abant İzzet Baysal Üniversitesi Eğitim Fakültesi Dergisi, 18*(4), 2270–2297. doi:10.17240/aibuefd.2018.18.41844-444422

Sucuoğlu, B., Bakkaloğlu, H., İşcen Karasu, F., Demir, Ş., & Akalın, S. (2014). Okul öncesi öğretmenlerinin kaynaştırmaya ilişkin bilgi düzeyleri. *Kuram ve Uygulamada Eğitim Bilimleri, 14*(4), 1467–1485. doi:10.12738/estp.2014.4.2078

Tican-Başaran, S., & Aykaç, N. (2020). Evaluation of 2018 Turkish early childhood teacher education curriculum. *Pegem Journal of Education and Instruction, 10*(3), 889–928. doi:10.14527/pegegog.2020.028

Turkish Statistical Institute (TÜİK). (2021). *İstatistiklerle çocuk, 2020.* https://data.tuik.gov.tr/Bulten/Index?p=Istatistiklerle-Cocuk-2020-37228

Türkoğlu, B. (2020, September 16-19). *Review of the eligibility of the activity books in the Inclusive Early Childhood Education for Children with Disabilities Project to the acquisitions of the preschool education program of the Ministry of National Education* [Conference presentation]. International Pegem Conference on Education. https://2020.ipcedu.org/dosyalar/files/ipcedu_ozetlerv2.pdf.pdf

Turner, F., Brownhill, S., & Wilson, E. (2017). The transfer of content knowledge in a cascade model of professional development. *Teacher Development, 21*(2), 175–191. doi:10.1080/13664530.2016.1205508

UNESCO. (2021). *Right to pre-primary education: A global study.* https://unesdoc.unesco.org/ark:/48223/pf0000375332

Yılmaz, G. (2014). *Turkish middle income trap and less skilled human capital.* Working paper no: 14/30. Central Bank of the Republic of Turkey. https://www.tcmb.gov.tr/wps/wcm/connect/c56c98ef-1c49-4324-94af-f88191f00906/WP1430.pdf?MOD=AJPERES&CACHEID=ROOTWORKSPACE-c56c98ef-1c49-4324-94af-f88191f00906-m3fw68n

ADDITIONAL READING

Akdağ, Z., & Haser, Ç. (2017). Beginning early childhood education teachers' struggle with inclusion in Turkey. *Asia Pacific Journal of Education, 37*(2), 219–231. doi:10.1080/02188791.2016.1273197

Brown, C. P., McMullen, M. B., & File, N. (Eds.). (2019). *The Wiley handbook of early childhood care and education.* John Wiley & Sons. doi:10.1002/9781119148104

Gören Niron, D. (2013). An integrated system of early childhood education and care governance in Turkey: Views of policy-makers, practitioners, and academics. *Early Years, 33*(4), 367–379. doi:10.1080/09575146.2013.854738

Holochwost, S. J., DeMott, K., Buell, M., Yannetta, K., & Amsden, D. (2009). Retention of staff in the early childhood education workforce. *Child and Youth Care Forum, 38*(5), 227–237. doi:10.100710566-009-9078-6

Institute of Medicine and National Research Council. (2012). *The early childhood care and education workforce: Challenges and opportunities: A workshop report.* The National Academies Press. doi:10.17226/13238

Rentzou, K., & Slutsky, R. (Eds.). (2020). *Early childhood education and care quality in Europe and the USA: Issues of conceptualization, measurement and policy.* Routledge. doi:10.4324/9780429283185

Wilinski, B. (2017). *When pre-K comes to school: Policy, partnerships, and the early childhood education workforce.* Teachers College Press.

Yaya-Bryson, D., Scott-Little, C., Akman, B., & Cassidy, D. J. (2020). A comparison of early childhood classroom environments and program administrative quality in Turkey and North Carolina. *International Journal of Early Childhood, 52*(2), 233–248. doi:10.100713158-020-00268-2

KEY TERMS AND DEFINITIONS

Early Childhood Care and Education: Care and education provided in settings where children are cared for and taught by individuals other than their parents or primary caregivers with whom they live.

Early Childhood Program Quality: The characteristics of early childhood programs that promote the physical, cognitive, emotional, and social development of children. High quality programs typically go beyond the minimum requirements, utilize Developmentally Appropriate Practice, and prioritize sufficient teacher and administrative qualifications, among others qualities.

Early Childhood Workforce: The wide range of individuals engaged in the care and education of young children including caregiving, teaching, and administrative staff, as well as consultants, learning specialists, and others.

In-Service Education: Refers to professional development activities that working educators participate to enhance their skills and remain up to date about knowledge and practices in the field.

Preservice Education: The education, training and/or professional experiences that an educator may undergo before they assume a particular role or position within an education program.

Chapter 3
The Core of Professional Development for English Language Teachers:
The Case of Bahrain

Hasan Mohsen Al-Wadi
Bahrain Teachers College, University of Bahrain, Bahrain

ABSTRACT

The lesson study strategy or what was called 'research lesson' has recently been a global mode in professional development programmes that can assist in filling the gap between what, how, and why teachers need to change and improve their teaching practices inside the classroom. This chapter provides a systematic review of the application of the lesson study strategy as an approach for seeking professional development on the part of the English language teachers in some Bahraini schools through a tailored school-based professional development programme. A comparison of the lesson study practice in Bahrain to the international practices will be made through determining the aims and procedures followed in this programme and the impact after its implementation. Lessons and consideration for future implementation of professional development programmes that are based on the lesson study strategy for ESL/EFL teachers in Bahrain will also be highlighted and discussed.

BACKGROUND ABOUT THE PROJECT CONTEXT

The Kingdom of Bahrain is an archipelago made up of more than 35 islands (about 700 sq.km.) located just over 20 km off the east coast of Saudi Arabia and about

DOI: 10.4018/978-1-7998-9278-6.ch003

30 km to the west of the peninsula of Qatar. This strategic location has provided Bahrain with a leading role in the Gulf region to accept initiative strategic projects in finance, commerce, transportation but more fundamentally in education where many educational developments have been carried out since the beginnings of the last century. This has had an obvious impact on the development of the teachers in that they have become better able to think openly and accept the culture of change during their work and interact throughout the implementation of these educational developmental projects which they have been exposed to.

With regard to formal education, official schooling in Bahrain started in the second decade of the last century. The first school for boys was opened in 1919 while the first school for girls was opened in 1928. Formal education started in 1930 announcing the era of public education and higher education was part of it when the students who had successfully finished their secondary school were sent abroad to pursue their university studies in medicine and engineering. The first batch of college students was sent to Beirut in Lebanon in 1938.

In terms of the initial teacher education programmes, both one year pre-service and two-year in-service programmes were offered to secondary school graduates in the 1960s to qualify them to act as certified teachers in the public schools and teach the core subjects. Since then, education in Bahrain has gone through several phases of development and reform.

After the new millennium in 2006, the government of Bahrain launched a new education reform plan to respond to the Kingdom of Bahrain's Education Reform initiatives as outlined in the Government of Bahrain's Vision 2030 proposed by the Economic Development Board (EDB). The focus of these initiatives is to improve the quality of teaching and learning for all Bahraini teachers and students. Consequently, new pre- and in-service training programmes have been designed and offered through the foundation of the Bahrain Teachers' College (BTC) in collaboration with international institutions such as the National Institute of Education (NIE) in Singapore to be the only and main provider for teacher professional development programs outside the Ministry of Education (MOE) to ensure quality and consistency with the government's vision. In 2018, the BTC formed new strategic collaborations with MOE by facilitating in-school training and professional development and in 2020 it launched a new strategic plan that focuses on improving school leaders, specifically senior teachers, in their professional and academic knowledge and skills. Currently, the BTC offers the following programs with the support and funding of the MOE:

- Bachelor (B.Ed) programs for Cycle 1 and Cycle 2 (primary school teachers)
- Part-time Postgraduate Diploma in Education (PGDE) (specialised subjects' teachers for intermediate and secondary schools)

- Teacher Leadership Programs (TLP) for head teachers and Senior Leadership Programme (SLP) for school principals.
- The Continuous Professional Development Programme for Private School Teachers (CPD for private school teachers)

These programmes have been designed and directed to equip the teacher candidates, employed teachers, and school leaders with the needed skills and knowledge to implement better teaching and learning practices in their schools. This enables them to better fulfill requirements related to the main projects led by the MOE to enhance the quality and level of learning and teaching at an international level, such as literacy strategy & Trends in International Mathematics and Science Study (TIMSS) or primary learners, evidence-based teaching for intermediate and secondary learners, and achieving the view of school as an independent entity through a professional and effective leadership role.

English Language Teaching Context in Bahrain

English enjoys a prestigious status in the educational context in the Kingdom of Bahrain. It is taught as a core subject in all the three stages in the formal school system from the 1st grade primary to the 3rd grade secondary at a rate of five to six 60-minute periods per week. This indeed shows the important and essential role of English perceived by the curricula experts and policymakers in Bahrain (Curriculum Document for Primary Education, 2005 & Curriculum Document for Secondary Education, 2004). Furthermore, English is also used as the main medium of instruction in higher education including the initial teacher preparation programmes at the BTC. This implies that the aim of teaching English in the formal system is not limited to teaching English for communication purposes only but also for academic purposes, such as accessing recent knowledge resources, and for professional purposes in the workplace.

This all has granted English the same value and prestige as the mother tongue Arabic, on the other hand, it has demanded to ensure that English language teachers (ELTs) are frequently updated and equipped with modern and effective teaching strategies to enable them to provide 'good teaching' to their English Foreign Language/English Second Language (EFL/ESL) learners. Accordingly, the Bahrain MOE has been carrying out regular and continuous training programmes to the ELTs across the different educational stages (primary, intermediate & secondary) to achieve this goal. These training programmes range from the general professional programmes offered by the BTC, such as lesson planning, creative writing, curriculum development and classroom management techniques to the specialized courses offered by the ELT specialists at MOE or other specialized organisations, such as the British Council, and publishers in which these teachers are trained on methods and techniques that can be implemented while teaching the assigned textbook to their learners.

It can be inferred from the above that despite the fact of the continuity and variety of the offered professional development (PD) opportunities to the ELTs, they are either general profession-based or curriculum-based (Al-Nahar, 2001). For instance, both types of programmes focus on updating classroom techniques and teaching methods and/or introducing new teaching perspective. Changes in the curriculum or the adaptation of a new teaching technique or method usually bring the teachers in contact with state-of-the-art methodology or require them to develop a new teaching perspective, which often creates a deficit in their teaching skills and leads the trainers to adopt equipping aims, instead of the long-term enabling objectives (Mercer, 2018).

Another feature of these PD modes is the fact that it has to be carried out either at the very beginning or at the very end of the school year when there is no regular teaching. If training is required during other school days, timetables have to be re-arranged so that the teachers can leave school after completing most parts of their duties before the end of the school day. This means that PD sessions or modules must spread over a longer period of time, thus making it less efficient. Moreover, teacher participation in PD depends largely on the decisions made by school heads as to whether or not they can release their teachers to attend. Some school heads see that training in the morning as disruptive to the school day. Since there are no mandatory regulations that require teachers' participation after school hours, teachers' attendance in any PD programme or workshop depends on their motivation and professional commitment (Von Esch and Kavanagh, 2018).

As a result of the aforementioned constraints, the participant EFL/ESL teachers can normally only fulfil immediate issues arising from the implementation and follow-up of these PD programmes instead of long-term, developmental objectives. The time constraints require the prioritisation of topics or summarising them to cover the widest ground, while the prevailing culture of teaching for exams encourages participating teachers to prefer a methodology that is based on transmission of 'new' information, prescription of 'fail-safe' techniques, and demonstration of 'best' teaching models. These teachers would usually view the PD workshops or programmes they have joined as not offering them anything 'new' as they would have expected (Lopriore, 2020).

In addition, this design of PD provided for teachers has, so far, been top-down and skills-based, focusing on changing classroom behaviour, and taking the form of "a collection of isolated events" instead of a developmental process (Roberts, 1998:5; Peacock, 2009:1). This structure of PD is not underpinned by an explicit theory of learning/teaching, nor does it incorporate the teachers' earlier experiences and their perceptions of teaching. According to Wyatt and Oncevska (2016), the teachers in this mode of training and development are expected to be only recipients of a definite content or practice(s) under the label of "good" teaching practice(s), which will invalidate teachers' existing knowledge and teaching experiences, rather than allowing them to be used as a base for analysis, reflection and knowledge construction.

To conclude, this format of PD doesn't incorporate microteaching, a demonstration of a mini lesson simulating the practice in actual reality, in training activities. This limitation may not reinforce the participating teachers' apprehension of being observed and evaluated by their peers. Al-Darwish and Sadeqi (2016:127) suggest that "microteaching can become a valuable tool for teachers' conceptual development within a constructivist model". The analysis and discussions that stem from microteaching and peer observation can enhance the teachers' conceptual development, acceptance of personal differences as well as their ability to reflect on their own teaching practices. Hence, these restrictions and teachers' attitude to PD may not nurture a culture of reflective teaching in which teachers become more aware of their teaching by reflecting upon their classroom practices in the light of the newly constructed knowledge derived from the conducted PD sessions/programmes.

Lesson Study as an Alternative PD: Design – Content Focus – Coherence and Duration

Before explaining the lesson study project that was implemented with the Bahraini EFL/ESL teachers in their schools, it will be helpful to provide a background about lesson study as one of approaches for teachers' professional development nowadays.

In fact, the first attempts to adopt the lesson study practice as a PD approach was originated in Japan. According to Dotger (2015), the Japanese educators utilised lesson study as a method to support their teachers to analyse their practices and identify areas for significant improvement through a collaborative style of work. Ustuk and Comoglu (2019) explain that lesson study appeared in the west as an official form of PD for teachers in the mid-1990s and was led by the scholars Stigler and Heibert (1999) and Lewis (2004).

With regard to the lesson study design and focus, Lewis (2000) mentions it is a process-based model in which the participating teachers collaboratively plan to research a lesson. All the participating teachers should take a role in the lesson planning and preparation but only one of them will perform it while the rest will stay observing him/her. After implementation, all the teachers will hold a meeting in which they will discuss to what extent the goal or vision of the lesson was successfully achieved. Based on the discussion, another teacher of the same group will perform the lesson trying to achieve the specified goal or vision more sufficiently.

Dudley (2013), on the other hand, mentions another form of lesson study that is analysis-based model. According to him, the lesson study starts with an initial meeting of the participating teachers in which they identify what aspect(s) of performance they want to improve when delivering a specific lesson. After that, one member of the group can perform the lesson while the others collect data from the students through interviews and surveys about what they liked and disliked in the lesson. The same team meet again and decide what change should be made to the lesson and who to perform it in the next time.

Alternatively, Cajkler and Wood (2016a) introduced a more practical model where the teachers are asked to identify a challenge they normally face in their teaching/learning context, implement a possible solution to resolve it, and measure its effect on students' learning. The lesson is revisited after conduction by the teachers through reflections focusing mainly on students' learning and how it should be re-taught in the future.

In the Bahraini context, an eclectic model was adopted from the three models mentioned above. The lesson study project was implemented with ESL/ESL teachers (n=12) in different schools (n=3) of different educational stages (primary, intermediate & secondary). During the project, the teachers were exposed to a workshop on doing action research and reflective practice in their profession. Then, each ESL/EFL group in the three schools was asked to collaborate with their head teacher to decide on a constant challenge they face while teaching English to their learners and identify a possible solution to implement in their teaching through their reference and reading of relevant literature (practical model – Cajkler and Wood, 2016b). The teachers were also requested to collaborate by doing peer observations on the first phase of implementing the change in their practice and discuss their reflections in a series of meetings (analysis model – Dudley, 2014). The teachers were also asked to do a second phase of their teaching in which they all decided on an improvement that should be added to the change they had decided about on phase one to implement in their teaching (process model – Lewis, 2000). In addition to this all, arrangements were made for peer observations among the teachers' groups in each school with the association of the researcher trainer as an external guide and evaluator. The following diagram illustrates the mechanism for conducting the designed eclectic approach of lesson study:

As it can be found in Figure 1, the teachers developed a transformative understanding of the change they needed to consider in their teaching under the guidance in a workshop in which they were equipped with the required skills of reflective practice and research skills to study and analyse their lessons in order to decide what action to be taken to improve their practice. This is indeed the opposite of the norm followed in the traditional professional development modes provided for the teachers in which they would act as passive learners who receive content from

Figure 1. Mechanism of Lesson Study Implementation in Bahraini School Context

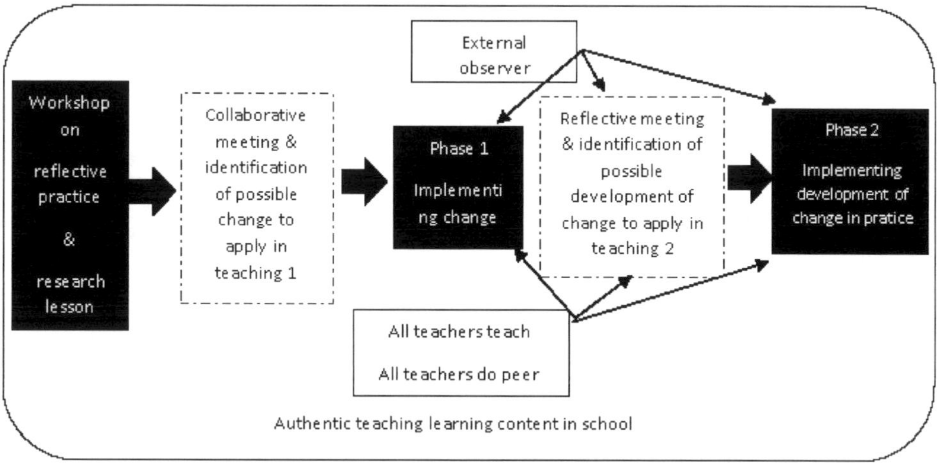

[Figure: Flowchart showing: Workshop on reflective practice & research lesson → Collaborative meeting & identification of possible change to apply in teaching 1 → Phase 1 Implementing change → Reflective meeting & identification of possible development of change to apply in teaching 2 → Phase 2 Implementing development of change in pratice. External observer connects to Phase 1 and Phase 2. All teachers teach / All teachers do peer. Authentic teaching learning content in school.]

an external expert. On the contrary, in this lesson study model, the external expert himself acted as a participant who belonged to those teachers through observing their lessons and sharing the attendance of their meetings as well (Lamb and Aldous, 2016).

The implementation of the lesson study PD programme lasted for one month in which the change cycle and the development cycle that had been proposed by the teachers took two weeks for each (10 lessons per cylce). During this time, the teachers were asked to justify and rationalize their proposed change and its development through referring to the published literature and reflecting on their current school teaching and learning context. Accordingly, four major teaching practices were identified as the change to be implemented by those ESL/EFL teachers with their learners:

- Using Socratic discussions to promote oral communications in ESL/EFL lessons.
- Improving writing skills through gallery walks and painting.
- Utilizing presentation skills for increasing students' confidence while speaking as ESL/EFL learners.
- Reinforcing team work through group projects and collective feedback.

What was noticeable about the above practices was that the participating teachers managed to rationalise their proposed changes and their development depending on different sorts of data in addition to the literature they had read and reviewed. The data were both quantitative through measuring their learners' progress by tests and homework and qualitative through systematic group interviews with students every 3 lessons and before each test or homework. This enabled the teachers to not only share their experiences with their peers, i.e., ESL/EFL teachers in other schools, but also theorise about their practices to their colleagues within the same school. Hunter and Back (2011:110) describe this practice and consider it as the core for establishing "professional learning communities" because when the participating teachers are involved in lesson study, they will be allowed to explore the possibility that any one participant might aim to identify himself or herself in multiple ways, in service of more than one social purpose. According to Hunter and Back (2011, p. 96), teachers' involvement in the lesson study project as part of their professional development motivates these teachers to position themselves as participants in the lesson study community in which they are engaged with social work associated with developing the study lesson and developing their professional identities within the group without being conscious of their act since it is embodied in the act of their participation.

As an assertion to the above, the outcomes of the conducted lesson study PD programme with those groups of ESL/EFL teachers was shaped into four action research reports that were presented and shared with the cluster schools where participating teachers' work. In addition, the schools' managements of the participating teachers were also supplied with data on students' and teachers' performance to facilitate the decision-making policy regarding the implementation of the target practices, specifically the ones examined and experienced in the lesson study project, by considering them in the strategic plans for those schools for the next school year.

COMPASSING FUTURE DESIGN OF PD FOR TEACHERS IN LIGHT OF LESSON STUDY

Experience with lesson study as an approach for developing the ESL/EFL teachers' teaching skills show that this approach can well support the participating teachers in achieving the following:

a. *Emphasising the central role of teachers to achieve the national goals.* It was apparent during the practice of the lesson study that the participating teachers felt a sense of "autonomy", "initiative", "desire to change/learn", and "problematise actual reality". This was reflected in their suggestions and interactions during their discussion meetings in which each member of the group was able to provide his/her suggestion(s) and involve the others to share how to implement that suggestion in real practice. This was also supported with guidance and leadership from the head teacher who was attending those meetings and represented the middle leadership of the school management in this regard. As well, the participating teachers managed to publicise, share and exchange their studied teaching practices with their peers in the cluster schools within their districts because their practices were found contextualized and responded to similar challenges or needs. Carjkler and Wood (2016b) assert this result of applying lesson study in teachers' PD and explain that it is a powerful means through which the practitioner teachers can develop agency in their teaching practice. Simultaneously, Lamb and Aldous (2016) report that lesson study can provide a way for the teachers to rise to the national priorities while still remaining in the classroom. According to the researchers, though the participating teachers in lesson study do not receive financial reward when they are conducting lesson study, they do get an opportunity to disseminate their practices and ideas without leaving their classrooms.

b. *Promotion of reflective practice culture in teaching.* Another evident result of applying lesson study in teacher PD is the promotion of reflective teaching practice. This important mental practice was witnessed throughout the applications of the two phases and it supported the teachers' engagement in identifying and elaborating specific teaching styles and strategies to enhance their teaching skills. Consequently, this has enabled these teachers to transform their understanding of their student learning as well as their teaching practices to be more contextualized since the issues they have investigated throughout their lesson study were meaningful to their local teaching context (Tasker, 2011; Olteanu, 2016).

c. *Practicing 'transformative pedagogy' in real context & achieving institutional reform* Overall, the implementation of lesson study has proven that researching the lesson and examining the new practices directly in the actual practice by the practitioner teachers can be an effective means to bridge the research-pedagogy gap and reinforce the concept of "transformative pedagogy". Several studies assert this result. For instance, Sato and Loewen (2019) discuss that transforming pedagogical practices usually comes as a result from the communities of practice which are formed during the lesson study practice. This was seen in the implemented lesson study project with the ESL/EFL teachers when the participating teachers established transformative dialogues with the external observer (the researcher) and took part in shaping the teaching style they had read about in their literature. In this regard, Dudley (2014) views this type of action as a potential to change the institutional norms and dynamics in the way the teachers' involvement in lesson study can assist in creating safe and trustworthy environments where they can get engaged in examining knowledge taken from research as well as exchanging experiences with peers. In addition, Saito et al (2014) explained how lesson study can play a part in the school reform project by directing the lesson study practice to achieve long-term goals for the teaching practices like the phases done in this regard which lasted for more than one week during which new beliefs and social and professional interactions occurred that have led to constant professional development on the part of the participating teachers.

CONCLUSION

The rationale, structure and outcomes resulted from implementing the lesson study PD programme for ESL/EFL Bahraini teachers support the argument that engaging teachers in lesson study activity is an effective way to support them in sustaining a proper level of PD throughout facilitating awareness of effective teaching pedagogies in ESL/EFL and the teachers' use of these pedagogies to fulfill their learners' language needs. This has managed to demonstrate 'good teaching' practices on the part of the participating teachers as well as their school leadership to go over part of their challenges and fulfill some strategic goals related to their schools' initiatives.

However, the experience of lesson study PD programme also informs that a more systematic and cohesive PD structure should be designed that guarantees going beyond 'good practices' by coordinating the efforts to fulfill the needs of the ESL/EFL learners as well as achieving the general teaching learning professional goals of the school. This can only happen when the lesson study PD programme consists of specific knowledge and applications of English language, proficiency skills and cultural implications needs that the participating ESL/EFL teachers are drawn attention to while they are in the programme. According to Freeman (2004) and Gandara et al. (2003), addressing general teaching and cultural implications or content will not necessarily positively impact the ESL/EFL teachers' pedagogies nor will it add to their professional growth. In this regard, de Jong and Harper (2005) clarify that the gap between 'good teaching' and 'effective ESL/EFL instruction' in lesson study projects can be filled in through ensuring that in any lesson study PD programme for ESL/EFL teachers, the research lesson activities must be guided by three main dimensions, they are: 1) second language learning process; 2) language and culture as a medium of instruction, and 3) language and culture as a goal of learning English as a foreign or second language.

Accordingly, and based on what has been achieved in the Bahraini experience, future lesson study projects that intended to be conducted with in-service ESL/EFL teachers should incorporate more emphasis on incorporating content regarding language and culture that are also consistent and coherent with the other professional development efforts priorities and practices that are shared with teachers of other subjects.

REFERENCES

Al-Darwish, S., & Sadeqi, A. (2016). Microteaching impact on student teachers' performance: A case study from Kuwait. *Journal of Education and Training Studies*, *4*(8), 126–134. doi:10.11114/jets.v4i8.1677

Al-Nahar, T. (2001). Evaluation of the Effectiveness of the Training Programmes for the Basic Subjects (Arabic & English Languages and Science). Directorate of Training: Bahrain.

Cajkler, W., & Wood, P. (2016a). Adapting lesson study to investigate classroom pedagogy in initial teacher education: What student-teachers think. *Cambridge Journal of Education*, *46*(1), 1–18. doi:10.1080/0305764X.2015.1009363

Cajkler, W., & Wood, P. (2016b). Mentors and student-teachers "lesson studying" in initial teacher education. *International Journal for Lesson and Learning Studies*, *5*(2), 84–98. doi:10.1108/IJLLS-04-2015-0015

de Jong, E., & Harper, C. A. (2005). Preparing mainstream teachers for English-language learners: Is being a good teacher good enough? *Teacher Education Quarterly*, *32*, 101–124.

Dotger, S. (2015). Methodological understandings from elementary science lesson study facilitation and research. *Journal of Science Teacher Education*, *26*(4), 49–369. doi:10.100710972-015-9427-2

Dudley, P. (2013). Teacher learning in lesson study: What interaction level discourse analysis revealed about how teachers utilized imagination, tacit knowledge of teaching and fresh evidence of pupils learning, to develop practice knowledge and so enhance their pupils' learning. *Teaching and Teacher Education*, *34*, 107–121. doi:10.1016/j.tate.2013.04.006

Dudley, P. (2014). *Lesson study: Professional learning for our time*. Routledge. doi:10.4324/9780203795538

Freeman, D. (2004). Teaching in the context of English language learners. In M. Sadowski (Ed.), Teaching immigrant and second-language students: Strategies for success. Cambridge, MA: Harvard Education Press.

Gandara, P., Rumberger, R., Maxwell-Jolly, J., & Callahan, R. (2003). English language learners in California schools: Unequal resources, unequal outcomes. *Education Policy Analysis Archives*, *11*(36), 1–52.

Hunter, J., & Back, J. (2011). Facilitating sustainable professional development through lesson study. *Mathematics Teacher Education and Development Journal, 13*(1), 94–114.

Lamb, P., & Aldous, D. (2016). Exploring the relationship between reflexivity and reflective practice through lesson study within initial teacher education. *International Journal for Lesson and Learning Studies, 5*(2), 99–115. doi:10.1108/IJLLS-11-2015-0040

Lewis, C. (2000). Lesson study: The core of Japanese professional development. *The Annual Meeting of the American Educational Research Association – Conference Proceedings.*

Lewis, C. (2004). Does lesson study have a future in the united states? *Journal of Social Science Education, 3*(1), 115–137. doi:10.4119/jsse-321

Lopriore, L. (2020). EFL awareness in ELT: Emerging challenges & new paradigms in teacher education. *Lingue e Linguaggi, 38*, 259–275.

Mercer, S. (2018). Psychology for language learning: Spare a thought for the teacher. *Language Teaching, 51*(4), 504–525. doi:10.1017/S0261444817000258

Ministry of Education. (2004). *Curriculum Document for English language curriculum for secondary education.* Kingdom of Bahrain: Directorate of Curricula – Secondary Education.

Ministry of Education. (2005). *Curriculum Document for English language curriculum for basic education.* Kingdom of Bahrain: Directorate of Curricula – Basic Education.

Olteanu, C. (2016). Reflection and the object of learning. *International Journal for Lesson and Learning Studies, 5*(1), 60–75. doi:10.1108/IJLLS-08-2015-0026

Peacock, M. (2009). The evaluation of foreign-language-teacher education programmes. *English Language Teaching Research, 13*(3), 259–278.

Roberts, J. (1998). *Language teacher education.* Arnold.

Saito, E., Murase, M., Tsukui, A., & Yeo, L. (2014). *Lesson study for learning community: A guide to sustainable school reform.* Routledge. doi:10.4324/9781315814209

Sato, M., & Loewen, S. (2019). Do teachers care about research? The research-pedagogy dialogue. *ELT Journal, 73*(1), 1–10. doi:10.1093/elt/ccy048

Stigler, J. W., & Hiebert, J. (1999). *The teaching gap: Best ideas from the world's teachers for improving education in the classroom.* The Free Press.

Tasker, T. (2011). Teacher learning through LS: An activity theoretical approach toward professional development in the Czech Republic. In K. E. Johnson & P. R. Golombek (Eds.), *Research on second language teacher education: A sociocultural perspective on professional development*. Routledge.

Ustuk, O. & Comoglu, I. (2019). Lesson study for professional development of English language teachers: Key takeaways from international practices. *Journal on Efficiency and Responsibility in Education and Science, 12*(2), 41-50. doi:10.7160/eriesj.2019.120202

Von Esch, K. S., & Kavanagh, S. S. (2018). Preparing mainstream classroom teachers of English learner students: Grounding practice-based designs for teacher learning in theories of adaptive expertise development. *Journal of Teacher Education, 69*(3), 239–251. doi:10.1177/0022487117717467

Wyatt, M., & Ončevska-Ager, E. (2016). Teachers' cognitions regarding continuing professional development. *ELT Journal, 71*(2), 171–185. doi:10.1093/elt/ccw059

Chapter 4
Turkish Postdoctoral Scholar Teaching Experiences and Professional Learning Opportunities From a Phenomenological Lens

Saadet Kuru-Çetin
Mugla University, Turkey

Nihan Demirkasımoğlu
Hacettepe University, Turkey

ABSTRACT

The purpose of this study is to analyze the professional learning and development opportunities of postdoctoral researchers from the faculty of education with phenomenological design to discover the experiences of the Ph.D. research assistants and assistant professors working for a teaching university at non-tenure status. The data were gathered through semi-structured interviews and analyzed using content analysis. The findings revealed that postdoctoral scholars experienced difficulties such as material development, teaching methods, and classroom management skills. Results suggested that postdoctoral scholars' teaching experiences mostly improved by their individual efforts and more university support is needed to to manage this stressful experience. The postgraduate's abroad experience is another factor that requires special attention in the role transition of academics since the cultural contexts of the studied and teaching may differ to a large extent. Universities should develop programs that are well-designed and include practice-based learning opportunities.

DOI: 10.4018/978-1-7998-9278-6.ch004

Copyright © 2022, IGI Global. Copying or distributing in print or electronic forms without written permission of IGI Global is prohibited.

INTRODUCTION

Postdoctoral scholars are the main source of future academia. Postdoctoral scholars' professional skills need several development opportunities including teaching among the other responsibilities such as research, publishing, and service to society (Nowell, 2018). A few research has been conducted to examine the viewpoints of Turkish postdoctoral scholars related to their teaching experiences and professional learning opportunities. One of the related researches (Hidiroğlu, et al., 2010) showed that faculty members, experts and assistant doctors working at a medical school in Turkey perceived their knowledge levels high, while continuous professional development levels were perceived to be low. In a recent study examining the postdoctoral scholars' current professional learning opportunities and required competencies, results revealed that although academics participate in a variety of professional learning, the perceived usefulness of the activities varies greatly and the types of professional learning and development they participate in may not be sufficient to best support their future careers (Nowell et al, 2020a). Postdoctoral scholars in universities seek professional learning and development opportunities through informal or formal activities to increase current or future knowledge, skills, and abilities. Formal activities can be exemplified as seminars, conferences, and workshops while informal activities cover mentoring, co-teaching and communities of practice (Nowell et al, 2019). This issue is a multifaceted phenomenon including the institution's role. Therefore, deepening our understanding related to the professional learning possibilities, and teaching activities of postdoctoral students may help to redesign the learning environment of young scholars to reach their full potential.

This study, focusing on the experiences of Turkish postdoctoral scholars, has the potential to contribute the current literature by describing teaching and learning experiences from different fields of education comparatively..

Research Questions

The purpose of this study is to examine the academic development of postdoctoral researchers through their teaching experiences. For this purpose, answers to the following questions were sought.

1. How do the doctoral research assistants and doctor faculty members in the first years of their career (1-3 years) define their teaching experience?
2. What are their perceptions of teaching roles?
3. What do they think about the professional learning opportunities that graduate studentship provides them in terms of teaching and learning? (adapted from McGugan, 2012)

4. What kind of processes are required to be successful in teaching roles from the perspectives of those postdoctoral students"? (adapted from McGugan, 2012).

LITERATURE

There is not consensus about the definition of postdoctoral positions. It is used to refer "non-tenured research-only academic positions whose holders have a PhD or equivalent qualification' (Marceau and Preston, 1996) and "early-career researchers' as those in the first five years of academic or research related employment following completion of postgraduate and postdoctoral (Bazeley et al., 1996, as cited in Åkerlind, 2005) research training" by different authors. Within the context of Turkish higher education system, postdoctoral scholars in universities refer to the research assistants with Ph.D. degree called as doctor research assistants. Most of the professional learning and development of postdoctoral academics occurs in the first years because at this stage, depending on their new start to the profession, the deep difference between their professional ideals and their daily working practices is felt and the different roles of faculty members (Bakioğlu & Yaman, 2004).

Examining the problems experienced by faculty members who have just started their careers, Gümüş and Gök (2016) revealed that new faculty members have problems such as having too much course load, not being able to spare time for research, having trouble adapting during the transition to teaching, and not being able to establish academic cooperation with colleagues. One reason is that institutional support for the teaching roles of postdoctoral scholars and academic mentoring is not satisfactory in general. Boice (1991) empirically proved that postdoctoral academics feel alone because of the faculty administration's passive position for the sake of academic autonomy. For this reason, besides their other roles and responsibilities, teaching roles are also left to the academic's personal efforts and successful transition to these roles becomes problematic many times (Cawyer, Simonds & Davis, 2002). Studying abroad also can contribute to this feeling of loneliness. Gümüş and Gök (2016) found that the new academic staff who completed their doctorate abroad experience serious problems and feel alone in the system. Education is one of the most important issues that faculty members need support in the first years of their profession.

In a study focusing on the teaching experiences of postdoctoral researchers in the United Kingdom (UK), it was determined that teaching roles have a complex structure and the interaction of faculty members with these roles occurs in five basic processes. These processes are: informal meetings with colleagues, feedback on their teaching performance, observation of other teaching staff, collaborative work, and training (McGugan, 2012). Nerad (2012), on the other hand, argues that people with a doctorate should have abilities such as traditional skills and competencies, professional competencies. These processes and abilities constitute the main blocks in the development of the teacher's identity as a lecturer. (McGugan, 2013; Nerad 2012). These processes and abilities that contribute to the development of postdoctoral researchers are also the output of the knowledge and skills they need to obtain before the doctorate (Sharmini, & Spronken-Smith). These processes, which are supported during and after the doctorate, can contribute to the development of the faculty. When institutions provide supportive contextual conditions for faculty members, new faculty members can adapt to the new work environment easier (Kondakçı & Haser, 2019). Besides the universities, some other institutions work for the preparation of postdoctoral researchers in some countries. For example, in the UK and Australia, research funding bodies support the broader skills development opportunities of postdoctoral researchers as part of government policy (Åkerlind, 2009). In developing the professional learning experiences of young scholars in the early years of their postdoctoral career, research-based and experiential learning opportunities can improve their learning outcomes and early career experiences (Nowell et al., 2020b). The importance of formalized teacher training and experiences for postdoctoral academics has been recognized by many universities. They prepare certified training programs to support the teaching and learning needs of postdoctoral researchers in their transitional roles. Recently, more attention is directed to the authentic experiences of university teachers as learners from experiencing the "real world skills" through the formalized programs. These programs have enough evidence to enrich their content including the courses such as communication, problem-solving and leadership (Nowell et al., 2020b).

In a study investigating the effectiveness of one of these programs (Nowell et al., 2020), it is reported that doctoral students and postdoctoral academics demand learning opportunities where they can gain meaningful learning experiences. According to the authors, at this point, experiential learning opportunities are increasingly coming to the fore because of their positive impact on the quality of the learning experience in the field of higher education by enabling learners to develop real-world skills and making it meaningful to the beneficiaries. One of the most important skills for new faculty is instructional design. Developing these skills during graduate or postdoctoral studies can contribute to a confident start to a faculty member's career (Hoffmann et al., 2021). In a study conducted to determine their views on current professional learning and development opportunities used by postdoctoral academics, it has been determined that the professional development support given directly by the supervisors is mostly directed towards researcher roles and that postdoctoral professionals need quality guidance and support to develop a broader skillset compatible with their expanding career trajectory (Nowell et al.,

2020). Educational opportunities to develop the teaching skills of Ph.D. scholars in faculty roles are more limited compared to opportunities to prepare them for roles such as research skills and writing. Moreover, when these programs are offered as just-in-time training for urgent needs such as teaching roles, the content and presentation style of the training programs may differ (Hoffmann et al., 2021). In a competitive global economic environment, approaches that go beyond apprenticeship models include formal and informal initiatives that take care of faculty professional socialization skills at the departmental level including peer cooperation and learning communities are recommended for the successful preparation of doctoral students for future teaching roles (Nerad, 2012).

Teaching and Learning Opportunities for Postdoctoral Scholars in Turkey

The general framework of the higher education system in Turkey is regulated by the Council of Higher Education (CoHE). In Turkey, there are four processes applied to research assistants during their graduate education to train faculty members. The first of these processes is the university's program. If the university has its program, research assistants complete their postgraduate education here. The second option is for research assistants to do their postgraduate education abroad. The third option that universities that do not have graduate programs apply to train faculty members is to send research assistants to developed/central universities within the scope of Articles 33 and 35 of the 2547 Higher Education Law No.2547. In Article 33 of the relevant Law, the status of research assistant is explained as follows to meet the need for academic staff: "Research assistants are members of the ancillary staff who assist with research, studies, and experiments in higher education institutions, as well as carrying out other duties assigned by authorized bodies". Again, according to Article 35 of the same law, research assistants constitute the basic human resources and talent pool of the higher education system in the future. Article 35 of this law states: "To meet their own needs and those of other higher education institutions either newly established or yet to be established, higher education institutions are responsible for the training of their faculty members, at home or abroad, and in accordance with the principles and objectives of development plans and also in accordance with the needs and principles set down by the CoHE." The fourth option is to train faculty members within the framework of the Faculty Member Training Program which was created by combining the 35th and 33rd articles of the Law No. 2547 in the 2001-2002 academic year. Faculty Member Training Program is a model developed by blending the 33rd and 35th articles of the Higher Education Law No. 2547, which covers foreign and domestic doctoral education, and operates as a domestic-foreign integrated doctoral program (Yalçınkaya, Koşar & Altunay, 2014).

Within the scope of the "Mission Differentiation and Specialization Project" initiated by the CoHE in 2017, it was decided to designate some state universities in Turkey as "research universities" to contribute to the efficient use of infrastructure and human resources in higher education and to increase the international visibility of the universities (YÖK, 2017). As of 2021, ten state universities in Turkey are within the scope of research universities. The participants interviewed within the scope of this research work at a university that focuses on teaching. Although the paths followed in the training of faculty members in Turkey have changed over the years, it is seen that this process continues with different options. It can be stated that the existence of the ways followed in the training of faculty members is an indication that the process is not fully settled. The differentiation of these processes inevitably also affects the education and training activities of post-doctoral faculty members. However, there is no regulation regarding the orientation of academics during the transition to teaching staff after doctorate, and some universities are trying to fulfill this function with their own programs. Therefore, some approaches differ from university to university and even between faculties. This research analyzes the phenomenon of teaching roles of Turkish postdoctoral academics from their perspectives adding new insights concerning their professional learning and development experiences. Understanding this neglected phenomenon in Turkish higher education setting will contribute to professional learning and development initiatives of policy makers.

METHOD

Design

This qualitative study is designed with phenomenological design to discover the experiences of the Ph.D. research assistants and assistant professors in their first years of the academic journey.

Research Setting

The research setting was a faculty of education with a variety of undergraduate and graduate programs in Turkey. The university does not have a legal policy for the orientation of postdoctoral academics to prepare them for their new career roles. In such cases in Turkey, doctoral education is considered to be sufficient for faculty roles including research and teaching or left to the initiative of the university's policy or the department's discretion. Almost all the postdoctoral academics learn on their own or through informal channels such as peer assistance. In this phenomenological qualitative study, doctor faculty members were also included as postdoctoral researchers because this is one of the positions in which research assistants perform their first teaching duties as independent academics if they can find a position right after Ph.D. In other words, doctor research assistants and doctor faculty members refer to the two academic status that the teaching responsibility starts in the academic career.

Participants

Participants are composed of postdoctoral students representing the fields of social sciences and natural and applied sciences in a public university. The first group is selected among the postgraduate research assistants and assistant professors in their first three years from the faculty of education representing the field of social sciences. According to the legislation of the Turkish Council of Higher Education, graduate students who are at the same time research assistants cannot be assigned for the graduate studentship process. Thus, this group has a very limited role in contributing their teaching experience opportunities. The second group will be composed of postgraduate research assistants and assistant professors from the field of natural and applied sciences. This group has the opportunity to assist the laboratory courses in their departments under the supervision of their professors. Despite not being a formal and structured professional learning opportunity in terms of teaching, this group seems to be more advantaged after postgraduate positions for teaching roles and responsibilities. This difference may result in their variations in professional learning and teaching experiences. Participants are the postdoctoral scholars with the titles of doctor research assistant and doctor faculty member (so-called in Turkish Higher Education Law, the synonym of assistant professor) who are working for a teaching university at non-tenure status. Participants are working in several departments of education colleges and some of them have abroad graduate studentship experience. Maximum variation sampling is applied to cover a wide range of experiences among; women and men, Ph.D. research assistants and assistant professors, different departments of educational sciences. More information is presented in Table 1.

As can be seen from Table 1, participants composed of different faculties and departments with varying teaching fields and experiences. Two of the participants work in the faculty of technology, five in the faculty of education, one in the faculty of letters, and one in the Faculty of Economics and Administrative Sciences. There are five men and five women participants. Participants' experiences vary from one to five years.

Table 1. Characteristics of participants

Participant	Gender	Academic Title	Years of Experience after Postdoctoral Degree	Type of Faculty	Department
P1	Female	Research Assistant	3 years	Faculty of Education	Department of Turkish and Social Sciences Education
P2	Male	Research Assistant	1 years	Faculty of Technology	Department of Woodworking Industrial Engineering
P3	Female	Doctor Faculty Member	3 years	Faculty of Education	Department of Educational Sciences
P4	Male	Research Assistant	1 years	Faculty of Education	Department of Educational Sciences
P5	Male	Research Assistant	5 years	Faculty of Education	Department of Educational Sciences
P6	Male	Research Assistant	2 years	Faculty of Technology	Department of Woodworking Industrial Engineering
P7	Female	Doctor Faculty Member	3 years	Faculty of Letters	Department of Modern Turkish Dialects and Literatures
P8	Male	Research Assistant	2 years	Faculty of Education	Department of Educational Sciences
P9	Female	Research Assistant	3 years	Faculty of Education	Department of Special Education
P10	Female	Doctor Faculty Member	5 years	Faculty of Economics and Administrative Sciences	Department of Business Administration

Data Collection

Tha data were gathered by the semi-structured interview form. The semi-structured interview form was mostly based on the research questions of McGugan (2012) investigating the postdoctoral researchers' teaching experiences. Draft interview forms were forwarded to the field experts for feedback, and the final version of the form was created considering their views. All the participants will be ensured anonymity and confidentiality. The interview form included the following questions:

1. How do you feel about teaching?
2. How do you see yourself in terms of teaching knowledge and skills?
3. Do you remember your first teaching experience? How was it?
4. What opportunities did you have to improve your teaching skills during your doctoral studies?
5. What factors in your current situation help or hinder your teaching roles?
6. What kind of support do you need to develop their skills?

Data Analysis

Data were analyzed using the content analysis approach. Content analysis is based on the division of data into categories and subcategories (Yıldırım ve Şimşek, 2013). In this study, the academic development of postdoctoral scholars was examined in the context of their teaching experiences and professional learning opportunities. Thereupon, the findings were independently re-themed and interpreted. Accordingly, six themes were identified as: "Postdoctoral's perceptions of the teaching roles of academics", "Self-perceptions of Participants' related to their Teaching Skills", "Challenges of First Teaching Experience", "Opportunities supporting postdoctoral scholars' teaching skills", "Factors help or hinder postdoctoral scholars' teaching roles" and "Postdoctoral scholars' need for learning opportunities". The themes were evidenced with the direct quotes (Yıldırım & Şimşek, 2013) of the participants. The responses were analyzed separately by two researchers and the inter-research consistency coefficient was calculated as %91 between two resarchers coding and analyzing schemas. In the analysis of the data, the participants were coded as P1-P10 and the information of the participants was kept confidential.

FINDINGS

The findings of the research were presented under six main themes, their sub-themes, and codes.

Postdoctoral's Perceptions of the Teaching Roles of Academics

Postdoctoral's perceptions of the teaching roles of academics were categorized under two subthemes and several categories within these themes. Participants have a positive perception related to their teaching roles (Table 2).

Table 2. Postdoctoral's perceptions of the teaching roles of academics

Theme	Sub-theme	Codes	Participants
Postdoctoral's perceptions of the teaching roles of academics	Positive attributes	Guide	P10, P3, P2, P6, P5
		Artist	P1
		Effort and dedication	P10, P4, P9
		Holy	P4, P7, P8
		Leader	P3
		Manager	P1
		Enjoyable	P9
	Negative attributes	Difficult	P4
		Tiring	P4

As can be seen from Table 2, one of the participants evaluated their teaching roles as difficult and tiring, while the other participants described their teaching roles with positive words such as "guidance, artist, holy, leader, manager, enjoyable". In addition, participants perceived the academic profession as requiring effort and dedication. For example, one participant expressed the teaching role as follows, expressing almost all of these characteristics:

"Teaching profession is a very valuable profession that requires significant effort, dedication and emotional labor" (P8).

Another participant expressed that the teaching role is differed from the past by the wide use of technology and emphasized the guiding role of faculty as follows:

"With the new changing situations, I think I can define my definition of teaching as a leader teacher. In the past, it was like taking and transferring information one-to-one, but with the changing technology, I think it is ideal that the student has access to different course resources, I think that the teacher should help the teacher how to reach which resources or help the student a little more in problem-solving, rather than transferring the information, I think that the teacher should guide the student (P3)."

Self-Perceptions of Participants' Related to their Teaching Skills

"How do you see yourself in terms of teaching knowledge and skills?" The responses of the participants are summarized in Table 3.

Table 3. Participants' perceptions related to their teaching skills

Theme	Sub-theme	Codes	Participants
Self-perceptions of Participants' related to their Teaching Skills	Sufficient	In terms of methodology	P1, P5, P6
		In terms of theoretical knowledge	P4
		In terms of communication	P6
	Insufficient	In terms of transferring knowledge	P8, P4, P2
		In terms of methodology	P6, P10, P1, P7
		In terms of communication	P3, P4

In Table 3, the opinions of the participants were examined in two sub-themes in terms of being sufficient and insufficient. While some participants found themselves sufficient in terms of communication with method and technique, some participants stated that they felt inadequate. K6 emphasized the advantage of a few age differences with the students, which in turn, provided easy communication with students. Below are examples of the participants' views on this theme.

"Before the doctoral process, I felt like I had learned everything, now I was a teacher. But as I saw the details of the subject during the doctoral process, I realized that this was not true, that I still had many things to learn. I realized I didn't know a lot of things. I know I'm at a certain level for my department. I think I'm good. However, I know that I have a long way to go to improve. Due to the fact that I had a small age difference with students in communication, I communicated comfortably with students. I tried to learn how to tell students through formation training. I also studied their behavior when I entered their classes with my professor" (P6).

"Although I feel more competent in terms of transferring knowledge and creating learning environments, I think I can improve myself more in terms of the variety of methods and techniques used" (P8).

First Teaching Experience and Challenges

Participants' first teaching experiences and memories of these experiences were asked with these questions: "Do you remember your first teaching experience? How was it?" In their responses, participants first mentioned their initial teaching experiences and then the difficulties they experienced. For example, K2 stated that entering some laboratory courses with his advisor prior to the teaching experience as an independent teacher improved his teaching skills:

I didn't teach before I got my doctorate. We were partially entering lab classes, and we were going in with them to assist him with our supervisor. If I hadn't assisted, would my situation be different now? I think I'd be further behind. Because when you analyze the lesson as a student, is very different from your psychology when you are a real teacher. I mean, while assisting my supervisor, I was actually putting myself in his shoes. How would I teach this lesson? I had the opportunity to observe his presentation technique and teaching technique, which was very effective in my teaching (P2).

Almost all of the participants answered this question by explaining the difficulties they experienced more than their memories of the first teaching experience. Participant postdoctorals' challenges of first teaching experience are presented in Table 4.

Table 4. Challenges of First Teaching Experience

Theme	Codes	Participants
Challenges of First Teaching Experience	Preparation of course material	P2
	Lack of knowledge of teaching methods and techniques	P6
	Differences between abroad experience and Turkish experience	P3
	Communication problems with the student	P3
	Deficiencies in classroom management skills	P5

From Table 4, it can be understood that postdoctoral scholars struggle with from course design, teaching methods, communication problems, and classroom management skills. Almost all the participants reported that they did not have teaching experience before Ph.D. graduation. Thus, many of the participants had difficulty in their first teaching experiences. A doctoral lecturer (P8) who took the course for the first time during the doctoral process and had no previous teaching experience, expressed his own experience as follows: "Rather than having difficulties while lecturing the preparation phase for the lesson was more tiring. Since I don't have any previous teaching experience, what methods and techniques will I use to convey the content, which examples will I choose as a basis, what kind of evaluation system will I set up, etc. I had to think and work on it. But after I started the lesson, I did not feel that I had difficulties in the teaching process. My systematic preparation also contributed to this. Otherwise, it would be a difficult and more tiring process "(K8).

K2 explained his stressful experience as follows: *"Of course, I had a hard time getting used to it. In other words, I had a difficulty in preparing and finding course material. It was a research study for me. There was some stress due to the limited time, but with the experience, I gained by both preparing and collecting these materials and giving lessons, I reached a very comfortable and good level at the end of this first semester"*. Another postdoctoral scholar with a Ph.D. degree abroad stressed the difference in academic culture between the abroad university and Turkey's higher education system she is working: *"Since I have studied with students abroad for a very long time, their point of view is different from the point of view of those here. Also, I couldn't apply the methods and techniques that I learned in theory. I wanted to do something different from the lecture. I didn't know exactly how to do it. In that sense, I had an adaptation problem. At first, it was difficult like that, I attended the classes of friends here and even took physics classes for about a semester, I gained experience by attending classes here, at least by listening to what the students are doing at class"* (K3).

Opportunities During Ph.D. Studentship

The question "What opportunities did you have to improve your teaching skills during your doctoral studies?" explored postdoctoral scholars' perception of opportunities that help them improve their teaching skills (Table 5).

Table 5. Opportunities during PhD studentship supporting postdoctoral scholars' teaching skills

Theme	Codes	Participants
Opportunities supporting postdoctoral scholars' teaching skills	Giving lectures with an advisor in undergraduate and graduate courses	P1, P2, P3, P4, P6
	Pedagogic formation	P4, P6
	Individual efforts (certificate programs, participation in projects)	P5, P6, P7, P4, P8 P9, P10
	Not provided	P7

One of the participants (P7) stated that he could not receive any support from the university in the development of his teaching skills; on the contrary, he could not find the opportunity to improve himself by being given drudgery. Therefore, it is understood that some of the participants tried to improve their teaching skills with their individual efforts. Emphasizing the importance of teaching assistantship among these opportunities, the participant stated as follows: *"We were teaching assistants, it was like an internship course. It was a lesson like special teaching methods with a teacher, but I was co-teaching. he usually lectured himself and gave some of it to me... once or twice when he went to the conference, I gave the whole lecture"* (K3). K4 stressed the role of pedagogical formation training as follows: *"In our time, there were formation courses like learning programs in doctoral courses. I have discussed a lot whether this should happen or not, especially in social sciences, teachers do not give much importance. They say that I care because I am in education, but it is not like that, the lesson is not just telling and going. The importance of classroom management is not understood."*

Another participant noted the absence of the university's training opportunities that prepare the prospective postdoctoral scholars for their future roles: *"A professional development program, etc., prepared by the university in this regard did not happen. All I remember is that a program was prepared for all lecturers during the distance education process and it was useful. Since I did not conduct distance lessons, I did not have the opportunity to practice. However, I conducted some theoretical and applied courses opened within the scope of the certificate program. This was an opportunity for me to improve my teaching skills. However, I can say that it is mostly the result of my individual efforts in terms of improving teaching skills"* (K8).

Opportunities and Challenges during COVID 19 Pandemics

Participants were asked "What factors in your current situation help or hinder your teaching roles?" to capture their current perceptions. Their responses were presented in Table 6.

From Table 6, it is understood that multiple roles of postdoctoral scholars such as research and publication and intense workload are the main challenging factors that they face during teaching. One participant complaining about course workload and variety of courses expressed his situation as follows (K3): "There are so many lessons. According to the people here, it's not too much, I take the minimum and do not take the rest, and I do my best not to take it. I am a newcomer, when there are 5-6 different lessons that I will teach for the first time, which one will I prepare in the best way and I am expected to research at the same time. None of them is complete, sometimes you prepare a little less for a lesson, other lessons are taught

Table 6. Factors that help or hinder postdoctoral scholars' teaching roles

Theme	Sub-themes	Codes	Participants
Factors help or hinder postdoctoral scholars' teaching roles	Challenges	Focusing on multiple workloads with publication and other academic work	P1, P9
		High course load and course variety	P3, P7, P9
		Distrust of the instructor and mistrust in some subjects	P8
	Helping factors	Learning from mistakes by watching online course recordings	P2
		Opportunity to do research with students	P5, P9
		Autonomy in teaching course content and choosing materials	P8

as much as possible now, there are too many lessons, of course, and nothing good comes out of these lessons."

One participant (K2) expressed the advantage of recorded courses during the pandemic to make a self-evaluation of teaching: *"Now, this period that we teach coincided with the distance education period. Therefore, we had the chance to watch the recordings created after the lessons. By watching these records, I realized the mistakes I saw in myself and the shortcomings I saw in teaching, and I started to change them"*.

Learning Opportunities Needed to Enhance the Teaching Role

Lastly, participants were asked, "What kind of support do they need to develop their skills?" Most of them needed a support at the university level (Table 7).

Table 7. Postdoctoral scholars' need for learning opportunities

Theme	Codes	Participants
Postdoctoral scholars' need for learning opportunities	To make the necessary cooperation for them to conduct lessons in private and public schools for a while.	P1
	Providing development opportunities for the university/department	P1, P2, P5, P8
	Individual effort and curiosity	P5, P9
	Reducing the course load	P9
	Getting educational formation during the doctoral period	P6
	Benefiting from the knowledge of experienced instructors	P7
	Get support for technological developments	P9

As can be seen from Table 7, early career scholars mostly emphasized the need for university or department-supported opportunities designed to provide them with skills such as collaboration with public and private schools coordinated by the university. For example, K8 highlighted the importance of collaborations in the department with these thoughts: *"Meetings, where good practices are shared, can be organized within the department. Again, the feedback received from the students at the end of the semester can be considered as useful opportunities in this regard. These feedbacks are directly specific to your teaching activity and are meaningful feedbacks. Based on this feedback, the missing dimensions in the teaching process can be analyzed and turned into learning opportunities. At the same time, constructive professional development programs organized on the basis of faculties and universities can be organized. However, I think that these programs can be beneficial if they are realized with an experience-sharing perspective, not as a course. On the other hand, national programs organized with the support of institutions can be supportive at this point. While individual efforts are valuable and meaningful, large field-specific experience-sharing meetings can be helpful"*.

Another participant suggested a collaboration between university and schools within this context (K1): *"The university can provide us with the following opportunity (it was on the agenda from time to time before): academic staff and members can be provided to conduct classes in public and private schools for a certain period and to be in the school environment... for this, academic points – incentives should also be provided"*.

DISCUSSION

This research analyzes the phenomenon of teaching roles of Turkish postdoctoral scholars from their perspectives concerning their professional learning and development experiences. The data analysis revealed six themes. Within the first theme, postdoctorals' perceptions of the teaching roles were mostly positive. They described their teaching roles as "guidance, artist, holy, leader, manager, enjoyable". Also, being an academic is perceived to involve significant effort, dedication, and emotional labor. This finding coincides with the findings of Tülübaş (2017) that come to the fore in the definition of the profession of mid-career academicians. Academicians are of the belief that service to humanity is at the core of academics. Accordingly, the academic profession needs emotional labor and dedication.

In the second theme, the opinions of academicians revealed their self-perceptions of teaching skills. While some of them felt inadequate in terms of methodology, theoretical knowledge, and communication skills, some of them felt adequate while teaching. The findings of Boice (1991) are parallel to our findings showing that new academics feel themselves alone and try to handle their responsibilities through their personal efforts which turn out to be a problematic role transition (Cawyer, Simonds & Davis, 2002).

The third theme is related to the challenges of the first teaching experience. The participants expressed several difficulties related to their initial teaching efforts such as material development, teaching methods, classroom management skills. Further, course design and planning before the class were found to be more exhaustive than the teaching during the course time. As a result, when new scholars do not know how to organize the instruction processes, the first teaching experiences of postdoctoral scholars turned out to be a stressful event. This finding is consistent with the past research revealing the first years' challenges of academics in different areas (Fantilli & McDougall, 2009; Stanulis, Fallona & Pearson, 2002; Gourneau, 2014). The postgraduate's abroad experience is another factor that requires special attention in the role transition of academics since the cultural contexts of the studied and teaching may differ to a large extent. Faculty candidates having long term experience in a different country and/or culture are likely to have more adaptation problems than the faculty's own graduates. This finding is supported in the research of Gümüş and Gök (2016) who found that the faculty with abroad Ph.D. degree had difficulties in adapting to both their institutions and the education-teaching process.

The fourth theme highlighted the opportunities of Ph.D. studentship. Participants expressed that distance education creates both challenges and opportunities similar to the findings of previous research (e.g. Sen & Kızılcalıoğlu, 2020). It is noteworthy that if postdoctoral scholars have previous teaching experience during graduate education, their transition to new teaching roles is easier. Additionally, postdoctoral scholars' main challenge was the intense workload, especially the intensity of teaching hours and the variety of courses to be taught. Besides, professional development programs seemed to be less than the new faculty needs. However, when these programs were provided by the university it was found to be supportive. As one participant (K3) reported, professional development programs offered by the university are more useful if the participant has the opportunity to practice. Finally, participants were asked about learning opportunities needed to enhance their teaching roles. Although participants expressed that there were different learning opportunities, the development opportunities of the university were limited, and the need for more, especially experience-based learning opportunities was emphasized. When institutions provide supportive contextual conditions for new academics, they can adapt to the new work environment more easily (Kondakçı & Haser, 2019). As Nowell et al. (2020b) stated, universities' professional learning programs that are research based offer valuable experiential learning opportunities which are critical in meeing the unique needs of their participants and are contextually appropriate. When based on experiential learning opportunities, instructional enhancement programs such as these certificate programs can strengthen teaching and learning approaches and practices and improve students' learning outcomes and experiences for both program participants and the undergraduate students they teach.

RECOMMENDATIONS

According to the research findings, the teaching skills acquired during and after the doctorate are considered important in the development of the self-confidence of the academicians in their teaching roles. Being an academician is accepted as a profession that has a lot of social outputs, and it is thought that the profession of the academics can be performed effectively only if it is done with a conscious choice and dedication. For this reason, it can be recommended to follow an approach that takes these qualifications into account in the selection of academics. In this respect, it would be useful to review the existing regulations neglecting these personal characteristics while entering the academic profession. Faculty members have difficulties due to the high course load and the diversity of the workload. Also, they need more guidance and feedback during their career transition. Since career transitions are stressful phases, their teaching workloads should be reduced. Supporting new postdoctoral scholars in publishing, participating in academic activities, and encouraging academic solidarity among faculty members will facilitate positive first experiences and successful career transitions. Lastly, international graduate experience causes an adaptation problem if there is a notable difference between the academic cultures of the universities where the graduate assistant obtained the Ph.D. degree and started to work. The orientation of this group of new academics needs a special design in professional development programs. Considering these findings holistically, the results of this research provide important clues to the universities and authorities that plan, develop and evaluate the process of career transition of graduate students to their new academic roles revealing their real professional learning and development opportunities.

FUTURE RESEARCH DIRECTIONS

There are many factors affecting postdoctoral scholars' teaching experiences and professional learning opportunities. This research is limited to the experiences of academics from the faculty of education. Further research may enlighten the different needs of postdoctoral scholars from different disciplines such as medicine, arts, engineering, and other. In the present study, the demographic characteristics of the academicians were not analyzed due to the qualitative nature of the research. Future research may consider the role of individual characteristics.

CONCLUSION

This qualitative study highlighted that Turkish postdoctoral scholars' teaching experiences mostly improved by their individual efforts and more university support is needed to start with positive motivation to manage this stressful experience. Although new scholars have some opportunities for teaching during graduate studentship, these experiences remain insufficient because they rely on the advisor's initiative. In other words, if professional learning and development opportunities of the new scholars' are not designed by the university or department as a part of its policy, new scholars need to find their own way, and this problem is tried to be solved by their personal efforts. Universities should develop programs that are well-designed and include practice-based learning opportunities. They should also take into account the field of study and needs of the new academic staff in the professional learning programs they will prepare for this purpose. Consequently, this research provides rationale for Turkish higher education legislation to develop better structured professional learning and development opportunities facilitating postdocotoral scholars' career transition phase.

ACKNOWLEDGMENT

This research received no specific grant from any funding agency in the public, commercial, or not-for-profit sectors.

REFERENCES

Åkerlind, G. S. (2005). Postdoctoral researchers: Roles, functions and career prospects. *Higher Education Research & Development*, *24*(1), 21–40. doi:10.1080/07294360520003 18550

Åkerlind, G. S. (2009). Postdoctoral research positions as preparation for an academic career. *International Journal for Researcher Development*, *1*(1), 84–96. doi:10.1108/1759751X201100006

Bakioğlu, A., & Yaman, E. (2004). Career developments of research assistants: Obstacles and solutions. *Marmara University Atatürk Education Faculty Journal of Educational Sciences, 20*(20), 1-20. https://dergipark.org.tr/en/download/article-file/1715

Boice, R. (1991). New faculty as teachers. *The Journal of Higher Education, 62*(2), 150–173. doi:10.2307/1982143

Cawyer, C. S., Simonds, C., & Davis, S. (2002). Mentoring to facilitate socialization: The case of the new faculty member. *International Journal of Qualitative Studies in Education, 15*(2), 225–242. doi:10.1080/09518390110111938

Fantilli, R. D., & McDougall, D. E. (2009). A study of novice teachers: Challenges and supports in the first years. *Teaching and Teacher Education, 25*(6), 814–825. doi:10.1016/j.tate.2009.02.021

Gourneau, B. (2014). Challenges in the first year of teaching: Lessons learned in an elementary education resident teacher program. *Contemporary Issues in Education Research, 7*(4), 299–318. doi:10.19030/cier.v7i4.8844

Hıdıroğlu, S., Önsüz, M. F., Topuzoğlu, A., & Karavuş, M. (2010). Evaluation of the perspectives of the academic medical staff and residents concerning continuing professional development in a medical faculty. *Marmara Medical Journal, 23*(3), 360-369. http://hdl.handle.net/11424/1919

Hoffmann, D. S., Kearns, K., Bovenmyer, K. M., Cumming, W. P., Drane, L. E., Gonin, M., Kelly, L., Rohde, L., Tabassum, S., & Blay, R. (2021). Benefits of a multi-institutional, hybrid approach to teaching course design for graduate students, postdoctoral scholars, and leaders. *Teaching & Learning Inquiry, 9*(1), 218–240. doi:10.20343/teachlearninqu.9.1.15

Kondakçı, Y., & Haser, Ç. (2019). Socialization at the university: A qualitative investigation on the role of contextual dynamics in the socialization of academics. *Research in Educational Administration and Leadership, 4*(2), 272–301. doi:10.30828/real/2019.2.3

McGugan, S. A. (2013). *Academic Development Through Teaching: A Study into the experiences of Postgraduate and Postdoctoral Researchers* [Unpublished doctoral dissertation]. The Open University.

Nerad, M. (2012). Conceptual approaches to doctoral education: A community of practice. *Alternation (Durban), 19*(2), 57–72. https://www.ufs.ac.za/templates/journals.aspx?article=1264

Nowell, L., Grant, K. A., Berenson, C., Dyjur, P., Jeffs, C., Kelly, P., Kenny, N., & Mikita, K. (2020b). Innovative certificate programs in university teaching and learning: Experiential learning for graduate students and postdoctoral scholars. *Papers on Postsecondary Learning and Teaching, 4*, 85–95.

Nowell, L., Ovie, G., Kenny, N., Hayden, K. A., & Jacobsen, M. (2019). Professional learning and development initiatives for postdoctoral scholars. *Studies in Graduate and Postdoctoral Education, 11*(1), 35–55. doi:10.1108/SGPE-03-2019-0032

Nowell, L., Ovie, G., Kenny, N., & Jacobsen, M. (2020a). Postdoctoral scholars' perspectives about professional learning and development: A concurrent mixed-methods study. *Palgrave Communications, 6*(1), 1–11. doi:10.105741599-020-0469-5

Şen, Ö., & Kızılcalıoğlu, G. (2020). Covid-19 pandemi sürecinde üniversite öğrencilerinin ve akademisyenlerin uzaktan öğretime yönelik görüşlerinin belirlenmesi [Determining the views of university students and academicians on distance education during the Covid-19 pandemic process]. *International Journal of 3D Printing Technologies and Digital Industry, 4*(3), 239-252. . doi:10.46519/ij3dptdi.830913

Sharmini, S., & Spronken-Smith, R. (2020). The PhD–is it out of alignment? *Higher Education Research & Development, 39*(4), 821–833. doi:10.1080/07294360.2019.1693514

Stanulis, R. N., Fallona, C. A., & Pearson, C. A. (2002). Am I doing what I am supposed to be doing?: Mentoring novice teachers through the uncertainties and challenges of their first year of teaching. *Mentoring & Tutoring, 10*(1), 71–81. doi:10.1080/13611260220133162

Tülübaş, T. (2017). *Orta kariyer evresinde bulunan akademisyenlerin mesleki kimlik algıları: Kolektif araçsal durum çalışması* [Professional identity of mid-career academics: A collective instrumental case study] [Unpublished doctoral thesis]. Kocaeli Üniversitesi Eğitim Bilimleri Enstitüsü.

Yalçinkaya, M., Koşar, D., & Altunay, E. (2014). Araştırma görevlilerinin bilim insanı yetiştirme sürecine ilişkin görüşleri [Research assistants' views on the training process of scholars]. *Kastamonu Eğitim Dergisi, 22*(3), 1009–1034.

Yıldırım, A., & Şimşek, H. (2013). *Sosyal bilimlerde nitel araştırma yöntemleri* [Qualitative research methods in social sciences]. Seçkin yayıncılık.

YÖK. (2017). *YÖK'te "Araştırma ve aday araştırma üniversiteleri" ile toplantı* [Meeting with "Research and candidate research universities"]. https://www.yok.gov.tr/Sayfalar/Haberler/yok-te-aday-ve-aday-arastirma-universiteleri-ile-toplanti.Aspx

Chapter 5
Masters of Change?
Reflections on the Use of an MA Programme to Upskill the College Sector in Bangladesh

Lucy Bailey
University of Bahrain, Bahrain

ABSTRACT

This chapter reflects on the author's experiences as Director of the Master Trainers strand of the Bangladesh College Education Development Project, a World Bank-funded programme to upskill pedagogical skills of Bangladeshi college teachers. The chapter contextualises the project in terms of educational and economic challenges in Bangladesh and discusses the challenges and opportunities afforded by the model of professional development adopted. Although the programme is still in process, which precludes detailed programme impact analysis, three dimensions of the project are identified as promoting effective change in college education: teacher ownership of the initiative, master trainers' engagement in their masters studies, and attention to means to maximise large-scale change. It is argued that cohort delivery of a Master's degree is more economic than sending individuals overseas for post-graduate study. In addition, although issues of teacher ownership are complex, the chapter describes how participants were given opportunities to evaluate and implement their own priorities for change.

DOI: 10.4018/978-1-7998-9278-6.ch005

INTRODUCTION

This chapter reflects on the author's experiences contributing to a 5-year World Bank-funded development of the college sector in Bangladesh. Working with a consortium of partner institutions in Bangladesh, the author's off-shore campus of a British university was contracted to upskill over 8000 teachers, leaders and policy makers across the college education sector as part of the Bangladesh College Education Development Project. This was achieved primarily through training 250-300 'master trainers' – that is, college teachers who were then responsible for training the remainder of the teachers. This chapter describes the approach taken to this upskilling, critically reflects on the challenges involved, and concludes with discussion of the wider implications of such a project.

It was the World Bank's decision to focus on college education rather than compulsory schooling, and the university received a structured brief from the World Bank. To complement this, a detailed Training Needs Analysis was conducted at the start of the project. Both of these pointed to economic, social and educational features of Bangladesh that informed the approach taken. I begin this chapter by providing an overview of these.

Thereafter, I describe the approach adopted for the training of the 'master trainers', before discussing the three principles that underpinned the approach. The principles are used to identify shortcomings and tensions in the programme, as well as to note its strengths. It is suggested that these three principles could be used as an evaluation framework for future similar projects.

BACKGROUND TO THE PROJECT

The Bangladeshi Socio-Economic Context

Bangladesh is a large developing country, with a diverse population. The population is predominantly Bengali, and approximately 90% Muslim (Hindus constituting most of the remaining 10%). There is a disputed number of indigenous ethnic groups, nevertheless Bangladeshis do largely share a common language. The eight most populous country in the world, Bangladesh encompasses both sprawling metropolises such as Dhaka and rural areas with sparse infrastructure; just under 40% of the population lives in rural areas. Agriculture remains its largest economic sector, although this now employs less than half of the workforce, and accounts for only about 42% of GDP (Central Intelligence Agency, 2021). The workforce is predominantly young; the median age within the population is only 27.9 years. Despite change in recent years, a range of measures point to ongoing economic and social disadvantage across the country; the mean age of mothers when giving birth to their first baby is 18.6 years, and more than 1 in 5 children under the age of 5 is underweight (Central Intelligence Agency, 2021).

In their report for the World Bank, Rahman et al (2019) note that Bangladesh is undergoing rapid economic transformation, moving from this largely agrarian focus to an industrial and service based economy. This has created new challenges, including high unemployment amongst tertiary graduates, who often have not developed the skills for required by employers. The development of human capital has long been seen as central to Bangladesh's economic development (Hossain & Jahan, 2000; Bhattacharya & Borgatti, 2012). Raising the quality of the education system is therefore critical to addressing these challenges, with the World Bank eager to pay particular attention to the development of tertiary education. Whilst problems persist in primary and secondary level education, such as high drop-rates for children from poorer families, it was the issues faced at tertiary level that were the focus of our intervention and which will therefore be discussed in the following sub-section.

The Bangladeshi College Education System

The college sector in Bangladesh is both large and diverse. It includes institutions that admit students from the age of 14 but also institutions awarding a range of degree qualifications, and it encompasses both private and public institutions. In total, according to the World Bank, there are currently 1,862 colleges in Bangladesh, of which 85% are private colleges. These colleges serve 1.81 million students, with 45% of those students being in the private sector (Rahman et al, 2019). These numbers speak to the scale of the sector; however, it should be noted that the percentage of the Bangladeshi population enrolled in tertiary education continues to be below both the average for lower-middle-income-countries and lower than the rates of enrolment enjoyed by neighbouring countries (Rahman et al, 2019). Moreover, the rapid development of this mass college education system has come at a price – first, in terms in teaching quality (Ahmed, 2016a), and second with lack of equity of access. I shall briefly discuss each of these in turn; however, it should be stressed that issues of quality and equity are inter-related, with efforts to ensure quality across the sector ensuring greater equity in access to appropriate education (Rahman et al, 2019).

Historically, Bangladesh's education system has been highly centralised (Gibson, 2020), with teachers having curtailed autonomy, poor facilities, few opportunities for professional development and consequently low job satisfaction (Alam & Khalifa, 2009; Nagashima et al, 2014). There are high rates of both teacher and student absenteeism (Al Faruki, 2020). Students are typically taught using traditional pedagogies; a didactic approach is usual and student-centred learning is rarely employed (Al Faruki, Haque & Islam, 2019; Akareem & Hossain, 2012), with rote-learning predominating (Rahman et al, 2019). As a result, students do not experience the active learning and innovative assessment practices which are needed to develop students' higher-order thinking skills. Rahman et al (2019) note of tertiary education:

'Classroom teaching mainly involves rote learning, non-creativity, and passivity of students that impedes higher-order critical thinking and soft skills development. Assessment of learning is conducted mainly through written exams, providing little scope for feedback to students other than conventional grades.' (Rahman et al, 2019: vi)

Large class sizes in colleges (Al Faruki, Haque & Islam, 2019; Anny, Mishra & Rahman, 2020) may explain this reliance on traditional teaching approaches. However, educational improvements have also been hampered by low job satisfaction across all levels of education, with salary levels, facilities, and limited opportunities for professional development all being sources of dissatisfaction (World Bank, 2013). Additionally, although college teachers may have masters or doctoral degrees in their teaching subjects, very few have any pedagogical training (World Bank, 2014). Consequently, efforts to reform the curriculum and assessment in higher education are hampered by a need for increased teacher training (Hossain & Khan, 2015).

Research into some of the challenges faced by those working in Bangladeshi college education offer insight into further reasons for low job satisfaction. Intimidation by students, acute staffing shortages, delays to remuneration and inadequate preparation for roles of responsibility are some of the issues reported in the focus groups conducted by Gibson (2020). College teachers seeking to use ICT face several impediments: most urban areas do not have more than eight hours of electricity per day and rural areas have even greater problems; there is a lack of reliable hardware and software, and what exists is often out of date; and internet connectivity is often poor or absent (Sultana & Shahabul, 2018). Additionally, there is some evidence that the efficiency of the education sector has been further impeded by corrupt practices, particularly in the private sector (Chongwoo et al, 2011; Aziz and Graner, 2011).

Issues of equity have exacerbated the difficulties faced by the sector. There has historically been unequal access to educational resources, which has led to huge variability in the college sector (World Bank, 2014). These inequalities include rural-urban differences, and socio-economic disparities and discrepancies in access by gender (Rahman, 2019). Whilst nearly two-thirds of the population live in rural areas, approximately 63% of tertiary provision is in urban areas (World Bank, 2014), and some researchers have pointed to the 'culture shock' that students from rural areas may experience when moving to university dormitories in urban settings (Ali et al, 2021). The recent expansion of higher education in urban areas has primary benefited affluent families (Nagashima et al, 2014). Less-affluent students are also more likely to attend rural colleges, which face greater infrastructural challenges (Nagashima et al, 2014). In addition, students from less-affluent backgrounds are more likely to attend private colleges, which have fewer facilities and enjoy lower status than public institutions.

Gender inequalities in access to tertiary education merit particular attention. Female educational qualifications have been a driving factor behind a diminishing of the gender wage gap in Bangladesh (Ahmed & McGillivray, 2015), although stereotypical subject choices, limited job skills (especially IT competence), and gendered career aspirations mean that female employment has not kept pace with increased female participation in higher education (Ahmed & Hyndman-Rizk, 2020). Although gender equality in enrolment has been achieved at the primary and secondary levels, it has not yet been reached in tertiary education (Ahmed, 2016b); only 43% of college students are female (World Bank, 2014). As the cost of a girl's dowry rises with age, girls from poorer families may drop out of college to marry (Del Franco, 2010). The urban-rural divide in college education creates particular issues for girls' education since for cultural reasons many families do not countenance daughters living away from home. Moreover, the number of women teachers in tertiary education continues to be low, although Asadullah & Choudhury (2015) have evidenced a move towards more women leaders at secondary and tertiary level. There are a number of possible reasons for this, including family responsibilities, cultural factors that discourage women from travelling to work, and a general male dominance of organisations across Bangladeshi society.

In summary, addressing these quality issues whilst being mindful of the impact on questions of equity was central to the project. As we sought to upskill the college teachers, we needed to focus on giving them teaching tools and techniques that could be employed in colleges facing these contextual challenges. We further sought to foster their motivation and give them opportunities for increased agency over the teaching. We also sought to give them strategies that could be used to address inequalities in a culturally appropriate manner.

Training Needs Analysis

An extensive Training Needs Analysis (TNA) was conducted, which included mixed methods data collection to evaluate college needs. The quantitative part of the TNA comprised two online surveys, one for college principals and the other for college teachers. The qualitative data collection involved college site visits, which included college tours, focus groups with faculty and students, and individual interviews with principals.

Particular attention was made to ensuring the perspectives of diverse stakeholders were included in the Training Needs Analysis, so that the issues of inequity facing the sector (World Bank, 2014) could be addressed. Visits were paid to both women's and men's colleges in order to observe the resources available and perspectives of participants in both. Owing to security concerns, the visiting delegation was advised by the World Bank only to visit colleges in the Dhaka area; however, it was considered essential to include the perspectives of rural colleges. To achieve this, college principals from other parts of Bangladesh were invited to the project headquarters and several focus groups of such principals were conducted in Dhaka.

We spoke to teachers, principals and students to ascertain current practice and explore some of the barriers to change. It was evident from our interviews, focus groups and site observations that teacher-centred classrooms are the norm in Bangladesh. We also saw the considerable difficulties many colleges faced in squeezing large numbers onto small campuses with few educational resources. There is insufficient space to report in detail on the TNA here; however, a summary of the perspectives of teachers, students and principals provides an important backdrop to the project.

Teachers identified a number of barriers to student-centred teaching, including low student motivation, and large class sizes. They were unsure how they could differentiate their instruction in large-group settings. Teachers expressed concern about high drop-out rates, particularly amongst female students. They reported being eager to develop their English language skills. Many said they currently struggled to keep up with recent developments in their subject area without the language skills to follow international research literature. They said they would welcome the change to pursue an internationally-recognised qualification at a well-ranked university, despite the challenges of studying in English.

The principals were concerned about high student-teacher ratios and low teacher motivation. They reported that multimedia facilities were available in their colleges, but under-utilised. They suggested that many of their teachers had poor subject understanding as well as weak pedagogical skills.

The students reported that their classes were boring, although they appreciated that their teachers made efforts to engage them. For example, some students told us that their instructors sang songs or told stories, but in each example these were diversions to amuse the students, and did not have any connection to the subject being studied. The students were frustrated by long exams that tested only their recollection of the textbook. They were interested in the possibility of more student-centred approaches, and very receptive to changes that included the use of educational technologies.

Throughout the TNA, we were sensitised to the richness of Bangladesh culture and a strong sense of national pride. We were also aware that innovative examples of best practice are already taking place in some colleges. For example, at one college we observed an extra-curricular scheme that the principal had introduced to develop soft skills that received little emphasis in the academic programmes. It was therefore evident that the participants in our programme would benefit from opportunities to share existing best practice in Bangladesh.

PROJECT DESCRIPTION

There was an extended period of negotiation between the university, the World Bank and our project partners in Bangladesh before the scope and content of the project was finalised. University leaders (including the author of this chapter) visited Dhaka for discussions and site visits, so that they had a strong understanding of the context. As a result of this process, a complex, large-scale intervention agreed with the World Bank, which encompassed:

1. Completion of an MA Education by 250-300 selected college teachers. Successful completion of the MA was a precondition for being appointed as a 'master trainer'; the master trainers would then be responsible for upskilling 7000-8000 college teachers across the country. This was complemented by:
2. Completion of an MA Educational Leadership by 500 college leaders. This approach of simultaneously upskilling both teachers and leaders reflects the research evidence suggesting that effective leadership support is essential to building teacher expertise in developing countries (Ziyadin et al, 2018).
3. Professional development with a small number of senior administrators. These sessions were offered to officials accompanying the leaders and master trainers to Malaysia.

Although these latter two elements are not discussed in this paper, they were integral to addressing the educational issues identified in the TNA. The remainder of this chapter therefore only discusses number 1. above.

The Bangladeshi government established a project headquarters to manage the project and to facilitate coordination between the various partners. This oversaw the recruitment of master trainers and the logistics related to their studies, although final decisions over admission to our academic programmes and the teaching itself remained the province of the university.

IMPLEMENTATION OF THE MASTER TRAINERS STRAND

The masters trainers strand of the project constitutes the focus of the remainder of this paper; the author of this chapter was the Director of this element and Programme

Coordinator of the Masters in Education for the university in Malaysia. This section provides details regarding the content of the training provided, and the logistics of delivery of this training.

The Training Needs Analysis had identified two key issues that the masters trainers element sought to address:

1. Learner-centred teaching. Both our own observations and our focus group data confirmed the suggestion in the literature that teacher-centred classrooms were the norm (Akareem & Hossain, 2012; Rahman et al, 2019), but also suggested that students in particular were very receptive to change. Teachers identified areas with which they would most welcome support, particularly strategies for large group teaching; developing student and teacher motivation; the use of educational technologies; and strategies for developing communities of practice, including mentoring skills. As a result of this, a new module entitled Teaching, Training and Technology was developed to enable in-depth exploration of these topics. In addition, the material covered in two other taught modules (Understanding, Curriculum, Learning and Assessment, and Leading Learning) was adapted so that it was made more relevant to the Bangladeshi context while achieving the usual learning outcomes.
2. Language. It was clear that the teachers were eager to develop their English skills and felt that this would enable them to keep abreast with recent developments in their teaching subjects. It was also evident that language support would be needed to enable college teachers to access the MA programme, which was delivered and assess in English. Consequently, students were given intensive English support classes during their visits to Malaysia.

'Block delivery' of modules in Malaysia was adopted – that is, where a module was taught intensively over a compressed amount of time, typically four teaching days, with one day's break in the middle. This approach was adopted since the focus group data suggested that faculty motivation would be increased by the prospect of face-to-face study in Malaysia. Selected participants travelled to Malaysia in cohorts of approximately 100 master trainers, and stayed on campus (during university vacations) to study their academic modules and receive language support. In order to minimise travel and accommodation costs, master trainers studied two modules concurrently, so that completion of all four taught modules necessitated only two three-week visits to Malaysia. The dissertation was the only module which did not include such a face-to-face component. Each module was then completed by independent study completed in Bangladesh, supported online by their module instructor. Although students usually have choice of modules within our MA Education, it was decided to

Masters of Change?

have fixed modules for this cohort. Table 1 provides an overview of the programme content, and Figure 1 provides an overview of the delivery structure.

During the block visits, the master trainers were able to focus exclusively on their studies, whereas when in Bangladesh they had to juggle study with work responsibilities. In addition, they had the opportunity to imbue a university atmosphere. Malaysia was seen as an example of a country with cultural and economic similarities to Bangladesh which had been able to transform its economy and educational system in recent decades; faculty were therefore particularly keen to learn lessons from Malaysia which they could emulate in Bangladesh.

Table 1. Programme Summary

Module Title	Comments
Understanding Curriculum, Learning and Assessment	Material adapted for Bangladeshi context
Teaching, Training and Technology	New module developed in light of TNA
Leading Learning	Material adapted for Bangladeshi context
Practice Based Inquiry	Compulsory module
Dissertation	Compulsory module

Figure 1. Delivery Structure

DISCUSSION

Three principles underpinned the model of teacher education adopted during this project: teacher ownership of change, student engagement, and cost-effective large-scale change. In this section, each of these key challenges will be discussed in turn. The discussion notes the strategies taken to adhere to each principle, as well as acknowledging limitations of the programme. It is suggested that these three criteria could provide a framework for evaluating the effectiveness of future large-scale interventions of this kind.

Ownership

An extensive literature has established that teacher ownership is a key feature of successful educational reform (Saunders et al, 2017). Consequently, one concern shared by both the university and our Bangladeshi partners was that the masters trainers should develop a sense of ownership over the project to improve college education through their studies. In this section, I explore how a sense of 'ownership' was promoted in relation to both their teacher and national identities.

Teacher ownership refers to 'a teacher's sense of alignment with an improvement effort and agency to influence it' (Saunders et al, 2017: 1). In other words, teacher ownership suggests that teachers should not be seen as passively implementing reform, but rather as having an active role in shaping and adapting it for their contexts. Teacher ownership may improve teacher satisfaction and improve student outcomes (Saunders et al, 2017). It can also ensure that reforms can be brought to both scale and sustainability (Bonner et al, 2020) Professional development opportunities have been shown to promote teacher ownership (Saunders et al, 2017). However, there can be tension between large-scale reform and a sense of teacher ownership (Niesz & Ryan, 2018).

Although the scale of Bangladesh's college sector posed a challenge for achieving teacher ownership, teacher ownership was seen as key to the project. Given the diversity of Bangladesh's college sector (Rahman et al, 2019), it was particularly important that teachers felt able to adapt their learning to their specific context. We employed a number of strategies to achieve this. The Training Needs Analysis data had suggested that faculty would be motivated by the prospect of achieving an international qualification; hence the decision was made to build the training of master trainers around a masters qualification rather than custom-designing a professional development programme for the project. The delivery model, with intensive block delivery in Malaysia, sought to give importance to their role of being a master trainer. Although it would have been more cost-effective for instructors to travel to Bangladesh than for students to travel to Malaysia (an issue discussed further below), the travel to Malaysia brought at least two benefits. It enabled them to focus on their studies, and was seen as a reward for their involvement in the project.

The learning approach taken during modules was the co-construction of knowledge, enabling the master trainers to experience the kind of learner-centred education that is rare in Bangladesh (Akareem & Hossain, 2012; Rahman et al, 2019). In addition, each module studied on the programme culminated in an assessment based on action research, to be conducted in the master trainer's own institution. In both these ways, the learning approach focused on the master trainers establishing their own priorities for implementation of learner-centred approaches. It also gave them opportunities to experience, evaluate and adapt the effectiveness of strategies studied.

Alongside these measure to promote teacher ownership of college reforms, we were anxious to promote master trainers' belief in national (as well as individual teacher) ownership of the project. The 'internationalisation' of higher education has been subjected to decolonial critique by Ndlovu-Gatsheni (2021), who argues that Europe and North America have self-positioned as 'the sole teachers of the world' (p.81), thereby relegating the rest of the world to being their students. The involvement of a British university in the improvement of Bangladeshi education could have lent to resentment. To address this, we recruited faculty to deliver the MA programme who saw the Bangladeshi participants as partners in change, and not merely their students. In addition, the dual positioning of the institution, as a Western university situated in a Muslim-majority country, was actively welcomed by the master trainers. The Western certification was seen as adding status to the project, whilst the Malaysian location connected the project to a country which is seen in Bangladesh as a positive example of a developing Muslim nation.

Engagement

A second key feature of successful professional development that has been identified by the literature is student engagement, yet research has shown that college faculty in Bangladesh have experienced curtailed autonomy and have low job motivation (Alam & Khalifa, 2009; Nagashima et al, 2014). Consequently, a number of further measures were adopted to promote master trainers' engagement in their studies.

There are many factors inhibiting tertiary teachers' engagement in professional development in Bangladesh. Practical challenges include low English language skills, which can impede access to international resources; inequities in pay which can demoralise instructors; and poor IT network and infrastructure (Shiddike & Rahman, 2019). It has also been suggested that faculty are more incentivised to engage in partisan politics than professional development, and that there is a poor legal framework for ensuring values and ethics in higher education (Shiddike & Rahman, 2019). Although some of these issues lay beyond the scope of the project, we paid close attention to developing the language skills needed for meaningful engagement in ongoing professional development. The project office also prioritised ensuring access to the necessary IT resources for all participants, and training in use of the university's various online resources, was a part of the project.

Student engagement in online education is particularly challenging in the Bangladeshi context (Sultana & Shahabul, 2018). The use of online delivery is at a nascent stage in Bangladesh higher education, and technical problems such as poor connectivity have hampered the adoption of online approaches (Sarker et al, 2019). Nevertheless, the project was able to employ several features that promote engagement in the online teacher development being provided. The programme began with a face-to-face component, required enactment of new strategies in practice, and was linked to a sense of career progression in becoming a master trainer – all measures identified by Popova et al (2018) as components of effective online teacher development programmes in developing contexts. Second, our project offered participants extensive feedback and support from instructors, which Philipsen et al (2019) has identified as a key design feature of successful online/blended professional development. Third, there was also attention to the need for adaptation to context in construction of our modules, another key feature which Philipsen et al (2019) have determined.

It was been noted above that issues of gender equity have challenged the college education sector, including under-representation of women teachers and leaders (Asadullah & Choudhury, 2015). To address this, the consortium had agreed that equal representation from women's and men's colleges should be sought amongst the master trainers. In practice, this was not achieved, with male participants considerably out-numbering female participants by approximately 10:1 on the initial cohort. Female participants noted that overseas travel for study was unusual for women in Bangladesh, and several attributed their participation in the programme to support from their mother-in-law; delivery of the programme within Bangladesh might therefore have been preferable for some social groups. Addressing this limitation is a priority for subsequent stages of the project.

Scale of Change

The aim of this project was not just to improve the master trainers individually but to effect large-scale change across Bangladesh college education. Consideration was therefore given not just to the ownership and engagement experienced by individual master trainers, but also the degree to which large-scale change could be effected by employing this model of professional development. It is too soon to formally evaluate the project impact, as the master trainers are still being upskilled and therefore the trickle-down has not commenced. Nevertheless, it is still pertinent to reflect on how the project was structured in the light of research to maximise the impact of postgraduate study. This was done by including opportunities for immediate change and by offering a cost-effective way to train a large number of master trainers.

The trickle-down approach of training the master trainers and then using them to upskill their colleagues is the long-term aim for the project. We also sought to explore ways in which immediate changes could be introduced in the colleges. The use of action research projects to assess each masters module was a key means by which seeds of change were introduced into colleges. Participants were instructed to identify an issue in their college related to the focus on the module, and then guided by their lecturers to implement and evaluate small-scale reform. In this way, the project built up a portfolio of successful action research projects to introduce learning-centred approaches and adapt them successfully to the diverse college contexts in Bangladesh.

The blended cohort approach employed for this project, using an off-shore campus of British university, contrasts with the historical reliance, common across many countries, of sending sponsored individuals overseas to pursue post-graduate qualifications at Western universities. Such study programmes may work more to the advantage of British universities than to their non-British students. Many British universities are now heavily dependent on the revenue generated from onshore international students, whereas the financial gains from offshore delivery are considerably lower (Bennell, 2019). I suggest that sending sponsored students to Western universities may be less effective than off-shore delivery for two reasons: it is less likely to meet the specific needs of the sponsoring nation, and the costs per student are higher.

Research has indicated several reasons why post-graduate study overseas may not meet the needs of overseas students. It can involve cultural challenges, with, for example, contrasting approaches to teaching and learning held by students and supervisors, and conflicting expectations of feedback (Elliott & Kobayashi, 2019). Students studying overseas may find that their supervisors/ examiners are not sensitive to culturally-inflected research topics, and may not understand that a topic or question that seems unimportant to them is crucial in another cultural context (Wisker & Robinson, 2012). Moreover, postgraduate students studying overseas may feel they are operating at a linguistic disadvantage beside Anglophone peers (Ozdemir, 2014). By contrast, the programme we offered in Malaysia was adapted to the specific needs of our Bangladeshi cohorts. This was achieved by adapting the topics discussed, the approaches to learning employed, the use of extensive linguistic support, and the recruitment and training of our own lecturers to ensure in-depth understanding of the Bangladeshi context.

The programme could be offered at lower cost in Malaysia than would have been the case at a British campus. This enabled the benefits of international academic mobility, such as bringing additional knowledge and skills to Bangladesh (Rahman, 2018), to be afforded to the large cohort of master trainers. Financial pressures on scholarship programmes have led several countries to explore more economical ways to receive overseas degrees, such as getting recognition for study at local universities, thereby only requiring part of the degree to be financed overseas (Bennell, 2020); however, these measures reduce student exposure to the benefits of overseas travel. Our model of delivery at an off-shore campus ensured that the Bangladesh consortium could benefit from the lower fees charged to off-shore students than to those studying at our UK campus. A further benefit was that such off-shore study was more readily compatible with our master trainers' responsibilities of full-time employment; studying in the UK for a qualification is usually more accessible to those who are younger and are not employed (Wilkins & Juusola, 2018).

CONCLUSION

This chapter has described a large-scale project for professional development of college teachers in Bangladesh. It has described the contextual challenges that needed to be addressed through this project, detailing the problems of both quality and equity of provision faced by college education. The chapter has outlined the professional development project that was created to address these issues. Three key aspects of an effective programme for professional development were then discussed, explaining how the project had been designed to promote teacher ownership, foster their engagement in the professional development, and ensure that the project led to larger-scale change.

Our project partners and the World Bank felt that the model developed in our master trainers programme was a cost-effective way of upskilling college teachers that combined the prestige of a British qualification with the cost advantage of studying in South-East Asia and cultural familiarity of a Muslim nation. Whilst the valorisation given to English-language qualifications such as the one we were offering could be seen as contributing to linguistic imperialism (Inoue & Stracke, 2013), participants were eager to gain a qualification perceived as having international currency. In addition, participants frequently referred to Malaysia as a role model for an Islamic economy, which had undertaken rapid and successful development within a short period of time.

This project offered an invaluable opportunity for the university to reflect on its practices and re-evaluate the needs of its students through detailed discussion with a range of stakeholders in Bangladeshi education. With universities increasingly marketing themselves internationally, it offers an example of how established programmes may need adaptation and how modes of delivery can be creatively adapted to maximise impact. The three themes of teacher ownership, student engagement, and scalability of reform offer a framework for evaluation of future professional development collaborations in diverse contexts.

REFERENCES

Abd Rahman, S., Puteh, F., Ahmad, U. K., Deris, F. D., Azizan, A. R., Busri, R. D., ... Ramli, N. S. (n.d.). *A Symbiotic UTM-UNMC Collaboration: Supporting Postgraduates of Bangladeshi College Education Development Project (BCEDP) with English Language Proficiency through MyLinE*. Academic Press.

Ahmed, J. U. (2016a). Massification to marketization of higher education: Private university education in Bangladesh. *Higher Education for the Future*, *3*(1), 76–92. doi:10.1177/2347631115610222

Ahmed, M. (2016b). The education system. In A. Riaz & M.S. Rahman (Eds.), Routledge Handbook of Contemporary Bangladesh (pp. 340-351). London: Routledge.

Ahmed, R., & Hyndman-Rizk, N. (2020). The higher education paradox: Towards improving women's empowerment, agency development and labour force participation in Bangladesh. *Gender and Education*, *32*(4), 447–465. doi:10.1080/09540253.2018.1471452

Ahmed, S., & McGillivray, M. (2015). Human capital, discrimination, and the gender wage gap in Bangladesh. *World Development*, *67*, 506–524. doi:10.1016/j.worlddev.2014.10.017

Al Faruki, M. J. (2020). A critical approach to active learning: A case study of two Bangladeshi colleges. *International Journal of Research in Business and Social Science, 9*(3), 165-174.

Al Faruki, M. J., Haque, M. A., & Islam, M. M. (2019). Student-Centered Learning and Current Practice in Bangladeshi College Education. *Journal of Education and Practice*, *19*(13), 95–107.

Alam, G. M., & Khalifa, T. B. (2009). The impact of introducing a business marketing approach to education: A study on private HE in Bangladesh. *American Journal of Business*, *3*(9), 463–474.

Ali, S., Sarker, M. F. H., Islam, M. S., Islam, M. K., & Al Mahmud, R. (2021). Pursuing higher education: Adaptation challenges and coping strategies of rural students at urban universities in Bangladesh. *Tertiary Education and Management*, *27*(2), 1–16. doi:10.100711233-021-09067-3

Anny, N. Z., Mishra, P. K., & Rahman, M. S. R. (2020). Teaching sociology in large classes: Issues and challenges in Bangladeshi colleges. *International Journal of Research in Business and Social Science, 9*(1), 46-54.

Bennell, P. (2019). The financial returns to onshore and offshore overseas students at British Universities. *International Journal of Educational Development*, *70*, 102097. doi:10.1016/j.ijedudev.2019.102097

Bennell, P. (2020). The internationalisation of higher education provision in the United Kingdom: Patterns and relationships between onshore and offshore overseas student enrolment. *International Journal of Educational Development*, *74*, 102162. doi:10.1016/j.ijedudev.2020.102162

Bhattacharya, D., & Borgatti, L. (2012). An Atypical Approach to Graduation from the LDC Category: The Case of Bangladesh. *South Asia Economic Journal*, *13*(1), 1–25. doi:10.1177/139156141101300101

Bonner, S. M., Diehl, K., & Trachtman, R. (2020). Teacher belief and agency development in bringing change to scale. *Journal of Educational Change*, *21*(2), 363–384. doi:10.100710833-019-09360-4

Central Intelligence Agency. (2021). Bangladesh. In *The World Factbook*. Available at: https://www.cia.gov/the-world-factbook/countries/bangladesh/#economy

Del Franco, N. (2010). Aspirations and self-hood: Exploring the meaning of higher secondary education for girl college students in rural Bangladesh. *Compare: A Journal of Comparative Education*, *40*(2), 147–165. doi:10.1080/03057920903546005

Elliot, D. L., & Kobayashi, S. (2019). How can PhD supervisors play a role in bridging academic cultures? *Teaching in Higher Education*, *24*(8), 911–929. doi:10.1080/13562517.2018.1517305

Gibson, M. T. (2020). Student intimidation, no pay and hunger strikes: The challenges facing Heads of Department in Bangladesh colleges. *Journal of Higher Education Policy and Management*, *42*(3), 365–379. doi:10.1080/1360080X.2020.1733735

Hossain, M. A., & Jahan, S. (2000). *Bangladesh. Globalization and living together: The challenges for educational content in Asia*. United Nations Educational, Scientific and Cultural Organization.

Hossain, M. M., & Khan, A. M. (2015). Higher education reform in Bangladesh: An analysis. *Workplace: A Journal for Academic Labor*, *25*, 64-68.

Inoue, N., & Stracke, E. (2013). Non-native English speaking postgraduate TESOL students in Australia: Why did they come here? *University of Sydney Papers in TESOL*, *8*, 29–56.

Nagashima, Y., Rahman, M., Al-Zayed Josh, S. R., Dhar, S. S., Nomura, S., Rahman, M. A., & Mukherjee, H. (2014). *A Study on National University and Affiliated Colleges in Bangladesh* (Vol. 65). International Bank for Reconstruction and Development/The World Bank.

Ndlovu-Gatsheni, S. J. (2021). Internationalisation of higher education for pluriversity: A decolonial reflection. *Journal of the British Academy*, *9*(s1), 77–98. doi:10.5871/jba/009s1.077

Niesz, T., & Ryan, K. (2018). Teacher ownership versus scaling up system-wide educational change: The case of Activity Based Learning in South India. *Educational Research for Policy and Practice*, *17*(3), 209–222. doi:10.100710671-018-9232-8

Ozdemir, N. O. (2014). The role of English as a lingua franca in academia: The case of Turkish postgraduate students in an Anglophone-centre context. *Procedia: Social and Behavioral Sciences, 141*, 74–78. doi:10.1016/j.sbspro.2014.05.014

Philipsen, B., Tondeur, J., Roblin, N. P., Vanslambrouck, S., & Zhu, C. (2019). Improving teacher professional development for online and blended learning: A systematic meta-aggregative review. *Educational Technology Research and Development, 67*(5), 1145–1174. doi:10.100711423-019-09645-8

Popova, A., Evans, D., Breeding, M. E., & Arancibia, V. (2018). *Teacher professional development around the world: The gap between evidence and practice.* World Bank Policy Research Working Paper (8572).

Rahman, S. (2018). Globalisation, Migration and Knowledge Generation: A Study on Higher Education Institutions in Bangladesh. In *Engaging in Educational Research* (pp. 263–278). Springer. doi:10.1007/978-981-13-0708-9_14

Rahman, T., Nakata, S., Nagashima, Y., Rahman, M., Sharma, U., & Rahman, M. A. (2019). *Bangladesh tertiary education sector review: Skills and innovation for growth.* World Bank. doi:10.1596/31526

Sarker, M. F. H., Al Mahmud, R., Islam, M. S., & Islam, M. K. (2019). Use of e-learning at higher educational institutions in Bangladesh: Opportunities and challenges. *Journal of Applied Research in Higher Education, 11*(2), 210–223. doi:10.1108/JARHE-06-2018-0099

Saunders, M., Alcantara, V., Cervantes, L., Del Razo, J., Lopez, R., & Perez, W. (2017). *Getting to Teacher Ownership: How Schools Are Creating Meaningful Change.* Annenberg Institute for School Reform at Brown University.

Shiddike, M. O., & Rahman, A. A. (2019). Engaging faculty in professional development: Lessons from Bangladesh. *Journal of Educational and Developmental Psychology, 9*(2), 124–137. doi:10.5539/jedp.v9n2p124

Sultana, M., & Shahabul, H. M. (2018). The cause of low implementation of ICT in education sector considering higher education: A study on Bangladesh. *Canadian Social Science, 14*(12), 67–73.

Wilkins, S., & Juusola, K. (2018). The benefits and drawbacks of transnational higher education: Myths and realities. *Australian Universities' Review, 60*(2), 68–76.

Wisker, G., & Robinson, G. (2014). Examiner practices and culturally inflected doctoral theses. *Discourse (Abingdon), 35*(2), 190–205. doi:10.1080/01596306.2012.745730

World Bank. (2013). *Bangladesh Education Sector Review (Report 80613-BD)*. Available at: https://openknowledge.worldbank.org/handle/10986/17853

World Bank. (2014). *A Study on National and Affiliated Colleges in Bangladesh. Discussion Paper.* South Asia Human Development Sector, Report No. 65. Available at: https://openknowledge.worldbank.org/bitstream/handle/10986/17743/844280NWP0BD0U00Box382120B00PUBLIC0.pdf?sequence=1&isAllowed=y

Ziyadin, S., Shash, N., Kenzhebekova, D., Yessenova, G., & Tlemissov, U. (2018). Data on the role of leadership in developing expertise in teaching in developing country. *Data in Brief, 18*, 1127–1133. doi:10.1016/j.dib.2018.03.137 PMID:29900285

Chapter 6
Teacher Professional Development for Inclusion in England and Bahrain

Hanin Bukamal
University of Birmingham, UK

ABSTRACT

The global pursuit for inclusion officially started with the United Nations Salamanca Statement, which called for the integration of children with special educational needs (SEN) into mainstream schooling. This triggered a substantial universal restructure of education systems, which includes a major reconsideration of teacher education for inclusion in order to prepare teachers to teach their diverse learners. Through a comparative case study design, this study explores inclusive practices in primary education in England and Bahrain. More specifically, the study examines the way in which schools support teachers' in-service professional development (PD) which then aid in the implementation of inclusive education. The findings reveal PD practices for inclusion in England which focus on support for SEN and improving teacher attitudes towards inclusion as well as PD practices in Bahrain that emphasise the assimilation of new teachers and the promotion of a collaborative teaching environment.

INTRODUCTION

The global pursuit for inclusion officially started with the United Nations Salamanca Statement in 1994, which called for the integration of children with special educational needs (SEN) in mainstream schooling (UNESCO, 1994). This agreement, signed by

DOI: 10.4018/978-1-7998-9278-6.ch006

92 governments, triggered a substantial universal restructure of education systems. Some countries were faster than others in adopting this policy. Nations also had different incentives for embracing inclusion which were either driven by the desire to reduce the expenditure associated with segregated special education (Armstrong, Armstrong, & Spandagou, 2010), or the strive for social justice. The implementation of inclusive education by developing countries might also be in response to the pressures of competing with developed countries. Regardless of the motivations for pursuing inclusive education, the benefits on an individual and societal level can still be attained.

Since the initiation of inclusive education, the field has witnessed different modifications not only on an educational level, but also on a societal level. Over the years, inclusion has influenced changes in policy, structural levels, teacher education, home-school relations, curriculum, and teaching techniques (Slee, 2013; Strogilos, 2012). More specifically, there is a major reconsideration of teacher education for inclusion in order to prepare teachers to teach their diverse learners. Despite decades of research on inclusion, the absence of a universal definition and consensus on inclusive practice, along with the inconsistent impact of inclusion policy, are all widely acknowledged in the literature (Ainscow, Dyson, & Weiner, 2013; Farrell, Hick, & Kershner, 2008; Spratt & Florian, 2015). Booth, Nes, and Strømstad (2003) discuss that the different conceptualisations and understandings of inclusive education pose barriers to developing inclusive teacher education, particularly the problematic perspective of inclusion as mainly related to teaching students with special educational needs. Booth et al. (2003) indicate that appropriate teacher education is crucial for the success of inclusive education, as teachers are considered instigators of inclusion. Most of the existing research on teacher education for inclusion additionally focuses on developing initial teacher education for inclusion, with a less substantial focus on developing professional development for inclusion.

Given the lack of research in the area of in-service teacher education for inclusion, it is vital to explore the way schools conceptualise inclusion through teacher support and professional development. This will help evaluate whether teachers have sufficient guidance to implement and practise this international policy of inclusive education. This chapter critically discusses the findings from a comparative study on the state of inclusive education in England and Bahrain and the associated practices. This broader study is part of the empirical work of my PhD thesis as a Bahraini teacher educator researching inclusive teaching practices in primary schools in England and Bahrain. A minor aspect from the findings of this broader study will be the highlight of this chapter and it pertains to the inclusive practices in schools in supporting teachers' professional development, which then aids teachers' implementation of inclusive education. Inclusive education initiated in England decades prior to its implementation in Bahrain; it is thus anticipated that the countries will be at different stages of progress with inclusion. It is essential to note that the purpose of this comparative study between England and Bahrain is not for the aim of benchmarking one country to another. The comparison is for the purpose of both countries to learn about the practices of the other, bearing in mind the cultural traditions of each and how that influences the practise of inclusion observed. One of the inclusive school practices obtained from this study concerns professional development opportunities for teachers to implement inclusion in the participating schools. The chapter will thus discuss the following more thoroughly: background and literature in the area of in-service teacher education for inclusion; the state of in-service teacher education for inclusion in the contexts of England and Bahrain; and the method and data collection instruments used to explore inclusive practices in each country. The chapter will then outline and critically discuss the findings of PD practices for inclusion in England which focus on support for SEN and improving teacher attitudes towards inclusion; as well as PD practices in Bahrain that emphasise the assimilation of new teachers and the promotion of a collaborative teaching environment.

LITERATURE REVIEW

Woodcock and Hardy (2017) differentiate between two forms of teacher professional development (PD) for inclusion: formal PD, such as workshop attendance; and informal PD, accumulated through teaching experience and school interactions. Appropriate professional development for inclusion is associated with positive teacher attitudes towards inclusive education (Avramidis, Bayliss, & Burden, 2000). These benefits can only be attained with suitable teacher support and training that equips teachers with the relevant practices to teach in a diverse classroom. However, specific guidance in the literature on the content of in-service teacher education for inclusion is lacking. Teacher education for inclusion is frequently associated with training on SEN (Avramidis & Kalyva, 2007). O'Gorman and Drudy (2010) believe that a background in special education is an essential prerequisite to enable teachers to eventually teach diverse learners. Strogilos and Tragoulia (2013) report that teachers indicate their need for PD related to specific SEN groups, particularly in the area of classroom management and how to respond to students with: Emotional and Behavioural Difficulties (Avramidis et al., 2000), Autism Spectrum Disorder (Humphrey & Symes, 2013), and Attention Deficit Hyperactivity Disorder (Braude & Dwarika, 2020). Avramidis and Kalyva (2007) speculate that more training on SEN can be acquired through the experience of teaching pupils with SEN and teachers' presence in an inclusive education environment, rather than a specific course. Forlin (2010), and Woodcock and Hardy (2017) suggest that teacher education for inclusion should focus on training teachers to cater for student diversity instead of predominantly special educational needs. This is in response to the change in perspective of inclusive education to cater for all learners' needs as opposed to focusing on one group of learners. Avramidis, Bayliss, and Burden (2002) also endorse PD that addresses student diversity and the associated teaching strategies and curriculum modifications.

Some of the practices recommended to be included in PD for inclusion include differentiated instruction for the inclusion of all students, rather than only for students with SEN as an approach to inclusive education (Strogilos, Tragoulia, Avramidis, Voulagka, & Papanikolaou, 2017). According to Strogilos and Tragoulia (2013), teachers indicate their need for training on co-teaching for general education teachers and special education teachers to work together in an inclusive classroom. This is earlier emphasised by Segall and Campbell (2012) who believe that SEN training and training specifically on the use of individualized education plans (IEPs) should be directed towards mainstream education teachers (MET), special education teachers' (SET), and school psychologists. This will therefore promote collaborative practices between teachers. Co-teaching activities could also include educator study groups, which encourage MET and SET collaboration. Herner-Patnode (2009) explores educator study groups as PD for inclusion where teachers get together in weekly sessions to conduct research. The sessions can be organised by a school coordinator who also provides supportive learning materials for the teachers to use. This group allows teachers to share practices and research developments with each other, which leads to an improvement in the knowledge and skills of the group members. Such co-teaching practices can be facilitated through the school leadership by permitting teachers the time in their teaching schedules to attend these sessions (Chrysostomou & Symeonidou, 2017).

It is essential to evaluate the current state of teacher training for inclusion in England and Bahrain as the research contexts of this study. One of the main provisions of in-service training for inclusive education in England is through the role of the Special Educational Needs Coordinator (SENCO). According to the Department for Education (DfE) (2015), the SENCO must be a qualified teacher who completed the 'National Award in Special Educational Needs Coordination'. This is a postgraduate degree which can be obtained from a recognised higher education institution. This award enables the SENCO to be part of the school leadership team and attain a leading role in shaping the school's SEN policy; supporting learning with an Education Health and Care plan (EHC); as well as coordinating between teachers, parents of children with SEN and different external agencies. The role of the SENCO varies from one school to another, but SENCOs primarily provide support for the mainstream teacher (Lindqvist & Nilholm, 2014). The role of the SENCO is essential for an inclusive school and acts as an inclusion manager, who is responsible for organising support for students with SEN in mainstream schools (Ainscow et al., 2013). SENCOs are also responsible for supervising teachers and staff, and maintain a record of assessments (Lindqvist, Nilholm, Almqvist, & Wetso, 2011). School leaders believe SENCOs should also coordinate with school nurses and educational psychologists to work on pupil welfare (Lindqvist & Nilholm, 2013). From a policy as well as a literature perspective, the SENCO role in England appears to be heavily focused on supporting students with SEN in mainstream education rather than the perspective of inclusion for all.

As for Bahrain, it is challenging to determine the state of PD for inclusion given the lack of local research in the area. The main source of PD training identified is through the Bahrain Teachers College (BTC), the sole teacher education entity in the country, which provides the following in-service training programmes: post-graduate diploma in education, teacher leadership and continuing professional development program, and the school leadership program (BTC, 2021). AlMahdi and AlWadi (2015) indicate that BTC is the second main in-service training provider after the Ministry of Education. It is however unclear whether or not these programs address teacher education for inclusion. One study in Bahrain specifically explores inclusive education from the perspective of in-service teachers where teachers indicate the need for support from the Ministry of Education, the school administration, and special education teachers for the implementation of inclusion (Bukamal, 2018). From a wider regional context, Amr (2011) reviews teacher education for inclusive and special education in the Arab world and states that the majority of the content seems to focus on special educational needs and disabilities and lacks focus on the pedagogical practices associated with teaching inclusive classrooms. The absence of teacher education for inclusion could then influence teachers' ability to teach in inclusive classrooms as well as their attitudes. Al-Manabri, Al-Sharhan, Elbeheri, Jasem, and Everatt (2013) indicate that the majority of professional development programmes for teachers in the Middle East do not address the teaching methods appropriate for student diversity. The authors believe that the lack of appropriate teacher education for inclusion is the main reason for unsuccessful practices in inclusive education in the Arab world. While Keller, Al-Hendawi, and Abuelhassan (2016) express the need for teacher education in the region to comprise skills necessary to teach children of exceptionalities.

It is vital to investigate how schools translate these practices to provide training support for teachers to implement inclusion policy given the ambiguity of specific in-service teacher education for inclusion in England and Bahrain, the overall scarcity of guidance and research on practices for teacher training for inclusion, and the ubiquitous influence of SEN on inclusive education practice. It is essential to explore as it has important implications for the practice of inclusion in schools, schools' response to students' diverse needs, and schools' support for their staff to implement inclusion.

METHOD

The remainder of the paper comes from research that is being conducted for my PhD thesis. The study involves 15 school staff from participating primary schools from England and Bahrain. From each school the participants included the school principal, SENCO in England or assistant principal in Bahrain, and two teachers. The data collection methods included semi-structured one-to-one interviews with the school principal, and SENCO or assistant principal. This is done in order to gain an understanding of the local context in which the school leaders are operating in, and how this context supported the implementation of inclusive education in the school from their perspective, as well as the school's own view and practice of inclusion. This was followed with unstructured classroom observations and follow-up interviews with teachers to examine teaching practices used to be inclusive of all learners. The purpose of the observations was to observe teachers' use of inclusive teaching practices. The study revealed inclusive practices on a country level, a school level, and classroom level. One of the main inclusive school practices identified by the participants included the school's approach to teacher's PD for inclusion. For this current chapter, teacher's PD is the only sub-theme which will be illustrated and discussed as it pertains directly to in-service teacher training to improve the implementation of inclusion. This is discussed next.

FINDINGS

The exploration of inclusive practices through interviews with the school leadership and teachers revealed specific school practices related to teacher training for inclusion in England and Bahrain. In England, teacher professional development for inclusion was generally for the purpose of improving teachers' attitudes towards inclusive education, as well as increasing teachers' knowledge on special educational needs. While in Bahrain, in-service teacher training sought to equip teachers with a variety of teaching strategies that enables them to respond to their diverse student needs. The approaches in each country will therefore be examined next.

Improving Attitudes and SEN Knowledge in England

Schools invest in teachers' PD to influence positive teacher attitudes towards inclusion. Internal school training is mostly led by the school's educational psychologist, SENCO, and principal. External training is delivered by Pupil School Support (PSS) and the Communication and Autism Team (CAT). The school leadership believes that the more knowledge teachers acquire on SEN, the more positive their attitudes will be towards inclusion. This PD encourages teachers to assume responsibility for all learners in the classroom including students with SEN. The participants also acknowledge the high costs associated with external PD. Teachers' inclusive practices are also built into performance evaluations, where teachers are expected to illustrate their adoption of inclusive practices.

We have to make sure that we trained everyone up as highly as we can. So that they're able to deal with the barriers and issues that arise… I do training at the beginning of every year, and say these are your statutory duties as a teacher. You are a teacher of SEN children and that is the law. So, if you're not doing that you are not performing as a teacher and that may come up in your performance management (SENCO).

The school leadership prioritises PD for teachers, and the principal attempts to build a professional learning community in the school by permitting teachers the time to work on projects together. Teachers also do exchange classroom visits and observations which is enabled by the time given by the school leadership. The principal and SENCO acknowledge that teachers in this school have struggled with having negative attitudes towards inclusion, which is why the school dedicates a big portion of the budget to improve staff knowledge. Recent staff training opportunities focus on improving students' reading skills, metacognition and Education Health and Care plans.

So, we try and pinpoint half term, based on the needs of the school what kinds of training staff need mm and that's a work in progress because staff.. there's always staff turnover, the children's needs change as they grow and develop and new children come in. So definitely ensuring that staff have the knowledge and confidence to deal with different situations is something that I think we need to work on improve even further with the inclusion within the classroom (Principal).

Internal training is customised based on current issues encountered in the classrooms and the identification by the school leadership to address the issues on a school level. For instance, the focus on improving students reading is in response to that the majority of learners have English as their Second Language (ESL). Teachers are therefore trained on how to best support this group of learners. External training is also provided to the SENCO by the local authority which brings together SENCOs from different schools, and then requires the SENCOs to transfer this training to their school staff.

Assimilating New Teachers and Collaborative Teacher Training in Bahrain

In Bahrain, teachers are also provided with internal and external training to the school to promote the use of inclusive teaching strategies. This is done in order to allow teachers to respond more efficiently to their non-Arabic learners. One school has a program especially designed for novice teachers to help them adjust to the school situation. It is a way for the school to manage teacher attitudes towards including large numbers of students who are non-Arabic speakers. The principal refuses to accept the excuse from teachers that they cannot implement the strategies only because they have a large proportion of the class who are non-Arabic speakers. This programme was implemented as a result of the school's previous experiences with new teachers who were unable to adjust to the school and appropriately respond to their diverse learner needs. In another school, teachers discuss how abundant professional development opportunities are available for them both externally to the school and internally. If any teacher is sent by the school to attend external training, that teacher is then required to share what she has learned with all the teachers in the school through a school training workshop. Other teachers are then required to implement that teaching strategy they acquired from the workshop. According to the participating teachers, the school also provides equal opportunities for all teachers to attend external training and there is no favouritism in the opportunities presented. The participants explain one of the main ways of training is through a school program called 'My Best Ideas', which are weekly sessions where each week one teacher shares a teaching method that is effective for her. The school administrator prepares a schedule of weekly sessions where teachers are encouraged to share their teaching practices with their colleagues. These sessions are advertised in the school staff's Whatsapp group with daily reminders of sessions are sent by the school administrator. During the sessions, teachers engage in discussions and later trial the strategy they learned about.

So, every teacher presents her ideas and everyone attends and learns, the teachers' response to 'My Best Ideas' is actually really positive, teachers try to switch periods with other teachers just so they would get a chance to attend 'My Best Ideas' (Principal).

I presented in it last year, I discussed the role play strategy, I explained it to my colleagues and conducted a workshop where I showed them videos of my students learning through this teaching strategy (Teacher).

One of the teachers explained how this programme is particularly effective for novice teachers as it exposes them to a variety of effective teaching methods, and enables them to accumulate experience on suitable teaching strategies for them to implement. The school leadership specifically targets new teachers in order to introduce them to the way of teaching in this school and the school's overall approach. This then leads to teaching practices to be unified across the school.

DISCUSSION

The findings of this study reveal comparable approaches to PD for inclusion between England and Bahrain with subtle differences. In both research contexts, the schools offer internal and external training, and the participants identify that PD is an essential variable in determining teacher attitudes towards inclusion. That could either be in a reactive manner to correct misconceptions and previous negative teacher attitudes towards inclusive education, or in a more proactive manner to prevent negative teacher attitudes from ensuing. In England, providing teachers with PD is schools' method to combat teachers' negative attitudes towards inclusion and is hence reactive. The schools believe that the more knowledge teachers have on inclusion issues, the less likely they are to have negative attitudes towards inclusion, as they will feel more capable of teaching students with SEN. In Bahrain, PD is more proactive in order to equip novice teachers with the knowledge necessary to teach in the schools' unique environment and be able to deal with its challenges, as well as avoid teachers' negative reactions to the challenging school circumstances. The positive association between PD and teacher attitudes is acknowledged by Avramidis et al. (2000) and Mónico et al. (2018), who assert that the more knowledge teachers have of inclusive teaching, the more positive their attitudes will be towards inclusive education.

Woodcock and Hardy (2017) similarly identify a strong association between teachers' PD and attitudes towards inclusive education. The authors find that teachers have more positive attitudes towards inclusion if they have had informal PD rather than formal PD and qualifications. Informal PD is similar to that in Bahrain through the implementation of the in-school PD programme 'My Best Ideas'. That is due to the fact that teachers with less formal PD tend to view inclusion in the broader sense of inclusion of all learners, hence adopting positive attitudes towards inclusion. Teachers who complete formal PD encounter more content related to special educational needs, which influences negative teacher attitudes towards inclusion. Woodcock and Hardy (2017) suppose that formal PD exposes teachers to the variety of issues encountered in responding to students' SEN, which can intimidate teachers and lead to their negative attitudes towards inclusion. Perhaps this has implications for PD for inclusion in that it should focus less on SEN categories, and instead prepare teachers to respond to their diverse learners as a more inclusive approach. This would be in line with more progressive notions of inclusive education, rather than the traditional view of inclusion being primarily related to the integration of learners with SEN in mainstream education. While SEN elements are integrated in PD in both England and Bahrain, SEN is more emphasised in the England context through the SENCO role and CAT support. PD in the Bahrain schools focuses on equipping teachers with a variety of teaching strategies that suit their diverse learners, as well as discusses some SEN topics. Ainscow and Miles (2008) explain that it is vital to provide teachers with a range of support and knowledge to increase teacher confidence. That is because teacher practices in the classroom are the result of their attitudes and beliefs. Another alternative for SEN focused PD would be for it to address more inclusive practices such as training teachers on effective co-teaching practices with teaching assistants and other teachers.

Collaborative approaches to PD for inclusion are present in both countries, they are however used more extensively in Bahrain. The collaborative learning community in England occurs more occasionally and on an ad-hoc basis, while the learning community in Bahrain is regulated with a sense of teacher accountability of their learning. PD in Bahrain is more focused on fostering collaborative practices between teachers and facilitating the coaching and mentoring of new teachers. Teachers are provided with coaching and mentoring opportunities upon entry into the school and continuously after. The focus on the training is to equip teachers with a variety of teaching strategies that suit their diverse learners through the use of student-centred learning. The schools also ensure their sustainable investment in external PD by having the trained teachers share their training experiences with their colleagues in school upon their completion of the external programme. This internal PD programme 'My Best Ideas' is considered an inclusive practice, as the programme focuses on introducing teachers to a variety of teaching strategies implemented by other teachers in the school that are effective in supporting diverse learners. This programme mirrors the educator study groups discussed earlier by Herner-Patnode (2009). 'My Best Ideas' thus encourages teacher collaboration, sustainable investment in PD, mentoring, and encouraging collective teacher responsibility and accountability. According to Conderman and Johnston-Rodriguez (2009), teachers are more likely to perform collaborative roles in collaborative cultures such as Bahrain, than individualistic cultures such as England. The authors indicate the importance of more experienced teachers mentoring novice teachers for inclusive practice, which is consistent with the purpose of 'My Best Ideas' programme.

In both countries, the school leadership encourages teachers to pursue collaborations with their colleagues, either through classroom visits in England, or the opportunity to attend internal PD sessions in Bahrain. The leadership's investment of the school budget in teachers' education demonstrates the leadership's dedication to inclusive education. Howes, Frankham, Ainscow, and Farrell (2004) suggest that a school can only move forward in its inclusive practices if there is a common understanding within the school of the meaning of inclusion. The schools therefore must seek ways to implement consistent values of inclusive education in all of their practices, in order to ensure a unified inclusive school culture. The school leaders in this study communicated the importance of teachers' continuous professional development for the benefit of teachers and students. The school leadership in England and Bahrain additionally indicate that PD in their schools is designed based on the schools' needs and circumstances. In England, teachers' PD emphasises the response to students with SEN and ESL, while in Bahrain PD seeks to cater for non-Arabic speakers and novice teachers.

CONCLUSION

This examination of approaches to PD in each country revealed an association with the ideology of inclusive education in the research contexts. In other words, the ideology of inclusive education determines the PD offer and design of the programmes, and vice versa. In England, the emphasis on SEN training and EHCs is linked more to a special needs focus of inclusion, while Bahrain's response to student diversity through the provision of a variety of teaching strategies reveals a more contemporary view of inclusion. Davis and Florian (2004) find that it is unnecessary to have specific SEN pedagogy, and that some teaching practices that are effective with some learners with SEN can also be effective for other learners. Generally, the authors consider that research should focus less on specific pedagogy for learners with SEN and more on pedagogy that suits diverse learners. Yet, the authors assert it is still necessary for mainstream educators to be equipped with special educational knowledge to inform their overall practice. The latter PD approach in Bahrain and ideology share the values of the inclusive pedagogical approach and its rejection of deterministic beliefs of student abilities (Florian & Black-Hawkins, 2011), as a more conducive approach to inclusion.

This paper is the first study to examine in-service teacher training for inclusion within primary schools in England and Bahrain. The findings are indicative of the national state of inclusive education and national practices to implement this policy in each research context. While background and knowledge on SEN is valuable for PD for inclusion, it should not be its primary focus. In-service training for inclusion should also incorporate elements of multicultural education, support for students who do not speak the home language of the school, co-teaching with teachers and support staff, and a variety of teaching practices that respond to different learners' needs and preferences. It will also be valuable to strategically plan teachers' training in a way to maximise schools' investment and to cope with staff turnover and changes in the student composition. Such training and teaching strategies will likely enhance students' sense of belongingness and motivation to learn.

REFERENCES

Ainscow, M., Dyson, A., & Weiner, S. (2013). From exclusion to inclusion: A review of international literature on ways of responding to students with special educational needs in schools. En-clave pedagógica. *Revista Internacional de Investigación e Innovación Educativa, 13*, 13–30.

Ainscow, M., & Miles, S. (2008). Making education for all inclusive: Where next? *Quarterly Review of Comparative Education, 38*(1), 15–34. doi:10.100711125-008-9055-0

Al-Manabri, M., Al-Sharhan, A., Elbeheri, G., Jasem, I., & Everatt, J. (2013). Supporting teachers in inclusive practices: Collaboration between special and mainstream schools in Kuwait. *Preventing School Failure, 57*(3), 130–134. doi:10.1080/1045988X.2013.794325

AlMahdi, O., & AlWadi, H. (2015). Towards a sociocultural approach on teachers' professional development in Bahrain. *Journal of Teaching and Teacher Education, 3*(1).

Amr, M. (2011). Teacher education for inclusive education in the Arab world: The case of Jordan. *Quarterly Review of Comparative Education, 41*(3), 399–413. doi:10.100711125-011-9203-9

Armstrong, A. C., Armstrong, D., & Spandagou, I. (2010). *Inclusive education: international policy & practice*. Sage Publications.

Avramidis, E., Bayliss, P., & Burden, R. (2000). A survey into mainstream teachers' attitudes towards the inclusion of children with special educational needs in the ordinary school in one local education authority. *Educational Psychology, 20*(2), 191–211. doi:10.1080/713663717

Avramidis, E., Bayliss, P., & Burden, R. (2002). Inclusion in action: An in-depth case study of an effective inclusive secondary school in the south-west of England. *International Journal of Inclusive Education, 6*(2), 143–163. doi:10.1080/13603110010017169

Avramidis, E., & Kalyva, E. (2007). The influence of teaching experience and professional development on Greek teachers' attitudes towards inclusion. *European Journal of Special Needs Education, 22*(4), 367–389. doi:10.1080/08856250701649989

Booth, T., Nes, K., & Strømstad, M. (Eds.). (2003). *Developing inclusive teacher education*. Routledge Falmer. doi:10.4324/9780203465233

Braude, S., & Dwarika, V. (2020). Teachers' experiences of supporting learners with attention-deficit hyperactivity disorder: Lessons for professional development of teachers. *South African Journal of Childhood Education, 10*(1), 1–10. doi:10.4102ajce.v10i1.843

BTC. (2021). *Academic Programs*. Retrieved from http://www.btc.uob.edu.bh/post-graduate-diploma-in-education

Bukamal, H. (2018). *The influence of teacher preparation programmes on Bahraini teacher attitudes and challenges with inclusive education*. Paper presented at the Sustainability and Resilience Conference: Mitigating Risks and Emergency Planning, Bahrain. 10.18502/kss.v3i10.3107

Chrysostomou, M., & Symeonidou, S. (2017). Education for disability equality through disabled people's life stories and narratives: Working and learning together in a school-based professional development programme for inclusion. *European Journal of Special Needs Education, 32*(4), 572–585. doi:10.1080/08856257.2017.1297574

Conderman, G., & Johnston-Rodriguez, S. (2009). Beginning teachers' views of their collaborative roles. *Preventing School Failure, 53*(4), 235–244. doi:10.3200/PSFL.53.4.235-244

Davis, P., & Florian, L. (2004). Teaching strategies and approaches for pupils with special educational needs: A scoping study. *Research in Reproduction, RR516*, 1–90.

DfE. (2015). *Special educational needs and disability code of practice: 0 to 25*. Retrieved from https://assets.publishing.service.gov.uk/government/uploads/system/uploads/attachment_data/file/398815/SEND_Code_of_Practice_January_2015.pdf

Farrell, P., Hick, P., & Kershner, R. (Eds.). (2008). *Psychology for inclusive education: new directions in theory and practice*. Routledge.

Florian, L., & Black-Hawkins, K. (2011). Exploring inclusive pedagogy. *British Educational Research Journal, 37*(5), 813–828. doi:10.1080/01411926.2010.501096

Forlin, C. (Ed.). (2010). *Teacher education for inclusion: changing paradigms and innovative approaches*. Routledge. doi:10.4324/9780203850879

Herner-Patnode, L. (2009). Educator study groups: A professional development tool to enhance inclusion. *Intervention in School and Clinic*, *45*(1), 24–30. doi:10.1177/1053451209338397

Howes, A., Frankham, J., Ainscow, M., & Farrell, P. (2004). The action in action research: Mediating and developing inclusive intentions. *Educational Action Research*, *12*(2), 239–258. doi:10.1080/09650790400200247

Humphrey, N., & Symes, W. (2013). Inclusive education for pupils with autistic spectrum disorders in secondary mainstream schools: Teacher attitudes, experience and knowledge. *International Journal of Inclusive Education*, *17*(1), 32–46. doi:10.1080/13603116.2011.580462

Keller, C., Al-Hendawi, M., & Abuelhassan, H. (2016). Special education teacher preparation in the Gulf Cooperation Council countries. *Teacher Education and Special Education*, *39*(3), 194–208. doi:10.1177/0888406416631125

Lindqvist, G., & Nilholm, C. (2013). Making schools inclusive? Educational leaders' views on how to work with children in need of special support. *International Journal of Inclusive Education*, *17*(1), 95–110. doi:10.1080/13603116.2011.580466

Lindqvist, G., & Nilholm, C. (2014). Promoting inclusion? "Inclusive" and effective head teachers' descriptions of their work. *European Journal of Special Needs Education*, *29*(1), 74–90. doi:10.1080/08856257.2013.849845

Lindqvist, G., Nilholm, C., Almqvist, L., & Wetso, G. M. (2011). Different agendas? The views of different occupational groups on special needs education. *European Journal of Special Needs Education*, *26*(2), 143–157. doi:10.1080/08856257.2011.563604

Mónico, P., Mensah, A., Grünke, M., Garcia, T., Fernández, E., & Rodríguez, C. (2018). Teacher knowledge and attitudes towards inclusion: A cross-cultural study in Ghana, Germany and Spain. *International Journal of Inclusive Education*, *24*(5), 527–543. doi:10.1080/13603116.2018.1471526

O'Gorman, E., & Drudy, S. (2010). Addressing the professional development needs of teachers working in the area of special education/inclusion in mainstream schools in Ireland. *Journal of Research in Special Educational Needs*, *10*(1), 157–167. doi:10.1111/j.1471-3802.2010.01161.x

Segall, M. J., & Campbell, J. M. (2012). Factors relating to education professionals' classroom practices for the inclusion of students with autism spectrum disorders. *Research in Autism Spectrum Disorders*, *6*(3), 1156–1167. doi:10.1016/j.rasd.2012.02.007

Slee, R. (2013). How do we make inclusive education happen when exclusion is a political predisposition? *International Journal of Inclusive Education*, *17*(8), 895–907. doi:10.1080/13603116.2011.602534

Spratt, J., & Florian, L. (2015). Inclusive pedagogy: From learning to action. Supporting each individual in the context of 'everybody'. *Teaching and Teacher Education*, *49*, 89–96. doi:10.1016/j.tate.2015.03.006

Strogilos, V. (2012). The cultural understanding of inclusion and its development within a centralised system. *International Journal of Inclusive Education*, *16*(12), 1241–1285. doi:10.1080/13603116.2011.557447

Strogilos, V., & Tragoulia, E. (2013). Inclusive and collaborative practices in co-taught classrooms: Roles and responsibilities for teachers and parents. *Teaching and Teacher Education*, *35*, 81–91. doi:10.1016/j.tate.2013.06.001

Strogilos, V., Tragoulia, E., Avramidis, E., Voulagka, A., & Papanikolaou, V. (2017). Understanding the development of differentiated instruction for students with and without disabilities in co-taught classrooms. *Disability & Society*, *32*(8), 1216–1238. doi:10.1080/09687599.2017.1352488

UNESCO. (1994). *The Salamanca Statement and framework for action on special needs education*. Retrieved from Paris: https://www.right-to-education.org/resource/salamanca-statement-and-framework-action-special-needs-education

Woodcock, S., & Hardy, I. (2017). Probing and problematizing teacher professional development for inclusion. *International Journal of Educational Research*, *83*, 43–54. doi:10.1016/j.ijer.2017.02.008

ADDITIONAL READING

Ainscow, M., Booth, T., Dyson, A., Farrell, P., Frankham, J., Gallannaugh, F., Howes, A., & Smith, R. (2006). *Improving schools, developing inclusion*. Routledge. doi:10.4324/9780203967157

Allan, J. (2015). The rhetoric of inclusion. *British Journal of Sociology of Education*, *36*(7), 1108–1114. doi:10.1080/01425692.2015.1076247

Allan, J., & Brown, S. (2001). Special Schools and Inclusion. *Educational Review*, *53*(2), 199–207. doi:10.1080/00131910120055624

Booth, T., & Ainscow, M. (2002). *Index for inclusion: developing learning and participation in schools* (Rev. ed.). Centre for Studies on Inclusive Education.

Florian, L., & Camedda, D. (2020). Enhancing teacher education for inclusion. *European Journal of Teacher Education, 43*(1), 4–8. doi:10.1080/02619768.2020.1707579

Messiou, K. (2017). Research in the field of inclusive education: Time for a rethink? *International Journal of Inclusive Education, 21*(2), 146–159. doi:10.1080/13603116.2016.1223184

Slee, R. (2008). Beyond special and regular schooling? An inclusive education reform agenda. *International Studies in Sociology of Education, 18*(2), 99–116. doi:10.1080/09620210802351342

Slee, R. (2011). *The irregular school: exclusion, schooling, and inclusive education* (1st ed.). Routledge. doi:10.4324/9780203831564

Thomas, G., & Loxley, A. (2007). *Deconstructing Special Education and Constructing Inclusion* (2nd ed.). Open University Press.

KEY TERMS AND DEFINITIONS

Communication and Autism Team (CAT): A team of specialists within the United Kingdom schooling system to support learners, school staff, and families to improve the learning experience of students with autism.

Education Health and Care Plan (EHC): A document which outlines the detailed support and provision for learners with special educational needs in the United Kingdom schooling system.

Inclusion or Inclusive Education: Concerned with the presence, active participation, and achievement of all learners in a mainstream school.

Integration: The physical placement of students with special educational needs from special education to mainstream education.

Local Authority: The organisation responsible for a group of schools in a specific region in the United Kingdom schooling system.

Non-Arabic Speakers: Learners in the Bahrain public school system, who are predominantly from South Asian countries, whose first language is not Arabic.

Pupil School Support (PSS): A service provided by the United Kingdom schooling system in support of learners with learning difficulties and vulnerable groups. This support can be provided to school staff through training which in turn will support this groups of learners.

Special Educational Needs (SEN): Includes students with emotional and behavioural difficulties, autism spectrum disorder, learning difficulties, hearing impairment and deafness, physical and health difficulties, profound and multiple learning difficulties, deaf-blindness, speech difficulties, visual impairment, non-native language speakers, and gifted learners.

Chapter 7
The Triple Entente in Brazil:
In-Service English Language Professional Development

André Hedlund
Pontifical Catholic University of Paraná, Brazil

ABSTRACT

This chapter aims to discuss the current scenario of Brazilian English language professional development opportunities through the lens of two organizations: Brazil's English Language Teachers (BrELT), an online learning community, and the Brazilian Teachers of English to Speakers of Other Languages (BRAZ-TESOL). The third perspective of PD will be described through the role of an emerging trend in the last decade: bilingual education solutions and their ongoing mentoring programs. These three levels of PD are quite representative of what is done in Brazilian in-service training and can offer insightful lessons to other countries. BrELT symbolizes the more informal, free-adherence type of PD through an online community. BRAZ-TESOL requires a paid membership and offers more formal PD opportunities to teachers as well as the possibility of joining chapters and SIGs. Bilingual programs such as Edify make on-demand mentorship available to private school teachers who adopt the program.

INTRODUCTION

Brazil faces a number of challenges when it comes to Professional Development (PD), mainly related to English Language Teaching (ELT). Access to proper qualification, number of English speakers, proficiency, and practical knowledge are some of the

DOI: 10.4018/978-1-7998-9278-6.ch007

major issues. However, three PD contexts offer insights into the reality of millions of Brazilian teachers. This chapter explores this Triple Entente of Brazilian PD and reflects on the benefits, limitations and lessons that can be learned and implemented by other professionals in similar and diverse contexts.

As a member of the Brazil's English Language Teachers (BrELT) virtual learning community, I described how it evolved from a relatively small number of participants in 2010 to one of the largest online learning and sharing spaces with nearly 20 thousand members, a blog, frequent webinars and chats, as well as three in-person conferences with important names of the ELT industry as speakers. According to Andrade (2017), BrELT is a community run by volunteers responsible for moderating the group on Facebook and organizing other initiatives.

The Brazilian Teachers of English to Speakers of Other Languages (BRAZ-TESOL) association currently has 16 Special Interest Groups (SIGs) ranging from topics such as *Business English* (BESIG), *Bilingualism* to *Leadership and Management* (LAMSIG), and *Mind, Brain, and Education* (MBE SIG), the SIG I represent in the Midwest of Brazil. The committee publishes a quarterly newsletter, keeps a YouTube channel with more than 2 thousand subscribers, has multiple social media profiles via the regional chapters, and SIGs, and has held seventeen International Conferences with prominent speakers from many countries. BRAZ-TESOL has successfully hosted its first major online conference (the 17th International Conference) (BRAZ-TESOL, 2021).

Lastly, I explored bilingual programs. I work as a bilingual program mentor for Edify Education, a bilingual solution provider, and my main role is to oversee the implementation of our bilingual programs by liaising with school managers and delivering PD to teachers in the form of mentoring. Our main bilingual program is present in more than 20 Brazilian states in over 150 schools almost totaling 40 thousand students. We hold annual events, a blog, and an accredited training center. (EDIFY Education, 2021).

These three levels of PD are quite representative of what is done in Brazil in terms of in-service training and can offer insightful lessons to other countries. My personal accounts of each of these PD opportunities illustrate how they can help professionals from different levels and backgrounds become more successful in their career. BrELT symbolizes the more informal, free-adherence type of PD through online communities and volunteer work. BRAZ-TESOL requires a paid membership and offers more formal PD opportunities to teachers from different backgrounds as well as the possibility of joining chapters and SIGs. Bilingual Programs such as Edify make on-demand mentorship available to private school teachers where the program is adopted.

BACKGROUND

Brazil has been a multilingual country since its origin. Before its colonization, millions of indigenous people lived on the land with their customs, culture and, of course, languages. European languages were brought to the territory from 1500 onwards. From Portugal came Portuguese, the country's official language and spoken by most of the population. However, the successive invasions and migratory waves, in addition to the need for communication with the indigenous people, created an environment in which many languages were used. Today more than 220 languages are present in Brazil (Megale, 2019).

Concerning ELT, it was only in 1996 when the *Lei de Diretrizes e Bases* (LDB) or Law of Guidelines and Bases made the inclusion of a foreign language in the curriculum mandatory in primary and secondary school. In 1998, when the *Parâmetros Curriculares Nacionais* (PCN) or National Curricular Standards were established, the importance of English teaching was even more emphasized (BRASIL, 1998). Nevertheless, most regular schools offer 1 or 2 hours of English a week in their curriculum (Megale, 2019).

These changes did not impact most of the Brazilian population. According to the British Council (2014), in 2014 only 5% of the Brazilian population could speak English at some level and only 1% could do it proficiently. To make matters worse, Education First (EF) places Brazil at 53rd in its English Proficiency Index in 2020, which is considered low and behind other South American neighbors such as Uruguay, Bolivia, Cuba, Chile, and Argentina for instance (EPI, 2020).

This situation also reflects on teacher education. Brazilian English teachers in regular schools are required to have a Bachelor's Degree in Modern Languages. Teachers working in Early Years education must have a degree in Pedagogy. However, these courses are known for focusing too much on theoretical aspects of the profession neglecting relevant practical knowledge and skills. Also, Modern Language students do not always have high enough English proficiency and they do not achieve high proficiency in their course on many occasions. (British Council, 2014)

According to a report conducted by the British Council (2015) in association with *Instituto de Pesquisas Plano CDE*, the Brazilian public school English teacher mostly:

- receives low wages;
- does not have the proper higher education institution qualification;
- does not have English proficiency certificates;
- does not have opportunities to practice the language;
- needs to invest in their own PD;

That scenario only reinforces that effective English teaching has happened mostly outside regular schools at language teaching centers or in more privileged schools. This also seems to be aligned with the perception that English is still an elite language and that public school students have fewer opportunities due to lack of access and less prepared teachers. However, as I demonstrate ahead, there are options for teachers to engage with PD that do not necessarily involve high costs (some are actually free). Let's explore these options starting with an online community that grew incredibly fast and now impacts tens of thousands of teachers.

THE TRIPLE ENTENTE: BrELT, BRAZ-TESOL, AND BILINGUAL PROGRAMS

BrELT: A Community for Teachers by Teachers

Founded by Bruno Andrade following a successful chat initiative on Twitter in 2010, BrELT kicked off as a Facebook group with the mission of connecting Brazilian English teachers who needed and/or could offer support. Its early format focused on making frequent chats available to participants on subjects ranging from understanding the importance of English teaching in Brazil, how to teach English online, lesson planning, school management, and ELT materials to innovation, teacher linguistic development, methodology, and learning strategies.

According to Andrade (2017), BrELT is a space for collaboration, sharing, and reflections. Among its many initiatives, we can mention the CoLAB, which brought teachers to either write articles or lessons about several topics, BrELT webinars streamed live on YouTube, BrELT Interviews with ELT professionals, a blog, monthly posts on Facebook, a calendar of ELT events in Brazil and the world, and **#RovingBrELT**, a hashtag created to promote, within and outside the community, content and insights experienced by participants who attend ELT events by sharing them on social media.

BrELT has also created a Language Development Special Interest Group with the objective of helping teachers develop language competencies through activities planned by a moderator who promotes interaction and participation via WhatsApp.

From November 2013 to June 2017, the number of participants on BrELT's Facebook group increased more than seven times, moving from 2000 to 15000 people (Andrade, 2017). Today, August 2021, it has reached the mark of 19.4 thousand participants (Facebook, 2021).

PD Through BrELT

Some of the initiatives previously mentioned demonstrate the level of commitment of BrELT as well as its multifaceted approach. Although they all form a much more complex network of PD, I will focus on the dynamic of interactions on BrELT's Facebook group and how the community connects teachers.

Two of the most effective PD ideas BrELT has promoted on Facebook have been the BrELT chats (#breltchat) and simply answering its members' requests on the group feed. BrELT chats started on Twitter and moved to Facebook when the group was created in mid-2011. These would normally start with a topic that could be chosen by the community members via poll voting and then a live discussion under a post with the topic, some housekeeping instructions, and the work of moderators to help it flow. Some examples of topics discussed are:

- Warm-ups & Wrap-ups
- Video in the ELT classroom
- Five-minute activities to save any lesson
- Content and Language Integrated Learning (CLIL)
- What did you learn at BrELT on the Road 2018?

BrELT chats were generally set up to take place every fifteen days in the evening when most teachers were available, they lasted 1 hour and often passed the 200-comment mark on the post with tens to hundreds of participants. As these chats were part of the community's feed, participants could come back to the discussion later on and read the whole thread. It was a great opportunity to connect famous ELT professionals to school directors, and novice teachers. This initiative was discontinued in 2018.

For anyone who's a member of BrELT on Facebook, while scrolling down, it takes no time to see that many teachers post questions to problems they are having in the classroom, new ideas for activities, requests for specific materials or resources, and basically anything that might help them teach more effectively. The community has grown so much that posts are not left unanswered for very long. Oftentimes, a request for a recommendation of Young Learners' materials or a course on pronunciation can turn into a fruitful discussion.

Lastly, one of BrELT's most interesting initiatives is to connect teachers, many of whom never attended events before, to local, national, and even international conferences. Besides having hosted three face-to-face events in major Brazilian cities (Rio de Janeiro, 2017; São Paulo, 2018; and Brasília, 2019), with the hashtag **#RovingBrELT**, Facebook group members and non-members can follow what's going on in the world of English Teaching on social media.

It is worth noting that according to Andrade (2017), who applied a questionnaire on 119 teachers, most respondents think of BrELT as a community where interaction and learning, as well as a sense of belonging, are central pillars. Teachers relied on BrELT for PD and PD-related news and most believed that this community positively impacted their teacher practice through exchange and ongoing pedagogical support. Fewer than 8% of the respondents claimed that BrELT did not significantly and positively impact their practice and a little over 9% did not perceive the community as an important source of PD.

BRAZ-TESOL: Opportunities Through Paid Membership

BRAZ-TESOL celebrated its 35th anniversary in 2021. Since 1986, it has been promoting PD initiatives to teachers, managers, and other professionals involved with language teaching in the country. According to its latest bulletin (BRAZ-TESOL, 2021):

BRAZ-TESOL is Brazil's largest association of teachers of English to speakers of other languages. A non-profit organization with a membership of approximately 1700 professionals, BRAZ-TESOL is an affiliate of TESOL International (US) and IATEFL (UK). The organization is also a member of the Southern Cone TESOL, formed by associations from Argentina, Uruguay, Paraguay, Peru, Colombia and Chile.

Organized with a National Executive Board, an Advisory Council (both with elections and 2-year terms), Regional Chapters, and Special Interest Groups (SIGs), BRAZ-TESOL impacts thousands of people in Brazil. Its mission is to foster and support research in ELT, including Applied Linguistics, Education Technology, and Second Language Acquisition, to promote teacher development and networking with other like-minded institutions, as well as organize local and international events.

Table 1. BRAZ-TESOL Special Interest Groups (SIGs)S

Assessment	Leadership and Management	Voices	Wellbeing
Bilingualism	Pronunciation	Mind, Brain, and Education	Translation
Coaching in ELT	Young Learners and Teens	Online Teaching	Business English
Intercultural Language Education	Teacher Development	Public School	English for Specific Purposes

Source: (BRAZ-TESOL, 2021)

BRAZ-TESOL has had chapters in 20 out of 27 Brazilian states. Currently there are active chapters in 16 states whose structure generally follows that of the national committee's. There are also 16 Special Interest Groups (SIGs) as shown in Table 1.

Regional chapters and SIGs promote local events and other PD initiatives. It is important to mention that they are run by volunteers and that many events are free for members or charge a small fee to cover operational costs.

PD Through BRAZ-TESOL

BRAZ-TESOL offers a number of PD opportunities through its paid membership. Individual members pay around 36 US dollars a year while institutions can join for about 144 US dollars annually (dollar rate regarded as 1 to 5 Brazilian Reais). The committee has just held its 17th International Conference, which had to be postponed in 2020 due to the COVID-19 pandemic. This was the first time the BRAZ-TESOL International Conference (BTIC) was delivered online. Besides BTIC, which is held biannually, BRAZ-TESOL holds major events with national and international reach (BRAZ-TESOL, 2021).

In 2021 alone, BRAZ-TESOL's website lists 20 events organized by different chapters or SIGs. Two examples are the São Paulo Chapter's "No brain, no gain" event about neuroscience and teaching, and the Young Learners and Teens SIG's "Tech'n'Teach" event about the use of technology in YLT classes. Members and non-members can sign up for these events on the website and BRAZ-TESOL issues certificates of participation for attendees (BRAZ-TESOL, 2021).

Another PD opportunity is represented by BRAZ-TESOL's newsletter. The first newsletter was launched in 2005 and, ever since, there have been 54 issues. There were four issues a year until 2018. Since 2019, BRAZ-TESOL has been launching two annual issues and it has recently been renamed (it is now called BRAZ-TESOL Echoes). Articles are written by important ELT names, members, and non-members on a variety of subjects that go beyond the spectrum of the area such as non-violent communication, burnout, innovation, and the new Brazilian Common Core. Members receive a printed copy of the newsletter by mail and they can download the PDF on the website under *Member Area* (BRAZ-TESOL, 2021).

Still under *Member Area,* BRAZ-TESOL offers discounts for products and services provided by sponsors (such as books and courses), access to the recordings of previous webinars (some of which can be found on BRAZ-TESOL's YouTube channel), and even job offers (BRAZ-TESOL, 2021).

Bilingual Programs

Bilingual education in Brazil forms a complex network with different players. This section focuses on bilingual programs, that is, a service package offered by an unrelated outsourced company without any prior connection to the school. This company is responsible for the elaboration of teaching materials and professional development training based on approaches and methodologies related to the development of bilingualism and the idea of student-centeredness. Therefore, the bilingual program has all the necessary structure, including books, online platforms, commercial and pedagogical support, as well as expertise to carry out the implementation in any given school.

It is important to mention that the new document drafted by the *Conselho Nacional de Educação* (CNE) or National Education Council in Brazil labels this modality **Extended Curriculum in Additional Language** because it is not implemented in all levels by the whole school and it increases the number of contact hours with the additional language from 1 or 2 classes to at least 3 classes a week. If this document is approved and comes into force, the denomination Bilingual Programs will most likely stop being used.

Bilingual schools, on the other hand, offer more hours of contact (30% to 50% of the curriculum) in the additional language to all students and need to have teachers who are experts in their subjects as well as linguistically proficient since the teaching of these subjects is done in that language. In the case of a bilingual program, the teachers at the school that adopts the program are usually the English-speaking teachers that the school has hired and they can vary greatly in terms of proficiency. These professionals undergo a linguistic assessment and, if they have the appropriate level of competence, go through the initial training about the program. They receive constant support from the program's coordinators (who are normally called advisors, tutors, or mentors) and follow didactic-pedagogical recommendations prepared by the program.

PD Through Bilingual Programs

PD in bilingual programs usually means ongoing mentoring within the schools. According to Asención Delaney (2012, p. 185), mentoring:

is important not only to inform new teachers about the standards in teacher training programs, but also to help them implement them within the unique contexts of their schools. Mentors can facilitate the implementation of standards by acculturating the new teacher into school policies and identifying contextual factors that foster or hinder standards implementation.

Mentoring can be done on an individual basis or in groups. Most of the work involves initial training, constant visits to the school, assistance with lesson planning, observation and feedback, recycling and improvement sessions. The continuous education axis is essential and one of the pillars of the successful implementation of a bilingual program. The mentors create, together with the teachers, an individualized development plan to promote reflection on teaching practices and develop competencies as the program progresses.

Since teachers in bilingual contexts might not be qualified to work in this scenario, most of the PD will be divided into two areas: 1) linguistic development; and 2) teaching or methodological development. The first area covers teachers' language training and proficiency. Sessions are normally carried out in English and a goal is set so that teachers can keep up with their progress. The second area involves theoretical and practical training on approaches, methods, techniques, and skills required for teaching English in bilingual contexts. Mentors will share resources and plan training sessions based on their mentees' demands and on what they observed in the classroom. Two examples that certainly became more popular due to the pandemic are blended learning and online/remote teaching resources.

As a mentor, my main role is to make sure my mentored teachers are taken care of. I travel to their schools, meet with them, listen to their struggles and demands, and offer my expertise to help in any way I can. This involves brainstorming ideas for their lesson plans or classroom management strategies as well as delivering workshops, setting up a date to observe their lessons and to give them feedback afterwards. We usually set up weekly meetings and I spend one of two days in loco. I may also serve as a mediator between teachers and managers, as well as between teachers and families.

Teachers who are being mentored in such programs normally refer to them as essential in their professional transition from more traditional teaching to teaching according to the demands of bilingual education contexts. Unlike publishers that offer specific training to cover how to use their materials, both printed and online, mentoring programs are ongoing, long-term, more personalized, and they cover other aspects not entirely related to pedagogical issues.

SOLUTIONS AND RECOMMENDATIONS

Based on the three PD scenarios depicted above, this section looks at some of the benefits and limitations of each (Table 2), their potential through my personal account, and what can be done to improve the experiences they offer.

Table 2. PD comparative table with benefits, limitations, and possible solutions

PD Type	Benefits	Limitations	Possible Solutions
BrELT (free membership)	-Free access -Networking -Sense of belonging -Questions almost immediately answered -Use of Portuguese is accepted -More distance from members	-Large number of members -Relies on volunteer work -Some initiatives have been discontinued -No sustained or long-term development program -Lack of personalized PD	Reboot initiatives that engaged the community in discussions, increase number of moderators, create ongoing mentoring programs
BRAZ-TESOL (paid membership)	-Exclusive access to recordings and newsletters -Networking -Sense of belonging -Possibility of joining chapters and/or SIGs -Discounts in events and courses -May be distant from members	-Large number of members -Not present in every state -Some initiatives are paid -No sustained or long-term development program -Lack of personalized PD -Use of Portuguese is discouraged	Hold more events in Portuguese, offer more benefits to public school teachers, offer some long-term PD programs
Bilingual Programs (for schools that hired this service)	-Restricted to school staff -Exclusive access to program's own resources -Sustained or long-term development program -Personalized PD -Use of Portuguese is accepted -Close proximity & Emotional support	-Almost no networking -Not much sense of belonging -Underqualified teachers -Lack of adequate materials	Create networking opportunities among schools, insist on hiring more qualified teachers, reformulate materials to fit the bilingual education context

BrELT

Despite its many initiatives and reach, some of the limitations of BrELT seem to be directly connected with its reliance on volunteer work. Two of the main issues that apparently arose from BrELT's rapid growth are: 1) the discontinuation of frequent and themed events on Facebook such as BrELT chat; and 2) the need for more constant moderation. As the community grew on Facebook, it became more dependent on moderators' judgement to ensure that its purpose was maintained. However, on a number of occasions, posts against the rules of the community cause some friction as they do not only move away from its scope but also offend the community due to extremist views.

BrELT has been and still is a powerful tool to connect English teachers from different contexts in Brazil and its benefits overweigh its limitations. Some of the most important lessons BrELT has to offer have to do with the fact that Virtual

Learning Communities can have a positive impact on teachers' PD and this can certainly be reflected on their students' outcomes. BrELT also shows that an active PD community can start small and rely on free or inexpensive resources.

Allan & Lewis (2006) suggest that Virtual Learning Communities can have a lasting impact on PD and are successful in supporting major life changes. I would like to illustrate this point through a personal anecdote. It was during the first edition of BrELT on the Road in 2017 that I learned about a scholarship opportunity to the UK. I decided to attend a session delivered by two quite active members of the community (one of them a moderator). Because of this connection we had, I decided to apply in the same year and was awarded the Chevening Scholarship for 2018-2019. BrELT connected me with a moderator and her session and that allowed me to study abroad and now hold an MSc in Psychology of Education from the University of Bristol.

The solution for BrELT, and any other virtual learning community, might come from its most active members. They can become moderators and they might be able to create a frequent flow of events. I recommend BrELT chat is rebooted, that BrELT promotes local events hosted by members, and that it helps connect more experienced teachers who can offer a few hours to mentor groups of novice teachers. Long-term and more personalized programs seem to yield better results.

BRAZ-TESOL

BRAZ-TESOL does have some limitations worth mentioning. The first one might be the reluctance, although justified, to host events or sessions mostly in Portuguese. Teachers whose English proficiency is low might feel intimidated to attend all-English sessions and they are the ones who could certainly benefit the most from the insights shared in these events. Secondly, I must say that even though BTICs and other major events are incredibly rich, they can be quite costly to many teachers from public schools. Scholarships and discounts are available, but they do not always cover all the costs

However, Alencar (2010) discusses how teachers tend to join teaching associations to develop their linguistic skills and learn about new methodologies and innovations for their practice. Falcão (2004) investigated BRAZ-TESOL and suggests that its organizational structure helped members pursue more professionalism, networking, and support.

In my case, I started attending BRAZ-TESOL conferences in 2015 through the local chapter. It was an opportunity for me to do some networking and meet references in ELT during the plenary sessions. Since then, I have participated in dozens of events hosted by BRAZ-TESOL both as an observer and as a speaker, including two BTICs. It was my connection with BRAZ-TESOL that allowed me to find my niche and grow professionally. In 2017 I published my first ELT-related article in BRAZ-TESOL's newsletter. Later that year, I was invited by the head of the still unborn MBE SIG to join as a board member. I had always had an interest in neuroscience and becoming one of the members of the MBE SIG helped me choose my master's program.

With that being said, BRAZ-TESOL is certainly an association worth joining and it has been bringing together regional chapters and SIGs to offer quite comprehensive PD opportunities. If I had not attended local events, published in the newsletter, as well as joined the SIG and spoken at the International Conference, I have no doubt I would not have accomplished what I have professionally. Being part of this association can have an enormous positive effect on one's career.

Bilingual Programs

Bilingual programs can be considered a quite recent trend in the Brazilian Language Teaching scenario. The absence of legislation regarding bilingual education contexts, with a few exceptions, allowed many schools to call themselves bilingual even though they did not have the proper curriculum and specialized staff. That meant, for many stakeholders, that they could not trust the type of service these schools were offering. To make matters more complicated, bilingual programs often have to deal with hiring issues as many schools are unwilling to replace their underqualified teachers. In extreme cases, where teachers do not have the right proficiency level or methodological knowledge and skills, mentoring can hardly help.

Many of the bilingual programs rely on materials that were first intended for widely different contexts and highly qualified professionals. These materials are either provided by larger publishers or repeat their formula, which basically means replicating their approach, layout, and sequence. They were made for English as a Foreign Language (EFL) contexts, with more homogeneous and smaller groups, and mostly aligned with the Communicative Language Teaching Approach. In that sense, underqualified teachers dealing with 30 students or more, whose levels of English are mixed, teaching from materials made for more prepared professionals can be a recipe for failure.

On the other hand, Hobson, Ashby, Malderez, and Tomlinson (2009) suggest that mentoring enhances problem-solving skills and increases self-reflection. It is also an effective way to make positive changes in the teaching context (Wang & Odell, 2002). Mentoring alone cannot be the only solution if teachers do not get the proper qualification.

The solution, at least partially, might be the one proposed by the National Education Council in Brazil concerning training requirements for teachers working in bilingual education contexts. These professionals will have to adapt to the demands set forth in the draft, provided it is approved by congress. That means that all professionals teaching bilingual curricula must have:

1. a Bachelor's Degree in Pedagogy, Education, and/or Tesol/Modern Languages;
2. at least a CEFR-B2 certificate;
3. a 120h qualification course specifically addressing bilingual education;

Except for requirement 1, the others are new and will enter into force as soon as the legislation becomes a reality. Many teachers in Brazil are taking this qualification course as of now as an in-service development program (when it should be pre-service) in order to adapt to a future demand that has not yet been confirmed. This also means that many institutions, particularly private universities, have started offering such course, and since the draft has no specifications regarding the curriculum (only the amount of hours), different universities offer different subjects. To illustrate this PD option, here's what the course I teach at the Pontifical Catholic University of Paraná (PUCPR) is offering:

1. Language and Cognition (30h)
2. Active Methodology and Technology (30h)
3. Building Academic Literacy (30h)
4. Curriculum and Assessment in Bilingual Education (30h)

Meeting the criteria required by the National Education Council may guarantee teachers are better prepared, at least with minimal linguistic and methodological requirements, to benefit from mentoring, through which they will be in touch with more practical elements of teaching in bilingual education contexts.

CONCLUSION

This chapter described three PD contexts in Brazil. The first addressed how teachers can find development opportunities through joining an online community free of charge on social media. The second looked at how having a paid membership to Brazil's biggest TESOL committee, as well as joining its chapters or SIGs, can provide teachers with excellent and relevant PD options. Finally, the third focused on how teachers in a bilingual education scenario, a bilingual school or a bilingual program, benefit from mentoring and ongoing pedagogical assistance.

Since Brazil has a history of overlooking in-service teacher education, these options certainly offer teaching professionals the possibility of improving their skills. Andrade (2017) has found that most of the teachers surveyed about the role of

BrELT attributed positive qualities to it such as *a sense of community, professional growth, a repository of shared best practices, learning and networking space, source or news and latest developments in ELT.*

Nevertheless, one must not neglect that these options might not (or should not) replace the role of well-structured and ongoing PD programs promoted by the teaching institutions and school managers themselves. Except for teachers in bilingual programs or members of BRAZ-TESOL, most teachers might not access frequent PD opportunities that are so essential to the development of new knowledge, insights, skills, and competencies. It is important to realize that BRAZ-TESOL members, despite paying the fees, might also choose not to attend many events.

Another concern is that these options may leave out the professionals who could benefit the most from them as suggested by the British Council (2015). Public school teachers who receive low wages and may not have good or frequent access to the internet are the ones who suffer the most.

That said, I do believe that this Triple Entente in Brazil can offer valuable lessons regarding English teachers' PD. Teachers can benefit a great deal from an online community where they can simply participate in chats or ask for help. This does not take much to build and can rely on the work of volunteers. Also, national TESOL committees can expand their reach through the creation of regional chapters and SIGs as well as a newsletter. Finally, bilingual programs teach us that ongoing mentoring with mutually established personal development goals, recycling, and improvement sessions based on lesson observations can do wonders when it comes to PD.

REFERENCES

Alencar, E. B. A. (2010). *Um galo sozinho não tece um (a)manhã": o papel de uma associação de professores de inglês no desenvolvimento da competência profissional de seus associados* [Unpublished master's thesis]. Universidade de Brasília, Brasília, Brazil.

Allan, B., & Lewis, D. (2006). The impact of membership of a virtual learning community on individual learning careers and professional identity. *British Journal of Educational Technology, 37*(6), 841–852. doi:10.1111/j.1467-8535.2006.00661.x

Andrade, B. C. (2017). *Comunidades Virtuais Na Prática E Na Formação Continuada De Professores De Inglês - Um Estudo De Caso Sobre A Comunidade* [Unpublished master's thesis]. Universidade Federal do Rio de Janeiro, Rio de Janeiro, Brazil.

Asención Delaney, Y. (2012). Research on mentoring language teachers: Its role in language education. *Foreign Language Annals, 45*(s1), s184–s202. doi:10.1111/j.1944-9720.2011.01185.x

BRASIL. (1998). *Secretaria de Educação Fundamental. Parâmetros curriculares nacionais: terceiro e quarto ciclos do ensino fundamental: língua estrangeira/ Secretaria de Educação Fundamental*. Brasília: MEC/SEF. Accessed at: http://portal.mec.gov.br/seb/arquivos/pdf/pcn_estrangeira.pdf

BRAZ-TESOL. (2021). Accessed at https://braztesol.org.br/site/view.asp?p=1

British Council. (2014). *Learning English in Brazil 2014: Understanding the aims and expectations of the Brazilian emerging middle classes*. Author.

British Council. (2015). *O Ensino de Inglês na Educação Pública Brasileira*. Author.

EDIFY. (2021). Accessed at https://www.edifyeducation.com.br/

EF EPI. (2020). *EF English proficiency index*. EF Education First.

Falcão, A. (2004). *A Brazilian teacher association for teachers of English: organisational improvement through an international and comparative educational perspective* [Unpublished master's thesis]. University of Leeds, Leeds, UK.

Hobson, A., Ashby, P., Malderez, A., & Tomlinson, P. (2009). Mentoring beginning teachers: What we know and what we don't. *Teaching and Teacher Education, 25*(1), 207–216. doi:10.1016/j.tate.2008.09.001

Megale, A. (2019). *Educação bilíngue no Brasil*. Fundação Santillana.

Wang, J., & Odell, S. (2002). Mentored learning to teach according to standards-based reform: A critical review. *Review of Educational Research, 72*(3), 481–546. doi:10.3102/00346543072003481

Chapter 8
School-Based In-Service Teacher Training and Peer-to-Peer Learning as an Element of Professionalization

Wiltrud Weidinger
Zurich University of Teacher Education, Switzerland

Rolf Gollob
Zurich University of Teacher Education, Switzerland

ABSTRACT

The IPE (International Projects in Education) Centre of the Zurich University of Teacher Education (PHZH) deals with questions of lifelong learning of teachers in many of its international collaborations. The chapter deals on the one hand with the question of how the continuing education of teachers is organized in Switzerland, what successful forms and approaches are, and on which learning theories they are based. Learning from colleagues in peer-mentoring programs as one element of school development is presented from various perspectives. The concept of school-based in-service teacher training (SITT) is presented and discussed for a successful implementation on school level. In addition, practical examples from various cooperation projects around the world are briefly presented to explain how experiences can be further developed thanks to careful cooperation and to learn from this that teachers around the world perhaps learn most effectively from their colleagues if there is a good concept behind this approach.

DOI: 10.4018/978-1-7998-9278-6.ch008

SITUATION AND COUNTRY CONTEXT OF SWITZERLAND

Teacher Education and the Educational System of Switzerland

In Switzerland, pre-and in-service teacher training is organized and implemented by teacher training Universities that view teachers' professional biographies from a lifelong learning perspective. Primary school teachers are trained for three years in a Bachelor's program, and Secondary school teachers finish their qualification with a master thesis after four years of training (European Commission/Eurydice 2021). Compulsory education in Switzerland lasts for eleven years, dividing a student's educational biography into two years of kindergarten, six years of primary school, and three years of lower secondary school. However, depending on their academic achievement, students can change into a cantonal high school (Gymnasium) after primary school leading up to "Matura," the qualification for entering University. If students remain in lower secondary school, they follow up with a vocational or technical school and soon enter the labor market (swissuniversities 2021). It is called the Swiss "dual education." The percentages of students entering Gymnasia after primary school and students aiming at vocational or technical training are around 20:80 with slight differences in urban and rural areas, imparting high reputation to the vocational track. The reason for this phenomenon, which guarantees highly skilled and qualified professionals in the labor market, lies in the extreme permeability of the Swiss educational system. Taking the vocational track itself does not represent a dead-end street.

On the contrary, students can decide to meander through the educational system aiming at a higher education degree at various points in their educational biography (swissuniversities 2021). Moving around the educational landscape implies high competencies in transversal/life skills, such as cooperation, communication, problem-solving, critical thinking, creative thinking, decision-making, etc. Teachers have to be prepared for this in their pre-service training but have to be followed up once they enter a classroom's and a school's reality.

In the Swiss educational system, several educational reforms have been undergone in the past years. National reforms in school education have tackled objectives such as digitalization, harmonization of curricula between the Cantons, and improvement of language and Mathematics competencies (European Commission/Eurydice 2020). The introduction of the reformed competence-oriented "Curriculum21" (Lehrplan 21) across all grades of the compulsory school system resulted in in-service training programs in 21 Swiss cantons. Apart from these nationally decided strategies by the only national board, the Swiss Conference of Cantonal Ministers of Education (EDK), all other strategies are dealt with and decided in the different Cantons. For the Canton of Zurich, the current issues in in-service teacher training relate to societal phenomena which strongly influence education and schooling and the corresponding educational reforms: Digitalization, competence-orientation, the introduction of whole-day schools, school leadership, elementary education – focus on 4 – 8-year-old students, education for sustainable development and German as a second language (Bildungsdirektion Kanton Zürich 2021). In schools in the Canton of Zurich, one-third of the students' population does have a migrant background and a different language than German.

IN-SERVICE TEACHER TRAINING IN SWITZERLAND

In-service teacher training starts at the entry point into the educational system as a class teacher, subject teacher, or teacher with a specifically assigned role (e.g., special education, integrative support, German as a second language, etc.). Schools in Switzerland are organized on a municipality level, with a school governing board forming an independent authority. School leaders are experts, members of the lay authority are politicians with an affinity to education. All schools decide in agreement with the school governing board which school-based in-service training they want to organize for their staff. Each school receives a yearly budget that can be spent on whole-school training opportunities or sending teachers to courses or programs offered by the teacher training Universities. In educational reforms or specific demands, the canton declares the related in-service training activities as compulsory and finances them (Kantonsrat Kanton Zürich 2015). School leaders develop together with their teaching staff and discuss with the school governing board their school program, including specific focus points and measures for quality assurance and school development (ibid).

In-service training formats at the University include single courses, modules as parts of a certificate program, and whole programs. However, tailormade in-service training activities are adapted to the school's specific needs between University experts and school leaders (PH Zürich 2021a). Contents of both possibilities – University in-service training as well as school-based in-service training – represent a wide range of topics from more general issues relating to teaching and learning (e.g., assessment, team-teaching, communication, etc.) to more specific topics (e.g., dealing with multicultural settings, introducing new didactic concepts, prevention of violence and mobbing, etc.) to particular subject-related issues (e.g., literacy skills, didactics of Maths and Natural Science, etc.). Apart from sending teachers as compulsory in-service training and an additional qualification (e.g., school leader, ICT teacher or coordinator, German as a second language), more and more schools decide on starting internal school development processes together with a University expert. The schools' demands are manifold, depend on a school's direct surroundings, and involve various topics mentioned previously.

School Development Processes as Another Level of In-Service Training

During the last years, it became evident that the demands of schools and teachers sometimes do not match the financial possibilities of the school for in-service training. Moreover, evaluation results of in-service training courses indicate a high need for mutual exchange among teachers and a lack of inter-communication among colleagues. Expertise, knowledge, and skills remain isolated in their classrooms, and teachers also do not have any low-level opportunity to receive feedback on their teaching and the students' learning processes (apart from a formal evaluation by the school governing board). The school's decision to start its school development process, including changes and activities on organization, teaching and learning, and human resource level, can ensure that in-service training elements are adapted to the specific needs of all involved. It is up to the school to involve University experts to accompany change processes or deliver inputs on specific topics. A school development process aiming to change teaching and learning culture involves peer-to-peer learning and feedback elements, expert teachers or mentoring systems, or some other kind of school-based mutual support.

In the past years, specific projects have started increasing this exchange and motivating teachers to learn from each other. For example, at the compulsory school level, the project "Good Practice" was initiated between the Zurich University of Teacher Education and the Cantonal Unit for School Evaluation (PH Zürich 2021b). "Good Practice" aims at exchanging innovative ideas for school development among schools. Each year seven schools act as exchange agents, making knowledge, experience, and materials available to each other. Another program, "Schools learn from schools" (original: "Schulen Lernen von Schulen"), puts the focus on the exchange of innovative practice in a network of schools.

Similar initiatives have started on an upper secondary level where peers are involved in the formal evaluation process of upper secondary schools by the Institute for External School Evaluations on Upper Secondary Level – "ifes" – (ifes/ipes 2021). Each evaluation team consists of four experts, two evaluation experts of ifes, and two peers who volunteer to participate in the evaluation process and at the same time use this opportunity for mutual exchange, practice-based in-service training "on-the-job," and reflection on their gained insights and learnings.

However, in-service training does not necessarily have to be built up in a cross-school project or school network using peer learning and peer support. In-service training as part of school development is most easily implemented as a school-based initiative. The potential of school-based peer-learning and peer exchange connected with mentoring systems is still not entirely used even though experience shows promising results. What are precisely the elements of a school-based in-service training (SITT) program? The following subchapter describes the concept of SITT in more detail, defining the different elements.

The Concept of School-Based In-Service Training as a Part of School Development (SITT)

School-based in-service training programs are usually part of a whole-school school development process aiming at teacher professional development. In most cases, SITT programs include elements such as mentoring, peer-coaching, and peer-feedback/learning among teachers as fixed elements. A structured process that includes inputs by mentors or expert teachers can be added depending on the school development process's focus. For this purpose, expert teachers will have to acquire the necessary knowledge, expertise, and experience in adult learning. Reflection as the central idea of SITT as a motor for professionalization can be viewed as another element. Based on the experiences in various activities of the department of International Projects in Education, a SITT program leads to a school culture where communities of practice are established in the long run.

Table 1. Elements of SITT programs

	Elements of SITT programs	
Mentoring – peer-to-peer learning – peer feedback	Structured in-service training: inputs, workshops	Reflection
Communities of practice		

Mentoring

International data shows that school-based mentoring programs on students' levels (e.g., adult-student mentoring, peer-mentoring) support the academic achievement of students as well as the development of transversal competencies positively (e.g., self-concept, self-efficacy, friendship etc.) (Wang & Odell 2002). Mentoring on the teacher- and student-level is often associated with an apprenticeship model with a younger, inexperienced person seeking guidance from an experienced expert (Halai 2006; Wang & Odell 2002). Recent definitions of mentoring among students and teachers in schools also point out the transformation of formerly hierarchical roles between mentors and mentees to a lateral relationship on an eye-to-eye level (Halai 2006; Wang & Odell 2007).

Mentoring in school-based in-service programs can be differentiated from other forms of counseling (e.g., supervision, coaching) with one significant distinction: in mentoring, *both* involved partners – mentor and mentee – are supported in their professional development (Finn 1993). In a school context, mentoring among teachers, therefore, is understood as the personal and professional development of teaching staff (Fischer 2008). Through the continuous exchange, cooperation can be intensified, and the sense of belonging to the school can be supported by all involved. Usually, the mentoring element is adapted according to the specific needs, goals, and context of the involved teachers. The following table gives an overview of the different forms of mentoring in a school context (adapted from Fischer & van Andel 2002 and Raufelder & Ittel 2012).

Table 2. Forms of teacher-mentor-mentee relationships (adapted from Fischer & van Andel 2002 and Raufelder & Ittel 2012)

Mentor	**Mentee**	**Situation**	**Main Purpose**
Schoolteacher	Student-teacher	Pre-service short-term practicum or one-year practicum	Learn how to teach from a model-teacher
Experienced school teacher	Novice teacher	Beginning at school: introduction phase	Develop basic teaching competencies
Teacher of subject matter	Teacher of subject matter	In-service: school-based/internal co-operative partnership; team model	Reflection, problem-solving, curriculum developing
Expert teacher (coach, supervisor)	Teacher	In-service: external partnership	Improve and extend teaching competencies
Headteacher	Teacher	In-service: external partnership	Staff development, develop leadership qualifications; career promotion

According to this overview, mentoring programs in schools can be implemented at different stages of teacher education. In Switzerland, Austria and Germany, Teacher Training Universities organize mentoring programs for student teachers or novice teachers as mentees like it is the case for the Zurich University of Teacher Education (PH Zürich 2021; Dammerer 2020; Strauß & Rohr 2019; Fraefel et al. 2017). In some programs, class teachers and teacher students also form peer-tandems and organize school internships as peer-mentoring possibilities, involving joint planning, teaching, and reflection sessions on eye-level (Fraefel et al. 2017). Other programs put the focus on peer-coaching between student teachers, installing tandems of more experienced student teachers with less experienced student teachers or same-level student teachers with each other (Kreis & Schnebel 2017). Mentoring programs within school-based in-service training programs are initiated and implemented by the schools themselves as staff development and quality assurance measures. Through mentoring, peer learning takes place. In this respect, it is essential to note that the term "peer-support" is not identical with "peer-mentoring" or "peer-learning". Peer support refers not to a format or method but describes the grassroots process of like-minded colleagues to support each other informally (Strauß & Rohr 2019, 112).

Scientific literature distinguishes three basic approaches to peer mentoring programs (Fischer 2008). They do not necessarily follow a chronological order and can also be described as phases.

- Apprenticeship approach: The focus lies in acquiring methodical hints, techniques, and approaches in classroom management and teaching practice. In the apprenticeship approach, the mentor takes up the role of technical supporter and instructor.
- Humanistic approach: The focus lies on counseling in different learning areas. The mentor takes up the role of an active counselor, provides feedback, and acts as a coach. He/She serves as a role model for the mentee.
- Critical-constructive approach: The focus lies in developing an autonomous and professional attitude towards teaching and supporting reflection competencies. The mentor takes up the role of a partner/motivator who keeps an eye on the mentee's professional development. The mentor also helps the mentee finding his/her way by sharing knowledge, experience, and network opportunities.

The third role within the critical-constructive approach is where mentors should find themselves in a sustainable working process (Dammerer 2018; Dammerer, Ziegler & Bartonek 2019).

As described at the beginning of this chapter, mentoring programs are defined by a mutual professional (and personal) development of mentors and mentees. Moreover, the relationships within a mentoring process are described as follows (Eby, Rhodes & Allen 2007):

- Mentoring represents a unique relationship between two individuals.
- Mentoring always means a relationship geared towards the gain of knowledge and new experiences.
- Mentoring always means a process.
- The relationship between mentor and mentee is asymmetrical but not reciprocal.
- Mentoring partnerships are dynamic relationships.

Mentors in a SITT program can be experienced teachers or fellow teachers who received additional training in the subject area, making them "expert teachers" and in skills and competencies needed for mentoring and accompanying learning processes of individuals. What are the competencies of mentors in schools? Teachers who act as mentors need a set of competencies in different areas. The well-known model of teachers' competencies by Baumert and Kunter (2013) can be adapted and used as a framework and starting point for detecting necessary competencies for mentors even though it was not explicitly developed for SITT programs. According to this, the model uses professional competencies as a set of

- motivational orientations,
- beliefs, values, and goals
- self-regulation as well as
- professional knowledge

Baumert and Kunter (2013) break down the dimension of professional knowledge using the example of Mathematics into content knowledge (e.g., deep understanding of school Mathematics), pedagogical content knowledge (e.g., explanatory knowledge, knowledge of students' mathematical thinking, knowledge of mathematical tasks) and pedagogical/psychological knowledge (e.g., knowledge of students' assessment, knowledge of learning processes, knowledge of effective classroom management). Apart from this, teachers also need organizational as well as counseling knowledge.

Table 3. The COACTIV model of professional competence (adapted from Baumert and Kunter 2013)

			Motivational orientations		
		Beliefs/values/goals		Self-regulation	
			Professional knowledge		
Domains of knowledge	Content knowledge	Pedagogical content knowledge	Pedagogical/ psychological knowledge	Organizational knowledge	Counselling knowledge
Facets of knowledge	Deep understanding of school Mathematics	Explanatory knowledge, knowledge of students' mathematical thinking, knowledge of mathematical tasks	Knowledge of students' assessment, knowledge of learning processes, knowledge of effective classroom management		

Organizational knowledge in this respect includes knowing different roles within the school and an understanding of different stakeholders outside the school, and a notion of the mechanisms of the school system. In the context of SITT, organizational knowledge also means knowledge about different networking possibilities and knowledge and agility of switching the roles from teacher – colleague to mentor-mentee. Counseling knowledge involves all communication, feedback, and steering counseling processes in the light of a critical-constructivist view on professional identity. Ideally, mentors/expert teachers receive training before starting their roles as mentors in a SITT program.

Lessons Learned

The implementation of peer mentoring as an element of school and staff development showed promising results on a qualitative level. From among the three presented approaches of mentoring programs (apprenticeship, humanistic, critical constructive), the critical constructive approach was set as a school goal. Within this goal, schools tried to bring teachers and schools into an autonomous and professional community that wants to start a lifelong learning professional learning experience. Critical-constructive peer mentoring – once it was installed – became a welcomed opportunity for teachers and practitioners to get into mutual exchange. However, for national and international contexts, implementation of mentoring in a school highly depends on school leaders and principals as critical people, especially in the introduction phase of a mentoring program. A thorough introduction (and ideally a separate training phase for future mentors) became necessary and desired element in this context. This needed training focused on the changed roles of mentors and their organizational knowledge, taking a rather systemic view on teaching practice and not only on content. When considering the COACTIV competence model of Baumert & Kunter (2013), it became evident that mentoring programs especially need to focus on two competence areas in recruiting and training future mentors: organizational and counseling knowledge. Another factor that can strongly influence the success of a school-based mentoring program is the creation of incentives for teachers to take part in it, especially as mentors. By introducing the COACTIV model as a competence model to future mentors, awareness could be raised for valuing the additional competencies as part of the professional portfolio of teachers.

Peer-to-Peer Learning and Peer-Feedback

The concept of peer-to-peer learning and peer-feedback in schools can be distinguished from mentoring approaches by four specific characteristics (Funk 2016, 44):

Table 4. Peer-to-peer learning and feedback (adapted from Funk 2016)

Concept of Little (1990)		Concept of Gräsel et al. (2006)		Concept of Steinert et al. (2006)	
Levels	Characteristics	Levels	Characteristics	Levels	Characteristics
Storytelling and scanning of ideas	Unsystematic and unregular exchange of experiences (e.g., short talks in the staff room)	Exchange	"low-cost" form of cooperation by chance, cooperation for mutual information (e.g., materials, methods), offering of advice	Differentiation	Global goal concept, formal information, cooperation in planning in grades or stages, formal exchange about curricula, contents, and grades, individual in-service training, self-reflection
Aid and assistance	Support in school-related tasks (e.g., mentoring)	Specialized cooperation	Cooperation to enhance efficiency, joint planning, structuring, sharing responsibility	Co-ordination	Global goal concept, extensive information, subject-based actions, partial cooperation for planning and implementing teaching, exchange about contents, didactics, assessment scales, self-evaluation, individual and school-based training
Sharing	Exchange (e.g., materials, methods, ideas, opinions)	Co-Construction	"high-cost" cooperation, joint development of tasks, joint problem-solving, relating one's knowledge to generate new knowledge, product-based cooperation	Interaction	Detailed goal concept, aligned actions between teachers of same grades and stages, extensive cooperation in planning and implementation, mutual counseling in content, didactics, diagnostics, extensive training
Joint work	Joint work and responsibility for tasks and decisions or individual actions are aligned with joint goals (e.g., using specific methods, implementing curricula etc.)			Integration	Systematic goal concept, aligned actions, transparency and mutual adaptation of teaching practice, systematic observation of actions and learning processes, self-evaluation and evaluation by others, systematic training

- Hierarchical status: Sender and receiver of feedback are at the same hierarchical position
- Knowledge and information status: The sender and receiver of feedback often have a similar level of expertise
- Organizational integration: Sender and receiver of feedback share the same organizational information
- Relation to tasks and situation: sender and receiver of feedback share the same framework of professional action and situational tasks

This framework implies that both peer-to-peer learning and peer-feedback partners have equal rights and duties, even though biographical and professional backgrounds can differ. However, especially for younger – less experienced – teachers opening one's classroom to a colleague can be associated with feelings of stress and anxiety due to formerly experienced test situations. Even though peer-to-peer learning and peer-feedback are not connected to any legal consequences, on a psychological level, this needs to be clarified and worked on carefully. Scientific literature defines different forms and phases of peer-to-peer learning and differentiates in its findings between aspects of cooperation and aspects of tasks or actions (Funk 2016, 45ff). From a cooperation point of view, peer-to-peer learning and peer feedback can support different levels of cooperation. The Table 4 illustrates these different levels, referring to three main theoretical concepts.

Peer feedback will also take a specific shape, depending on the phase or form of peer-to-peer learning that a school practices. From a task- or action perspective, peer feedback needs to be planned and defined beforehand to bring all participants in a defined cooperative relationship (Funk 2016, 50). In this respect, the peer-feedback concept as a "high-cost" form of cooperation can help define different stages and questions of peer-feedback design and steps to take (Funk 2016, Gallacher 1997):

Why do we do peer-to-peer learning, and do we plan it?

Table 5. Motives for peer-to-peer learning

Motive	
Initiative	**Development**
- The decision to get benefit from feedback - Organizational assignment to accomplish feedback - The decision who in the professional organization might function as a feedback source	- Select a topic/skill/practice - Clarify the purpose/goal - Clarify the specific information/behavior to gather/observe - Determine where, when, and how the information will be gathered. - Define where, when, and how the results will be feedbacked and discussed - Propose the "ground rules."

How do we organize peer feedback, and how do we process it?

Table 6. Organization and processing of peer-to-peer learning

Design		Processing
Accomplishment		Analysis and reflection
- Conduct a session as planned - Gathering and collect information with a focus on the skill, practice, topic that was identified: - Use of particular skill - Occurrence of a particular interaction - Existence of a particular situation - Quality of written products …by using methods that were agreed on	- Receive/give feedback regarding the use of a specific skill or practice based on performance information gathered	- Consider whether what occurred was the intended - Determine what factors influence what happened - Consider what to do differently the next time - Refine or adapt the use of a skill or practice - Generate ideas/options regarding things that might be done differently - Request ideas/suggestions regarding alternative strategies - Develop plans for the continued development to refine or adapt the use of targeted skill or practice

Apart from clarifying motives, engagement for development, design, and forms of processing institutional frameworks in the school play an important role. Aspects of institutional quality criteria are discussed in the last section of this chapter.

Lessons Learned

Peer-learning and peer-feedback as part of a SITT program were installed in different forms in schools in the canton of Zurich and our international project regions. Whereas many schools decide to use peer-learning and peer-feedback as low-level in-service training, a smaller number of schools decide to use both elements simultaneously: mentoring and peer-learning/peer-feedback. In the first case, it became evident that a sole implementation of peer-learning and peer feedback not only works through offering time and space to do so but also needs structured coordination and reflection by participating teachers and school leaders/principals. Peer learning and peer feedback became very welcome for new and inexperienced teachers who report a considerable benefit from this opportunity. At the same time, experienced teachers generally report a value they see in two aspects: coaching and supporting younger colleagues and exchanging and discussing with fellow experienced teachers. It became crucial to introduce the concept of peer-learning and peer-feedback in all its facets to avoid the fear of exposure or consequences of perceived "failures". In the framework of the presented approaches to peer-learning by Little (1990), Gräsel et al. (2006), and Steinert et al. (2006), the desired concept of implementation in most schools was the differentiated model of Steinert et al. (2006), which puts a focus on deeper reflection and integration of made experiences. In case the introductory part was missed, or if school leaders/principals left the entire implementation process up to their staff, peer-learning was endangered to remain on a superficial level. It meant, in some cases, a reduction to an exchange of valuable teaching materials among each other and did not include structured, planned, and mutual lesson observation, including peer feedback and reflection. In these cases, peer learning followed a relatively unstructured and spontaneous exchange of experiences according to the Little (1990) approach. Regardless of the practiced approach of peer learning, most schools used the concept of Gräsl et al. (2006) for cooperation in case of specific purposes (e.g., project-oriented planning, activity week, etc.) but not as a regular form of peer-learning. For this reason, a particular focus was given to the organization of peer-learning and peer-feedback structures within a school (frequency, time, low-level registration, etc.), on the preparation of practical tools for lesson observation and feedback, and on the training of giving and receiving feedback.

Structured In-Service Training: Inputs and Workshops

A variety of SITT programs uses structured in-service training elements such as joint workshops, content inputs, or seminars as training elements to use as a foundation of the necessary pedagogic or didactical concepts depending on the character of the SITT program (e.g., the introduction of participatory students' activities, introduction of a new subject etc.). SITT programs that implement mentoring/peer coaching without a specific content focus often use workshops and inputs to introduce the model itself and raise awareness of the different roles of mentors and mentees. Ideally, inputs and workshops involve all teachers within a school who are part of the SITT program and do not exclude anybody (e.g., mentors-only training etc.). Structured workshops are half-days are also often used as milestones within a SITT program, forming a structural element within the school development process. Organization of structured in-service training elements often lies with the school principal or the head of the steering group (if there is one), being responsible also for the planning, invitation of guest speakers, financial resources for external experts, and time management.

Once a school has successfully trained mentors/expert teachers for a specific content/topic, they can act as multipliers and internal trainers in structured in-service training workshops and inputs. Again, the most critical part is their awareness of shifting the roles. Additionally, a school's culture that develops itself towards installing communities of practice also opens possibilities for "new" expert teachers/mentors who might take over a structured in-service training workshop in the future. If the school's culture values this potential of their staff and does not punish internal exposure with feelings of envy or jealousy, new or more hesitant teachers will get motivated to also play an active role in knowledge transfer to their colleagues.

Lesson Learned

Most schools in past activities have chosen to include structured in-service training as part of their SITT programs at some point in their development. In most cases, this was also dependent on the financial resources of schools or authorities (especially in regions where schools do not have direct access to an allocated budget). If schools can choose, they choose concrete pedagogic-didactic issues such as cooperative learning settings, project-oriented work methods, classroom management, or assessment questions. In some cases, schools showed high interest in receiving input on relevant topics in their specific local context (e.g., inter-/transcultural questions, working with traumatized children, preventing violence or mobbing etc.). Inputs directly connected to the implementation of mentoring or peer-learning were planned and coordinated by the schools' heads or the schools' steering groups (in case they installed one). However, experiences showed that connecting inputs and workshops chosen through a participatory approach in the school's staff created a positive starting point for introducing peer-learning and mentoring with a clear focus on a topic of interest. In the long run, solid implementation of mentoring and peer-learning activities became regular and self-functioning when connected to an actual field of interest.

When schools plan to use their multipliers (often also referred to as "expert teachers"), it becomes essential to thoroughly clarify the shifting of their role together with the entire team. For the moment of the in-service training part, their colleagues became experts for the topic and could act as coaches and facilitators for their colleagues. Experiences show that this aspect became vital in regions or school districts characterized by a traditional teacher-centered teaching and learning culture, hierarchical structures within the institution, and traditional forms of leadership. In some cases, awareness-raising became especially important when involving the schools' leadership in this process. An element that was used in some cases was a structured exchange with "good-practice schools" (similarly to the Swiss program "Schulen lernen von Schulen (Schools learn from schools")) presented in section 1 of this chapter. Teachers received the opportunity to meet colleagues from other schools, ask questions, see documentation of the SITT program and discuss critical issues.

REFLECTION

Within a SITT program, the reflection of learning processes is essentially independent of which forms were chosen. It includes self-reflection and reflection done by all participants. In self-reflection, a vital part consists of "tracing the internalized images of school and teachers from one's personal school career and questioning them self-critically about their importance for personal pedagogical identity" (Berner et al. 2019, 299). This kind of self-reflection can also be viewed as "biographical reflection" and constitutes the key for teacher professionalism (ibid.). In this respect, questioning one's subjective theories and traditional cognitive patterns can be the first step. "Tradition is not only a way of seeing and acting, but also a way of hiding" – a crucial statement by Maturana & Varela (1984) in their book "The tree of knowledge" describes that "tradition stands for the usual everyday theories which enable a pedagogical vision on the one hand, and impede it on the other hand" (Berner et al. 2019, 307). According to the theory of Maturana & Varela, behavioral patterns that have become regular and acceptable shape this tradition. More explicit, subjective theories are "complex aggregates of conscious and/or unconscious automatized beliefs about fundamental questions of teaching and learning, which are reflected in classroom teaching" (Groeben et al. 1988, 22).

Self-reflection is not something that happens only individually. It should always be complemented with cooperation (Helmke 2012, 284 – 288). Mentoring or peer-to-peer learning within a SITT program can facilitate this process.

A simple and valuable instrument for peer feedback and reflection is the Johari window, developed by Joseph Luft and Harry Ingham (Luft 1989). The Johari window is divided into four areas: open for the free area (public area), blind area (blind spot), hidden area (private area), and unknown area (unconscious area).

By using the Johari window in peer-to-peer learning or mentoring programs, differences in external and self-perception become visible and can be discussed. It can trigger important insights into performed actions – for the feedback receiver and the sender, especially when the feedback conversation is made in a critical-constructive way.

Table 7. Johari window according to Luft (1989, 28) adapted from Berner et al. (2019, 309)

	Self-perception Known to me	Self-perception Not known to me
External perception Known to others	**Public** Facts that are public. Behavior that is known to me and others.	**Blind spot** Aspects of behavior that I do not know and are only perceived by others.
External perception Not known to others	**Private** Aspects which we consciously hide and which are not perceived by others.	**Unknown** Things that are not immediately accessible and not known to us and others.

In SITT programs, the quality of peer feedback strongly depends on the way a lesson was observed. Therefore, the observer must receive precise suggestions on what to observe and for what purpose the feedback is intended. Find below three examples of observation requests (Berner et al. 2019, 311f):

1. Observe my lesson and provide feedback about the quality of my questions, mainly if the questions are open or closed.
2. Observe my lesson and give me feedback about the quality of my task assignments. For example, are the instructions clear, concise, and understandable? Did all students listen? Did they have to ask follow-up questions?
3. Observe my lesson and provide feedback about whether I am narrating in an exciting and age-appropriate fashion. If the students listened and did not, at what point did their attention fade, and why.

If time is minimal, lesson observation can also only be limited to micro-teaching sequences within a group of teachers. According to studies by John Hattie (2013), micro-teaching with an efficiency rate of $d=0.88$ is a highly effective teacher training method that affects teaching success. Micro-teaching usually consists of a short teaching sequence of about 5 – 10 minutes with a follow-up discussion among colleagues.

Lessons Learned

During the implementation of a SITT program it became evident that teachers need concrete tools not only for giving and receiving peer-feedback but also for reflecting on it. For this reason, we decided to use existing forms of self-reflection that also can prompt discussion among colleagues, as provided by Hattie (2012) or Becker (2005) for checking the quality of classroom teaching with a set of questions like the selection below. (Becker 2005, 217).

- How did I encourage the teaching-learning process?
- Was the interest in the learning content topic maintained?
- Were the central questions or problems pointed out to the students?
- Was the emphasis of the lesson discernible?
- How many questions did I ask?
- What kinds of questions did the students ask?
- Did I listen to the students?
- Were the agreed-upon rules for discussion observed?
- How did I react to the students' contributions?

- Were the students' comments repeated verbatim by me?
- Did I use stereotypical forms of reinforcement?
- How significant was my proportion of speaking in class?
- How significant was the students' proportion of speaking in class?
- Were there individual students with an exceptionally high proportion of speaking in class?
- How strong was the female student participation in class compared to the male student participation rate?
- What kinds of contributions were made by particular "problem students"?
- Did I concentrate on particular students?
- Did specific conflict situations arise?
- How were the conflicts temporarily overcome?
- Were the work assignments understandable and clear?
- How were the work assignments introduced into the teaching-learning process?
- What kinds of learning assistance was offered by me?
- How were the work results presented?
- How were the knowledge, insights, or perceptions recorded?

Development of a SITT Program and Quality Criteria

Once a school has made the decision to install a SITT program, an internal school development process starts. Several decisions need to be made. The department IPE provided a checklist for school leaders or school steering groups that was used as a first step before planning concrete implementation. These decisions involve:

- How will the team be taken on board for the process?
- Who will act as mentors/expert teachers? How are these mentors/expert teachers selected? Are all teachers mentors and mentees at the same time? Does the concept follow a strict peer-coaching and peer-feedback approach?
- How is SITT organized? Does SITT start with a joint workshop and follow-up training for the mentors/expert teachers? How regularly does this take place?
- How are mentors and mentees matched?
- How is peer mentoring organized? By whom? How often does peer mentoring take place?
- How is the SITT program monitored? How are reflections and learnings recorded?

All SITT initiatives, national and international, show standard criteria that make them successful and sustainable. The criteria connected with implementing the SITT program range from relevance, quality of training, and coaching to participatory processes in the school development itself.

Independent from the different forms and phases of SITT and peer mentoring, several institutional factors determine the success or failure of peer mentoring (Herrera 1999). Thus, apart from exploring and using personal resources, structural setups strongly influence the solid implementation of a SITT program in a school. The following institutional frameworks, therefore, represent quality criteria for implementation (Raufelder & Ittel 2012, 151f):

- *Decision*: If a school and its staff decided to start a SITT program including peer mentoring, all involved need to follow this goal. It includes the readiness to pursue pedagogical and personal-professional goals and processes in everyday teaching.
- *Time and money*: The time allocated for SITT programs and peer mentoring by the participants and the institution plays a vital role in the school context. This accounts for the coordination of the program itself, choosing teachers who will act as mentors or expert teachers and who are granted the necessary time for this task by the school leadership or the authority. Moreover, direct contact persons need to be appointed on the institutional level who steer the SITT processes in the long run. Time and financial resources for regular training – or input sessions – as part of the professionalization process need to be budgeted (Orland 2001).
- *Development*: Installing a SITT program as a solid element within a school's professionalization process can shift traditional patterns and sustainable empowerment of teaching staff for co-operatively and responsibly designing the school's culture. Different experience backgrounds and the growing heterogeneous composition of teaching staff in schools can thus also be valued and used (Bastian 2006, 37; von der Groeben 2003).
- *Adequate training of mentors*: This quality criterium is added by Ziegler (2009) as an additional element. Mentors need some kind of initial training to take up the role of a critical-constructive person. However, this is difficult to fulfill in some cases, especially in cases where teacher training Universities or authorities offer no adequate training formats (depending on the school system and on resources). Thus, in various SITT programs, schools have taken this task on themselves by developing expert teachers responsible for a specific subject or learning area and investing in their professional understanding of a mentor with individualized training.

OUTLOOK

What becomes evident in the presented SITT program is that the overall concept of SITT builds on a participatory approach of staff development with a clear focus on autonomy and self-directed learning. This implies a certain mindset of teachers but also school leaders. This mindset includes understanding leadership roles that empower staff, give space for autonomy, and allow a fearless atmosphere. Supporting schools in taking this shift can bear a challenge. Experiences with the SITT program show that even though mentoring, peer learning and peer feedback are very much part of a bottom-up initiative of teachers, school leaders are critical people in coordinating, structuring activities, and motivating their staff. However, teachers need to understand that sharing their experiences, challenges, doubts, and, most importantly, their success is key to a professional view on their teaching profession. Our experiences with the SITT program show that integrating new and inexperienced teachers is part of a professional understanding in most schools. However, creating openness for opening their classroom doors also in senior teachers needs time and practical experience. Apart from all the lessons learned described for the different elements of the SITT program, we strongly believe in the approach of "primary experiences or first-hand experiences". This means that teachers need to experience structured peer exchange already in the first phases of implementing a SITT program. In concrete terms, setting activities such as showing model lessons and model feedback sessions, micro-teaching sessions with activities of practicing feedback, giving room for mutual exchange on defined aspects of teaching can be helpful methods to lay the basic foundation and openness for an ongoing peer learning process. If teachers start to value that peer learning is a vital part of their self-reflection process and a natural element in their everyday professional life, motivation and the spirit for taking up new school development activities and programs will rise. SITT programs show from the authors' point of view that this can be a chance for changing schools and their teaching and learning culture for meeting challenges of the 21st century.

For a long time, the idea prevailed that the representatives of the institutions know best what teachers need in terms of further training. For example, new curricula or teaching materials for foreign language teaching are oriented towards new social needs or scientific findings. In this case, it may make sense or be necessary to plan and implement training systematically and top-down. However, when it comes to teaching practice, to questions of the social design of school life, cooperation with parents or other teacher teams, teachers and school leaders have their views of topics that need to be addressed. They are the ones who either look for solutions together and need an external facilitator who knows how to accompany such processes. Alternatively, a school might need an expert on specific content, perhaps on a specific subject or pedagogical or psychological issue. It is the task of education authorities or universities of education to guarantee that good specialists are available and that they are also willing and able not only to lecture on content but also to respond to the schools' realities. This also includes preparing the knowledge and content together so that they can be applied.

SITT programs with their elements of mentoring, peer learning, peer feedback, structured in-service training, and space for reflection are a way to strengthen teachers' and schools' professional identity and understanding of the teaching profession.

REFERENCES

Bastian, J. (2006). Gesamtschule – Umgang mit Heterogenität. *Pädagogik*, 58, 7–8.

Baumert, J., & Kunter, M. (2013). The COACTIV model of teachers' professional competence. *Online (Bergheim)*, 25–48. Advance online publication. doi:10.1007/978-1-4614-5149-5_2

Berner, H., Isler, R. & Weidinger, W. (2019). *Simply good teaching*. Bern: hep.

Bildungsdirektion Kanton Zürich. (2021). https://www.zh.ch/de/bildungsdirektion.html

Dammerer, J. (2020). Mentoring für beginnende Lehrpersonen – ein Instrument der Personalentwicklung. In Mentoring im pädagogischen Kontext. Professionalisierung. Pädagogik für Niederösterreich, Band 10. Studienverlag.

Dammerer, J., Ziegler, V., & Bartonek, S. (2019). Tutoring and Coaching as Special Forms of Mentoring for Young Eachers Starting Their Careers. *Yaroslavl Pedagogical Bulletin*. Advance online publication. doi:10.24411/1813-145X-2019-10278

Eby, L., Rhodes, J., & Allen, T. (2007). Definition and Evolution of Mentoring. In T. Allen & L. Eby (Eds.), *The Blackwell Handbook of Mentoring*. Blackwell. doi:10.1002/9780470691960.ch2

European Commission/Eurydice. (2020). *Switzerland. National reforms in school education*. https://eacea.ec.europa.eu/national-policies/eurydice/content/national-reforms-school-education-89_en

European Commission/Eurydice. (2021). *Switzerland. Teachers and education staff*. https://eacea.ec.europa.eu/national-policies/eurydice/content/teachers-and-education-staff-106_en

Finn, R. (1993). Mentoring – the effective route to school development. In H. Green (Ed.), The School Management Handbook (pp. 62–88). Academic Press.

Fischer, D. (2008). Mentorieren. Zwischen kollegialer Begleitung, professionellem Anspruch und persönlichem Zuspruch. *Schulverwaltung Spezial, 1*.

Fischer, D., van Andel, L., Cain, T., Žarkovič-Adlešič, B., & van Lakerveld. (Eds.). (2008). *Improving school-based mentoring. A Handbook for Mentor Trainers*. Münster.

Fraefel, U., Bernhardsson-Laros, N., & Bäuerlein, K. (2017). Partnerschaftliches Lehren und Lernen im Schulfeld – Aufbau von Professionswissen mittels Peer-to-Peer Mentoring in lokalen Arbeits- und Lerngemeinschaften. In *Lehrerbildung auf dem Prüfstand 2017* (pp. 30–49). Sonderheft.

Funk, C. M. (2016). *Kollegiales Feedback aus der Perspektive von Lehrpersonen*. Springer VS. doi:10.1007/978-3-658-13062-6

Gallacher, K. K. (1997). Supervision, mentoring and coaching: Methods for supporting personnel development. In P. Winton, McCollum, J.A. & Catlett, C. (Eds.), Reforming personnel development in early intervention: Issues, models, and practical strategies (pp. 173 – 191). Paul Brookes.

Gräsel, C., Fussangel, K., & Pröbstel, C. (2006). Lehrkräfte zur Kooperation anregen – eine Aufgabe für Sisyphos? *Zeitschrift für Pädagogik, 52*(2), 205–219.

Halai, A. (2006). Mentoring in-service teachers: Issues of role diversity. *Teaching and Teacher Education, 22*(6), 700–710. doi:10.1016/j.tate.2006.03.007

Hattie, J. (2012). *Visible Learning for Teachers. Maximizing Impact on Learning*. Taylor and Francis. doi:10.4324/9780203181522

Hattie, J. (2013). *Visible Learning. A Synthesis of Over 8¢000 Meta-analyses Relating to Achievement*. Taylor and Francis.

Helmke, A. (2012). Unterrichtsqualität und Lehrerprofessionalität. In Diagnose, Evaluation und Verbesserung des Unterrichts (4th ed.). Seelze: Klett-Kallmeyer.

Herrera, C. (1999). *School-based mentoring: A first look into its potential*.

IFES/IPES. (2021). *Peers*. https://www.ifes-ipes.ch/ueber-das-ifes-ipes/peers

Kantonsrat Kanton Zürich. (2005). *Volksschulgesetz*. http://www2.zhlex.zh.ch/appl/zhlex_r.nsf/WebView/E797088926DBBD28C125864500284C64/$File/412.100_7.2.05_111.pdf

Kreis, A. & Schnebel, S. (2017). Peer Coaching in der praxissituierten Ausbildung von Lehrpersonen. *Lehrerbildung auf dem Prüfstand 2017*, 1 – 7.

Little, J. W. (1990). The persistence of privacy: Autonomy and initiative in teachers' professional relations. *Teachers College Record*, *91*(4), 509–536.

Marti, S. (2019). *Toolbox Führung. Kompendium zeitgemässer Führung*. Eigenverlag.

Orland, L. (2001). Reading a mentoring situation: One aspect of learning to mentor. *Teaching and Teacher Education*, *17*(1), 75–88. doi:10.1016/S0742-051X(00)00039-1

PH Zürich. (2021a). *Übersicht Weiterbildung*. https://phzh.ch/de/Weiterbildung/

PH Zürich. (2021b). *Good Practice von Zürcher Schulen*. https://phzh.ch/de/Weiterbildung/volksschule/veranstaltungen/Themenreihen/good-practice/

Raufelder, D., & Ittel, A. (2012). Mentoring in der Schule: Ein Überblick. Theoretische und praktische Implikationen für Lehrer/-innen und Schüler/-innen im internationalen Vergleich. *Diskurs Kindheits- und Jugendforschung, 2,* 147 – 160. https://elibrary.utb.de/doi/epdf/10.3224/diskurs.v7i2.04

Steinert, B., Klieme, E., Maag-Merki, K., Döbrich, P., Halbheer, U., & Kunz, A. (2006). Lehrerkooperation in der Schule: Konzeption, Erfassung, Ergebnisse. *Zeitschrift für Pädagogik*, *52*(2), 185–204.

Strauß, S., & Rohr, D. (2019). Peer-Learning in der Lehrer*innenbildung. *Journal für lehrerInnenbildung, 10(3)*, 106 – 116. Advance online publication. doi:10.35468/jlb-03-2019_11

Swissuniversities. (2021). *Swiss Education System*. https://www.swissuniversities.ch/en/topics/studying/swiss-education-system

Von der Groeben, A. (2003). Lernen in heterogenen Gruppen. Chance und Herausforderung. *Pädagogik*, *55*(9), 6–9.

Wang, J., & Odell, S. J. (2002). Mentored learning to teach according to standard-based reform: A critical review. *Review of Educational Research*, *54*(2), 143–178. doi:10.3102/00346543072003481

Wang, J., & Odell, S. J. (2007). An alternative conception of mentor-novice relationships: Learning to teach in reform-minded ways as a context. *Teaching and Teacher Education*, *23*(4), 473–489. doi:10.1016/j.tate.2006.12.010

APPENDIX

Case Study: Romania

Type of activity: After-school program for children coming from vulnerable groups
   SITT program elements: mentoring, peer learning and peer feedback
   Qualitative description of the program and its challenges:

At the heart of the multi-year project in Romania is the realization that children from vulnerable families are running behind in school every day. Many educational foundations have not been laid, the time and sensitivity for parental support are weak or missing altogether, and the learning gaps are widening. In cooperation between a Swiss development organization and local NGOs, an approach has been developed which is well known in the respective regions of the country under the name 'after school classes'. Regularly trained education specialists offer daily supplementary services in school classrooms or youth centers for children with specific needs. As evaluators, we were tasked with visiting these services and making recommendations for adaptations. We were impressed by the complexity of the task. It is certainly important that all children never again have to stand in front of the teacher and the class the next day without having done their homework or feel ashamed or compensate for lack of performance through conspicuous behavior. However, homework help is by no means the only activity in these programs. It is also essential that all children have a good lunch and that they brush their teeth afterward. Play activities are also a must, whether in the form of free play outdoors or in the rooms. The social dynamics in the respective groups is also a central topic. How does one react to arguments and disputes? How are small groups formed and made fit for cooperation? How does one react as a leader to the personal concerns of individual children whose private lives are sometimes extremely challenging? The role of the educators is an extremely diverse one. They have to meet school demands, and they have to be animators for play, they have to be able to offer handicrafts, comfort, and support; they have to recognize family problems and cooperate with social workers where necessary. They have to provide medical assistance and organize large groups; they have to cooperate with teachers and always be cheerful. In short, they perform an impossible and almost inhuman task. How can they stay fit and healthy? With whom can they exchange and recharge their batteries? For such situations and professional groupings, so-called intervision groups or peer support groups are recommended. Together with those responsible in Romania, we have therefore recommended installing such groups and the training of corresponding coordinators. The principle of peer support is a form of collegial practice counseling. The group members are in a collegial relationship with each other and provide each other with a kind of "thinking service". In contrast to supervision, intervision is not led by an outside professional. This central aspect was new for many. Don't we have to ask professionals to offer us solutions to our problems? To realize that the solutions often lie in the field of experience of other colleagues took some time and, above all, much trust in one's competence. It was also important that everyone realized: the content of the discussions comes from the participants, but the form and procedure of the group sessions are strictly regulated and offer security. Working method In intervision, a highly structured procedure is deliberately used. The structure gives the participants security and prevents unwanted boundary crossings. For example, a moderator is appointed alternately within the group to ensure that the agreed procedure is adhered to. In addition, agreements must be made in a peer support group. These include the confidential handling of information and the principle of personal responsibility. Not all concerns can be dealt with satisfactorily within this framework. Therefore, the concerns should contain an open, concrete, and current question, be related to one's practice, be within the sphere of influence of the participants present, be workable in the time available, and correspond to the group's resources. It was striking that at the beginning, many did not realize that there are no insignificant topics. Especially the social dynamics in the groups or the relationship of the educators to individual children were seen as 'secondary' at the beginning and became more and more relevant. Hearing that others have similar questions, challenges and problems was perfect for everyone. In each of the fortnightly meetings, the focus is always on one participant and his or her topic. Focusing on one case ultimately helps everyone because everyone listens, asks questions, gives feedback, and thus thinks about their situation. The colleagues in Romania have experienced that this form of exchange is also an effective way of recognizing and combating possible burnout and not stumbling over the same problems over and over again in a lonely job. However, the most central element was certainly the realization by many participants that we all have the solutions to problems within ourselves but need the exchange with others to do so. This strengthens us and gives us courage.

Case Study: Bosnia-Herzegovina

Type of activity: Implementation of democracy education in schools
 SITT program elements: Structure in-service training, peer learning and peer feedback
  Qualitative description of the program and its challenges:
   After the Dayton Peace Treaty in 1995, the Council of Europe became intensively involved in various areas. Bosnia and Herzegovina and the entire Western Balkans were in a period of intense change, and the education system was no exception. On the one hand, there were the war years with their isolation and the horrific private experiences of many families. Then there was also a social, economic, and

political transition that confronted the entire country with almost insurmountable hurdles. From the very beginning, we at the Zurich University of Teacher Education were involved in developing concepts for a learner-centered democracy education under the title Education for Democratic Citizenship and Human Rights Education (EDC/HRE) and implementing them in the form of teaching materials and training programs. The same teachers who previously taught defense education in a socialist system should now champion concepts of democracy. As difficult as the task may seem, it proved to be a pragmatic one. At the center of the chosen approach was the realization and the plan that nothing should be taught in class that is not also lived in class and school, and that, moreover, can be implemented in everyday life. This approach can be described under the title 'about democracy, through democracy, for democracy as a short formula. It was special that many teachers (first from Bosnia, then from other Western Balkans countries) were involved in the initial development of related teaching materials. Developing, testing, and improving for colleagues - this motto was at the center of a unique development of lesson plans for all levels and age groups. After many different phases, the six volumes published by the Council of Europe were put in a digitalized form thanks to the financial support of the Swiss authorities and supplemented with democracy materials for school leaders and parents (www.living-democracy.com). However, the big challenge is how the teaching models and the didactic and methodological approaches integrated into them can be learned about and applied quickly and effectively by as many teachers as possible. The forms that have been further developed and intensively used for this purpose will be briefly described here under the titles of model teaching and micro-teaching, whereby micro-teaching, in particular, is of importance for the present technical article. Teaching is a craft that is based on well-founded theories but is primarily learned in reflective practice. Instead of providing theoretical information about lesson planning, we organized so-called model lessons in hundreds of training sessions (started in Bosnia and then continued in all countries of the region). A local school can implement a selected lesson in cooperation with the author of the teaching material. As all lesson models are designed for high pupil activity, there were hardly any language difficulties. The lesson assignments were given in English, all participants (both the pupils and the teachers who often watched up to 150) had headphones and were served by a simultaneous translator with the appropriate language. In the same way, the teaching expert could listen to all the students' contributions and discussions. In this way, all teachers got to know the teaching models in the application and under local conditions. After subsequent discussions, questions, and intensive exchange, everyone had the opportunity to deal with the teaching materials more deeply and plan the next day. This was the personal testing and application day for all participants. Each teacher either tested the same lesson they had experienced or chose a new one from the teaching materials available in their own school. Invited colleagues from the same school could follow this lesson and give feedback. The following day, all participants come back to the workshop loaded with student products, photos, and experiences. In an intensive exchange, impressions are mutually reflected, and further lesson planning for the coming weeks is set out in writing, including the curriculum and democracy materials. The second chosen pattern is used either in separate workshops or attached to the one just described. In micro-teaching, all participants prepare extracts from the lessons in small teams. The participants are divided into groups of about 20. A separate classroom is available for each group. Each team now has the task of teaching the lesson sequence they have prepared. With this model, all participants are either in the role of the teacher or the student. Teaching sequences of about 15 minutes are followed by a reflection session of about 30 minutes. Then it is the turn of another team to teach the sequence they have prepared. Micro-teaching requires intensive preparation time (to plan a sequence of 15 minutes well, a team needs about half a day, because first, the teaching materials have to be read, then a sequence is selected, and the necessary learning materials, blackboard texts, worksheets etc. have to be prepared. Also, in this model, teaching is experienced 1:1 (hereby adults for adults) and necessarily reflected on by peers afterward. Even if the impression is given that these are time-consuming models, the reality experienced several times shows that subsequent subject and theory discussions are based on experienced practice. No participant leaves a workshop here without having experienced and reflected on teaching themselves and/or having taught themselves. The focus is on practice reflected by colleagues.

Chapter 9
Embedding Authentic and Effective Awareness About Mental Health in Pre-Service Teacher Training

Frederic Fovet
https://orcid.org/0000-0003-1051-4163
Royal Roads University, Canada

ABSTRACT

The chapter examines the urgent need for pre-service teacher training programs to integrate content on mental health. In the current neo-liberal context, there is increasing pressure on universities to streamline and shorten these programs, when in fact there might be a need to add content to their existing structure. Developing pre-service teachers' awareness around student mental health is a pressing need but one campuses are usually reluctant to address when it may represent a widening of their scope. The chapter analyzes phenomenological data collected by the author around his lived experience of delivering a course on mental health within a Canadian pre-service teacher training program. It examines the complex, rich, and diverse outcomes that are achieved (1) on teacher candidates' approaches to inclusion, (2) on their ability to navigate their own mental health issues, and (3) more widely on their willingness to embrace social model approaches to disability. The chapter examines the repercussions of this reflection on the transformation of pre-service teacher programs.

DOI: 10.4018/978-1-7998-9278-6.ch009

INTRODUCTION AND CONTEXT

There has been a tendency over the last decade in Canada, within the current neo-liberal climate which prevails in higher education (HE) (Bamberger et al., 2019; Morgan, 2021), to shorten pre-service teacher training and to make these programs as palatable, hands-on, fast-paced, and cost-effective as possible (CBC, 2018; Teaching Certification, 2021). Institutions have been competing within each of these dimensions in order to maintain their share of what is increasingly a weakening and highly coveted market (Rust & Kim, 2012). This has meant that two ambivalent and contradictory pressures have emerged within these programs nationally. On the one hand, there is an increasing realization that early career teachers are ill prepared for the field and that attrition is rising (Goldhaber et al., 2021; Phillippo & Kelly, 2014; Vagi et al., 2019). The implication is that pre-service training should be enriched, both in terms of scope of experiences and in depth of knowledge (Krieg et al., 2020; Ronfeldt et al., 2021). On the other hand, marketing pressures are leading to the elimination of an increasing number of courses and topics for the sake of expediency (Gilroy, 2005; Mergler & Spooner-Lane, 2012). One such topic is mental health (MH). Stakeholders in the field are stressing the fact that specific and detailed training in relation to mental, social and emotional health is essential when preparing early career educators for the realities of classroom practice (Murano et al., 2019). Few programs, however, nationally have succeeded in integrating this training in their pre-service credentials format (Brown et al., 2019; Schwartz et al., 2017).

The chapter will discuss the experience of an Atlantic province campus in integrating, developing and prioritizing mental health training within a pre-service teacher qualification program. The author will more specifically explore and analyze phenomenological data related to his lived experience, as an instructor, in developing and teaching a course focusing on adolescent mental, social and emotional health within a BEd program. He has offered this course within this faculty of education, on five occasions, in both French and English over a period of five years.

The chapter will describe first the format the author adopted when offering these courses. The second part of the chapter will examine and analyze the impact of these courses on the development of pre-service teachers' professional development and their awareness around mental health. The third part of the chapter will examine and explain the extent to which the delivery of these courses goes beyond raising awareness and offers trainee teachers the opportunity to reflect on their own experiences with mental health, and their own strategies to develop and maintain resiliency in this context. This section will also explore the degree to which these courses support and encourage the development of a post-modern lens on mental health – and disability more generally - among pre-service teachers; this in turn helps shift them from a medical model view of mental health to a social model of disability perspective. It is argued, in the chapter, that these learning opportunities contribute to the pre-service teachers' wider ability to conceptualize effective approaches to inclusion in the classroom

LITERATURE

It is tempting when discussing this topic to seek to formulate and present a cohesive definition of what MH issues amount to (Granlund et al., 2021). This should be resisted, however, as it will be argued that MH issues represent a concept which is multifaceted, complex, and changes shape depending on the theoretical lens through which it is approached ((Richter & Dixon, 2020). There is also always a risk of being ethnocentric when attempting formal definitions and it is clear that interpretations of what constitutes MH issues are heavily influenced by cultural parameters (Vaillant, 2012). Defining MH and MH issues too rigidly would run the risk of locking the chapter in a unique theoretical lens and of missing opportunities broader reflection. The chapter will argue that in fact much of the value of pre-service courses on MH lies in having the potential of shifting teacher candidates' views and conceptualization of MH, more particularly of making them conscious that bio-medical models are not the sole approach to MH issues (Fennig & Denov, 2019). It is important, however, to explicitly stress that exploration of MH is schools cannot be limited to Social and Emotional Learning (SEL) – a literature which is currently extremely popular but remains limited to interactions among peers within the class itself (Allbright et al., 2019; Weissberg, 2019). The main focus of MH in schools instead should be conceptualized more widely as the ability of students - but also of all school stakeholders – to navigate and function emotionally effectively in complex and changing environments, beyond the classroom itself (Galderisi et al., 2015).

There is an increasing body of literature which relates to MH in the K-12 sector (Cavioni et al., 2020). First, it has become apparent that the MH of students must become the focus of specific attention on the part of educators and administrators (García-Carrión et al., 2019; Shelemy et al., 2019; Waldron et al., 2918). MH issues have for some time been seen as a post-secondary issue (Khanlou, 2019). Within the post-secondary sector, indeed, statistics and quantitative data are regularly collected with regards to MH issues among students via accessibility services (Linden et al., 2021; Treleaven, 2020). Awareness of the impact of MH issues on students' performance and wellbeing is therefore much greater in this sector. The reality - that these students do not suddenly develop MH issues as they arrive in the post-secondary sector - has become apparent over time, and the K-12 sector is progressively understanding that it must improve both its awareness of the impact of MH and its processes to collect data around these issues (Pascoe et al., 2020).

When awareness exists among teachers around MH, it tends to be very clinical in nature (Caldwell, 2019). This is problematic in many cases as teachers are not clinicians and the adherence to the medical model often reveals a wider misunderstanding around the role of educators in the MH of students. The medical model is a conceptualization of MH which looks exclusively to bio-medical factors to understand disorders and an individual's inability to function effectively in their daily contexts (Deacon, 2013; Handerer et al., 2021). Teachers' adherence to medical model views also leads to a disempowering culture of referral within which teachers may feel that as soon as MH is discussed or brought up, a clinical specialist must be involved and take over (Rusch et al., 2018). The broader concern within this literature is the fact that a deficit model view is still prevalent (Dudley-Marling, 2015). The deficit model, which often serves as a subtext to the bio-medical perspective, makes three assumptions within educational landscapes: (i) that the individual with MH issues is essential faulty or lacking in a key competency of characteristic; (ii) that the individual with MH issues must strive to fit into a societal model and structures that are designed for the mainstream, and (iii) that the individual with MH issues must be 'fixed', treated, or 'repaired', and that this intervention must happen outside the classroom or the educational space (Ashton & Arlington, 2019).

While awareness of the MH issues that impact students is growing, there is still very little scholarship which focuses on teacher's knowledge and understanding of MH, or on their level of comfort with this topic (Atkins & Rodger, 2016; Mazzer & Rickwood, 2015). Initiatives around MH First Aid have become popular in the post-secondary sector, but are still rare in the K-12 sector (Mantzios et al., 2019). Even when it is delivered in the K-12 sector, MH First Aid – while definitely contributing to awareness – can be confusing to a degree in the sense that it is short in format but overly ambitious in content (Morgan et al., 2019). There is otherwise, currently, very little emphasis on MH within pre-service teacher training in North America, or Global North countries more generally (Brown et al., 2019). Such training and awareness is not regularly included in the formal structure of these programs (Ball et al., 2016). Neither does this represent a set of competency that is monitored or assessed in the practicum portion of the training. There is, more broadly, very little professional development (PD) in the field – for in-service teachers themselves - that adequately provides training or key competencies on student MH (Pandori-Chuckal, 2020). It would be fair to assert that there is a certain degree of fear around this topic generally and the overall tendency in the field is to shy away from these concerns, rather than embrace them proactively (Dhort et al., 2016; Wei et al., 2019). The root cause of this fear is difficult to identify and formulate with precision, but it is clear that teachers' own battles with MH trigger a reticence to discuss these issues openly (Lever at al., 2017).

There is in fact a growing body of literature which also examines the MH issues of teachers (McLean et al. 2017). Here too there is generally hesitancy and ambivalence, rather than proactive policy and explicit direction. Teacher attrition is increasing in most Global North countries, and reaching dangerous proportions (Harris et al., 2019). While it is very difficult to assess what factors are responsible for teachers' departure from the profession, it is fair to presume that MH issues play a significant role (Lever et al., 2017; Wong et al., 2017). Exhaustion and stress are certainly demonstrated as being instrumental in many of these cases, and it is fair to assume that they eventually snowball into wider MH issues (Oberle & Schonert-Reichl, 2016; Von der Embse et al., 2016). There is also literature focused on leadership which discusses the need for school administrators and leaders to acknowledge the impact of MH on teacher performance, wellbeing, job satisfaction, and longevity in the profession (Bamberger et al., 2019; Berkovich & Eyal, 2015; Skaalvik & Skaalvik, 2014).

Research into MH in schools has exploded overnight during the COVID pandemic (Vaillancourt et al., 2021). It has examined the impact the school closures and the pivot to online learning have had on teachers and students. Educators have experienced phenomenal stress amidst the often unrealistic expectations and overwhelming timeframes (Gadermann et al, 2021; Sokal et al, 2020). School closures and the shift to online teaching and learning has caused isolation amidst learners, loss of social capital, anxiety and depression (Hawrilenko et al., 2021). The COVID pandemic has also increased social inequities and support, online efforts, and services for racialized students, Indigenous students, culturally diverse learners and students with disabilities has been poorly lacking (Goudeau et al., 2021). This, in turn, has accentuated – often even triggered – MH issues among these student populations (Dorn et al., 2020).

METHODOLOGICAL REFLECTION

The chapter adopts a phenomenological approach to data analysis. Phenomenology is both a theoretical stance and a methodology that focuses on the relevance and richness of stakeholders' lived experience of a phenomenon (Wilson, 2015). The data collection and analysis hone in on the meaning making that these stakeholders develop when confronted with challenging phenomena in their private or professional life (Emiliussen et al., 2021; Wiles et al., 2013); meaning making in itself becomes pertinent and worthy of analysis because it often reveals the deep existential motivations that shape individuals' interactions with others, and behaviours in social contexts (Joseph, 2014; van Manen, 2014). Phenomenology has been increasingly popular in the field of educational research, and helps investigators understand the meaning making that educators and administrators develop within their work environment when faced with challenges and key professional choices (Webb & Welsh, 2019).

The author will explore his own professional experiences with the teaching of mental health content within pre-service teacher training programs. The choice of phenomenology is particularly pertinent in this chapter as the author has been personally immersed in work related to MH with teacher candidates for a number of years. He therefore has a wealth of experiences, reflection and notes to draw from and to analyze. There is no doubt that other qualitative methodologies that focus on the student voice itself will be equally relevant in the future and form the basis for studies that will build on this work, but this initial exploration from an instructor lens of what is still a novel process – integrating MH in teacher training – lays the ground and identifies key themes and concerns. The author has worked, over time both as faculty and sessional instructor, on a Canadian campus situated in the Maritime Provinces; the Bachelor of Education program in this institution includes a course on adolescence mental health. He has had the opportunity to offer this course five times – twice in French and three times in English -, and in many ways has been able to shape it in unique ways. He draws here from his first-hand experience both of the way such a course unfolds, and of the impact such a course has on teacher candidates' positionality vis-à-vis mental health as a topic area. He reflects on key take-aways that will be crucial to faculty planning and designing courses of this type.

OBSERVATIONS

This section of the chapter examines the analysis of phenomenological data collected by the author through his five experiences with teaching this course. The section first examines how the course is delivered. It then goes on to draw conclusions, from his lived experience as an instructor, as to the impact this course has on teacher candidates' perceptions and their positioning towards MH.

Teaching a Course on Mental Health within a Teacher Training Program

The course is short in nature and offered over a three week period with two lectures or synchronous sessions a week. The course has been offered alternatively face to face or online, depending on the way the program schedule is finalized each year. This variety in format has not made a significant difference in the delivery of the course, and is not relevant to the reflection offered here. The course was offered in both French and English, as this is a pre-service teacher training program which is offered simultaneously in two languages. The language of instruction made no significance difference, for the purpose of this analysis, even though it must definitely be acknowledged that culture itself may undoubtedly have an impact on MH training within a wider landscape - beyond Canada itself or this specific Atlantic region (Higgen & Mösko, 2020). Conceptualization of what constitutes MH issues is inevitably shaped by cultural norms.

The course was mostly focused on practice but did include an overview of the various theoretical stances that are encountered in the field of education with regards to MH interventions. The stated objectives of the course are to introduce the students to the various theoretical frameworks that are used in the K-12 sector when addressing the needs of adolescent students with MH issues. It seeks to offer the students the necessary skills to recognize and navigate these frameworks, and understand the way each informs some of the strategies and interventions the students are likely to encounter in the field. Avenues explored are bio-medical (Handerer et al., 2021), social model of disability (Hogan, 2019), holistic and humanistic (Kazantzis & Stuckey, 2018), ecological (Hellblom-Thibblin & Sandberg, 2020), psycho-dynamic (Gatta, 2019; Morton & Berardi, 2017), and experiential (Kilbourne et al., 2018) approaches to the management of MH in schools. Within each model, the students explore specific classroom interventions, tools, and resources that align with that perspective. Students are encouraged to acknowledge how diverse and complex the landscape of intervention in fact is.

There are immediate and relatively straight-forward take-aways to the course, which amount to tangible content-based acquisitions of knowledge and skills. Some of the immediate gains resemble those which are reported in the implementation of First Aid MH courses which have emerged across North America (Hart et al., 2019). There are also some very immediate and pragmatic gains in the area of suicide intervention for example (Saewyc et al., 2014). Most participants in the course generally report to the instructor having no knowledge of suicide intervention policies and processes before the course begins (Breux & Boccio, 2019).

Students are generally excited about the content of this course. They often mention the fact that its inclusion in the structure of the program has been decisive in their choice of program and institution. They also regularly suggest that the course should be made longer and offer even more insights, as well as more opportunities to practice and implement some of the strategies introduced. The delivery of the course is usually overall a success and leads to positive outcomes and very satisfactory course evaluations. This chapter, however, will go beyond this simple examination of content, objectives and outcomes, to explore the impact that the course has more broadly on teacher candidates' attitudes and perceptions of MH in school. The course, it is argued, is not solely about content, but more importantly offers an opportunity for students to reflect – as individuals – on their own construct of MH issues.

Impact of these Courses on the Development of Pre-Service Teachers' Awareness around Mental Health

This section will examine three distinct areas of gains from the course. The first area of development relates directly to the students' perceptions of MH. The second area of development focuses on the opportunity that this course offers the students to reflect on their own lived experiences with MH. The third area of gains relates to the ways teacher candidates develop the ability to navigate theoretical approaches to MH, and evolve in their vision, from a societal perspective, of not just MH but also disability more generally.

Pre-Service Candidates' Perceptions of Mental Health

Beyond just offering teacher candidates a knowledge base around MH and some hands-on tools for classroom interventions, having access to such a course offers these pre-service teachers space to reflect on their actual understanding of MH, and to develop an awareness that there are multiple theoretical approaches to and constructs of MH. Many enter the course with firm preconceptions of what MH is, how MH issues are defined and identified, and what impact MH issues have on individuals' ability to function and remain in educational settings. Many of the first classes focus on shaking these preconceptions, and challenging presumptions. By this stage these teacher candidates have already developed firm beliefs about the bio-medical causes of MH issues, clinical stances with regards to MH in schools, and an exclusive reliance on medication and bio-medical treatments. This is characteristic of what the literature evidences as being the dominant culture in schools around MH (Reinke et al., 2011). The course uses a variety of texts, media sources, and testimonies to encourage the students to reconsider their assumptions in this area.

Opportunity for Teachers to Reflect on their own Experiences with Mental Health

The most surprising revelation within the delivery of this course is the fact that it systematically offers pre-service teachers an opportunity to reflect on their own experiences with MH issues. In an initial reflection on students' personal experiences with MH, which represents the first assignment in the course and is submitted in blog format, approximately a third of students discuss their own significant issues with MH. More share stories of experiencing MH issues as relatives, friends, or life partners of individuals directly affected. Over the duration of the course, a number of students always disclose much more complex diagnoses and MH conditions. This is particularly interesting as the literature highlights the degree to which MH issues are responsible for the high degree of attrition early in the profession. Despite these statistics and this evidence, pre-service teacher training programs provide very few spaces and forums that allow students to share their own experiences with MH, seek support, or develop competencies to manage these MH issues in their future practice. It may be that, currently, a course of this type is in fact the only window within which teacher candidates can reflect, to a degree, on the ways they will juggle their own MH issues and experiences with the pressures of the profession.

The course itself often serves as a bridge towards further conversations that take place with program coordinators, field coordinators, teacher mentors, and campus accessibility services – in terms of disclosure and self-management of their own MH issues. Within the course, the students formulate concerns about the way they will be able to address their own needs with regards to MH as they enter their practicum, and their future classrooms, and support is subsequently sought out by the students as a result. It is interesting to note that, despite the fact that steps are taken throughout the course to allow students never to feel pressured into disclosing these experiences or issues to their peers - the initial blog for example can be submitted as a confidential written assessment shared directly with the instructor instead of being shared on the learning management platform -, most students, almost without exception, decide to share these experiences freely with peers. It is quite clear in these moments, when lived experiences with MH are shared, that the students are glad that these spaces of support become available to them and that they wish to seek understanding and empathy from a community of peers.

One of the dimensions of the course examines the use of technology to support student MH, particularly in terms of development of social capital (Chou et al., 2019; Murray et al, 2020), access to support services (Iorfino et al., 2019; Pretorius et al., 2019), but also development of voice and identity through the implementation of critical pedagogy (Goodyear & Armour, 2021; Sullivan, 2021). Towards the end of the course, there is always a point when the teacher candidates realize that most of the strategies discussed in this section are also useful to them in terms of creating optimal conditions for their own MH issues to not impact their wellbeing in the school environment and their ability to function effectively in their future career. This exploration of the way technology can serve their own needs in relation to MH clearly amounts to an extension of the search for acceptance and support discussed above; they seek spaces – beyond the class and the course itself - where they might continue to benefit from such support networks, even if these are not based within their own schools, local networks, or face to face communities of practice (Hsu et al., 2019; Ridout & Campbell, 2018).

Supporting and Encouraging the Development of a Post-Modern Lens on Mental Health

The third outcome is one observed with regards to all learners, irrespective of their prior experiences with MH. Teacher candidates typically adopted, as a result of taking the course, a post-modern lens on MH which allowed them to begin to consider MH as a spectrum rather than a clearly delineated dichotomy between MH and mental illness. A post-modern perspective generally encourages one to consider disability as an interaction between individual embodiments and the design of experiences and environments (Murphy & Perez, 2002), rather than as an inherent characteristic of the individual. As such, it becomes a spectrum – and a fluid construct – rather than a clearly defined or rigidly delineated concept. Often referred to as the social model of disability, post-modern perspectives in this area have the advantage of fully acknowledging the degree to which it is the environment that creates a perception of disability for the individual, when there is a lack of fit with personal embodiments and characteristics (Hogan, 2019).

The social model of disability itself is rarely discussed in pre-service teacher training (Inclusive School Communities, 2019). While inclusion is discussed at length in such programs, it can be very challenging to lead teacher candidates towards genuine immersion and engagement with the concept of inclusion if they have not previosuly been introduced to the social model of disability (Graham et al., 2018; Lalvani & Broderick, 2013). Without this awareness of disability as a social construct, teacher candidates are likely to revert repeatedly and inevitably to a deficit view of disability, which makes it very difficult for them to develop and deploy whole classroom approaches that focus on a design thinking view of the inclusion of diverse learners (Gomez & McKee, 2020). This course becomes key therefore in the growth and development of teacher candidates, and their preparedness for the classroom, because it introduces them to social model of disability perspectives and shifts them away from deficit model approaches. It achieves this in respect to MH, but also more widely triggers an awareness and understanding, among these students, of the social model in relation to disability more broadly. This becomes a defining moment in the pre-service path of these students, and leads to a rich and transformative reflection in relation to inclusion. This is always apparent in the class discussions and the feedback to the instructor.

OUTCOMES FOR THE SECTOR AND REPERCUSSIONS FOR TEACHER TRAINING PROGRAMS

This chapter is not focused solely on the course which the author has taught on five occasions. From the onset, it was explicitly clear that the aim of discussing the delivery of this course and its impact on teacher candidates was to highlight the urgent need for the reform of teacher training programs. MH must feature more prominently in these programs, but there are wider repercussions still on the format of these programs.

Move away from Deficit Model Practices and Literature

The main take away from the reflection contained in this chapter is that it is essential to shift pre-service teachers away from a deficit model view of MH, and from an adherence to bio-medical literature aligned with this stance towards MH. This is a much more challenging task than may at first appear. Teachers, indeed, as a profession are highly likely to default back instinctively to a deficit perspective on MH because of the general ethos that is perpetuated by schools and school districts (Becher & Lefstein, 2021). Unfortunately, current funding models in the K-12 sector mean that support services and interventions in relation to MH are inevitably linked to a referral to a clinician, the identification of a diagnosis, the production of diagnostic information, and the implementation of individualized and specialized interventions – rather than whole class, design-focused strategies (AACTE, 2018). It is fair to say that the K-12 sector has in fact been key in perpetuating deficit model views of MH because of the welfare and bio-medical funding models within which it has been operating with for half a century (Kriewaldt & Turnidge, 2013; McLean Davies et al., 2013). At this stage, the profession requires more than a shift away from deficit model practices; it requires a major overhaul of practices, policies, funding practices training, and resources (Lombardi, 2016; Renkly & Bertolini, 2018).

Introduction of the Social Model of Disability within Pre-Service Teacher Training Programs

The main way to shift teacher mindsets away from deficit model approaches to learner diversity – particularly neurological, cognitive or psychiatric diversity – is to create opportunities for them to familiarize themselves with post-modern views of disability or MH (Bessa et al., 2013; Whittey, 2008). As has become apparent through the chapter, the most user-friendly, palatable, and accessible way for pre-service teachers to explore and embrace post-modern views is to introduce them to the social model of disability (Freedman et al., 2019; Elder et al., 2021; Mueller, 2021). The introduction of pre-service teachers to the social model of disability can normally be achieved fairly quickly, easily and effectively; this is not a resource issue but simply requires intentionality. It leads them to reconsider deficit approaches to student diversity, and encourages them to embrace their role as designers of the learning experience. It ensures that they successfully adopt a design mindset when examining students' MH issues (Connor & Olander, 2019). Unfortunately, however, there is currently very little effort to integrate the social model of disability into the pre-service curriculum (Annamma & Morrison, 2018; Buffington-Adams & Vaughan, 2019). This therefore represents an immediate need for reform. Universal Design for Learning (UDL) fits well within this post-modern approach to inclusion, and can be said to translate the social model of disability into classroom practices (Fovet, 2014). However, UDL itself is not frequently discussed in pre-service teacher training programs, nor is it commonly brought up in relation to MH (Fovet, 2020; Lister et al., 2021).

Need to Stretch this Reflection beyond Pre-Service Teacher Training

The explicit aim of this chapter was to analyze the phenomenological data accumulated by the author in relation to MH training within pre-service teacher training; this analysis emerged from the specific opportunities encountered by the author to reflect on this topic as he developed a course, and to dive deep into his lived experiences. Throughout the analysis, however, it has become clear that many of the observations made and assertions presented apply equally to in-service PD related to MH. Studies and further research must widen the scope of this analysis and will eventually help formulate additional recommendations for specific in-service PD in the area of MH. This, of course, gives rise to different but considerable challenges: PD is currently underfunded, under-utilized, and easily dismissed in much of the K-12 landscape (Fairman et al., 2020; Liu & Phelps, 2020). It can be fragmented, sporadic and disjointed. The outcomes and take-aways described in this chapter are sizable and pivotal for many students. It may be difficult to achieve deep engagement with these topics within the limited time available to teachers for PD each year. This means that effective in-service training in relation to PD may have to be provided through innovative and creative means: the level of engagement required to achieve the outcomes described in this chapter would perhaps be more easily achieved through the use of sustainable, virtual and interactive platforms available asynchronously and consistently through the year (O'Dowd & Dooly, 2021; Watkins, 2019).

Impact of this Reflection within the Landscape of the COVID Crisis

As discussed in the literature review above, students' issues with MH have significantly increased during the COVID crisis. Through much of 2019, and parts of 2020 in certain jurisdictions, the spread of the SARS-CoV-2 virus has led to the explosion of a pandemic and the closure of K-12 schools (Viner et al., 2020). This has brought about the overnight adoption of online and blended delivery while students remained at home in lockdown (Bordoloi et al., 2021; OECD, 2020). Many students have reported stress and anxiety during these times (Schwartz et al., 2021), loss of social capital opportunities (Bayrakdar & Guveli, 2020), challenges accessing support services effectively (Rusch et al., 2021), and a widening of existing social inequities in the class (Andrew et al., 2020; Frohn, 2021). The urgency of integrating MH awareness into pre-service teacher training programs has never been this acute or pressing (Hidalgo-Andrade et al., 2021).

Teachers themselves are also demonstrating increased anxiety and stress, isolation, lack of feelings of competency, and loss of job satisfaction (Aperribai et al., 2020; Kim & Asbury, 2020; Klapproth et al., 2020). This is having a considerable cumulative impact on teachers' MH (Gadermann et al., 2021), and has already led to a sizeable increase of attrition rate – despite the return to a degree of post-pandemic normalcy (Ozamiz-Etxebarria et al., 2021; Sokal et al., 2020). There has never been a more important conjuncture than this exceptional moment in the evolution of the K-12 sector, within which pre-service teachers require space and opportunity to reflect on their own MH issues, the support they need, and best practices to ensure that their MH issues are not exacerbated within daily classroom experiences (Roman, 2020; Yastibas et al. 2021).

There have been exceptional opportunities for change during the pandemic and the online pivot has, in many ways, been a cathartic moment that has allowed the emergence of topics and issues related to MH, which should have been discussed in schools for decades. It has forced a debate and made all stakeholders aware of the urgency of the need for effective teacher training in the area of MH. It would be perhaps bold to say that the issues which have arisen in the COVID context are new, but these have certainly been exacerbated and have put an end to the denial which was previously pervasive. There is therefore hope that the pandemic will have been a turning point for MH training and awareness. As is the case with most pandemic gains and encouraging outcomes, however, there is also a risk that lessons will be forgotten rather than embedded sustainably into a deliberate and formalized process of management of change. It will be essential for school leaders and academics to reflect on this journey, and to formulate specific action items that can lead to progress. In this sense, this chapter is a call to action which has a considerable degree of urgency.

CONCLUSION

The aim of the chapter was to demonstrate the urgency of integrating, in pre-service teacher training programs, not just content on MH, but also the opportunities for the development of specific competencies and awareness. Ideally these programs should offer teacher candidates the space to voice and process their own MH issues, and ways to address them successfully within their future practice. Addressing these priorities represents, in any 21st century teacher training program, essential preconditions for success and excellence. Indeed, as has been shown in the literature review contained in this chapter, that any failure to address these important needs with regards to MH awareness and training is likely to lead, among early career teachers, to a lack of feeling of competency, to cumulative stress, anxiety, and exhaustion, and eventually to teacher attrition. The chapter has demonstrated the immediate beneficial outcomes that adding such a course to pre-service teacher training programs can offer teacher candidates. The phenomenological analysis presented here has showcased the breadth, diversity, and scope of these beneficial outcomes. The repercussions of this reflection on the possible reform of pre-service teacher training programs suggest that what is required is not solely the integration of content on MH, but also the introduction of students to the social model of disability, and post-modern perspectives on inclusion. The COVID landscape has made the urgency of these needs appear much more sharply, and has highlighted the significant consequences, on school climates and school cultures, of not addressing them successfully and in a timely manner.

REFERENCES

Allbright, T. N., Marsh, J. A., Kennedy, K. E., Hough, H. J., & McKibben, S. (2019). Social-emotional learning practices: Insights from outlier schools. *Journal of Research in Innovative Teaching & Learning*, *12*(1), 35–52. doi:10.1108/JRIT-02-2019-0020

American Association of Colleges of Teacher Education (AACTE). (2018). *A pivot toward clinical practice, its lexicon, and the renewal of educator preparation.* A report of the AACTE Clinical Practice Commission.

Andrew, A., Cattan, S., Costa Dias, M., Farquharson, C., Kraftman, L., Krutikova, S., Phimister, A., & Sevilla, A. (2020). Inequalities in children's experiences of home learning during the COVID-19 lockdown in England. *Fiscal Studies*, *41*(3), 653–683. doi:10.1111/1475-5890.12240 PMID:33362314

Annamma, S., & Morrison, D. (2018). DisCrit classroom ecology: Using praxis to dismantle dysfunctional education ecologies. *Teaching and Teacher Education, 73*, 70–80. doi:10.1016/j.tate.2018.03.008

Aperribai, L., Cortabarria, L., Aguirre, T., Verche, E., & Borges, Á. (2020) Teacher's Physical Activity and Mental Health during Lockdown Due to the COVID-2019 Pandemic. *Frontiers in Psychology, 11,* 2673. doi:10.3389/fpsyg.2020.577886

Ashton, J. R., & Arlington, H. (2019). My fears were irrational: Transforming conceptions of disability in teacher education through service learning. *International Journal of Whole Schooling, 15*(1), 50–81.

Atkins, M. A., & Rodger, S. R. (2016). Preservice teacher education for mental health and inclusion in schools. *Exceptional Education International, 26*(2), 93–118. doi:10.5206/eei.v26i2.7742

Ball, A., Iachini, A. L., Bohnenkamp, J. H., Togno, N. M., Brown, E. L., Hoffman, J. A., & George, M. W. (2016). School mental health content in state in-service K-12 teaching standards in United States. *Teaching and Teacher Education, 60*, 312–320. doi:10.1016/j.tate.2016.08.020

Bamberger, A., Morris, P., & Yemini, M. (2019). Neoliberalism, internationalisation and higher education: Connections, contradictions and alternatives. *Discourse (Abingdon), 40*(2), 203–216. doi:10.1080/01596306.2019.1569879

Bayrakdar, S., & Guveli, A. (2020) *Inequalities in home learning and schools' provision of distance teaching during school closure of COVID-19 lockdown in the UK.* https://www.iser.essex.ac.uk/research/publications/working-papers/iser/2020-09.pdf

Becher, A., & Lefstein, A. (2021). Teaching as a Clinical Profession: Adapting the Medical Model. *Journal of Teacher Education, 72*(4), 477–488. doi:10.1177/0022487120972633

Berkovich, I., & Eyal, O. (2015). Educational leaders and emotions: An international review of empirical evidence, 1992–2012. *Review of Educational Research, 85*(1), 129–167. doi:10.3102/0034654314550046

Bessa, Y., Brown, A., & Hicks, J. (2013). Postmodernity and Mental Illness: A Comparative Analysis of Selected Theorists. *American International Journal of Contemporary Research, 3*(4), 64.

Bordoloi, R., Das, P., & Das, K. (2021). Perception towards online/blended learning at the time of Covid-19 pandemic: An academic analytics in the Indian context. *Asian Association of Open Universities Journal, 16*(1), 41–60. doi:10.1108/AAOUJ-09-2020-0079

Breux, P., & Boccio, D. E. (2019). Improving Schools' Readiness for Involvement in Suicide Prevention: An Evaluation of the Creating Suicide Safety in Schools (CSSS) Workshop. *International Journal of Environmental Research and Public Health, 16*(12), 2165. doi:10.3390/ijerph16122165 PMID:31248082

Brown, E. L., Phillippo, K. L., Weston, K., & Rodger, S. (2019). United States and Canada pre-service teacher certification standards for student mental health: A comparative case study. *Teaching and Teacher Education: An International Journal of Research and Studies, 80*(1), 71-82. https://www.learntechlib.org/p/202092/

Buffington-Adams, J., & Vaughan, K. P. (2019). The Curriculum of Disability Studies: Multiple Perspectives on Dis/Ability. Introduction: An Invitation to Complicated Conversations. *Journal of Curriculum Theorizing, 34*(1). https://journal.jctonline.org/index.php/jct/issue/viewFile/35/2019JCTVol34Iss1

Burkhauser, S. (2017). How much do school principals matter when it comes to teacher working conditions? *Educational Evaluation and Policy Analysis, 39*(1), 126–145. doi:10.3102/0162373716668028

Caldwell, N. (2019) *Teachers' Perception of Mental Health in the School System* (Master's thesis). Eastern Illinois University. https://thekeep.eiu.edu/theses/4581

Cavioni, V., Grazzani, I., & Ornaghi, V. (2020). Mental health promotion in schools: A comprehensive theoretical framework. *The International Journal of Emotional Education, 12*(1), 65–82. https://files.eric.ed.gov/fulltext/EJ1251771.pdf

CBC. (2018, November 23). *UPEI 1-year bachelor of education program attracting more students.* CBC News. https://www.cbc.ca/news/canada/prince-edward-island/pei-upei-bachelor-of-education-one-year-program-update-1.4918105

Chou, C. C., Chuang, H.-H., & Wharton-Beck, A. N. (2019). Fostering the Development of Social Capital to Enrich Student Experiences Through After-School Digital Tutoring Programs. *Journal of Educational Technology Development and Exchange, 12*(1), 1. Advance online publication. doi:10.18785/jetde.1201.01

Connor, D., & Olander, L. (2019) Influence of Medical and Social Perspectives of Disability on Models of Inclusive Education in the United States. *Oxford Research Encyclopedia of Education.* https://oxfordre.com/education/view/10.1093/acrefore/9780190264093.001.0001/acrefore-9780190264093-e-1244

Deacon, B. (2013). The biomedical model of mental disorder: A critical analysis of its validity, utility, and effects on psychotherapy research. *Clinical Psychology Review*, *33*(7), 846–861. doi:10.1016/j.cpr.2012.09.007 PMID:23664634

Dorn, E., Hancock, B., Sarakatsannis, J., & Viruleg, E. (2020). *COVID-19 and learning loss—disparities grow and students need help*. McKinsey & Company. https://www.mckinsey.com/industries/public-and-social-sector/our-insights/covid-19-and-learning-loss-disparities-grow-and-students-need-help

Dudley-Marling, C. (2015). The resilience of deficit thinking. *Journal of Teaching and Learning*, *10*(1). Advance online publication. doi:10.22329/jtl.v10i1.4171

Elder, B. C., Givens, L., LoCastro, A., & Rencher, L. (2021). Using Disability Studies in Education (dse) and Professional Development Schools (pds) to Implement Inclusive Practices. *Journal of Disability Studies in Education*. doi:10.1163/25888803-bja10010

Emiliussen, J., Engelsen, S., Christiansen, R., & Klausen, S. H. (2021). We are all in it! Phenomenological Qualitative Research and Embeddedness. *International Journal of Qualitative Methods*, *20*. Advance online publication. doi:10.1177/1609406921995304

Fairman, J., Smith, D., Pullen, P., & Lebel, S. (2020). The challenge of keeping teacher professional development relevant. *Professional Development in Education*, 1–13. Advance online publication. doi:10.1080/19415257.2020.1827010

Fennig, M., & Denov, M. (2019). Regime of Truth: Rethinking the Dominance of the Bio-Medical Model in Mental Health Social Work with Refugee Youth. *British Journal of Social Work*, *49*(2), 300–317. doi:10.1093/bjsw/bcy036

Fovet, F. (2014). Social model as catalyst for innovation in design and pedagogical change. *Widening Participation through Curriculum Open University 2014 Conference Proceedings*, 135-139.

Fovet, F. (2020). Exploring the Potential of Universal Design for Learning with Regards to Mental Health Issues in Higher Education. In *Pacific Rim International Conference on Disability and Diversity. Conference Proceedings*. Center on Disability Studies, University of Hawai'i at Mānoa.

Freedman, J., Applebaum, A., Woodfield, C., & Ashby, C. (2019) Integrating Disability Studies Pedagogy in Teacher Education. *Journal of Teaching Disability Studies*. https://jtds.commons.gc.cuny.edu/integrating-disability-studies-pedagogy-in-teacher-education/

Frohn, J. (2021). Troubled schools in troubled times: How COVID-19 affects educational inequalities and what measures can be taken. *European Educational Research Journal, 20*(5), 667–683. doi:10.1177/14749041211020974

Gadermann, A. M., Warren, M. T., Gagné, M., Thomson, K. C., Schonert-Reichl, K. A., Guhn, M., Molyneux, T. M., & Oberle, E. (2021). *The impact of the COVID-19 pandemic on teacher well-being in British Columbia.* Human Early Learning Partnership. http://earlylearning.ubc.ca/

Galderisi, S., Heinz, A., Kastrup, M., Beezhold, J., & Sartorius, N. (2015). Toward a new definition of mental health. *World Psychiatry; Official Journal of the World Psychiatric Association (WPA), 14*(2), 231–233. doi:10.1002/wps.20231 PMID:26043341

García-Carrión, R., Villarejo-Carballido, B., & Villardón-Gallego, L. (2019) Children and Adolescents Mental Health: A Systematic Review of Interaction-Based Interventions in Schools and Communities. *Frontiers in Psychology, 10*, 918. doi:10.3389/fpsyg.2019.00918

Gatta, M., Miscioscia, M., Svanellini, L., Spoto, A., Difronzo, M., de Sauma, M., & Ferruzza, E. (2019) Effectiveness of Brief Psychodynamic Therapy with Children and Adolescents: An Outcome Study. *Frontiers in Pediatrics, 7.* doi:10.3389/fped.2019.00501

Gilroy, P. (2005). The commercialisation of teacher education: Teacher education in the marketplace. *Journal of Education for Teaching, 31*(4), 275–277. doi:10.1080/02607470500280076

Goldhaber, D., Krieg, J., Theobald, R., & Goggins, M. (2021). Front End to Back End: Teacher Preparation, Workforce Entry, and Attrition. *Journal of Teacher Education.* Advance online publication. doi:10.1177/00224871211030303

Gomez, S.A., & McKee, A. (2020) When Special Education and Disability Studies Intertwine: Addressing Educational Inequities through Processes and Programming. *Frontiers in Education, 5*, 202. doi:10.3389/feduc.2020.587045

Goodyear, V. A., & Armour, K. M. (2021). Young People's health-related learning through social media: What do teachers need to know? *Teaching and Teacher Education, 102*, 103340. Advance online publication. doi:10.1016/j.tate.2021.103340 PMID:34083866

Goudeau, S., Sanrey, C., Stanczak, A., Manstead, A., & Darnon, C. (2021). Why lockdown and distance learning during the COVID-19 pandemic are likely to increase the social class achievement gap. *Nature Human Behaviour, 5*(10), 1273–1281. doi:10.103841562-021-01212-7 PMID:34580440

Graham, L. J., Tancredi, H., Willis, J., & McGraw, K. (2018). Designing out barriers to student access and participation in secondary school assessment. *Australian Educational Researcher, 45*(1), 103–124. doi:10.100713384-018-0266-y

Granlund, M., Imms, C., King, G., Andersson, A. K., Augustine, L., Brooks, R., Danielsson, H., Gothilander, J., Ivarsson, M., Lundqvist, L.-O., Lyngegård, F., & Almqvist, L. (2021). Definitions and Operationalization of Mental Health Problems, Wellbeing and Participation Constructs in Children with NDD: Distinctions and Clarifications. *International Journal of Environmental Research and Public Health, 18*(4), 1656. doi:10.3390/ijerph18041656 PMID:33572339

Handerer, F., Kinderman, P., Timmermann, C., & Tai, S. J. (2021). How did mental health become so biomedical? The progressive erosion of social determinants in historical psychiatric admission registers. *History of Psychiatry, 32*(1), 37–51. doi:10.1177/0957154X20968522 PMID:33143472

Harris, S. P., Davies, R. S., Christensen, S. S., Hanks, J., & Bowles, B. (2019). Teacher Attrition: Differences in Stakeholder Perceptions of Teacher Work Condition. *Education in Science, 9*(4), 300. doi:10.3390/educsci9040300

Hart, L. M., Bond, K. S., Morgan, A. J., Rossetto, A., Cottrill, F. A., Kelly, C. M., & Jorm, A. F. (2019). Teen Mental Health First Aid for years 7–9: A description of the program and an initial evaluation. *International Journal of Mental Health Systems, 13*(1), 71. doi:10.118613033-019-0325-4 PMID:31788023

Hawrilenko, M., Kroshus, E., Tandon, P., & Christakis, D. (2021). The Association Between School Closures and Child Mental Health During COVID-19. *JAMA Network Open, 4*(9), e2124092. doi:10.1001/jamanetworkopen.2021.24092 PMID:34477850

Hellblom-Thibblin, T., & Sandberg, G. (2020). A dynamic ecological approach to categorisation at school, past and present. *European Journal of Special Needs Education*. Advance online publication. doi:10.1080/08856257.2020.1790883

Hidalgo-Andrade, P., Hermosa-Bosano, C., & Paz, C. (2021). Teachers' Mental Health and Self-Reported Coping Strategies During the COVID-19 Pandemic in Ecuador: A Mixed-Methods Study. *Psychology Research and Behavior Management, 14*, 933–944. doi:10.2147/PRBM.S314844 PMID:34239334

Higgen, S., & Mösko, M. (2020). Mental health and cultural and linguistic diversity as challenges in school? An interview study on the implications for students and teachers. *PLoS One*, *15*(7), e0236160. doi:10.1371/journal.pone.0236160 PMID:32687515

Hogan A. J. (2019). Social and medical models of disability and mental health: evolution and renewal. *CMAJ: Canadian Medical Association journal/ journal de l'Association medicale canadienne*, *191*(1), E16–E18. doi:10.1503/cmaj.181008

Hsu, P. C., Chang, I. H., & Chen, R. S. (2019). Online Learning Communities and Mental Health Literacy for Preschool Teachers: The Moderating Role of Enthusiasm for Engagement. *International Journal of Environmental Research and Public Health*, *16*(22), 4448. doi:10.3390/ijerph16224448 PMID:31766127

Inclusive School Communities. (2019). Exploring Disability and Inclusion Tool 2: The Models of Disability. *Toolkit.* https://inclusiveschoolcommunities.org.au/resources/toolkit/exploring-disability-and-inclusion-tool-2-models-disability

Iorfino, F., Cross, S. P., Davenport, T., Carpenter, J. S., Scott E., Shiran, S., & Hickie, I. B. (2019). A Digital Platform Designed for Youth Mental Health Services to Deliver Personalized and Measurement-Based Care. *Frontiers in Psychiatry, 10*, 595. DOI= doi:10.3389/fpsyt.2019.00595

Joseph, D. (2014). Interpretative phenomenological analysis. In K. A. Hartwig (Ed.), *Research Methodologies in Music Education* (pp. 145–166). Cambridge Scholars Publishing.

Kazantzis, N., & Stuckey, M. E. (2018). Inception of a discovery: Re-defining the use of Socratic dialogue in cognitive behavioral therapy. *International Journal of Cognitive Therapy*, *11*(2), 117–123. doi:10.100741811-018-0015-z

Khanlou, N. (2019). Post-Secondary Student Mental Health and Well-being: A Systems and Intersectionality-Informed Approach. *International Journal of Mental Health and Addiction*, *17*(3), 415–417. doi:10.100711469-019-00105-1

Kilbourne, A. M., Smith, S. N., Choi, S. Y. E., Liebrecht, C., Rusch, A., Abelson, J. L., Eisenberg, D., Himle, J. A., Fitzgerald, K., & Almirall, D. (2018). Adaptive School-based Implementation of CBT (ASIC): clustered-SMART for building an optimized adaptive implementation intervention to improve uptake of mental health interventions in schools. *Implementation Science; IS*, *13*(1), 119. doi:10.118613012-018-0808-8 PMID:30185192

Kim, L. E., & Asbury, K. (2020). 'Like a rug had been pulled from under you': The impact of COVID-19 on teachers in England during the first six weeks of UK lockdown. *The British Journal of Educational Psychology*, *90*(4), 1062–1083. doi:10.1111/bjep.12381 PMID:32975830

Klapproth, F., Federkeil, L., Heinschke, F., & Jungmann, T. (2020). Teachers' experiences of stress and their coping strategies during COVID-19 induced distance teaching. *Journal of Pedagogical Research*, *4*(4), 444–452. doi:10.33902/JPR.2020062805

Krieg, J. M., Goldhaber, D., & Theobald, R. (2020a). *Disconnected development? The importance of specific human capital in the transition from student teaching to the classroom* (CALDER working paper no. 236–0520). https://eric.ed.gov/?id=ED605737

Kriewaldt, J., & Turnidge, D. (2013). Conceptualising an approach to clinical reasoning in the education profession. *The Australian Journal of Teacher Education*, *38*(6), 103–115. doi:10.14221/ajte.2013v38n6.9

Lalvani, P., & Broderick, A. A. (2013). Institutionalized ableism and the misguided "Disability Awareness Day". *Transformative Pedagogies for Teacher Education in Equity and Excellence in Education*, *46*(4), 468–483. doi:10.1080/10665684.2013.838484

Lever, N., Mathis, E., & Mayworm, A. (2017). School Mental Health Is Not Just for Students: Why Teacher and School Staff Wellness Matters. *Report on Emotional & Behavioral Disorders in Youth*, *17*(1), 6–12. PMID:30705611

Linden, B., Boyes, R., & Stuart, H. (2021). Cross-sectional trend analysis of the NCHA II survey data on Canadian post-secondary student mental health and wellbeing from 2013 to 2019. *BMC Public Health*, *21*(1), 590. doi:10.118612889-021-10622-1 PMID:33765965

Lister, K., Seale, J., & Douce, C. (2021). Mental health in distance learning: A taxonomy of barriers and enablers to student mental wellbeing. *Open Learning*, 1–15. Advance online publication. doi:10.1080/02680513.2021.1899907

Liu, S., & Phelps, G. (2020). Does Teacher Learning Last? Understanding How Much Teachers Retain Their Knowledge After Professional Development. *Journal of Teacher Education*, *71*(5), 537–550. doi:10.1177/0022487119886290

Lombardi, J. (2016) The Deficit Model Is Harming Your Students. *Edutopia*. https://www.edutopia.org/blog/deficit-model-is-harming-students-janice-lombardi

Mantzios, M., Cook, A., & Egan, H. (2019). Mental health first aid embedment within undergraduate psychology curriculums: An opportunity of applied experience for psychology students and for enhancing mental health care in higher education institutions. *Higher Education Pedagogies, 4*(1), 307–310. doi:10.1080/23752696.2019.1640631

Mazzer, K. R., & Rickwood, D. (2015). Teachers' role breadth and perceived efficacy in supporting school mental health. *Advances in School Mental Health Promotion, 8*(1), 29–41. doi:10.1080/1754730X.2014.978119

McLean, L., Abry, T., Taylor, M., Jimenez, M., & Granger, K. (2017). Teachers' mental health and perceptions of school climate across the transition from training to teaching. *Teaching and Teacher Education, 65*, 230–240. doi:10.1016/j.tate.2017.03.018

McLean Davies, L., Anderson, M., Deans, J., Dinham, S., Griffin, P., Kameniar, B., Page, J., Reid, C., Rickards, F., Tayler, C., & Tyler, D. (2013). Masterly preparation: Embedding clinical practice in a graduate pre-service teacher education programme. *Journal of Education for Teaching, 39*(1), 93–106. doi:10.1080/02607476.2012.733193

Mergler, A. G., & Spooner-Lane, R. (2012). What Pre-service Teachers need to know to be Effective at Values-based Education. *The Australian Journal of Teacher Education, 37*(8), 5. https://ro.ecu.edu.au/ajte/vol37/iss8/5. doi:10.14221/ajte.2012v37n8.5

Morgan, A. J., Fischer, J. A., Hart, L. M., Kelly, C., Kitchener, B., Reavley, N., Yap, M., Cvetkovski, S., & Jorm, A. (2019). Does Mental Health First Aid training improve the mental health of aid recipients? The training for parents of teenagers randomised controlled trial. *BMC Psychiatry, 19*(1), 99. doi:10.118612888-019-2085-8 PMID:30917811

Morgan, H. (2021). Neoliberalism's influence on American universities: How the business model harms students and society. *Policy Futures in Education*. Advance online publication. doi:10.1177/14782103211006655

Morton, B. M., & Berardi, A. A. (2017). Trauma-informed school programming: Applications for mental health professionals and educator partnerships. *Journal of Child & Adolescent Trauma*. PMID:32318170

Mueller, C. O. (2021). "I Didn't Know People With Disabilities Could Grow Up to Be Adults": Disability History, Curriculum, and Identity in Special Education. *Teacher Education and Special Education, 44*(3), 189–205. doi:10.1177/0888406421996069

Murano, D., Way, J. D., Martin, J. E., Walton, K. E., Anguiano-Carrasco, C., & Burrus, J. (2019). The need for high-quality pre-service and in-service teacher training in social and emotional learning. *Journal of Research in Innovative Teaching & Learning, 12*(2), 111–113. doi:10.1108/JRIT-02-2019-0028

Murphy, J. W., & Perez, F. D. (2002). A Postmodern Analysis of Disabilities. *Journal of Social Work in Disability & Rehabilitation, 1*(3), 61–72. doi:10.1300/J198v01n03_06

Murray, B., Domina, T., Petts, A., Renzulli, L., & Boylan, R. (2020). "We're in This Together": Bridging and Bonding Social Capital in Elementary School PTOs. *American Educational Research Journal, 57*(5), 2210–2244. doi:10.3102/0002831220908848

O'Dowd, R., & Dooly, M. (2021). Exploring teachers' professional development through participation in virtual exchange. *ReCALL*, 1–16. doi:10.1017/S0958344021000215

Oberle, E., & Schonert-Reichl, K. (2016). Stress contagion in the classroom? The link between classroom teacher burnout and morning cortisol in elementary school students. *Social Science & Medicine, 159*, 30-37. doi:10.1016/j.socscimed.2016.04.031

OECD. (2020). Strengthening online learning when schools are closed: The role of families and teachers in supporting students during the COVID-19 crisis. *OECD Policy Responses to Coronavirus (COVID-19)*. https://www.oecd.org/coronavirus/policy-responses/strengthening-online-learning-when-schools-are-closed-the-role-of-families-and-teachers-in-supporting-students-during-the-covid-19-crisis-c4ecba6c/

Ozamiz-Etxebarria, N., Santxo, N. B., Mondragon, N. I., & Santamaria, M. D. (2021). The psychological state of teachers during the COVID-19 crisis: The challenge of returning to face-to-face teaching. *Frontiers in Psychology, 11*, 620718. Advance online publication. doi:10.3389/fpsyg.2020.620718 PMID:33510694

Pandori-Chuckal, J. K. (2020). *Mental Health Literacy and Initial Teacher Education: A Program Evaluation* [PhD Thesis]. Western University. Electronic Thesis and Dissertation Repository, 6834. https://ir.lib.uwo.ca/etd/6834

Pascoe, M., Hetrick, S. E., & Parker, A. G. (2020). The impact of stress on students in secondary school and higher education. *International Journal of Adolescence and Youth, 25*(1), 104–112. doi:10.1080/02673843.2019.1596823

Phillippo, K., & Kelly, M. (2014). On the fault line: A qualitative exploration of high school teachers' involvement with student mental health issues. *School Mental Health, 6*(3), 184–200. doi:10.100712310-013-9113-5

Pretorius, C., Chambers, D., Cowan, B., & Coyle, D. (2019). Young People Seeking Help Online for Mental Health: Cross-Sectional Survey Study. *JMIR Mental Health*, 6(8), e13524. doi:10.2196/13524 PMID:31452519

Reinke, W. M., Stormont, M., Herman, K. C., Puri, R., & Goel, N. (2011). Supporting children's mental health in schools: Teachers perceptions of needs, roles, and barriers. *School Psychology Quarterly*, 26(1), 1–13. doi:10.1037/a0022714

Renkly, S., & Bertolini, K. (2018) Shifting the Paradigm from Deficit Oriented Schools to Asset Based Models: Why Leaders Need to Promote an Asset Orientation in our Schools. *Empowering Research for Educators*, 2(1), Article 4. https://openprairie.sdstate.edu/ere/vol2/iss1/4

Richter, D., & Dixon, J. (2020). Models of Mental Health Problems: A Quasi-Systematic Review of Theoretical Approaches. PsyArXiv. doi:10.31234/osf.io/s6hg5osf.io/s6hg5

Ridout, B., & Campbell, A. (2018). The use of social networking sites in mental health interventions for young people: Systematic review. *Journal of Medical Internet Research*, 20(12), e12244. doi:10.2196/12244 PMID:30563811

Roman, T. (2020). Supporting the Mental Health of Preservice Teachers in COVID-19 through Trauma-Informed Educational Practices and Adaptive Formative Assessment Tools. *Journal of Technology and Teacher Education*, 28(2), 473–481. https://www.learntechlib.org/primary/p/216363/

Ronfeldt, M., Matsko, K. K., Greene Nolan, H., & Reininger, M. (2021). Three Different Measures of Graduates' Instructional Readiness and the Features of Preservice Preparation That Predict Them. *Journal of Teacher Education*, 72(1), 56–71. doi:10.1177/0022487120919753

Rusch, A., Rodriguez-Quintana, N., Choi, S.Y., Lane, A., Smith, M., Koschmann, E., & Smith, S.N. (2021). School Professional Needs to Support Student Mental Health During the COVID-19 Pandemic. *Frontiers in Education, 6*, 193. doi:10.3389/feduc.2021.663871

Rusch, D., Walden, A. L., Gustafson, E., Lakind, D., & Atkins, M. C. (2018). A qualitative study to explore paraprofessionals' role in school-based prevention and early intervention mental health services. *Journal of Community Psychology*, 47(2), 272–290. doi:10.1002/jcop.22120 PMID:30161268

Rust, V., & Kim, S. (2012). The Global Competition in Higher Education. *World Studies in Education*, 13(1), 5–20. Advance online publication. doi:10.7459/wse/13.1.02

Saewyc, D. M., Konishi, C., Rose, H. A., & Homma, Y. (2014). School-based strategies to reduce suicidal ideation, suicide attempts, and discrimination among sexual minority and heterosexual adolescents in Western Canada. *Infant Journal Child Youth Family Studies*, *5*(1), 89–112. doi:10.18357/ijcyfs.saewyce.512014 PMID:26793284

Schwartz, K. D., Exner-Cortens, D., McMorris, C. A., Makarenko, E., Arnold, P., Van Bavel, M., Williams, S., & Canfield, R. (2021). COVID-19 and Student Well-Being: Stress and Mental Health during Return-to-School. *Canadian Journal of School Psychology*, *36*(2), 166–185. doi:10.1177/08295735211001653 PMID:34040284

Schwartz, T., Dinnen, H., Smith-Millman, M. K., Dixon, M., & Flaspohler, P. D. (2017). The urban teaching cohort: Pre-service training to support mental health in urban schools. *Advances in School Mental Health Promotion*, *10*(1), 26–48. doi:10.1080/1754730X.2016.1246195

Shelemy, L., Harvey, K., & Waite, P. (2019). Supporting students' mental health in schools: What do teachers want and need? *Emotional & Behavioural Difficulties*, *24*(1), 100–116. doi:10.1080/13632752.2019.1582742

Skaalvik, E. M., & Skaalvik, S. (2014). Teacher self-efficacy and perceived autonomy: Relations with teacher engagement, job satisfaction, and emotional exhaustion. *Psychological Reports*, *114*(1), 68–77. doi:10.2466/14.02.PR0.114k14w0 PMID:24765710

Sokal, L., Trudel, L. E., & Babb, J. (2020). Canadian teachers' attitudes towards change, efficacy, and burnout during the COVID-19 pandemic. *International Journal of Educational Research Open*, *1*, 100016. Advance online publication. doi:10.1016/j.ijedro.2020.100016

Sullivan, F. R. (2021). Critical pedagogy and teacher professional development for online and blended learning: The equity imperative in the shift to digital. *Educational Technology Research and Development*, *69*(1), 21–24. doi:10.100711423-020-09864-4 PMID:33192035

Teaching Certification. (2021) *Alternative Teaching Certification*. https://www.teaching-certification.com/alternative-teaching-certification.html

Treleaven. (2020, October 8). Inside the mental health crisis at Canadian universities. *Maclean's*. https://www.macleans.ca/education/inside-the-mental-health-crisis-at-canadian-universities/

Vagi, R., Pivovarova, M., & Miedel Barnard, W. (2019). Keeping Our Best? A Survival Analysis Examining a Measure of Preservice Teacher Quality and Teacher Attrition. *Journal of Teacher Education, 70*(2), 115–127. doi:10.1177/0022487117725025

Vaillancourt, T., Szatmari, P., Georgiades, K., & Krygsman, A. (2021). The impact of COVID-19 on the mental health of Canadian children and youth. *Facets, 6*(1), 1628–1648. doi:10.1139/facets-2021-0078

Vaillant, G. (2012). Positive mental health: Is there a cross-cultural definition? *World Psychiatry; Official Journal of the World Psychiatric Association (WPA), 11*(2), 93–99. doi:10.1016/j.wpsyc.2012.05.006 PMID:22654934

van Manen, M. (2014). *Phenomenology of Practice: Meaning-giving Methods in Phenomenological Research and Writing*. Left Coast Press.

Viner, R., Russell, S., Croker, H., Packer, J., Ward, J., Stansfield, C., Mytton, O., Bonell, C., & Booy, R. (2020). School closure and management practices during coronavirus outbreaks including COVID-19: A rapid systematic review. *The Lancet. Child & Adolescent Health, 4*(5), 397–404. doi:10.1016/S2352-4642(20)30095-X PMID:32272089

Von der Embse, N., Pendergast, L. L., Segool, N., Saeki, E., & Ryan, S. (2016). The influence of test-based accountability policies on school climate and teacher stress across four states. *Teaching and Teacher Education, 59*, 492–502. doi:10.1016/j.tate.2016.07.013

Waldron, S. M., Stallard, P., Grist, R., & Hamilton-Giachritsis, C. (2018). The 'long-term' effects of universal school-based anxiety prevention trials: A systematic review. *Mental Health & Prevention, 11*, 8–15. doi:10.1016/j.mhp.2018.04.003

Watkins, A. L. (2019). *Facilitating Sustainable Professional Development Programs: A Phenomenological Study of the Use of Online Professional Development* [EdD. Thesis]. School of Education, Manhattanville College. ProQuest Dissertations Publishing, 2019. 13865370. https://www.proquest.com/openview/dbcfdf768e1c2a19e0acece9899b7908/1?pq-origsite=gscholar&cbl=18750&diss=y

Webb, A. S., & Welsh, A. J. (2019). Phenomenology As a Methodology for Scholarship of Teaching and Learning Research. *Teaching & Learning Inquiry, 7*(1), 168–181. doi:10.20343/teachlearninqu.7.1.11

Wei, Y., Baxter, A., & Kutcher, S. (2019). Establishment and validation of a mental health literacy measurement in Canadian educators. *Psychiatry Research, 279*, 231–236. doi:10.1016/j.psychres.2019.03.009 PMID:30890275

Weissberg, R. P. (2019). Promoting the Social and Emotional Learning of Millions of School Children. *Perspectives on Psychological Science*, *14*(1), 65–69. doi:10.1177/1745691618817756 PMID:30799753

Whitley, R. (2008). Postmodernity and mental health. *Harvard Review of Psychiatry*, *16*(6), 352–364. doi:10.1080/10673220802564186 PMID:19085389

Wiles, R., Bengry-Howell, A., Crow, G., & Nind, M. (2013). But is it Innovation? The development of novel methodological approaches in qualitative research. *Methodological Innovations*, *8*(1), 18–33. doi:10.4256/mio.2013.002

Wilson, A. (2015). A guide to phenomenological research. *Nursing Standard*, *29*(34), 38–43. doi:10.7748/ns.29.34.38.e8821 PMID:25902251

Wong, V. W., Ruble, L. A., Yu, Y., & McGrew, J. H. (2017). Too stressed to teach? Teaching quality, student engagement, and IEP outcomes. *Exceptional Children*, *83*(4), 412–427. doi:10.1177/0014402917690729 PMID:30555178

Yastibas, A. E. (2021). Preparing Preservice English Language Teachers to Teach at Unprecedented Times: The Case of Turkey. *Journal of English Teaching, 7*(1). Advance online publication. doi:10.33541/jet.v7i1.2284

KEY TERMS AND DEFINITIONS

Bio-Medical Lens on Mental Health: This lens is a deficit model approach which tends to see as the only cause of mental health issue bio-medical disorders. It prioritizes clinical evaluation and treatment with drugs. It leads to a culture of referral in schools, within which teachers may feel that they are not equipped to address mental health issues in the classroom, and must instead systematically rely on clinicians to create inclusive provisions.

Deficit Model: An approach to mental health which construes individuals with mental health issues as inherently missing essential characteristics, not fitting into mainstream expectations, and requiring 'fixing'. Deficit model approaches to mental health are often described as bio-medical, and focus mostly on clinical treatment and medication.

Mental Health First Aid: A word commonly used to describe short, user-friendly, non-technical courses which seek to steer participants away from ready assumptions, and misconceptions about mental health. They are careful not to focus on clinical information, and instead encourage participants to develop attitudes, approaches and reflexes which increase awareness, facilitate and support the provision of services, and avoid stigma.

Post-Modern Approaches to Mental Health: A stance which seeks to dissect the way language and discourse perpetuate hegemonic views of mental health which lock the public in simplistic views which reinforce a sharp dichotomy between mental health and mental illness, instead of privileging a vision of mental health as a spectrum and a continuum.

Social Model of Disability: The social model of disability positions disability not as an inherent characteristic of individuals, but rather as a lack of fit or as a friction between individual embodiment and the design of experiences, spaces, or products. The social model of disability places back the burden on the designer of the environment, rather than focus on the individual's exceptionality.

Chapter 10
Quality Management Teacher Professional Development Model:
For Quality Education as Internal Efficiency

Cleophas Peter Chidakwa
University of Zimbabwe, Zimbabwe

ABSTRACT

The chapter presents the Quality Management: Teacher Professional Development model for quality education as internal efficiency in Zimbabwe's primary schools. The model is a product of a qualitative phenomenological doctoral study. The researcher analyzes quality management practices from three rural primary schools consistently awarded the Secretary's Merit Award for performance 'par excellence'. The model is cost effective and work embedded. Teachers get professionally developed daily as they work in schools. As a process quality management model, it involves planning, organizing, leading, monitoring, and controlling. Teachers participate in quality management by being members of school-based committees or teams. The QMTPD model develops teachers in some of these aspects: effective teaching; classroom management; setting, marking, and moderating tests; diagnosing and remedying weak learners. Effectiveness of the QMTPD model is manifested in the literacy rate of above 90% that Zimbabwe has attained.

DOI: 10.4018/978-1-7998-9278-6.ch010

INTRODUCTION

This chapter analyzes the quality management teacher professional development (QMTPD) model for provision of quality education as internal efficiency. To facilitate understanding of the model, key concepts are first defined for the following terms: Quality Management, Quality Education, Internal Efficiency and Teacher Professional Development. The chapter presents the QMTPD model as a school embedded, cost-effective in-service teacher professional development program. The presentation of the QMTPD model follows this outline: First, a survey of educational issues in both colonial and independent Zimbabwe that give rise to the model are discussed. Second, an overview of the model is given. A detailed analysis of how to implement the model, its impact and lessons about teacher professional development that are drawn from implementing the model will follow.

Definitions of Key Concepts

In this section, the following terms are defined: Quality Management; Quality Education, Internal Efficiency and Teacher Professional Development.

Quality Management: Chidakwa (2017a) defines *quality management* in education as a process or system of planning, organizing, leading, monitoring and controlling for achievement of quality education in educational institutions. Harris et al. (2021), Martin et al. (2021), and Doherty (1994) also note that quality management has an organisational structure, responsibilities, procedures and processes that facilitate how it is implemented in schools. The QMTPD model presents the quality management process as involving planning, organizing, leading, monitoring and controlling production of quality education as internal efficiency within collaborative and participatory teams in schools. The QMTPD model emphasizes involvement of key education stakeholders including Ministry of Primary and Secondary Education (MoPSE) officials, parents, school authorities and teachers in schools working collaboratively within school-based committees. The key stakeholders plan, organize, lead, monitor and control production of quality education in schools.

Planning for quality management involves participants sharing decisions on which quality goals schools need to attain, and formulating school program activities to achieve the goals. Organizing entails setting up quality management school-based teams for achieving quality education. Leading involves teachers in the schools leading teams that have been set up to achieve provision of quality education. Monitoring and controlling for quality management involves using agreed and established processes to give feedback on how quality management procedures are progressing in the schools.

Quality Management Teacher Professional Development Model

Quality Education as Internal Efficiency: Quality education is difficult to define. However, Chidakwa (2017a) cites Teesse & Polesol (2003); Kingdon (1996); Sharon, Ball & Howe (1995) Doherty (1994); Aspin et al. (1994); Garrison (1993); Lockheeed & Verspoor (1991) and Ramsden (1991) who describe quality education as a 'protean and nebulous term' that is contested and elusive. This perspective implies that the meaning of quality education is relative. Albeit, this observation, Machingura et. al. (2012) and Teese & Polesol (2003) identify five common indicators of quality education. These indicators include the following: accessible and participatory, equitable, efficient, effective, and relevant. Accessibility and participatory, suggests that quality education is made available to every learner without discrimination. In addition, instruction given caters for the different learners' individual learning needs. This indicator fulfills the global view of quality education as a fundamental right of every child. Equity indicates that quality education should be fairly and justly provided to everyone irrespective of their learning needs: physically, socially, culturally and economically. Efficiency is both internal and external. Internal efficiency refers to management of learners from the time they are admitted into schools and up to when they graduate, with minimal or no wastage that result from dropping out, failing and repeating grades/forms. External efficiency suggests that all graduates from the school system end up gainfully absorbed into the world of work. Effectiveness suggests that the education system always meets established goals and learners admitted therein graduate successfully. Lastly, relevance implies that the system imparts knowledge, skills and competencies that make school graduates self-reliant in producing work opportunities that gainfully occupy them.

Internal Efficiency: Tahar et. al. (2022); Konalasani et. al (2020); Munawaru (2010); and Mahere (2010) identify the following indicators of quality education as internal efficiency:

- Consistent achievement of above average academic examination pass rates;
- Effective implementation of the official school curriculum;
- Existence of good rapport among school administrators (school heads, deputy school heads, teachers-in-charge and heads of departments), the teaching and ancillary staffs, the students, the school development committee (SDC), and parents;
- Sustained and effective development of sports, arts and culture;
- Good school ethos, that promote unhu/ubuntu philosophy; and
- Upholding and maintenance of good staff and learner discipline.

The emphasis of the QMTPD model is to ensure that teachers in schools improve their performance in delivering quality education as internal efficiency.

Teacher Professional Development: Osborne (2021) argues that staff development, training and human resource development are terms that are used interchangeably with *professional development.* The Zimbabwean school system extensively refers to teacher professional development as staff development. Likewise, in this chapter, the terms staff development, in-service and teacher professional development are used interchangeably.

Sancar et al. (2021) and Villegas-Remers (2003) define teacher professional development as a life long process that includes regular opportunities and experiences that are systematically planned or unplanned to promote growth and development in the teaching profession. Postholm (2012) refers to staff development as how teachers learn to learn, and how they apply the learned knowledge in their line of work to support the learning of learners. OECD (2009) views staff development as all those activities that develop in teachers, teaching knowledge, skills and expertise. Staff development or teacher professional development then is a lifelong, continuous and socially interactive process where teachers learn from one another effective teaching and classroom ways of improving performance of the learners. Nakabugo, et al. (2011) reiterate that the pivotal role of staff development is improving the quality of education and student achievement in the classroom. Thus, the QMTPD model aims at improving the quality of education delivery and student achievement in schools.

Mukeredzi (2016) argues that staff development may be initiated by Ministry of Education officials, schools, teachers and parents. The QMTPD model, is an analysis of quality management practices that had responded to MoPSE's call in Zimbabwe for schools to produce quality education as internal efficiency in the 1990's. Schools had to devise cost-effective quality management practices with which to deliver quality education efficiently within an environment that had been created by the economic structural adjustment program (ESAP). To do this, schools adopted quality management principles and practices that involved everyone in the schools through collaborative teamwork. This is the crux of the QMTPD model.

Reynolds & Neeleman (2021) and Chikoko (2006) identify the following as some activities of staff development:

- Locally planned and conducted school meetings
- Workshops
- Conferences
- Seminars that are organized for the purposes of improving the professional performance of teachers to enhance learners' performance in the classroom.

The QMTPD is a work embedded staff development model that uses the above activities to provide quality education as internal efficiency in Zimbabwean schools. As a result, the schools end up by being awarded the Secretary's Merit Award/Bell

(SMA) for performance 'par excellence' (MoPSE 2005 and MoPSE 2007). Darling-Hammond et. al. (2017) visualize work-embedded staff development models as effective in providing learning that results in positive changes to teacher knowledge and practices that lead to improved learner outcomes.

SURVEY OF EDUCATIONAL ISSUES IN ZIMBABWE

Zimbabwe is a former British colony in Southern Africa. The Ministry of Primary and Secondary Education (2020) estimates the population of Zimbabwe to be slightly above fifteen million. The same report estimates the country's school age population between three (3) to eighteen (18) years to be slightly above one-third of the total country's population. According to Chiparausha & Chigwada (2021) and Gomo (2003), the United Nations Report ranks Zimbabwe as the first Southern African country with a literacy rate of above ninety (90) percent.

On gaining independence in 1980, Zimbabwe set to redress major inequalities in its education system. Colonial Zimbabwe had maintained a dual education system for its citizens. The first was the much-envied elitist education for white Europeans, Asians and Coloured that sought to create colonial masters. The other was the much-abhorred sub-standard education for black Africans that was designed to created responsible African servants to serve the colonial bosses. African education was selective with a lot of bottle-necks that African learners had to endure in their quest for education. Educational policies were discriminatory. Maravanyika (1990) observes that whilst white colonial education was compulsory, African education was not. Also, the colonial government spent twenty (20) times on white education than they did on African education. As a result, African learners were admitted into poorly funded and resourced schools that offered very little hopes of success. In 1966, the colonial government introduced so called F1 and F2 secondary schools. The F1 secondary schools admitted only one-third of the African learners from primary schools to purse a purely academic career. The curriculum offered in these schools was designed to make them skilled blue-collar workers for the colonial government. About fifty-percent of the remaining primary school leavers, found themselves in F2 secondary schools where they were subjected to a hybrid and watered-down mixture of technical, vocational and academic education. This education was designed to make them semi-skilled workers who would serve as literate handy men for the white bosses. The rest were left to fend for themselves. The colonial government was not interested in funding African education. Funding was left to white Christian missionaries whose interest was to produce literate Africans who would help them in spreading the Christian religion to the Africans.

In 1980, education became a fundamental right of every child. Primary education was declared free and compulsory. The government embarked on quantitatively expanding the education system. Kanyongo (2005) posits that primary schools in Zimbabwe rose from 2 401 to 4 504 from 1980 to 1989 and primary school enrolment rose from 819 586 to 2 274 178. Secondary schools increased from 177 in 1979 to 1502 in 1989. This reflects respective increases of 177.5% and 87.6% for both primary and secondary schools. This expressive quantitative expansion in school infrastructure and learner enrolments was followed by a corresponding demand of suitably qualified teachers to man the new classes thus created. According to Riddel (1998), about 51.48% of primary school teachers were trained in 1990. Trained secondary school teachers were only 48.1%. The Zimbabwe Integrated National Teacher Education Course (ZINTEC) was introduced. The ZINTEC philosophy is education with production. Using the ZINTEC teacher training model, students first undergo a college residential session to learn education theory. After this they are then deployed into schools where they will practice applying learned theory during teaching. After teaching practice, they go back for a residential session where they then consolidate what they learned during teaching practice with the theory of education. Thus, the teacher so produced can easily integrate teaching theory and practice whilst undergoing training. ZINTEC boosted production of teachers such that Riddel (1998) posits that by 1996, qualified secondary school teachers had risen to 89% and in 1997 qualified primary school teachers were 77.2%. Today, Zimbabwe boasts of fully qualified teachers in its schools.

Zimbabwe adopted the Economic Structural Adjustment Program (ESAP) advised by the International Monetary Fund and World Bank when it began experiencing an economic downturn in the 1990's. ESAP prescribed reducing government expenditure on social services programs. Resources for quantitative and qualitative expansion of education in the country were drastically reduced. Paid manpower development leave (MDL) for teachers wishing to go for in-service or staff development training was abolished. It is at this point that Zimbabwe decided to qualitatively expand its education system. Given this catch twenty-two situation, Zimbabwe's Ministry of Primary and Secondary Education had to devise a way of encouraging school administrators to produce the needed quality education in schools. MoPSE introduced the SMA to incentivize and recognize schools that managed to provide quality education as internal efficiency by producing the best pass rates in the annual public examinations that their learners sat for. It was through analyzing the quality management practices that were obtaining in those schools that were consistently being awarded the SMA that gave rise to the QMTPD model which is the subject of discussion in this chapter.

Zimbabwe's Education System

The education system in Zimbabwe is divided into primary, secondary and tertiary levels. The primary education level is subdivided into infants and junior classes. The infant classes consist of early childhood development (ECD) A; B; Grade 1 and 2 classes. Grade 3, 4, 5, 6 and 7 make up the junior classes. At the end of grade seven, learners write the national grade seven examinations which are administered by Zimbabwe School Examination Council (ZIMSEC). Candidates are examined in seven areas namely; English; Mathematics; indigenous language; Agriculture and ICT; Social Science; Physical Education and Visual Performing Arts (VPA), and Science and Technology. The Social Science paper combines Family and Religious Studies (FAREME) and Heritage Studies. Performance is measured on a sliding scale of grades 1-9. Grade 1 represents the best performance and grade 9 the least performance. Learners are admitted into secondary schools based on the aggregated performance units in the examination. Candidates with the least number of aggregate units in the grade seven examination get first preference when enrolling into secondary schools. Thus, all primary schools need to produce candidates with the best performance results for them to be admitted into good secondary schools. Secondary education in Zimbabwe is made up of six classes or forms. After Form four, leaners write the ZIMSEC Ordinary ('O') level examination. Those who pass the 'O' level examinations can either proceed to Form 5 (Lower Sixth) or Form 6 (Upper Sixth) classes. Those who fail can proceed to tertiary institutions to pursue vocational and technical education of their choice. Those who go for Forms 5 and 6, write the ZIMSEC Advanced ('A') level examination. Passing candidates enroll for university education. Failing candidates can enroll for technical and vocational education.

OVERVIEW OF THE QUALITY MANAGEMENT TEACHER PROFESSIONAL DEVELOPMENT MODEL: FOR QUALITY EDUCATION AS INTERNAL EFFICIENCY DELIVERY

The QMTPD in-service model is a product from a qualitative ethno-graphic doctoral study by Chidakwa (2017a) entitled *Quality Management Practices in Rural Primary Schools in the Mashonaland Provinces of Zimbabwe: Implications for Policy*. In the study, the candidate analyses the quality management practices that were obtaining in rural primary schools consistently awarded the coveted Secretary's Merit Award (SMA) in Zimbabwe for performance *'par excellence.'* Every year the Ministry of Primary and Secondary Education in Zimbabwe presents the Secretary's Merit Bell to one selected primary and one secondary school in each of the ten administrative provinces in Zimbabwe. The chief criterion for the award is that the chosen schools consistently produce the best results in the annual public examinations that the learners write.

To come up with the QMPTD model, three (3) rural primary schools in the Mashonaland provinces of Central, East and West respectively, were studied (Chidakwa, 2017a). The provinces from which the schools were located are shown in Figure 1. The schools whose quality management practices were studied were purposefully selected from lists provided by MoPSE showcasing schools that had been awarded the coveted and prestigious Secretary's Merit Award (SMA) between 1990 and 2010 more than once for performance 'par excellence'. According to Directors' Circular Minutes Numbers 4 of 2005 and 11 of 2007, the SMA is a prestigious award that is given to one primary and one secondary schools in each of the ten administrative provinces of Zimbabwe for producing the best results in the annual public examinations that learners will write. Selection of the schools targeted representation of the three types of primary schools in Zimbabwe. Primary schools in Zimbabwe are categorized as either P1, P2 or P3. P1 schools are located in what used to be whites' only residential areas before independence, in urban,

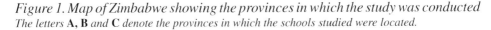

Figure 1. Map of Zimbabwe showing the provinces in which the study was conducted
The letters **A, B** and **C** denote the provinces in which the schools studied were located.

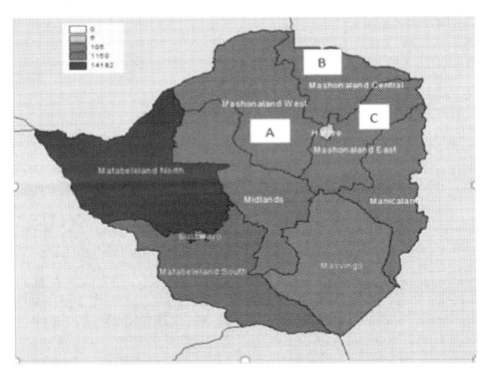

peri urban and rural farming areas. P2 schools are located in what used to be black African residential areas in commercial business urban, peri urban and rural areas before independence. P3 schools are located in what was referred to as rural African Tribal Trust Lands. P1 schools are high fee paying, and patronized by the rich elite in the country. P2 are patronized by learners from relatively well to do middle class families. P3 schools cater for rural learners whose families survive mostly on subsistent farming.

Data for the qualitative study that were analyzed to come up with the QMTPD model were generated through face to face and telephone interviews of personnel in the schools. Those interviewed included school heads (SHs), deputy school heads (DSHs), teachers in charge (TICs) of the infants' sections, selected teachers teaching in the infants' section, Grades 3-4, and Grades 5-7, and selected parent members of the School Development Committees (SDCs). Selection of the study's participants was based on those who were conveniently in the schools when the researcher visited to generate data and on the advice of school heads of those who were knowledgeable and experienced with the quality management processes in the schools. Follow up telephone interviews were conducted to check and confirm what had been said during the face-to-face interviews. On site observations focused on describing the ambience of the schools' grounds, infrastructure and any projects that were being undertaken in the schools. Document analyses focused on the performance pass rates in the end of year Grade Seven (7) examinations, pass rates of the different grade classes within the schools, supervision tools used to supervise teachers, schedules of programed quality management meetings and minutes of quality management meetings conducted in the schools.

Qualitative ethno-methodology studies are largely accused of lacking validity and reliability. However, Randall et al. (2021) and Chisaka (2006), contend that the researcher is also a research instrument in qualitative studies. This makes him/her more reflexive of the issues under study. Chidakwa (2017a) cites Chisaka (2006) who argues that validity and reliability of qualitative studies lie in the close contact and prolonged engagement of those involved in the phenomena under study. Thus, data generated under such circumstances are likely to be rich and more valid in capturing and describing the events that take place than data that are collected by a researcher at a distance, and far removed from the place where the events under study are taking place.

The Quality Management Teacher Professional Development for Quality Education Model

The Quality Management Teacher Professional Development model for Quality Education as Internal Efficiency departs from traditional in-service teacher professional development models widely in practice. Staff development takes place in school-based quality management committees that are institutionalized in the schools. The model is cost effective. Teachers do not leave their work stations to attend the in-service teacher professional development programs. In addition, school do not need to hire additional teachers to replace those who would have gone on teacher professional development. Teachers participate in the teacher professional development through the quality management process conducted in the school. The QMTPD model involves individual development of teachers who will be working in quality management school teams. School leaders monitor teacher development by supervising, using statistical control processes and periodic performance reviews and appraisals. During implementation the model can be instantly reviewed from immediate feedback from the school-based teams to ensure that it is producing required results. The model is hands on. Teachers immediately apply newly learned knowledge, skills and competencies in achieving school objectives. The model borrows heavily from the philosophy and theory of total quality management proposed by William Edwards Deming (October 14, 1900 - December 20, 1993), action research on quality causes and effects (fish) diagrams pioneered by Kaoru Ishikawa (July 13, 1915 - April 16, 1989) and Doctor Armand Vallin Feigenbaum (April 6, 1920 – November 13, 2014) who developed the Total Quality Control processes that inspired the theory of Total Quality Management.

Figure 2. A systematic illustration of the quality management teacher performance improvement model

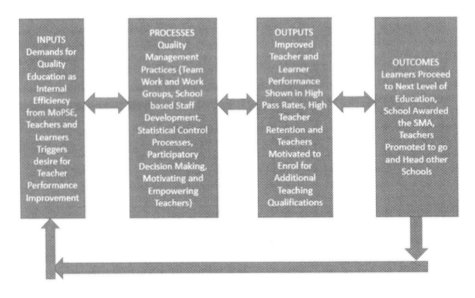

Quality Management Teacher Professional Development Model

The QMTPD model targets school leaders and ministry of education authorities who ideally favor school-embedded teacher professional development programs. During implementation, the QMTPD model becomes infused in the daily management duties of school leaders without requiring extra time for teacher professional development elsewhere. The model feeds directly into the schools' prime goal, of improving teacher performance so that it enhances learner performance. The QMTPD is a systems model. Figure 2 illustrates and summarizes the model.

Figure 2 illustrates the QMTPD as comprising inputs, processes, outputs and outcomes. The inputs are demands for quality education as internal efficiency from Ministry of Primary and Secondary Education officials, teachers, parents and learners. The process involves letting teachers participate in decision making matters on quality education, organizing quality management in school-based committees, empowering and motivating teachers to lead school-based staff development programs, monitor and control the quality management process in the schools. The outputs are improved teacher and learner performance manifested in very high pass rates that learners achieve in national public examinations that learners write at the end of every year. The high pass rates motivate teachers to want to stay in the schools for as long as it is necessary. The outcomes of the quality management teacher performance development model are that learners proceed to the next level of secondary education in high numbers. The schools will be awarded the prestigious Secretary's Merit Award for excellent performance and some of the teachers in the schools become eligible for promotion to higher administrative posts of deputy school heads or school heads. In the same figure, the double pointed arrows in-between the boxes represent symbiotic feedback between the boxes. The arrows below the boxes from the outcomes to the inputs, represent feedback that will result in evaluating and reviewing the whole quality management teacher improvement process. The process management theory of planning, organizing, leading and controlling form the basis of the model.

Quality Management Planning Practices

Alshourah (2021); Scheerens & Bosker (1997); Oakland (1995) and Donnelly, et al. (1992) describe planning for quality management as a basis for effective social processes of influencing others' efforts to achieve quality set goals and a future record of insightfully written quality activities. To successfully implement the QMTPD model, planning is needed. Quality management planning is a collaborative and participatory activity that involves the SHs, DSHs, TICs, teachers, parents and education officials in the Ministry of Primary and Secondary Education working together. Collaborative and participatory planning affords teachers to come to grips with how planning for quality education is done, thus enhancing their professional development. In addition, collaborative planning, enables teachers to experience different views and perceptions of the quality education shared and desired by the different stake holders. Involving teachers in quality management planning also exposes them to different roles and functions of stakeholders in the planning process. Through this backward mapping planning approach teachers are shown the strategic planning process; how quality visions, and missions are crafted; the value of quality management teamwork; and how to formulate quality education policy frameworks.

Quality Management Organizing Practices

Organizing is a managerial function that follows planning. According to Alshourah (2021) and Bradley (1993), quality management organizing thrives within a flat organizational structure that involves participatory teamwork in school-based quality management committees by synchronizing human, physical and financial resources to achieve quality education. In schools winning the SMA quality management organizing is a union of administration and quality management work functions. Figure 3 illustrates the convergence of governance/administration and quality management structures in schools with bureaucratic systems of governance.

Organizing for Administration in the Schools

The hierarchical structure shown in Figure 3 is the official structure of governing schools in Zimbabwe. The school heads (SHs) form the top of the hierarchy. Deputy school heads (DSHs) come next. These are followed by teachers-in-charge (TICs) of the infants' departments. Teachers are at the bottom of the hierarchy. The arrows pointing downwards show that authority and communication flows down from the SHs to the teachers. SHs as chief school executives have the final say on all school decisions and ensure implementation of MoPSE's policies. DSHs as 'school heads in waiting' are responsible for enforcing decisions of the school heads and ensuring proper implementation of ministry policies. TICs supervise infants' teachers teaching ECD, grade 1 and 2 classes.

Organizing for Quality Management Work

In Figure 3, the flat structure on the right of the tall structure illustrates that teachers were involved in quality management through participating in school-based teams. Snongtaweeporn et al. (2020); Jumady et al. (2021) and Bradley (1993) view teamwork as a form of flattening the bureaucratic hierarchy for quality management. The organizing structure for implementing quality management in schools is flatter than that for governance. It has only two ladders. The senior management team

Quality Management Teacher Professional Development Model

Figure 3. Convergence of administration and quality management organizational structures

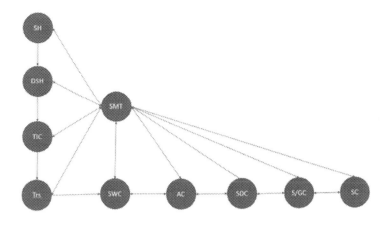

Key:

SH	School Head	DSH	Deputy School Head
TIC	Teacher-in-Charge	Trs	Teachers
SMT	Senior Management Team	SC	Sports Committee
AC	Academic Committee	S/GC	Subject/Grade Committee
SDC	Staff Development Committee	SWC	Staff Welfare Committee

(SMT) tops the hierarchy. The SMT consists of SHs, DSHs, and TICs. Below SMTs are school-based committees (SBCs) or quality management teams. The double pointed arrows from the teachers to the SMT and from the teachers to the quality management teams indicate that the flow of authority and communication during the quality management process is reciprocated in the schools. The SBCs are teacher led. Teachers join in as many SBCs as they want. The members of SMTs can also join in any SBCs they choose as ordinary members. The numbers of SBCs vary from school to school. However, basic teams include:

- Academic committee;
- Staff development committee;
- Staff welfare committee;
- Subject/Grade committees;
- Sports committee; and
- School tours committee.

The Academic Committee

This quality management team is responsible for these activities:

- Setting and maintaining the quality standards in the schools;
- Setting, marking, moderating and overseeing the administration and conduct of periodic tests, end of term and end of year test. Periodic tests are conducted either weekly, fortnightly, after three weeks or monthly depending on each school arrangement;
- Analyzing, ranking and publishing the performance of different classes in the tests written;
- Diagnosing performance of each class and conducting item analysis to note concepts well understood or poorly grasped by learners and suggesting remedial teaching;
- Organizing teachers to tour all classrooms in the schools. The tours are meant for the teachers to observe and learn from their colleagues how they are managing the quality of the learners' written exercises, classroom and learners' displays. After the visits, all the teachers discuss and evaluate their observations noting strengths, weaknesses and suggesting areas needing improvement; and
- Lastly, the academic committee also organizes demonstration lessons. Teachers are asked to plan and prepare a lesson they want to teach whilst others are observing. After the teaching, evaluative discussions/seminars are held to examine the lesson strengths, and weaknesses. Recommendations are proffered on how to improve overall lesson presentation.

Depending on school size, the above activities can either be taken as a whole school or decentralized to various sections or grades in the schools. Through the academic team, teachers are exposed to setting valid and reliable tests; marking and moderating tests; calculating item analyzes and diagnosing learner performance in examined concepts. Teachers are also exposed to proper class management and teaching approaches.

Staff Development Committee

This is central to all quality management in schools awarded the SMA. The function of this committee is to conduct teacher professional development on quality education on quality teaching, curriculum and assessment issues. Prior to coming up with the staff development program, the committee first conducts a needs analysis on aspects teachers need enlightening on. The committee then organizes for learning to take place in the form of workshops, conferences, symposia and seminars in the schools. In most cases teachers in the schools research, facilitate and present on the given topics. However, when teachers feel uncomfortable presenting on an issue, the schools often invite outside experts in the areas.

Staff Welfare Committee

The staff welfare committee is responsible for among other things:

- Organizing support for sick and bereaved members of staff or their close relatives;
- Organizing functions to celebrate special events in lives of staff members or their close relatives. These include birthday, wedding and graduation parties;
- Buying groceries, including meat (beef), in bulk at wholesale prices. The provisions are then shared amongst all contributing members monthly. This helps to lessen financial burdens of staff members; and
- Some welfare committees create financial revolving funds. Willing members contribute agreed amounts monthly. The amount thus collected is paid to a member monthly until all members have their turn. The cycle then starts again. Another version of the revolving funds is that members contributed an agreed amount every month. The amount thus collected is loaned out to anyone in need at an agreed interest on return. At the end of the year, the accumulated contributions plus interests will then be shared equally amongst all members to help boost their financial earnings.

Whilst the activities of the welfare committees do not appear to directly contribute to quality management, they however maintain high staff morale thereby motivating them to want to remain in the schools contributing meaningfully to the quality management processes.

The Sports Committee

This committee is responsible for ensuring that schools have vibrant co-curricular activities that permit maximum participation of all learners and teachers in the school. Participation of teachers is through coaching the different sporting activities. Through staff development programs teachers are assisted to coach in various sporting disciplines. The schools often invite sporting experts to coach in different sporting disciplines. Teachers are seconded to the experts so that they are mentored on how to coach thereby facilitating knowledge transfer.

Educational Field Trips and Tours Committee

Schools often conduct educational field tours to augment their quality management teaching and learning processes. Teachers are encouraged to include educational visits as part of their instructional packages whenever possible. Before the onset of the covid-19 pandemic, schools undertook educational visits to prominent heritage sites in the country. The visits are designed to add more learning insights in learners and as a form of recreation. Also, members of the various quality management teams are encouraged to visit other schools so as to observe and learn how their peers in parallel teams are conducting quality management business. Through this mode teachers in the schools are able to enhance quality management knowledge and skills.

Subject Committee

The subject committee is a natural grouping of teachers who teach the same subjects in schools that practice specialized subject teaching. Specialized subject teaching involves teachers instructing in specific subjects only across a grade or several grades. Although the practice in Zimbabwean primary schools is that one class teacher teaches all the curricular subjects in one grade class, some schools now practice subject specialized teaching. In this teaching mode, a grade classes' subjects' curriculum is shared amongst several teachers where each teacher specializes in teaching a subject to the grade class. The subject committees are responsible for deliberating on teaching methodologies of specific subjects across the grades in the school; coming up with school syllabi for the different subjects taught in the school; how to interpret the subjects' syllabi and then draw up schemes and plans for teaching the subjects across all grades in the school. In most of the cases the subject committees provide the expertise on how to teach various subjects across the different grades in the school.

Grade Committees

These operate in multi grade class streamed schools. The grade committee is made up of teachers teaching the same grade classes. Grade committees are in schools that do not practice specialized subject teaching. Focus of the committee is to improve instruction in the grades they represent. Key functions of the committees include:

- Establishing school syllabi, schemes and plans of work for the specific grade; and
- Conducting demonstration lessons and staff development programs on how to teach in a particular grade.

Information Communication Technology (ICT) Committee

The function of this team is to enhance ICT knowledge, skills and competencies of teachers and learners in schools. In this covid-19 era, the committees are experimenting and coming up with home-grown on-line pedagogies and learning packages to use with the learners during lockdowns. One of the schools has recently devised an ICT learning package that learners can access through WhatsApp. Teachers can also correct the learners' work on WhatsApp.

Quality Management Leadership Practices

Chidakwa (2017b) and Kruse (2013) define quality management leadership as a process of socially influencing others to achieve set quality goals. Effective quality management leadership demands one to be visible, visionary and able to steer the efforts of followers through the quality management process. The QMTPD model recommends that teachers at the grassroots of the authority hierarchy lead quality management teams in schools. An analysis of quality management leadership by Chidakwa (2017b) identifies these attributes:

- Democratic
- Visionary
- Supportive
- Communicative
- Participatory
- Exemplary
- Delegated
- Empowering and
- Open mindedness.

Democratic Leadership

Allows teachers to:

- choose grades and classes they feel able to teach effectively;
- select duties and responsibilities that they are able to accomplish effectively;
- quality management school-based committees that they believe they can contribute in meaningfully and confidently;
- bring to attention of school administrators' problems and challenges they are facing during teaching and throughout the quality management process;

- observe and learn from their colleagues how their classes and classrooms are managed and organized for effective teaching and learning

Democratic leadership practices help instill unity of purpose, a sense of ownership, working cooperatively in teams and togetherness by letting teachers speak up whenever they note issues that they feel needed to be addressed. These practices boost their confidence. Democratic leaders view teachers as mature individuals who are able to work independently and responsibly without tight monitoring and supervision. Democratic leaders settle for win-win compromises.

Visionary Leadership

Is purposive with clear goals and pursues these until attained. Visionary leadership manifests itself by establishing strategic plans whose clients' charters have clear mission statements. During strategic planning, views of key stakeholders are considered.

Supportive Leadership

Supportive leaders identify with and respond to concerns and plights of followers. In addition, supportive leaders always establish opportunities to draw closer to their followers. This enables the leaders to experience what followers are going through during quality management process and devise homegrown solutions to the challenges being faced.

Communicative Leadership

Communicative leadership makes known to followers what they need to know. Followers are aware of what needs to be done, how to do it and gives feedback on how it is being done. Through meetings that are conducted, teachers get opportunities to reflect, comment and come up with suggestions that help in alleviating any issues.

Participatory Leadership

Participatory leadership seeks collaborative engagement with followers in whatever is being done during the quality management process. Participatory leadership encourages close cross pollination of ideas between leaders and followers; is collegial and treats followers as equal. The QMTPD exposes teachers to participatory management in school-based committees. This enables the teachers to become well versed with quality management processes for quality education.

Quality Management Teacher Professional Development Model

Exemplary and Open-Minded Leadership

Exemplary leadership is hands-on and demonstrates to subordinates what is involved during quality management and how it is done. Also, exemplary leaders are supportive, encourage openness and collaborative work. Open minded leadership, is leadership open to suggestions and accommodates different opinions of subordinates on a situation. Open minded leaders see things from their subordinates' perspectives. Open minded leadership empowers followers to be creative, innovative and to experiment with new ideas on how to do assigned tasks in the ways they see fit. Open minded leadership brings into the organization new ways of thinking and doing things differently.

Delegated Leadership

This is hand-off leadership. The leader relinquishes authority, empowers followers through transferring their authority, autonomy, resources and effort needed to perform given tasks. This leaves the leader more time to focus on other tasks that need doing. The formation of quality management school-based committees, enable delegation of quality management functions to teachers in the school. This makes quality management a school community project with shared responsibilities. Delegating quality management tasks to teachers instill unity of purpose that make them want to see provision of quality education successful in schools.

Quality Management Monitoring and Controlling Practices

Quality management monitoring and controlling is a way of managing, assessing, examining and measuring the quality management process to determine that it is not deviating from set standards.

Quality management monitoring and controlling involves the following practices:

- Giving learners homework and early morning work to consolidate learned material;
- Allowing teachers and learners to go on field and educational tours to staff develop teachers and extend learners' learning experiences;
- Creating school-based quality improvement teams or functional natural work groups to practice quality management;
- Periodically testing and evaluating learners' progress on learned matter;
- Supervising teachers constantly; and
- Allowing teachers to observe their colleagues' work.

Homework and Early Morning Work

Routinely assigning learners' homework and early morning exercises enable them to revise, practice and consolidate what they learn at school during the day. Homework proves to parents of learners that teaching and learning is going on in the schools. Some schools have policies that stipulate the minimum quantities and quality of work that learners in different grades are given daily as homework.

Educational Field Trips and Tours

Teachers are encouraged to plan and use field trips and tours to enhance their teaching experiences. Educational trips and tours are ways of ensuring that learners experience how the knowledge they learn in class is applied in daily life. Schools can visit national heritage, commercial, agricultural and industrial sites. Teachers are encouraged to visit their colleagues in other schools to see how they teach and manage displaying teaching media and learners' work in their classrooms. By so doing teachers can note those areas that they feel they need to improve on.

School-Based Quality Management Teams

The school-based quality management teams give immediate feedback to school authorities on how quality management is progressing. Each team is allocated specific quality management areas and tasks to work and report on. For example, the academic committees are tasked with:

- Making statistical calculations of performance pass rates of the different classes in periodic, end of term and year tests;
- Staff developing teachers on designing grade test specification grids and using these to set tests that are valid, reliable and trustworthy. The test specification grids for each grade class are modelled along the Zimbabwe School Examination Grade Seven specification grid that learners will write at the end of the primary education level;
- Organizing administration, and moderation of tests;
- Conducting diagnostic item analysis of tests that will have been administered to identify those areas and concepts that learners were having difficulties with;

The information thus gained is used to enhance learner performance and adequately prepare the learners for the grade seven final examination.

Learner Assessment Testing Programs

These are ways of ensuring if the work being taught in various grade classes is appropriately suited to the grade level. After marking the tests, moderation is done to ensure fairness. Struggling classes are identified and assisted so that they can improve. Learners identified with serious learning challenges are remedied.

Supervision of Teachers

This is a way monitoring and controlling the work of teachers. The school heads, deputy school heads and teachers-in-charge of the infants' sections supervise. teachers' work by observing them conduct lessons, inspecting the quality and quantity of written work given to learners, and checking their official teaching records. Supervision is meant to guide teachers on how to do their work so as to enable the school to achieve quality education as internal efficiency. Clinical and developmental supervision models are ideally recommended for quality management work.

OVERVIEW OF THE IMPACT OF THE QMTPD MODEL

The quality management teacher professional development for quality education is quite beneficial to education in Zimbabwe. A number of schools have been awarded the Secretary's Merit Award (SMA) for producing quality education as internal efficiency. The SMA is a provincial award presented every year to one primary and one secondary school for producing the best performance in the national public examinations in each of the ten administrative provinces in the country. The award of the prestigious SMA started way back in the 1990s when the Ministry of Primary and Secondary Education (MoPSE) in Zimbabwe announced its intention to pursue provision of quality education as internal efficiency in its schools. Most provinces in Zimbabwe have now introduced district quality awards to those schools that also perform well in annual public examinations. Schools awarded the district award, automatically qualify as runners up for the provincial SMA. A school administration district in Zimbabwe has on average about sixty (60) primary schools and twenty (20) secondary schools all competing for this prestigious award for performance *'par excellence.'* This translates to all the schools in Zimbabwe following what is described in the QMTPD model so that they can be recognized and qualify as producing quality education. Thus 'the quest for quality education' is a reality in Zimbabwe. This gives credibility to the claims made that the country has an above ninety (90) percent literacy rate.

Lessons Learnt about Teacher Professional Development

The QMTPD for quality education model is a cost-effective, school institutionalized and work-embedded teacher professional development model. It is practiced as teachers conduct their daily teaching and learning activities. Teachers do not need to take leave to go on professional development leave. As a work-embedded teacher professional development program, it offers opportunities for instant feedback and correction whenever any of its aspects are found wanting. Being practiced in the school, it ensures that teachers are kept informed and updated about new changes and developments taking place at the workplace. Teachers through participation in school team-based committees own the model and can easily adapt changes within the framework of the quality management teacher professional development model for provision of quality education. The teamwork that is characteristic of the model promotes autonomy, collegiality, togetherness and a sense of unit and purpose (*esprit de corps*). This ensures hard work from all team members as they will be afraid of letting the team down. In addition, teachers learn and professionally develop from their colleagues without having to withdraw from the work station. The QMTPD is a content and hands-on program that imparts in teachers' knowledge, skills and competencies that enhance their daily work, thereby improving the performance of the learners they are teaching.

SUMMARY AND CONCLUSION

This chapter presented the quality management teacher professional development (QMTPD) model for provision of quality education as internal efficiency. Key terms: Quality Management; Quality Education; Internal Efficiency; and Teacher Professional Development were also defined. A survey of educational issues in Zimbabwe's colonial and post-independence eras that have given rise to the model have been highlighted. The QMTPD model is a product of a doctoral thesis that analyzed quality management practices that were obtaining in Zimbabwe's rural primary schools that were consistently being awarded the Secretary's Merit Award (SMA). The SMA is an award that is given every year to those schools that manage to produce high pass rates in the public examinations that learners write annually. The QMTPD model has been described as a school institutionalized, work-embedded and cost-effective staff development model. Teachers do not have to leave their work places to attend an in-service professional development programme on quality management for production of quality education as internal efficiency but can do so at the school during the course of their daily work activities. The model is viewed as empowering to teachers in the schools. It grants them autonomy to plan, organize, lead, monitor and control the quality management process that results in the schools achieving quality education as internal efficiency.

To conclude, school administrators whose goal is to achieve quality education as internal efficiency for their learning clientele are encouraged to try out the QMTPD with the teaching staffs at their schools.

REFERENCES

Alshourah, S. (2021). Total quality management practices and their effects on the quality performance of Jordanian private hospitals. *Management Science Letters*, *11*(1), 67–76. doi:10.5267/j.msl.2020.8.029

Aspin, D. N., Chapman, J. D., & Wilkinson, V. R. (1994). *Quality schooling: A pragmatic approach to some current problems, topics and issues*. Cassell.

Bradley, L. H. (1993). *Total quality management for schools*. Technomic Pub.

Chidakwa, C. (2017a). *Quality management practices in rural primary schools in the Mashonaland provinces of Zimbabwe: Implications for policy* [Unpublished doctoral thesis]. University of Zimbabwe, Harare.

Chidakwa, C. (2017b). *Leadership practices for quality management in three rural primary schools awarded the Secretary's Merit Award in Mashonaland provinces of Zimbabwe*. HRRC.

Chikoko, V. (2006). *Negotiating roles and responsibilities in the context of decentralized school governance: A case study of one cluster of schools in Zimbabwe* [Unpublished doctoral dissertation]. University of KwaZulu-Natal, Durban, South Africa.

Chiparausha, B., & Chigwada, J. P. (2021). *Promoting library services in a digital environment in Zimbabwe*. Retrieved from https://www.igi-global.com/chapter/promoting- library-services-in-a-digital environment-in-zimbabwe/274763

Chisaka, B. C. (2006). *Ability streaming: A stumbling block to teaching and learning*. University of Zimbabwe Publications.

Darling-Hammond, L., Hyler, M. E., & Gardiner, M. (2017). *Effective teacher professional development*. Retrieved from: https://learningpolicyinstitute.org

Doherty, G. D. (Ed.). (1994). *Developing quality systems in education*. Routledge and Kegan Paul.

Donnelly, J. H., Gibson, J. L., & Ivancevich, J. M. (1992). *Fundamentals of management* (8th ed.). Irwin.

Garrison, D. R. (1993). Quality and access in Distance Education: Theoretical Considerations. In D. Keegan (Ed.), *Theoretical principles of distance education* (pp. 9–21). Routledge.

Gomo, E. (2003). *Zimbabwe human development report*. United Nations Development Program.

Harris, F., McCaffer, R., Baldwin, A., & Edwin-Fotwe, F. (2021). *Modern construction management* (8th ed.). Wiley Blackwell.

Jumady, E., Suglarto, S., & Latief, F. (2021). Management Performance Analysis Based on Total Quality Management Principles. *Point of View Research Management*, 2(1). Retrieved from: journal.accountingpointofview.id/index.php/POVREMA/article/view/112

Kanyongo, G. Y. (2005). Zimbabwe's public education system reforms: Successes and challenges. *International Education Journal*, 6(1), 65–74.

Kingdon, G. (1996). The quality and efficiency of private and public education: A case study of urban India. *Oxford Bulletin of Economics and Statistics*, 58(1), 57–82. doi:10.1111/j.1468-0084.1996.mp58001004.x

Konalasami, K., & Arafat, Y., & MulYadi, M. (2020). Principal's management competencies in improving the quality of education. *Journal of Social Work and Science Education*, 1(2). Advance online publication. doi:10.5290/jswe.VIi2.47

Kruse, K. (2013). *What is leadership?* Retrieved from https:www.forbes.com/sites/kevinkruse/2013/04/09

Lockheed, M. E., & Verspoor, A. M. (1991). *Improving primary education in developing countries*. Oxford University Press.

Machingura, V., Magudu, S., Maravanyika, O. E., Moyo, P. V., & Musengi, M. (2012). Quality of education in independent primary schools in Zimbabwe: A national survey. *International Journal of Academic Research in Progressive Education and Development*, 1(4), 64–73.

Mahere, S. M. (2010). *Speech read on the occasion of awarding the Secretary's Merit Award to a primary school* [Unpublished speech]. Ministry of Primary and Secondary Education.

Maravanyika, O. E. (1990). Implementing Educational Policies in Zimbabwe: *World Bank Discussion Paper No. 91, Africa Technical Department Series.* World Bank.

Martin, J., Elg, M. Gremyr, I., & Wallo, A. (2021). *Towards a quality management competence framework: exploring needed competencies in quality management.* Retrieved from: doi:10.1080/14783363.2019.1576516

Ministry of Primary and Secondary Education. (2005). *The Director's Circular Minute Number 4 of 2005: The Secretary's Merit Award.* The Ministry of Primary and Secondary Education.

Ministry of Primary and Secondary Education. (2007). *The Director's Circular Minute Number 11 of 2007: The Secretary's Merit Award.* The Ministry of Primary and Secondary Education.

Ministry of Primary and Secondary Education. (2020). *2019 Primary and Secondary Education Statistics Report.* Retrieved from: http://mopse.co.zw/sites/default/files/public/downloads/2019%20Annual%20Education%20Statistics%20Report%20pdf%20for%20UPLOADING.pdf

Mukeredzi, T. G. (2016). Teacher professional development outside the lecture room: Voices of professionally unqualified practicing teachers in rural Zimbabwe secondary schools. *Global Education Review*, *3*(4), 84–106.

Munawaru, I. (2010). *An assessment of the internal efficiency of basic education in the Wa Municipality of the Upper West Region: Master's Thesis:* Retrieved from https://www.grin.com/document/461294

Nakabugo, M. G., Bisaso, R., & Masembe, C. S. (2011). *The continuum of teacher professional development: Towards a coherent approach to the development of secondary school teachers in Uganda.* Retrieved from http://homehiroshima-u.ac.jp/cice/publications/sosho42-14pdf

Oakland, J. S. (1995). *Total quality management: Test with cases.* Butterworth-Heinemann.

OECD. (2009). *Creating effective teaching and learning environments: First results from TALIS.* Retrieved from https://www.oecd.org/education/school/43023606.pdf

Osborne, D. (2021). *Professional development and growth: Instruction and pedagogy for youth in public libraries.* Retrieved from https: //publiclibraryinstruction.web.unc.edu/chapter-11-professional-development-and-growth/

Pollit, C. (Ed.). (1992). *Considering quality: An analytic guide to the literature on quality and standards in The Public Service*. Centre for the Evaluation of Public Policy and Practice, Brunel University.

Postholm, M. B. (2012). Teachers' Professional Development: A Theoretical. *Review of Educational Research, 54*(4), 405–429.

Ramsden, P. (1991). Evaluating and Improving Teaching in Higher Education. Legal Education Review, 149. doi:10.53300/001c.6008

Randall, D., Rouncefield, M., & Tolmie, P. (2021). Ethnograpy, CSCW and Ethnomethodology. *Computer Supported Cooperative Work, 30*, 189-214. Retrieved on: https://link.springer.com/article/10.1007/s10606-020-09388-8

Reynolds, D., & Neeleman, A. (2021). School improvement capacity: A review and a reconceptualisation from the perspectives of educational effectiveness and educational policy. In A. O. G. Beverborg, T. Feldhoff, K. M. Merki, & F. Radisch (Eds.), *Concepts and design developments in school improvement research: Longitudinal, multilevel and mixed methods and their relevance for educational accountability* (pp. 27–40). Zurich Rostock Springer Pub. doi:10.1007/978-3-030-69345-9_3

Riddel, A. R. (1998). Reforms of educational efficiency and equity in developing countries: An overview. *Compare: A Journal of Comparative Education, 28*(3), 227–292.

Sancar, R., Atal, D. & Deryakulu, D. (2021). A new framework for teachers' professional development. *Teaching and Teacher Education, 101*. doi:10.1016/j.tate.2021.103305

Scheerens, J., & Bosker, R. (1997). *The foundation of educational effectiveness*. Elsevier Science Ltd.

Sharon, G. B., Ball, S. J., & Bowe, R. (1995). *Markets, choice and equity in education*. Open University Press.

Snongtaweeporn, T., Siribensanont, C., Kongsang, W., & Channuwong, S. (2020). Total Quality Management in Modern Organisations by Using Participation and Teamwork. *Journal of Arts Management, 4*(3). https://so02tci-thaijo.org/index.php/jam/article/view/243921

Tahar, A., Sofyani, H., Arisanti, E. N., & Amalia, F. A. (2022). Maintaining Higher Education Institution Performance Amid the Covid-19 Pandemic: The Role of IT Governance, IT Capability and Process Agility. *Malaysian Online Journal of Educational Management, 10*(1), 45–61.

Teese, R., & Polesol, J. (2003). *Undemocratic schooling: Equity and equality in mass secondary education in Australia*. Melbourne University Publishing.

Villegas-Remers, E. (2003). *Teacher professional development: An international view of the literature*. Retrieved from UNESCO website: https://unesdoc.unesco.org/images/0013/001330/133010e.pdf

World Bank. (1992). *A review of primary and secondary education for successful expansion to equity of learning achievements: Report Number 8976-ZIM*. Retrieved from: https:/document1.worldbank.org/ curated/en/474521468167384035/pdf/multi-page.pdf

KEY TERMS AND DEFINITIONS

Collaborative and Participatory Teams: Functional social quality management groupings of teachers set up in schools to achieve quality education as internal efficiency.

Effective: Productive teaching and classroom management that results in high performance of learners.

Ministry of Primary and Secondary Education (MoPSE): The governing Ministry for Early Childhood Development, Primary and Secondary School Education in Zimbabwe.

School-Based Committees: Groupings of people that are established in schools to carry out quality management work.

Secretary's Merit Award (SMA): An annual award given by MoPSE to those schools that manage to produce the highest pass rates in public examinations that learners sit for.

Staff Development: An informal, lifelong, and socially interactive professional development programme. The term is used interchangeably with teacher professional development to refer to training of human resources in the workplace.

Work Embedded: A staff development programme that is infused or is part and parcel of the work activities, duties and responsibilities of a teacher that takes place at the workplace or in the school.

Chapter 11
Professional Development for Educators in Singapore, South Africa, and Zimbabwe:
Lessons to Learn From Each Other

Tawanda Chinengundu
https://orcid.org/0000-0002-9114-6368
University of Pretoria, South Africa

Jerald Hondonga
New Era College, Botswana

John Chakamba
University of Zimbabwe, Zimbabwe

Rumbidzayi Masina
University of Zimbabwe, Zimbabwe

Abigirl Mawonedzo
University of Zimbabwe, Zimbabwe

ABSTRACT

Teacher professional learning is an integral component to support the increasingly complex skills learners need in order to succeed in the 21st century. The purpose of this chapter is to compare teacher professional development in Singapore, South Africa, and Zimbabwe and identify gaps and share good practices between the countries to help teachers learn and refine instructional strategies. Continuous professional teacher development, which is managed by the South African Council of Educators, is a system that encourages educators to grow professionally. Zimbabwe has mainly relied on cascaded professional development workshops. However, critics of this model of professional development argue that this model often has no meaningful impact on classroom practice. In Singapore, most professional development is subject specific and provides teachers with opportunities for networked learning, collegial sharing, and collaboration. From the findings, the recommendation is that there is need for cooperation between countries to strengthen teacher professional development systems.

DOI: 10.4018/978-1-7998-9278-6.ch011

INTRODUCTION

Teacher professional development is an integral part of teacher education because only continued learning and training assures high level of expertise and ensures teachers keep up-to-date with new research on how to teach special needs children, emerging technologies for the classroom and new curriculum resources (Mullis, Martin, Goh & Cotter, 2016). Several educational comparative studies may have been done between different nations and Singapore, but a few, if any, of these studies have been on comparisons regarding teacher professional development (TPD) (Lam, 2015). This chapter reports on a comparative study of TPD systems in Singapore, South Africa and Zimbabwe. The reason for comparison is that the three countries had similar challenges in TPD at the point of independence from colonial rule and yet, they responded differently to those challenges (Milne & Mhlolo, 2021). For instance, Singapore upon realising that it had a few adequately qualified teachers and other resources, its policymakers decided early to invest in their teaching human resources and developed a comprehensive system for selecting, compensating, and developing teachers and principals (Mullis, et al., 2016). Currently, Singapore's TPD system is dominated by professional learning communities in schools which include collaborative approaches to teaching (OECD, 2019).

In South Africa, initial TPD takes place in universities. Zimbabwean universities are also involved in TPD but initial TPD starts in teachers' training colleges which are affiliated to the University of Zimbabwe. Although TPD is being proposed in current South African and Zimbabwean human resource development pronouncements, there is no evidence of coherence in terms of implementation (Gomba, 2019; Johns & Sosibo, 2019; Mukeredzi, 2016). Meanwhile, Singapore has a coherent system that ensures their policies move from theory into practice (Mullis, et al., 2016). This study situates TPD as one vital response to the attainment of the three countries' developmental programmes. TPD in South Africa is managed through the implementation of Continuous Professional Teacher Development (CPTD) system which is coordinated by the South African Council of Educators [SACE] (SACE, 2013). In Zimbabwe TPD is a cornerstone intended to drive the New Developmental strategy 1 (NDS1) anchored by the heritage based Education 5.0, National Vision 2030 and in keeping education delivery strategies in pace with the Fourth Industrial Revolution (4IR) (Gomba, 2019).

The practices in TPD in the three countries will be tracked to expose similarities and differences in the systems. It is worth noting that Singapore is believed to have one of the best TPD systems (Tan & Dimmock, 2014) while South Africa has a commendable TPD system in Southern Africa (Johns & Sosibo, 2019; OECD, 2019). Zimbabwe has mainly relied on particular cascaded national professional development workshops and individual teachers' professional development initiatives, in general

(Chikoko, 2007; Mhumure, 2017). All the three countries have transformed their curricula of learning areas at both primary and secondary school level several times and as such, there is always need to have TDP programmes to keep abreast with demands of the new curriculum changes and innovations. Hence, this chapter examines TPD in the three countries in a bid to address the following research questions.

- What teacher professional development models are adopted in Singapore, South Africa and Zimbabwe?
- What are the similarities and differences in the way teachers engage in TPD activities in the three countries?
- What challenges do these countries face in implementing TPD?

The chapter aims to generate debate and share ideas on how countries can learn from each other on innovative ways of improving efficiency of TPD. The chapter begins by conceptualizing TPD. This is then followed by an outline of the methodology and TPD systems and how they function in Singapore, South Africa and Zimbabwe. Similarities and differences on how teachers engage in TPD activities in the three countries are exposed. Challenges faced in trying to implement highly effective and/or innovative TPD mechanisms are then explained. Recommendations and future research directions are provided before wrapping up the chapter with a conclusion.

BACKGROUND

Definition of Teacher Professional Development

Teacher professional development can be defined in different ways. In general, TPD is regarded as a series of teacher-skills development processes that occur when teachers are working in schools after graduation from teacher education institutions. The Organisation for Economic Co-operation and Development [OECD] (2019) defines TPD as activities that develop an individual's skills, knowledge, expertise and other characteristics as a teacher. According to the European Commission (2010) TPD should be supported through a three-phase model: initial teacher education, induction and in-service teacher education. This continuum supports teachers' career-long development. Thus, professional development of teachers is a life-long process that starts at initial teacher education and ends at retirement. It is important for countries therefore, to ensure that provision for teachers' initial education, early career support and further professional development is well coordinated, coherent, adequately resourced and quality assured (Chen & McCray, 2012). Teachers need to be encouraged to become reflective practitioners and autonomous learners in their career-long professional development.

The definitions recognize that TPD can be provided in many ways ranging from formal to informal ways. It can be made available through external expertise in the form of courses, workshops or formal qualification programmes, through collaboration between schools or teachers across schools (observational visits to other schools or teacher networks) or within the schools in which teachers work. In the last case, TPD can be provided through coaching/mentoring, collaborative planning and teaching and the sharing of good practices (OECD, 2019).

Effective TPD updates teachers' content knowledge, exposes them to new teaching strategies, sustains teaching effectiveness and prompts continuous growth (Desimone & Garet, 2015). Numerous research studies indicate that the key to increasing teachers' proficiency in teaching is their continuing development and learning through effective professional development (Borko, 2004; Desimone & Garet, 2015; Wei, Darling-Hammond & Adamson, 2010). This assertion resonates closely with Borko, Jacobs and Koellner (2010) who argue that if we want schools to offer more powerful learning opportunities for students, we must offer more powerful learning opportunities for teachers. Studies including those by (Borko, 2004; Desimone, 2009; Wei, Darling-Hammond & Adamson, 2010) suggest that an inspiring and informed teacher is the most important school related factor influencing learner performance. Furthermore, this chapter has the potential to enrich the understanding of the mechanisms that underlie teacher learning in the current globalized world.

Conceptualising Teacher Professional Development

There are a range of conceptualizations of TPD. Some of the conceptualisations place the notion of change at the centre of the teacher. For example, Marcelo's (2009) Implicit Model and Guskey's (2005) Teacher Changing Process Model that is expounded by Marcelo (2009) can particularly be mentioned. Such models of TPD are recognizable when one places focus on the nature and content of change in the teacher. On the other hand, conceptualisations of TPD are expressed in terms of the format and driver of learning provision. For example, Gaible and Burns (2005) describe three TPD models. The standardised model is a centralised approach which is best used to disseminate information among large groups in the form of workshops, seminars or training sessions. The model commonly utilizes the cascading system where one/two master teachers at a school might attend a centralized workshop and when they return they provide TPD to their colleagues. The second model is the site-based TPD which involves intensive learning by groups of teachers in a school or region. The model promotes long-term changes in instructional methods usually via locally facilitated activities that build on communities of practice (Dalby, 2021). The third one is the self-directed TPD which involves independent learning sometimes initiated at the learners' discretion, using available resources that may include existing formal institutions, computers and internet. It focuses on individualized, self-guided TPD with little formal structure or support.

Different approaches to TPD can complement each other and can be implemented in a variety of forms, enabling TPD programmes to grow to reach large numbers of teachers while supporting teachers in their efforts to improve student learning. However, site-based TPD, since it addresses locally based needs and reflects local conditions, should be the cornerstone of teacher development across the education system (Mhakure, 2019). This chapter seeks to explore the models used by the three countries; Singapore, South Africa and Zimbabwe in a bid to compare notes and share the experiences.

MAIN FOCUS OF THE CHAPTER

Research Methodology

The chapter is based on a cross-cultural qualitative research in which the researchers adopted document analysis as the analytical approach. Data was collected from secondary literature to examine TPD programmes in Singapore, South Africa and Zimbabwe in a bid to find lessons that could be learnt from good practices in each country. This involved a process of examining, analysing, and interpreting various documents (Bowen, 2009, p.29). Some of the documents included government reports, and research papers on TPD. Government documents were investigated and triangulated with data from academic journal articles and reports from international organisations. Where necessary, data was buttressed with primary data collection through interviewing key informants.

TPD Systems and How they Function in Singapore, South Africa and Zimbabwe

Teachers need sound knowledge and skills in content, instruction and pedagogy, along with an understanding of child development and a strong sense of efficacy (Archibald & Coggshall, 2011). Countries that are recognised for having high-quality teachers and high student achievement levels typically also offer teachers with extensive and rigorous professional development opportunities (Guskey, 2005). They also provide teachers with study release time and the support necessary to enhance their qualifications.

Teacher Professional Development in Singapore

The Ministry of Education (MOE) in Singapore and the National Institute of Education (NIE) at Nanyang Technological University-the only teacher training college as well as the Academy of Singapore Teachers (AST) are the bodies responsible for TPD for Singapore's teachers. The three work very closely with each other and with the schools in order to identify their needs and design professional development programmes (Bautista, & Ortega-Ruiz, 2015; NIE, 2009). Each year senior managers-principal, vice principal, or head of department-discuss and plan with each teacher their yearly professional development agenda in response to their interests and school's needs as well as the requirements of the curriculum. This agenda then needs to be approved by the teacher reporting officer who is usually linked with the MOE (Bautista, Wong & Gopinathan, 2015). Singapore places much emphasis on collaborative and community-oriented forms of TPD, which are deemed to enhance not only teachers' content and pedagogical knowledge, but also to bring about a sense of belonging and solidarity among teachers.

NIE is the sole institution that offers pre-service teacher education programmes in Singapore, and one of the main TPD providers for in-service teachers and other stakeholders (NIE, 2009). NIE provides graduate degrees in education. The courses offer primarily focus on subject content, curriculum development, pedagogies, assessment and student learning. Most courses lead to the award of in-service diplomas and/or advanced professional qualifications. The MOE offers numerous scholarship opportunities for teachers who seek higher degrees in Singapore and overseas either full-time or part-time.

The delivery modes of NIE TPD courses and programmes include specialists' lectures and talks, hands-on workshops, project work, fieldwork, action research and a wide range of academic activities that require both individual and group work (Bautista et al., 2015). To complete the required coursework, teachers are generally requested to interact both face-to-face and online. NIE is also involved in numerous small-scale school-university partnerships with primary and secondary schools interested in improving specific aspects of their curriculum and/or pedagogies (Wang et al., 2014).

The Academy of Singapore of Teachers (AST) brings together teachers from different schools and engages them in multiple types of networked learning. The AST was designed to specifically enable teachers to discuss and share innovative pedagogical practices in their specific subjects, thereby raising professional standards of disciplines and fostering a stronger teacher-led culture of professional exchange, collegial sharing, and collaboration (MOE, 2010). The AST comprises four Subject Chapters (referred to as disciplinary networked learning communities), each divided into concrete school subjects. All MOE teachers who teach these subjects are invited to become members of the Subject Chapters, which provides them with numerous opportunities to learn with/from other fellow colleagues.

In addition to the Subject Chapters, there are six Centres of Excellence (also referred to as Academies or Institutes) (Bautista et al., 2015). Four Centres of Excellence offer TPD to the teachers of the different languages taught in Singapore schools, namely English, Mandarin, Malay and Tamil. The other two centres specialise in the TPD of Music and Arts teachers and Physical Education teachers. The Subject Chapters and the Centres of Excellence organize a wide variety of TPD initiatives for teachers, ranging from formal activities (e.g. workshops on school-based research methods, courses and seminars focus on content knowledge and pedagogical content knowledge, conferences, symposiums) to more reform-type TPD activities (e.g. action research, collaborative reflective discussions). Teachers' learning is supported by "One Portal All Learners" (OPAL), an online platform with several content management repositories containing useful information and learning materials.

Much of the professional development of Singaporean primary and secondary teachers occurs within school settings, where they have numerous work-embedded learning opportunities. For instance, in 2009/10, after more than a decade of innovative TPD initiative, the MOE mandated all public schools to become professional learning communities (PLCs). This policy made Singapore the first country in the world to adopt the PLC framework nation-wide (Tan & Dimmock, 2014). PLCs provide teachers with structures and to engage in a variety of inquiry-based TPD practices such as action research, lesson study, and a wide range of learning circles focused on different topics (e.g. curriculum innovation, student-centric teaching practices, new uses of ICT, collaborative lesson planning, and project-based learning). MOE schools are encouraged to provide at least one hour of curricular time per week for teachers to actively engage in these kinds of school-based TPD initiatives (Hairon & Dimmock, 2011). The learning teams commonly plan for about 8-10 two hour sessions speed over the entire academic year. These hours of work are acknowledged in teachers' appraisal contributing to the annual 100 hours of optional training entitlements.

The programme provides 100 hours of training per teacher per year, most of these hours are scheduled during working hours. Undertaking these hours is optional; although teachers are not obliged to participate; most of them do so (Bautista et al., 2015). The aim is to offer teachers the learning opportunities that meet their needs according to their personal motivation and goals (Bautista et al., 2015). This means that the system is highly centralized by the MOE and this type of learning is not compulsory, however, teachers are self-motivated to participate in some of learning activity. What may explain the high percentage of Singapore's teachers participating in teacher professional development activities is that teachers spend on average of only seventeen hours of teaching weekly, which is much lower than other countries according to TALIS 2013 (OECD, 2014).

Another form of school-based TPD that has gained momentum in Singapore is lesson study. Lawrence and Chong (2010) in their study of ten teachers from a secondary school, examined how lesson study which originated from Japan contributed to teachers' learning in Singapore. Lesson study means that teachers plan a class together, and then one of them teaches the class for the allotted period while the others observe (Postholm, 2012). After the teaching, they reflect on the lesson to assess whether the stipulated objectives were achieved. The study established that the lesson study approach strengthened teachers' sense of togetherness and teacher self-efficacy in a teaching context. Furthermore, the study shows that the approach allows teachers to learn new knowledge about the subject and education practices, thus gaining more understanding of learner needs and classroom management. However, participants in the study cited challenges in relation to finding time to observe and reflect on lessons.

With regards to supporting teachers in professional development, the MOE sponsors all teacher professional development programmes (MOE, 2010) Teachers who have at least six years of service can take half-pay leave for one month to give them time to undertake purposeful professional development, to recharge and renew their skills, and those who have at least twelve years of experience can take up to two-and-a-half months of full-pay leave.

Challenges of Teacher Professional Development in Singapore

Regardless of all the resources in place to support TPD in Singapore, there are also several challenges and constraints important to consider. Firstly, there is a challenge of accessibility. For example, teachers from some primary schools are often restricted only to attend PD that is related to the subject matter in which they specialise (e.g. mathematics), despite that most of them teach various other subjects like music or arts. This restriction results in lost opportunities to improve their teaching competences in areas that are out of their specialisation (Bautista et al., 2015).

There is overwhelming amount of work for teachers. Some teachers have high teaching loads, various academic responsibilities (e.g. marking, meeting with parents) and coupled with administrative duties like sitting in committees. Having to fulfill all these responsibilities make it difficult for teachers to bring all their energy, commitment and enthusiasm into the PD activities in which they participate. According to OECD 2018 Teaching and Learning International Survey [TALIS] (OECD, 2019) it was established that across OECD countries, developing advanced information and communication technology skills was one area in which teachers needed more training, along with teaching in multicultural/multilingual settings and teaching learners with special needs.

There are high stakes examinations. The Singapore education system is highly competitive and selective (Hogan & Gopinathan, 2008). Students test scores are one of the factors considered when appraising teachers' performance hence many educators in Singapore tend to 'teach to the test' and drill learners with lectures and reproductive learning activities ignoring what they learn in PD settings (e.g. innovative teaching approaches, learner-centred pedagogies, inquiry-based learning activities).

Teacher Professional Development in South Africa

To become a teacher in South Africa, one can follow one of the two routes, namely: a four-year Bachelor of Education (B.Ed.) degree or a three or four year Bachelor's degree, followed by a one-year Postgraduate Certificate in Education (PGCE). Once completed, both routes lead to classification as a professional qualified teacher. However, South African university programmes vary considerably; some focus on acquiring subject content knowledge, while others focus on pedagogic skills and knowledge. However, in general, there seems to be a challenge in the teaching of Mathematics and Science (Mullis et. al, 2015). For example, the Trends in Mathematics and Science Study (TIMMS) reveal that South African learners typically perform below the expected level at the international rating (Taylor, 2008; Ogegbo, Gaigher, & Salagram, 2019). To rectify this, institutions have developed qualifications that will assist in upgrading teachers' skills and providing them with the necessary knowledge for teaching mathematics and science. Currently, the Advanced Certificate in Education (ACE) is used as professional development for mathematics and science teachers who have no teaching qualifications. ACE is used to address the issue of underqualified teachers in the system. The Continuous Professional Teacher Development system, overseen by the SACE, began monitoring quality of TPD and recording teachers' professional development points. Upon qualifying all teachers are required to register with SACE.

In South Africa most of the TPD activities take place outside schools, where subject advisors and teacher education experts from institutions of higher learning take the lead (Mhakure, 2019; Ogegbo, et al., 2019). Teachers from disadvantaged schools attend generic TPD workshops facilitated by experts together with teachers from other schools. According to Little (2012) school-based TPD activities should be at the core of teacher learning and should also be linked purposefully and coherently to the external TPD activities. Therefore, lesson study is viewed as an alternative TPD paradigm for South African schools (Ono & Ferreira, 2010). Lesson study is a collaborative teacher-inquiry TPD with specific emphasis on reflection on practice and learners' cognition, leading to the development of a teacher's expertise and learning within the context of their work environment (Lee & Choy, 2017). In view of the success of lesson study in Japan, Ogegbo et al. (2019) confirm that South Africa adopted it. Lesson study was believed to be beneficial as a professional development strategy for South African teachers. Some studies carried out in South Africa found out that lesson study enhanced teachers' professional teaching strategies, networking skills, lesson plan writing, classroom management, self-efficacy and positive attitudes towards teaching (Mhakure, 2019; Ogegbo, et al., 2019). However, challenges such as lack of time, lack of institutional support and insufficient instructional materials pose a threat to teachers' participation in lesson study.

In South Africa TPD is managed through the implementation of CPTD system. Department of Education (2007), through the National Policy Framework for Teacher Education Development, mandates SACE to manage the system. SACE has overall responsibility for the implementation, management and quality assurance of the CPTD system'. The OECD report on reviews of national policies for education in South Africa (2008) emphasized the role of SACE in teacher development by mentioning that' SACE is one of the most important bodies for the teaching profession in South Africa and it is well positioned to improve the public image of teaching' (SACE, 2011). The system encourages educators to engage in professional development in order to achieve maximum benefits, hence the system awards points to the teachers for their development. CPTD is an integral part of teacher education because only continued learning and training assures a high level of expertise and ensures teachers keep up-to-date with new research on how children learn, emerging technologies for the classroom and new curriculum resources.

CPTD management system is provided to all teachers whether state-employed, employed by School Governing Bodies or employed by independent schools (SACE, 2013). SACE (2013) reiterates that the main ideas are to encourage teachers to become better at their job and to encourage school communities to become better sites of teaching, learning and development. So educators are expected to learn on a continued basis to be able to meet the global demands (Darling-Hammond, 2017). CPTD is one way to encourage professional development as part of SACE's Code of Professional Ethics for Educators. Each educator pledges to uphold the Code when they register with SACE. Section 7 of the SACE Code stipulates that all educators must keep abreast of educational trends and developments and promote the on-going development of teachers as a profession (SACE, 2013).

Research shows that an inspiring and informed teacher is the most important school-related factor influencing learner performance (Darling-Hammond, 2017). TPD is an integral part of teacher education because only continued learning and training assures a high level of expertise and ensures teachers keep up-to-date with new research on how children learn, emerging technologies for the classroom and new curriculum resources (Rauf, Ali, & Noor, 2017).

According to SACE (2013) each educator develops a Personal Development Plan (PDP) file as part of the CPTD system. The PDP is a resource document to assist each teacher with professional growth. The PDP is a resource file in which the teacher is expected to record his/her CPTD activities. The activities have value for professional development. Therefore, teachers will be allocated points based on such activities when they report them the CPTD system. These include the following: teacher-initiated activities; school-initiated activities and externally driven activities offered to outside service providers.

Challenges of TPD in South Africa

According to Steyn (2008) one of the greatest challenges of CPTD is to motivate teachers to become committed to their own development and learning and participate as active members in a community of practice. As a result there is poor or non-participation of teachers in CPTD activities (Gomba, 2019). There is generally non-participation of educators in the system due to inaccessibility of information technology resources, particularly for those schools where network is poor.

Guldenhuys, and Oosthuizen (2015) also cite lack of interest in CPTD activities by some teachers as another challenge. Most aging professionals or those near retirement are reluctant to participate. This is also coupled with the fact that some teachers are technophobic and would not be encouraged by any system that is technologically driven, particularly those who are old in the system and had little exposure to technology (Department of Basic Education (DBE), 2018).

In a study by Gomba (2019), it was established that SACE's CPTD Portal's capacity disadvantaged the teachers' reporting process. Most teachers had challenges of accessing or even operating the CPTD system. Furthermore, there was lack of support by school management. Generally, there was lack of systematic and regular monitoring of teachers' reporting progress. From Gomba's study (2019), it is evident that no one wants to take responsibility to manage CPTD activities in schools. Consequently, it becomes a neglected programme in the system.

To address some of these challenges South Africa launched the Integrated Strategic Planning Framework for Teacher Education and Development (ISFTED) in 2011. The primary aim of the framework was to improve the quality of teacher education and development in order to improve the quality of teachers and teaching. From the framework, the Teacher Professional Development Master Plan 2017-2022 was developed and approved in 2018 (DBE, 2018). The development of the Master Plan was intended to fast-track the implementation of ISFTED.

Teacher Professional Development in Zimbabwe

The Ministry of Primary and Secondary Education (MoPSE) rolled out a new curriculum in 2017 from grade 1 to advanced. According to MoPSE (2014, p.22) the curriculum is competence-based aimed at preparing learners for societal and global challenges. The curricular changes call for staff development programmes which develop both skills and consolidate knowledge needed to cope with the change (Maphosa & Chisango, 2016). Gasva and Moyo (2017) conducted a study in rural Zimbabwe on the implementation of the new curriculum and recommended the need for continuous teacher professional development courses to keep teachers abreast on the new curriculum.

Teacher education in Zimbabwe is done in teachers' colleges and universities, and knowledge levels vary among practicing teachers (Ministry of Higher and Tertiary Education (MoHET). The required minimum qualifications for primary and lower secondary school teachers (Form 1-4) is an 'Ordinary' Level academic certificate plus a teachers' diploma/certificate obtained after three or four years of teacher education in a teachers' college. Teachers for senior secondary (Form 5 & 6) require an 'Advanced' Level certificate plus a teachers' diploma/certificate, plus a three-year university degree. However, due to shortage of teachers the government often temporarily employs professionally unqualified graduates. The graduates are expected to register for the Post-Graduate Diploma in Education (PGDE) offered in universities after at least two years teaching experience. Formal long-term courses take the form of further education as trained teachers enroll with institutions of higher learning for Open and Distance learning or Block release programmes (Maphosa & Chisango, 2016). This is in line with international trends where professionally unqualified graduates are being persuaded to join teaching and given special dispensations to develop them to qualified status.

In Zimbabwe, the main vehicles for TPD are seminars, workshops and conferences using the cascade model. Personnel from the Ministry of Primary and Secondary Education's Curriculum Unit Division and universities facilitate the workshops. The model is relatively cheap in terms of resources and that new information can quickly reach a large population of teachers in the shortest possible time. However, the model is criticised for negating the principles of effective provision of TPD such as participation, collaboration and programme ownership by teachers (Bett, 2016).

Responding to societal demands for quality education in the country, the governments of Zimbabwe and the Netherlands launched a 'Better School Programme Zimbabwe (BSPZ)' in 1993 (Chikoko, 2007). This marked the introduction of localised school clusters and/or subject panels to help in TPD. Subject panels have a program of activities. Teachers from all high schools in a district are expected to attend the subject panel activities and each school provides travel and subsistence for their teachers. Teachers decide on how and what they want to discuss, including selection of facilitators. Subject panels represent a form of teacher network in Zimbabwe; however, it is unclear whether the teachers are in full control of their professional development through this innovation. Studies on subject panels/clusters established that they are beneficial to the teachers as they help to counter teacher isolation, reduce stress and provide teachers with unique instructional guidance system (Desimone, 2009; Jita & Mokhele, 2014; Mhumure, 2017).

Distance education has been and is still being used as a form of TPD. The Zimbabwe Open University (ZOU) is playing a pivotal role in providing self-initiated and paced opportunities for teachers to upgrade their qualifications (Kangai & Bukaliya, 2011; Tarusikirwa, 2016). Distance education has provided opportunities for many teachers, especially in developing countries, to acquire higher qualifications in various educational fields.

Zimbabwe introduced Learning Area Platforms (LAPs) in 2019. The LAPs are associations of teachers who teach closely related subjects which are re-configured to ensure greater integration, more efficient utilization of resources and enhanced effectiveness (MoPSE Secretary's Circular Minute No. 7 of 2018). For example, Science is a Learning Area Platform which brings together teachers who teach Biology, Chemistry, Physics, Combined Science, Geography and Information Communication Technology. The rationale for LAPs is to bring teachers together for the creation of collaborations and networks that facilitate professional development and lead to effective teaching and learning. The establishment of LAPs is thus one of strategies through which the Ministry of Primary and Secondary Education hopes to achieve its mandate of providing quality education to the whole nation. It is also hoped that LAPs will equip teachers with additional knowledge, skills and value relevant to each learning area for enhanced teaching and learning and the attainment of quality learning outcomes. The circular emphasized that the main function of LAPs is the workplace-based development of the teacher for effective teaching and learning.

In a study by Mtetwa, Chabongora, Ndemo and Maturure (2015), it was established that government in partnership with other stakeholders including non-governmental organisations provides TPD to practicing teachers. Teachers engage in TPD activities on voluntary basis. There are few mathematics teacher-targeted provisions outside standard university programme offerings. Furthermore teachers seem to value TPDs essentially for personal career advancement while providers value TPDs to improving students' performance and their pass rates. The observation was that the style of TPD provision for mathematics teachers in Zimbabwe is characterized by fairly stable structural arrangements, but the associated resource and support mechanisms render operational aspects largely dysfunctional.

Challenges of TPD in Zimbabwe

The study has established that teachers encounter. Some of the challenges include, including lack of support from school heads and poor funding for professional development activities. Mahere (2018) established that many school heads who were at the epicentre of teacher supervision did not adequately understand the concept of clinical supervision as part of professional development. Some school heads confused clinical supervision with inspection. In some cases, teachers were expected to use their own resources to attend professional development workshops (Maphosa & Chisango, 2013). The challenges made it difficult for primary school clusters to achieve their intended goals of improving teachers' instructional practices and student achievement (Delport & Makaye, 2009).

Esau and Mpofu (2017) cited increased load on the part of the teacher, mere negativity by teachers and unavailability of resources as some of the challenges in implementing TPD in Zimbabwe. They further argued that the new curriculum seemed not to be achieving some of the intended goals partly because of the unpreparedness of teachers to execute the new curriculum packages. Mangwaya, Blignaut and Pillay, (2016) conducted a research on the readiness of teachers to implement the early childhood curriculum and found out that teachers were not well acquainted with the new demands especially with the new assessment procedures.

Similarities and Differences of TPD Systems in Singapore, South Africa, and Zimbabwe

The study reveals that initial teacher training in Zimbabwe is conducted at teachers' training colleges. The colleges are affiliated to universities who are responsible for quality assurance and certification of graduates. Singapore has only one teachers' training college; National Institute of Education operating at Nanyang Technological University whilst in South Africa initial teacher training is done at universities. As for teacher professional development, it is generally done at universities in the three countries.

Singapore introduced an innovative TPD policy initiative where the MOE mandated all public schools to become professional learning communities. The PLCs provide teachers with structures and to engage in a variety of inquiry-based TPD practices such as action research, lesson study, and a wide range of learning circles focused on different topics like curriculum innovation and student-centric teaching practices. This policy made Singapore the first country in the world to adopt the PLC framework nation-wide (Dimmock & Tan, 2013). This initiative is contrary to Zimbabwe where there is no clear policy on teacher professional development. Mhumure (2017) confirms that the MoPSE (Zimbabwe) should come up with clear policies governing TPD. Furthermore, (ibid) recommends that the policies need to make it mandatory for school heads to release teachers for professional development meetings and provide resources as well. In South Africa, monitoring the quality of TPD and recording teachers' professional development points is done through a CPTD system, overseen by the SACE. This system is not found in Singapore and Zimbabwe.

It was established that three bodies namely: Ministry of Education, National Institute of Education and Academy of Singapore Teachers are responsible for TPD in Singapore. These bodies work very closely with each other and with the schools in order to identify their needs and design professional development programmes (Bautista et. al, 2015). Singapore places much emphasis on collaborative and community-oriented forms of TPD, which are deemed to enhance not only teachers' content and pedagogical knowledge, but also to bring about a sense of belonging and solidarity among teachers. According to TALIS (OECD, 2019), 84% of teachers in Singapore reported that they supported each other in implementing new ideas after attending collaborative TPD. The study reveals that much of the professional development of Singaporean primary and secondary teachers occurs within school settings, where they have numerous work-embedded learning opportunities. In South Africa most of the TPD activities take place outside schools, where subject advisors and teacher education experts from institutions of higher learning take the lead (Mhakure, 2019; Ogegbo, et al., 2019). Teachers from disadvantaged schools attend generic TPD workshops facilitated by experts together with teachers from other schools. Similarly, in Zimbabwe, the main vehicles for TPD were seminars, workshops and conferences (Chikoko, 2007; Mhumure, 2017).

The study found out that Subject Chapters and Centres of Excellence organize a wide variety of TPD initiatives for teachers, ranging from formal activities to more reform-type TPD activities. In Zimbabwe, subject panels have a program of activities of TPD. Teachers from all high schools in a district are expected to attend the subject panel activities and each school provides travel and subsistence for their teachers. Zimbabwe also introduced Learning Area Platforms in 2019. The LAPs are associations of teachers who teach closely related subjects which are re-configured to ensure greater integration, more efficient utilization of resources and enhanced effectiveness. Similarly, South Africa has subject clusters especially for science and mathematics teachers. Most of the TPD in subject panels/clusters is subject-specific and provides teachers with opportunities for network learning, collegial sharing, and collaboration.

The study established that in South Africa and Singapore the lesson study was also utilized as a form of TPD. According to Ogegbo, et al. (2019), lesson study being site-based enhanced teachers' professional teaching strategies, networking skills, lesson plan writing, classroom management, self-efficacy and positive attitudes towards teaching. A study by Mhakure (2019) in South Africa, advocates that site-based TPD through the use of lesson study can provide a solution to the TPD of mathematics teachers in disadvantaged schools. Site-based TPD adds vigor to the TPD programmes since training is embedded in the school and classroom contexts and this gives teachers the opportunity to see teaching and learning as it happens in real time in their school contexts (Lawrence & Chong, 2010). However, this type of TPD is not practiced in Zimbabwe. Furthermore, in Singapore teachers' learning is supported by "One Portal All Learners" (OPAL), an online platform with several content management repositories containing useful information and learning materials. In Zimbabwe, distance education has been and is still being used as a form of TPD to upgrade teachers' content knowledge. Similarly, the Advanced Certificate in Education is used as professional development for mathematics and science teachers who have no teaching qualifications in South Africa. The Advanced Certificate in Education is used to address the issue of underqualified teachers in the system.

The MOE in Singapore encourages schools to provide at least one hour of curricular time per week for teachers to actively engage in school-based TPD initiatives. Each teacher is provided 100 hours of training per year and most of these hours are scheduled during working hours. Although undertaking this training is optional, most teachers do participate (Bautista et al., 2015). Similarly, in Zimbabwe, teachers engage in TPD activities on a voluntary basis (Mtetwa et al., 2015). They further highlight that teachers seem to value TPDs essentially for personal career while providers value TPDs in terms of improving pass rates. By the same token, TPD in South Africa is also voluntary despite the CTPD system which leads to accumulation of points by teachers.

Challenges Faced in Trying to Implement Highly Effective and/or Innovative TPD Mechanisms

Generally the three countries seem to share common challenges. The economic challenges and the current COVID-19 pandemic demand training that will provide teachers with not only skills for work but also skills for life and livelihood opportunities. In Zimbabwe and South Africa there is poor or non-participation of teachers in TPD activities (Mahere, 2018; Mtetwa et al., 2015) alludes to the non-participation of educators to inaccessibility of information technology resources, particularly for those schools where network is poor. Outstanding also, as Buczynski and Hansen (2010) and Kennedy (2016) observed, is the mismatch between the skills being developed by the training system and the expectation of the labour market in the Zimbabwean system. In addition, teachers were also found to have outdated knowledge of the subject due to inadequate or non-existent internship programme

(Kennedy 2016; Meissel, Parr, & Timperley, 2016). The study also established that teachers encounter many challenges including lack of support from school heads and poor funding for professional development activities. In some cases, teachers were expected to use their own resources to attend professional development workshops (Maphosa & Chisango, 2013). However, in Singapore the MOE sponsors all teacher professional development programmes.

A significant number of researchers who have conducted research focusing on Contemporary Approaches to Teacher Professional Development (Hill, Beisiegel, & Jacob 2013; Meyers, Molefe, Brandt, Zhu, & Dhillon, 2016; Osborne, Borko, Fishman, Gomez Zaccarelli, Berson, Busch, Tseng, 2019;) concur that yesterday's TPD programmes have failed to produce a teacher for today's world and the authorities have therefore called for a paradigm shift guided by modern trends and the demands of the labour market. Other authorities (Borko, Jacobs, & Koellner, 2010; Buczynski & Hansen, 2010; Mtetwa et al., 2015; Mukeredzi, 2016) observed some common challenges contributing to the demise of TPD programmes. Among challenges cited were the system curricula which fail to address the employment needs of the learners, inadequate infrastructure, obsolete machinery and outdated course outlines.

Regardless of all the resources in place to support TPD in Singapore, there are also challenges and constraints important to consider. Marco-Bujosa, McNeill, Gonzalez-Howard, and Loper (2017), in a study focused on characteristics of academic programmes serving trainee teachers in Singapore, established the mismatch between technology used to train teachers and that used in the school system. The observed mismatch was attributed to the inadequate collaboration between training institutions, industries and ministerial policies. Furthermore, some teachers have high teaching loads, various academic responsibilities such as marking, meeting with parents and administrative duties like sitting in committees. In the Zimbabwean context, Esau and Mpofu (2017) concur that increased load on the part of the teacher and mere negativity by teachers are some of the challenges in implementing TPD.

RECOMMENDATIONS

Lessons to Learn from Each Other

Zimbabwe, which rolled out a new curriculum in 2017 can learn a lot from South Africa and Singapore for the teachers to adjust to the needs of the new curriculum. As established from the study, Singapore has a well-coordinated policy on TPD.

The CPTD system used in South Africa on monitoring and controlling its TPD activities is a practice that Singapore and Zimbabwe can explore. However, South Africa needs to improve the CPTD system since it seems to have many challenges for teachers as shown in the study. South Africa and Zimbabwe have most of their TPD taking place outside schools. They can learn from Singapore where TPD is conducted in school settings with emphasis on collaboration and enhancement of unity among teachers. This helps improve teacher effectiveness and willingness to adopt new innovations. However, for these collaborations to be productive, teachers must have reasons to collaborate and instructional support should be facilitated by a 'more knowledgeable other' (Burns et al., 2016).

The study established that in Singapore teachers are given at least one hour of curricular time to engage in TPD activities, a practice which could be emulated by South Africa and Zimbabwe. Since the study also established that Singapore operates an online platform (OPAL) it would be important for South Africa and Zimbabwe to find out how it operates. Such a platform would help teachers since it has several content management repositories containing useful information and learning materials. Real time instructional coaching using appropriate and available technologies to provide on-going support will also shift TPD from traditional workshops to more support-based interventions. Furthermore, technologies such as radios, telephones, televisions and internet can offer teachers in low-resource environment access to content, new curriculum and a variety of learning experiences (Burns et al., 2016).

South Africa and Zimbabwe were found to have challenges of funding TPD activities while Singapore sponsors all the activities. It would be essential to establish the funding mechanisms for TPD. From the study, it can be argued that Singapore's comprehensive set of TPD resources, considered as a whole, presents the features of high quality TPD described in the literature (Baustista et al., 2015). Therefore, South Africa and Zimbabwe can learn a lot from Singapore in order to improve their TPD activities. However, countries should not indiscriminately copy other countries' successful practices but should learn from each other and find out effective ways that suit their own circumstances. It is argued that TPD can be customized or contexualised to adapt to local situations (Darling-Hammond et al., 2017; Galaczi et al., 2018). For example, in Singapore teachers are offered different TPD training routes depending on the level of expertise (beginner, experienced, expert (Hairon & Dimmock, 2011). Staff developers are appointed in many schools to facilitate the matching between teachers' future career goals and available learning opportunities. This provides teachers with TPD that is tailored to their competencies, needs and interests.

FUTURE RESEARCH DIRECTIONS

The study focused on professional development for educators in Singapore, South Africa and Zimbabwe. The analysis of the discussion showed that much of the teachers professional development of Singapore in primary and secondary schools occur within school settings. In South Africa most of the teacher professional development activities take place outside schools and similarly in Zimbabwe teacher professional development are held as seminars, workshops and conferences outside the school setting. Thus, this suggests that further research on the effectiveness of school based teacher professional development programs could be done. The current study showed that in Zimbabwe there is a mismatch between skills being developed during professional development of educators and the expectations of the labour market. Therefore, a study to establish teacher professional development and its impact on teacher and student learning could be carried out. The study reveals that initial teacher training in Zimbabwe is conducted at teachers' training colleges. The colleges are affiliated to universities who are responsible for quality assurance and certification of graduates. Singapore has only one teachers' training college: National Institute of Education operating at Nanyang Technological University whilst in South Africa initial teacher training is done at universities. Therefore, a quantitative study on the influence of teachers' background and professional development on students' achievement could be established.

CONCLUSION

The purpose of the paper is to compare TPD systems in Singapore, South Africa and Zimbabwe. Professional development of teachers is a life-long process that starts at initial teacher education and ends at retirement. It is important for countries to ensure that provision for teachers' initial education, early career support and further professional development is well coordinated, coherent, adequately resourced and quality assured. From the study, it was established that the three countries have initial teacher education in universities and teachers' colleges. However, a variety of TPD activities were carried out at different levels in each country. Whilst Singapore has a clear policy on TPD, Zimbabwe does not have one. Although South Africa follows the CPTD system which is monitored by SACE more still needs to be done to ensure the engagement of all teachers. Therefore, Zimbabwe and South Africa can learn from Singapore on how to draft a TPD policy. Furthermore, it was found out that Singapore places much emphasis on collaborative and community-oriented forms of TPD, which are deemed to enhance not only teachers' content and pedagogical knowledge, but also to bring about a sense of belonging and solidarity among teachers.

The OECD (2019) TALIS confirms that 84% of Singaporean teachers supported each other in implementing new ideas due to collaborative and community-oriented TPD.

All the three countries utilised Subject panels although in different names. The effectiveness of Learning Area Platform introduced in Zimbabwe in 2019 still need to be evaluated. The Subject Chapters in Singapore were found to be effective since they ranged from formal TPD activities to reform type TPD activities. Subject Clusters in South Africa seemed to have challenges when they were implemented in Mpumalanga.

The three countries were found to have some challenges like poor or non-participation by teachers and high teaching loads. Zimbabwe and South Africa were found to have inadequate resources allocated for TPD activities. Despite all the resources for TPD, Singapore still faced challenges of inaccessibility especially for primary school teachers who could not attend TPD for other subjects which they did specialise in although they were teaching them. Lack of support from school heads and poor funding for TPD were cited as other challenges in Zimbabwe and South Africa. However, it was established that the MOE sponsors all TPD activities in Singapore. It can be concluded that South Africa and Zimbabwe have a lot to learn from Singapore which seems to have features of high quality TPD. Close collaboration between the teacher training colleges and the labour market is important in aligning the curriculum with requisite skills needed in the labour market. The active engagement of the industry through work placements and the design of training programmes are crucial for the success of the TPD programme. From the findings, recommendations are that there is need for cooperation between countries to strengthen teacher professional development systems to enhance learner performance. However, countries should not indiscriminately copy successful practices but should learn from each other and find out effective ways that suit their own circumstances.

REFERENCES

Archibald, S., & Coggshall, J. G. (2011). *High Quality Professional Development for All Teachers: Effectively Allocating Resources*. National Centre for Teacher Quality.

Bautista, A., & Ortega-Ruiz, R. (2015). Teacher Professional Development: International Perspectives and Approaches. *Psychology. Social Education, 7*(3), 240–251.

Bautista, A., Wong, J., & Gopinathan, S. (2015). Teacher professional development in Singapore: Depicting the landscape. *Psychology. Social Education, 7*(3), 311–326. doi:10.25115/psye.v7i3.523

Bett, H. K. (2016). The cascade model of teachers' CPD in Kenya: A time for change? *Cogent Education, 3*, 1–9. doi:10.1080/2331186X.2016.1139439

Borko, H. (2004). Professional development and teacher learning: Mapping the terrain. *Educational Researcher, 33*(8), 3–15. doi:10.3102/0013189X033008003

Borko, H., Jacobs, J., & Koellner, K. (2010). Contemporary approaches to teacher professional development. In E. Baker, B. McGaw, & P. Peterson (Eds.), *International encyclopedia of education* (3rd ed.). Elsevier. doi:10.1016/B978-0-08-044894-7.00654-0

Bowen, G. A. (2009). Document Analysis as a Qualitative Research Method. *Qualitative Research Journal, 9*(2), 27–40. doi:10.3316/QRJ0902027

Buczynski, S., & Hansen, C. B. (2010). Impact of professional development on teacher practice: Uncovering connections. *Teaching and Teacher Education, 26*(3), 599-607. doi:10.1016/j.tate.2009.09.006

Burns, M., Lawrie, J., & Inter-agency Network for Education in Emergencies Secretariat. (2016, October 5). *Education for All. Global Partnership for Education Blog.* http://www.inee.org/en/blog/new-publication-where-its-needed-most-quality-professional-development-for

Chen, J. Q., & McCray, J. (2012). A Conceptual framework for Teacher Professional Development: The Whole Teacher Approach, NHSA Dialog. *A Research-to-Practice Journal for the Early Childhood Field, 15*(1), 8-23.

Chikoko, V. (2007). The cluster system as an innovation: Perceptions of Zimbabwean teachers and school heads. *African Education Review, 4*(1), 42–57. doi:10.1080/18146620701412142

Dalby, D. (2021). Professional learning through collaborative research in mathematics. *Professional Development in Education, 47*(4), 710–724. doi:10.1080/19415257.2019.1665571

Darling-Hammond, L. (2017). Teacher education around the world: What can we learn from international practice? *European Journal of Teacher Education, 40*(3), 291–309. doi:10.1080/02619768.2017.1315399

Darling-Hammond, L., Heyler, M. E., & Gardener, M. (2017). *Effective Teacher Professional Development.* Learning Policy Institute. doi:10.54300/122.311

De Vries, S., Jansen, E. P. W. A., & Van de Grift, W. J. C. M. (2013). Profiling teachers' continuous professional development and the relation with their beliefs about learning and teaching. *Teaching and Teacher Education, 33*(1), 78–89. doi:10.1016/j.tate.2013.02.006

Delport, A., & Makaye, J. (2009). Clustering schools to improve teacher professional development: Lessons learnt from a Zimbabwean case study. *Africa Education Review, 6*(1), 96–105. doi:10.1080/18146620902857608

Department of Basic Education. (2018). Teacher Professional Development Master Plan 2017-2022. Republic of South Africa.

Department of Education. (2007). National Policy Framework for Teacher Education and Development in South Africa. Government Gazette 29832.

Desimone, L. M. (2009). Improving impact studies of teachers' professional development: Toward better conceptualisations and measures. *Educational Researcher, 38*(3), 181–199. doi:10.3102/0013189X08331140

Desimone, L. M., & Garet, M. (2015). Best practices in Teachers' Professional Development in the United States. *Psychology. Social Education, 7*(3), 252–263.

Esau, H., & Mpofu, J. (2017). The preparedness of primary schools to implement the grade 3 new curriculum in Zimbabwe: A Case study of Bulawayo metropolitan primary schools. *European Journal of Social Sciences Studies, 2*(4), 104–116.

Gaible, E., & Burns, M. (2005). *Using Technology to Train Teachers.* http://www.infodev.org/en/Publication.13.html

Galaczi, E., Nye, A., Poulter, M., & Allen, H. (2018). *Teacher Professional Development: Cambridge Assessment English Perspectives.* University of Cambridge.

Gomba, G. K. B. (2019). Challenges faced by Educators in Implementation of Continuous Professional Teacher Development in South Africa. *Teacher Education in the 21st Century.* . doi:10.5772/intechopen.84836

Guldenhuys, J. L., & Oosthuizen, L. C. (2015). Challenges influencing teachers' involvement in Continuous Professional Development: A South African Perspective. *Teaching and Teacher Education, 51*, 203–212. doi:10.1016/j.tate.2015.06.010

Guskey, T. R. (2005). Five key concepts kick off the process: Professional provides the power to implement standards. *Journal of Staff Development, 26*(1), 36–40.

Hairon, S., & Dimmock, C. (2011). Singapore schools and professional learning communities: Teacher professional development and school leadership in an Asian hierarchical system. *Educational Review*, *64*(4), 405–424. doi:10.1080/00131911.2011.625111

Hill, H. C., Beisiegel, M., & Jacob, R. (2013). Professional development research: Consensus, crossroads, and challenges. *Educational Researcher*, *42*(9), 476–487. doi:10.3102/0013189X13512674

Hogan, D., & Gopinathan, S. (2008). Knowledge management, sustainable innovation, and pre-service teacher education in Singapore. *Teachers and Teaching*, *14*(4), 369–384. doi:10.1080/13540600802037793

Johns, L. A., & Sosibo, Z. C. (2019). Constraints in the implementation of continuing professional teacher development policy in the Western Cape, South Africa. *The Journal of Higher Education*, *33*(5), 130–145.

Kangai, C., & Bukaliya, R. (2011). Teacher Development through open distance learning: The case for Zimbabwe. *International Journal on New Trends in Education and Their Implications*, *2*(13), 124–141.

Kennedy, M. (2016). How does professional development improve teaching? *Review of Educational Research*, *86*(4), 945–980. Advance online publication. doi:10.3102/0034654315626800

Lam, B. H. (2015). Teacher Professional Development in Hong Kong Compared to Anglosphere: The Role of Confucian Philosophy. *Psychology. Social Education*, *7*(3), 295–310. doi:10.25115/psye.v7i3.521

Lawrence, C. A., & Chong, W. H. (2010). Teacher collaborative learning through the lesson study: Identifying pathways for instructional success in a Singapore high school. *Asia Pacific Education Review*, *11*(4), 565–572. doi:10.100712564-010-9103-3

Lee, M. Y., & Choy, B. H. (2017). Mathematical teacher noticing: The key to learning from lesson study. In E.O. Shack, M.H. Fisher & J.A. Wilhelm (Eds.), Teacher noticing: Bridging and broadening perspectives, contexts, and frameworks. Springer.

Little, J. W. (2012). Professional community and professional development in the learning-centred school. In M. Kooy & K. van Veen (Eds.), *Teacher learning that matters: International perspectives*. Routledge.

Mahere, S. M. (2018). Clinical Supervision Model: Its role in the Professional Development of Teachers in Zimbabwe. *Zimbabwe Journal of Education*, *30*(3).

Mangwaya, E., Blignaut, S., & Pillay, S. K. (2016). The readiness of schools in Zimbabwe for the implementation of early childhood education. *South African Journal of Education*, *36*(1), 792. doi:10.15700aje.v36n1a792

Maphosa, A., & Chisango, F. F. T. (2016). Why Educational Practitioners Resist Staff Development Programmes: Evidence from Binga and Hwange Districts, Zimbabwe. *Greener Journal of Educational Research, 6*(2), 44-51.

Marcelo, C. (2009). Professional development of teachers: Past and Future. *Educational Sciences Journal*, *8*, 2–20.

Marco-Bujosa, L. M., McNeill, K. L., Gonzalez-Howard, M., & Loper, S. (2017). An exploration of teacher learning from an educative reform-oriented science curriculum: Case studies of teacher curriculum use. *Journal of Research in Science Teaching, 54*(2), 141-168.

Meissel, K., Parr, J. M., & Timperley, H. S. (2016). Can professional development of teachers reduce disparity in student achievement? *Teaching and Teacher Education, 58*, 163-173. doi:10.1016/j.tate.2016.05.01

Meyers, C. V., Molefe, A., Brandt, W. C., Zhu, B., & Dhillon, S. (2016). Impact results of the eMINTS professional development validation study. *Educational Evaluation and Policy Analysis*, *38*(3), 455–476. doi:10.3102/0162373716638446

Mhakure, D. (2019). School-based mathematics teacher professional learning: A theoretical position on the lesson study approach. *South African Journal of Education*, *39*(Supplement 1), S1–S8. doi:10.15700aje.v39ns1a1754

Mhumure, G. (2017). *Zimbabwean teachers' perspective on the History Subject Panels as an Innovation for professional development* [Unpublished PhD Thesis]. University of Free State.

Milne, A., & Mhlolo, M. (2021). Lessons for South Africa from Singapore's gifted education – A comparative study. *South African Journal of Education*, *41*(1), 1–8. doi:10.15700aje.v41n1a1839

Ministry of Education (MOE). (2010). *Schools as professional learning communities*. MOE.

Ministry of Primary and Secondary Education (MoPSE). (2014). *Curriculum Framework for Primary and Secondary Education 2015-2022*. Curriculum Development Unit.

Mtetwa, D., Chabongora, B., Ndemo, Z., & Maturure, E. (2015). Features of Continuous Professional Development (CPD) of School Mathematics Teachers in Zimbabwe. *International Journal of Educational Sciences*, 8(1), 135–147. doi:10.1080/09751122.2015.11917599

Mukeredzi, T. G. (2016). Teacher Professional Development outside the lecture room: Voices of Professionally Unqualified Practicing Teachers in Rural Zimbabwe Secondary Schools. *Global Education Review*, 3(4), 84–106.

Mullis, I. V. S., Martin, M. O., Goh, S., & Cotter, K. (2016). *Teachers, Teacher Education and Professional Development in South Africa. TIMSS 2015 Encyclopedia: Educational Policy and Curriculum in Mathematics and Science.* TIMSS & PIRLS International Study Centre.

National Institute of Education (NIE). (2009). A Teacher Education Model for the 21st Century. NIE.

OECD. (2019). TALIS 2018 Results (Volume 1): Teachers and School Leaders as Lifelong Learners. TALIS, OECD Publishing. doi:10.1787/1d0bc92a-en

Ogegbo, A. A., Gaigher, E., & Salagram, T. (2019). Benefits and challenges of lesson study: A case of teaching Physical Science in South Africa. *South African Journal of Education*, 39(1), 1–9. Advance online publication. doi:10.15700aje.v39n1a1680

Ono, Y., & Ferreira, J. (2010). A case study of continuing teacher professional development through lesson study in South Africa. *South African Journal of Education*, 30(1), 59–74. doi:10.15700aje.v30n1a320

Organisation for Economic Co-operation and Development (OECD). (2014). *A Teachers' Guide to TALIS 2013: Teaching and Learning International Survey.* Paris: TALIS, OECD Publishing.

Osborne, J. F., Borko, H., Fishman, E., Gomez Zaccarelli, F., Berson, E., Busch, K. C., & Tseng, A. (2019). Impacts of a practice-based professional development programme on elementary teachers' facilitation of and student engagement with scientific argumentation. *American Educational Research Journal*, 56(4), 1067-1112. doi:10.3102/0002831218812059

Postholm, M. B. (2012). Teachers' professional development: A theoretical review. *Educational Research*, 54(4), 405–429. doi:10.1080/00131881.2012.734725

Rauf, P. A., Ali, S. K. S., & Noor, N. A. M. (2017). The Relationship Between Models Of Teachers Professional Development And Teachers Instructional Practices In The Classrooms In The Primary Schools In The State Of Selangor, Malaysia. *International Journal of Education, Psychology and Counseling, 2*(5), 120–132.

South African Council for Educators. (2013). *CPTD Management Handbook*. South African Council for Educators.

South African Council for Educators (SACE). (2011). *Redefining the role and functions of South African Council for Educators*. South African Council for Educators.

Steyn, G. M. (2008). Continuing professional development for teachers in South Africa and social learning systems: Conflicting conceptual frameworks of learning. *Koers, 73*(1), 15–31. doi:10.4102/koers.v73i1.151

Tan, C. Y., & Dimmock, C. (2014). How 'top-performing' Asian School system formulates and implements policy: The case of Singapore. *Educational Management Administration & Leadership, 17*(4), 114–123. doi:10.1177/1741143213510507

Tarusikirwa, M. C. (2016). Modeling Teacher Development through Open and Distance Learning: A Zimbabwean Experience. *Universal Journal of Educational Research, 4*(12), 2706–2715. doi:10.13189/ujer.2016.041203

Taylor, N. (2008). *What's wrong with South African Schools?* Paper presented at what's working in School Development Conference, Boksburg, South Africa.

Wang, X., Kim, B., Lee, J. W. Y., & Kim, M. S. (2014). Encouraging and being encouraged: Development of an epistemic community and teacher professional growth in a Singapore classroom. *Teaching and Teacher Education, 44*, 12–24. doi:10.1016/j.tate.2014.07.009

Wei, R. C., Darling-Hammond, L., & Adamson, F. (2010). *Professional development in the United States: Trends and challenges*. National Staff Development Council.

ADDITIONAL READING

Admiraal, W., Schenke, W., De Jong, L., Emmelot, Y., & Sligte, H. (2019). Schools as professional learning communities: What can schools do to support professional development of their teachers? *Professional Development in Education, 47*(4), 684–698. doi:10.1080/19415257.2019.1665573

Avalos, B. (2011). Teacher professional development in Teaching and Teacher Education over ten years. *Teaching and Teacher Education, 27*(1), 10–20. doi:10.1016/j.tate.2010.08.007

Barni, D., Danioni, F., & Benevene, P. (2019). Teachers' Self-Efficacy: The Role of Personal Values and Motivations for Teaching. *Frontiers in Psychology, 10*, 1645. Advance online publication. doi:10.3389/fpsyg.2019.01645 PMID:31354604

Dimmock, C. (2016). Conceptualising the research-practice-professional development nexus: Mobilizing schools as 'research-engaged' professional learning communities. *Professional Development in Education, 42*(1), 36–53. doi:10.1080/19415257.2014.963884

Jensvoll, M. J., & Lekang, T. (2018). Strengthening professionalism through cooperative learning. *Professional Development in Education, 44*(4), 466–475. doi:10.1080/19415257.2017.1376223

Kraft, M. A., & Papay, J. P. (2014). Can professional environments in schools promote teacher development? Explaining heterogeneity in returns to teaching experience. *Educational Evaluation and Policy Analysis, 36*(4), 476–500. doi:10.3102/0162373713519496 PMID:25866426

Opfer, V. D., & Pedder, D. G. (2011). The lost promise of teacher professional development in England. *European Journal of Teacher Education, 34*(1), 3–23. doi:10.1080/02619768.2010.534131

Thornton, K., & Cherrington, S. (2019). Professional learning in early childhood education: A vehicle for professional growth. *Professional Development in Education, 45*(3), 418–432. doi:10.1080/19415257.2018.1529609

KEY TERMS AND DEFINITIONS

Cascade Model: One of the teacher professional development model used to train a large number of in-service teachers in a short span of time. In this model, a number of teachers are often trained in a particular content, and they in turn go ahead and train their colleagues on the same.

Collaboration: Means working together with one or more people to complete a project or task or develop ideas or processes. In the workplace collaboration occurs when two or more people work together towards a common goal that benefits the team or organisation like a school.

Lesson Study: Is a Japanese model of teacher-led research in which a group of teachers work together to target an identified area for development in their students' learning. Using existing evidence, participants collaboratively research, plan, teach and observe a series of lessons, using ongoing discussion, reflection, and expert input to track and refine their interventions.

In-Service Teacher Training: The process by which teachers engage in further education or training to refresh or upgrade their professional knowledge, skills, and practices in the course of their employment.

National Institute of Education (NIE): Is an autonomous institute of Nanyang Technological University in Singapore. The institute is the sole education institute for teachers in Singapore.

Policymakers: A member of a government department, legislature, or other organization for making new laws or rules.

Subject Cluster: Involves bringing together teachers of the same subject from different schools to facilitate pedagogical activities to improve quality of teaching and learning by addressing the diverse needs of all learners.

Teacher Self-Efficacy: Refers to teacher's belief in his/her ability to successfully cope with tasks, obligations and challenges related to his/her professional role like didactical tasks or managing discipline in the classroom.

Chapter 12
Using ICT and Digital Tools in Teacher Professional Development in the UAE

Ghadah Hassan Al Murshidi
UAE University, UAE

Elaine Wright
UAE University, UAE

ABSTRACT

The teaching profession is a constantly changing, diverse environment, striving to meet the needs of the youth of today. One aspect which has transformed teaching is information and communications technology. However, one area which has been slower to embrace this digital era is professional development. Even though continuous teacher professional development is seen as an important aspect of equipping teachers to be effective in the classroom leading to best practice, time constraints, budgets and timetabling difficulties can hinder teachers' access to high quality professional development programs. This chapter will aim to highlight ways the online learning environment has been maximized in order to enhance the professional practice of teachers within the country. The chapter will give a brief outline of other ways in which the UAE has sought to enhance education via online methods; how the visions and goals of the nation's leaders depend upon effective, efficient, and high-quality teachers; and an outline of various forms of online professional development.

DOI: 10.4018/978-1-7998-9278-6.ch012

INTRODUCTION

The teaching profession is a constantly changing, diverse environment, striving to meet the needs of the youth of today. One aspect which has transformed teaching is Information and Communications Technology (ICT). It has permeated every aspect of teaching and is used within the teaching community to further the education of children in all subject areas. However, one area which has been slower to embrace this digital era is professional development (PD). This is despite the fact that continuous teacher professional development (TPD) is seen as an important aspect of equipping teachers to be effective in the classroom leading to best practice, time constraints, budgets and timetabling difficulties can hinder teacher's access to high quality professional development programs. TPD can be considered in both the preservice and in-service aspects, with research showing that both ends of the teaching profession need to be invoked when promoting ICT in teacher professional development. Professional development is key for teachers to encourage and equip them to meet the needs and demands in the constantly changing environment of the modern school, especially within the rapidly developing and progressive country of the United Arab Emirates (UAE). This relatively young nation, which has seen rapid growth and globalization in recent years, strives for a world class education system, which must rely on well trained teachers. The UAE has invested heavily in teacher development and has embraced various forms of ICT and digital tools in teacher professional development. Therefore, this chapter will aim to highlight, through a case study, ways in which the UAE has maximized the online learning environment in order to enhance the professional practice of teachers within the country, how the visions and goals of the nation's leaders depend upon effective, efficient and high-quality teachers, along with an outline of how various forms of online professional development, from online courses to YouTube channels, are used in the UAE to enhance teacher professional development.

BACKGROUND

The UAE: A Country of Rapid Changes, Progressive Goals and an Aspiring Education System

The country of the United Arab Emirates is a relatively young nation. Situated in the Arabian Peninsula, the country was created in 1971 and has since developed at a remarkably fast pace, driven in large by the wealth created by the discovery of oil. Since the opening of the first modern school in the UAE, in the Emirate of Sharjah in 1930 (Alhebsi et al., 2015), there have been many changes in the UAE's schooling system which has given way to the modern, global education system the country has today. The country's "Vision 2021" is "to make the United Arab Emirates among the best countries in the world" (UAE Vision 2021, 2018a) and this vision is realized through investment into the education system.

By establishing state-of-the-art technological infrastructure in the UAE, the government has taken the initiative to develop proactive solutions and thereby keeping pace within a global economy. Therefore, the UAE has become a role model for other countries in the world (Al Grug, 2020). It is undeniable that the UAE places a huge focus on education. As His Highness (H.H.) Sheikh Zayed Bin Sultan Al Nahyan, founder of the UAE noted, "The greatest use that can be made of wealth is to invest it in creating generations of educated and trained people" (Embassy of the United Arab Emirates Cultural Division, 2011, para.1). He also said, "The real asset of any advanced nation is its people, especially the educated ones, and the prosperity and success of the people are measured by the standard of their education" (Embassy of the United Arab Emirates Cultural Division, 2011, para 1). Therefore, high quality education will enable the people of the UAE to fulfil the goals and aspirations of its leaders. In another directive, Vision 2030, the UAE government states that they wish to become focused on both learning and culture to provide high quality education for those in the country (Government of Abu Dhabi, 2008).

There have been several noted examples of how the country has embraced online learning in a wider sense. Hamdan Bin Mohammed Smart University established in 2002, is the first Ministry of Education accredited eLearning academic institution in the UAE and is a fine example of the sound ICT enabled education infrastructure in the country. The university over the years has created a framework which has designed, developed and implemented flexible and responsive platforms to facilitate learners' access, interactivity and learning as well as the ability to track their progress throughout their studies (Al Mansoori, 2020). Another ICT initiative in UAE was the establishment of Mohammed bin Rashid Smart Learning Programme in the year 2012. The programme was designed in such a way as to build a solid educational infrastructure, train teachers and prepare students to use technological devices in education (Al Hammadi, 2020)

Therefore, it is seen that as the UAE and its educational system has developed at a rapid pace and through the visions and directives of the nation's leaders, the country seeks to have a "first rate education system" (UAE Vision 2021, 2018a). As a result, teacher professional development needs to be at the crux of this movement to address existing challenges in the present era of modernization. Teachers must be provided with adequate training to play their part in becoming nation builders. The evidence presented in this section suggests that with the UAE building an efficient infrastructure in order to create a competitive knowledge economy (UAE Vision

2021, 2018a), the world of education in the UAE has been effectively utilizing this resource to provide online, high quality teacher professional development.

A Digital Age and Information and Communication Technology (ICT)

Information and communication technologies have occupied a predominant place in every discourse of life ranging from business and public policy to education and tele medicine. UNESCO (2021, para.1) defined ICT as "a diverse set of technological tools and resources that can be used profoundly to communicate, create, disseminate, store, and manage information." In the academic world it may be impossible to imagine a future learning environment without the support of any form of ICT enabled tools (Punie et al., 2006). Information and Communications Technology has the great potential to transform the social structure and operation procedures, and thereby enable educational institutions to react and change (Kozma, 2002; Oh, 2003)

Kozma (2002) is of the opinion that ICT is becoming the heart of preparing students and teachers for participation in a teaching and learning society. Therefore, ICT needs to be harnessed in teacher professional development in order to respond to changes happening on the global education front. By establishing a state-of-the-art technological infrastructure alongside a wealth of initiatives on the part of the government to develop proactive solutions to current situations, thereby keeping pace with changes and emergencies, the UAE has become a role model for other countries in the world (Al Grug, 2020). Even though the education system in the country is relatively young compared to other global counterparts, the nation has invested heavily in ensuring state of the art technological infrastructure when imparting high quality education, comparable to the best in the world.

Digital Tools in Teacher Professional Development: A Review of the Literature

Generally, teacher professional development is expensive, eats into staff members' time and is not personalized (ALLT 2020, January 3rd). These problems are not confined to one country or even continent, but are global issues (ALLT 2020, January 3rd). Jung (2005) found that globally, some countries such as Singapore, USA and Canada used ICT as means to deliver the teacher training itself. Other countries, for example, the UK, Korea, South Africa, and Sweden, as well as others, used ICT to enable teachers to have enhanced opportunities for professional development and networking. Jung (2005, p.95) noted "Teachers can be trained to learn HOW to use ICT or teachers can be trained VIA ICT" and both methods are being employed worldwide, depending on the situation. In an African context, Mwalongo, (2011) found that teachers in Tanzania used ICT in order to access self-study materials online for their PD, which in turn, aided them in their classroom practice. Carlson and Gadio (2002) shares that in Costa Rica, teachers have been trained using online training with appropriate support, which has encouraged these teachers to adopt more ICT in their classrooms. Universities in Malaysia, UK and Finland are using online professional development in higher education (HE) (ALLT 2020, January 3rd) and there are organizations who provide global, online professional development for HE institutions such as Qedex (ALLT 2020, January 3rd). Whilst online PD is still in the developing stages in the UAE, Alhashmi and Moussa-Inaty (2021) did find that teachers in the UAE valued online methods to share resources, whist finding traditional in-house training less than favorable. Recent studies have demonstrated a need for high quality PD in the education sector within the UAE (Alawani & Singh, 2018; Elatawneh & Sidek, 2021).

The Importance of Context

As with face-to-face professional development, not all online PD is the same. Carlson & Gadio (2002) identified four different types of teacher professional development, all of which, have an online component and can be used to either complement face to face teaching or be used as standalone methods of PD. They suggest that it is not a "one model fits all" approach when it comes to teacher professional development. It is clearly important to situate the course within the educational and cultural context where it sits in order to make it relevant (ALLT 2020, January 3rd; Carlson & Gadio, 2002). Despite many counties in the world employing similar models of ICT within schools, Albion et al. (2015) also calls for some cultural diversity and contextualization to teacher professional development programs. Alawani and Singh (2018) recognises that within the UAE, teachers need more bespoke training and mobile TPD is one way to achieve this goal. Studies have shown that within the UAE, teachers do see the need for teacher professional development which is relevant to the context and subjects they teach (Alawani & Singh, 2018; Alhashmi & Moussa-Inaty, 2021; Forawi, 2015). Whilst this is a gap, it could also be a challenge with online TPD in the UAE as many of the international courses for teachers may be offered in English and not all teaching staff may have a mastery of the English language. Alhashmi and Moussa-Inaty, (2021) found that UAE teachers expressed frustrations with courses in English as some staff had difficulties in understanding and would have found TPD in Arabic more beneficial. Therefore, care needs to be taken when considering online TPD to ensure there are no language barriers.

Community and Online Teacher Professional Development

From a pedagogical perspective, teachers working together online with instructors, peers, and experts share and collectively construct their skills and knowledge as well as provide feedback (Carlson & Gadio, 2002; Spiteri & Chang Rundgren, 2017) not only nationally, but globally, adding an international perspective to personal development (Jung, 2005). Electronic Personal Development (ePD) was the term used by Anderson and Henderson (2004) when considering teacher professional development in Australia. They saw that teachers could use a mix of face-to-face learning, which was then followed up by learning online. Although in this study using a VLE allowed collaboration, Anderson and Henderson (2004) notes that there needs to be "social presence" with online environments to allow for better communication and relationships. Vrasidas and Glass (2007) also advocate that PD through the medium of ICT allows for communities of practice to develop and encourages collaboration amongst teachers, allowing professionals to work together, share experiences (either synchronously or asynchronously) and learn from one another, which is key to good PD (Vrasidas & Glass, 2007). Wang et al., (2014) note that the formation of these virtual learning communities can encourage and support teachers in the development and implementation of new ideas. Teachers remarked that online collaboration encouraged them to actively participate in learning and the course was seen in a positive light as its contents directly related to classroom practice (Wang et al., 2014). Teachers fedback that they enjoyed belonging to a learning community, further strengthening the idea that teachers enjoy learning together. Prestridge and Tondeur's (2015) study found that blogs were seen as a helpful method to allow teachers to reflect on their practice. The ability to challenge others' opinions online was noted by Prestridge and Tondeur (2015) as being an important aspect of online PD, but there needs to be a sense of community between learners and mentors in order for this to happen. Spiteri and Chang Rundgren (2017) noted that Maltese teachers also highlighted the importance of collaboration which was enhanced through the use of digital technology. Communities of practice were also seen as helpful in Australia to allow ICT teachers to access resources and provide support for one another (Pearson, 2003).

Laurillard, (2016) described how the tailored design of a MOOC (Massive Open Online Course) could aid with ICT teacher PD. Teachers using this course for PD valued the online discussion and peer contributions. Despite pointing out the lack of collaboration which took place on the course, mainly due to the constraints of the MOOC platform used (Cousera), it was seen that this type of course could seek to provide PD to teachers in the subject area of ICT in many parts of the world (Laurillard, 2016). This is another challenge facing the use of ICT in teacher professional development, that is, how to design courses which encourage collaboration and are of interest to the user.

The Flexible Nature of Using ICT in Teacher Professional Development

Flexibility is one of the many benefits with the online model of professional development as it has the ability to adapt, especially to the lives of lady teachers who often juggle work and family life (Vrasidas & Glass, 2007) as well as giving greater autonomy to the teacher for their learning (Prestridge & Tondeur, 2015), which is a very attractive draw for busy teachers who desire a more personalized approach. Studies show that teachers face time pressures which prevents them investing in TPD (Bennison and Goos, 2010; Forawi, 2015). Forawi, (2015) identified that science teachers within the UAE had a lack of opportunities to take part in professional development, despite recognizing TPD as important for their career and that teachers felt held back from these opportunities due to heavy workloads, long working hours or the cost of face-to-face PD programs. Therefore, it is clear that the flexibility offered by online teacher professional development could allow more science teachers in the UAE to undertake courses at a time convenient to them. Whilst governments can make their own flexible, tailored online courses for teachers, there are other opportunities available over the internet which teachers can use to develop their practice. Koukis and Jimoyiannis (2019) found that MOOCs were an effective form of TPD. One participant, when highlighting the flexibility which online PD affords, said they "found the online professional development easily accessible, through a "click" and he could "see what was going on" (Prestridge & Tondeur, 2015). This is an attractive option for teachers who can undertake PD at their own time and pace (Carlson & Gadio, 2002).

The Use of E-Portfolios

The use of e-portfolios is another method of incorporating ICT into TPD. Bala et al., (2012) studied how twenty English language teachers used e-portfolios in Malaysia. The e-portfolio allowed the teachers to collate, not only items such as their CV, but also audio and video clips, which enabled the collection to be used for career planning and monitoring professional development. Results found that not only did the use of the e-portfolio enhance teacher professional development, but it facilitated teachers in collaborating with one another and allowed the teachers to become more proficient and confident in their use of technology. This, Bala et al., (2012) said would make teachers utilize ICT in the classroom more readily. Therefore, the use of ICT and digital tools in teacher professional development has not only been shown to benefit the teachers involved, but their students also. Vrasidas and Glass, (2007) also advocate for "web-based portfolios" to allow teachers to become reflective practitioners. E-portfolios have been used in the UAE to allow teachers to document their professional development in an electronic format. Ghany and Alzouebi, (2019) found that teachers in the UAE had positive experiences with e-portfolios as they align with many Smart objectives within the UAE, as well as allowing teachers to document large amounts of information in a simple, attractive way which can be shared easily. However, Ghany and Alzouebi, (2019) did note that there were sometimes issues due to technical difficulties as well as teachers being required to have hard copies as well as electronic copies of their portfolio.

Challenges of using ICT in Teacher Professional Development

As with any type of change, teachers must make time to accommodate to these new styles of PD (Vrasidas & Glass, 2007). Also, Stephenson (2010) identified that in the TPD field within the UAE, there had been a dependence on one off workshops and outside expertise being brought in to transmit knowledge. Therefore, this could be a challenge for online TPD, as it may take some time, within the UAE, for this method of professional development to be accepted. Albion et al., (2015) found that it is vital to gain the views and opinions of teachers when considering any professional development, especially in order to integrate the use of ICT successfully into a teacher's pedagogy. Therefore, it is a process which must not be rushed but implemented in a methodological way in order to encourage teachers to use and practice the idea. On a more global scale, Carlson and Gadio, (2002, p.127) cite problems such as "low bandwidth, telecommunications costs, limited computer access, etc" as problematic with online PD. Costs involved in learning are computers and internet, as well as the designing and maintenance of the course which must also be taken into consideration (Carlson & Gadio, 2002). Whilst online PD can be interactive, studies have shown that teachers in the UAE place value in classroom observations of colleagues and face to face discussions as effective methods of PD (Alhashmi & Moussa-Inaty, 2021). The value of these personal interactions cannot be underestimated, and this is an area where ICT cannot entirely fill the gap. In addition, the majority of schools in the UAE are staffed by expatriate teachers who are on short term work contracts, which can lead to a volatile staffing structure. Stephenson (2010) found that in the UAE, there was a high rate of staff turnover in education which made some aspects of TPD, such as building Communities of Practice, difficult. This is a specific challenge within the UAE which will need addressing to allow effective TPD through online communities.

Online Teacher Professional Development in the UAE

The UAE is one country which has contextualized its online P.D for teachers and has maximized the use of ICT to provide teachers with continuous opportunities for best practice within the context in which they are located. The UAE government clearly strives to push forward with progressive plans for the future of the nation. Once example is Vision 2021, which sought to incorporate the key aspects of a competitive knowledge economy as well as a first-rate education system throughout the country (UAE Vision 2021, 2018a). The UAE values investment in its youth and desires "for all schools, universities and students to be equipped with Smart systems and devices as a basis for all teaching methods, projects and research." (UAE Vision 2021, 2018b, para. 1). Therefore, it is of the upmost importance that teachers are well trained and equipped to meet these aspirations. The schooling system in the UAE is overseen by the Ministry of Education (MOE) whose vision is "Innovative education for a knowledge, pioneering, and global society" (United Arab Emirates Ministry of Education, 2020a, para 1). It is a vision of looking to the future and striving for the best possible outcomes in the field of education.

Therefore, one of the most important resources in this vision are the teachers who teach, encourage, and inspire the children to become active participants in the goals set forth by the leaders of the nation. It is well known that "the quality of an education system cannot exceed the quality of its teachers" (Schleicher, 2020, p iv). For this reason, teacher professional development has been prioritized within the UAE to build a strong education system where quality and skill drive education forward. In 2017, long before most of the educational world was accustomed to online training, the United Arab Emirates Ministry of Education spoke about "the transformation to smart teaching" (United Arab Emirates Ministry of Education, 2017). The desire was to maximize the use of ICT within schools in the UAE. When outlining a new plan for using more technology in education in 2017, the MOE spoke about their new, online training site "The Smart Training Platform" which aims at enrolling teachers in different training courses through the World Wide Web with the aim of upgrading their skills and developing their professional performance thus improving the outcomes of the Emirati school. This platform will also help the teacher attain relevant and modern experience and skills, and further enables him to manage the classroom utilizing modern methods and tools. (United Arab Emirates Ministry of Education, 2017, para. 4).

Therefore, the concept of teachers using ICT and online tools in teacher professional development has been a popular and well-known idea within the teaching community in the UAE for some time.

In addition, using modern online platforms such as YouTube, the channel "MOE training", by the UAE Ministry of Education has 2K subscribers and provides online videos which teachers can use formally and informally to further their professional development (MOE Training, n.d.). Teachers can access this at any time, at their own convenience, which is one of the benefits of online professional development. This is not only limited to teachers within the UAE, but is open to all, which demonstrates one of the strengths of using digital means of TPD, in that the resources are not confined to geographical boundaries, and it allows teachers to collaborate globally (Jung, 2005)

In recent days, in a rapid response to the Covid 19 pandemic, the UAE Ministry of Education, in collaboration with Hamdan Bin Mohammed Smart University in Dubai and the UNESCO Institute for Information Technologies in Education, developed two, free, online courses for teacher professional development, to prepare them for online teaching. The courses entitled "How to become a remote teacher in 24 hours" (available in 5 languages) and "How to design an online course in 24 hours" saw an impressive 81,000 student complete the online courses, in 60 countries, including teachers from the GCC and the United States of America (Hamdan Bin Mohammed Smart University, 2020a; Hamdan Bin Mohammed Smart University, 2020b). These courses cover various topics ranging from online learning design and learning management systems to planning an online lesson and practical examples (Hamdan Bin Mohammed Smart University, 2021a; Hamdan Bin Mohammed Smart University 2021b). This innovative approach has not only had benefits within the UAE but also further afield, highlighting the potential for cross collaboration amongst education professionals using ICT (Jung, 2005). Both courses were offered in Arabic (in addition to other languages), which made them directly applicable to not only the UAE but other Arabic speaking countries, as advocated by Alhashmi and Moussa-Inaty, (2021) who saw that teachers in the UAE expressed frustration at TPD courses only being offered in English. These courses received a range of very positive feedback from educators (Hamdan Bin Mohammed Smart University, 2021c) thereby highlighting the training gap which these courses filled. This is testament to the future vision of the nation and is another example where the UAE has the infrastructure and vision to utilize ICT and digital tools in online teacher professional development, not only to the benefit of their own teachers, but teachers worldwide also.

In December 2020, the UAE Ministry of Education held an online professional development virtual symposium for teachers. There were a variety of online workshops which teachers could "virtually attend" on topics ranging from multiple intelligences to career goals. Teachers could access these talks via Microsoft teams, in English and Arabic, over a period of two days (United Arab Emirates Ministry of Education, 2020b). This was a useful tool used to bring teachers together "virtually" to share and contribute to their field, an excellent example of collaboration and community in online professional development. Nonetheless, it is not only teachers who can benefit from online training. For schools to run effectively, school administration staff, teachers and senior leaders must work together to provide high quality education. March 2020 saw 25,000 school staff undertaking online training offered by the ministry of education (United Arab Emirates Ministry of Education, 2020c). It was identified that, through the training of a skilled workforce, the education system within the UAE can be "competitive" and "flexible" in order to meet the demands of the current climate (United Arab Emirates Ministry of Education, 2020c). These courses tackled topics such as online schooling and its associated platforms, as well as giving teachers an opportunity to see how to use these in online schooling. As advocated by several studies (Anderson & Henderson, 2004; Pearson, 2003; Prestridge & Tondeur, 2015; Spiteri & Chang Rundgren, 2017; Vrasidas & Glass, 2007; Wang et al., 2014), the UAE government utilized virtual learning communities to roll out the training (United Arab Emirates Ministry of Education, 2020c). This, as shown by Anderson and Henderson, (2004); Pearson, (2003); Prestridge and Tondeur, (2015); Spiteri and Chang Rundgren, (2017); Vrasidas and Glass, (2007) and Wang et al., (2014) would have promoted a sense of community and collaboration amongst those taking the course and thereby making the online learning more effective. In addition, through the MOE's online training system "learning curve", teachers were able to access fully online learning, either live, or through their virtual learning communities. The MoE website states: "the MoE has strived to lay the foundations of a smart education system that responds to the rapid technological developments in the field of education and employs them to improve the quality of its outputs" (United Arab Emirates Ministry of Education, 2020c, para.10).

With an established history of developing professional development for teachers online, the UAE continues to integrate this idea into new schemes. The MoE has recently launched the Education Professions Teachers License, to ensure "high quality" and "the best standards" in education (United Arab Emirates Ministry of Education, 2020d). This project is still in its infancy, however the MoE desires in the future, that teachers will compile an e-portfolio as part of their license renewal (United Arab Emirates Ministry of Education, 2020e), which has shown to be effective in other studies (Bala et al., 2012; Ghany & Alzouebi, 2019) thereby highlighting the integration of ICT into the professional development of the nation's teachers.

CONCLUSION

The literature points to the fact that there is a place in TPD to embrace digital and online tools and that there are many benefits to this style of PD. The UAE is an example of how high-quality teacher professional development can be carried out using ICT, in a form appropriate to the context, to place teachers in a globally connected community of quality teacher improvement. This chapter will be of benefit to school leadership, teacher trainers as well as teachers who are involved with both organizing, providing, and taking part in teacher professional development. Despite the use of ICT in TPD still being in its infancy in the UAE, this chapter is designed to encourage and challenge those in the education sector to maximize the opportunities which can be had with online TPD and to provide teachers with relevant, contextualized training which does not become a burden but seeks to be applicable to each and every teacher where they are at. There are few studies looking at using ICT for teacher professional development within the UAE. Further studies could look at teacher perceptions of using digital tools in TPD in the UAE and also on the most applicable tools to use within the UAE, when considering ICT in TPD.

REFERENCES

Al Grug, T. (2020). *UAE education system is a role model for other countries.* Gulf News. https://gulfnews.com/opinion/op-eds/uae-education-system-is-a-role-model-for-other-countries-1.72488846

Al Hammadi, H. I. (2020). *The Futures of Education after Covid 19. Regional Dialogue.* Unesco. https://en.unesco.org/sites/default/files/synthesis_report_future_of_education_webnair_1.pdf

Al Mansoori, H. E. H. (2020) *How the UAE's robust ICT infrastructure brought over 1 million students online amid COVID-19.* MyITU. https://www.itu.int/en/myitu/News/2020/09/21/08/01/UAE-ICTs-education-1-million-students-online-COVID-19

Alawani, A. S., & Singh, A. D. (2018). Exploring a New Innovative Approach for Teacher Professional Development in UAE: A Pilot Study. *Innovation Arabia, 11*, 101.

Albion, P. R., Tondeur, J., Forkosh-Baruch, A., & Peeraer, J. (2015). Teachers' professional development for ICT integration: Towards a reciprocal relationship between research and practice. *Education and Information Technologies*, *20*(4), 655–673. doi:10.100710639-015-9401-9

Alhashmi, M., & Moussa-Inaty, J. (2021). Professional learning for Islamic education teachers in the UAE. *British Journal of Religious Education*, *43*(3), 278–287. doi: 10.1080/01416200.2020.1853046

Alhebsi, A., Pettaway, L., & Waller, L. (2015). A history of education in the United Arab Emirates and Trucial Shiekdoms. *The Global eLearning Journal, 4*(1), 1-6.

ALLT. (2020, January 3rd). *Applied Linguistics & Language Teaching. Reframing Professional Development to be Effective, Efficient and Global* [Video]. YouTube. https://www.youtube.com/watch?v=yNlP0inr0iE

Anderson, N., & Henderson, M. (2004). e-PD: Blended models of sustaining teacher professional development in digital literacies. *E-Learning and Digital Media, 1*(3), 383–394. doi:10.2304/elea.2004.1.3.4

Bala, S. S., Mansor, W. F. A. W., Stapa, M., & Zakaria, M. H. (2012). Digital portfolio and professional development of language teachers. *Procedia: Social and Behavioral Sciences, 66,* 176–186. doi:10.1016/j.sbspro.2012.11.259

Bennison, A., & Goos, M. (2010). Learning to teach mathematics with technology: A survey of professional development needs, experiences and impacts. *Mathematics Education Research Journal, 22*(1), 31–56. doi:10.1007/BF03217558

Carlson, S., & Gadio, C. T. (2002). Teacher professional development in the use of technology. *Technologies for Education,* 118-132.

Elatawneh, H. A. A., & Sidek, S. B. (2021). Formulation of Theoretical Framework of Teaching Quality Factors Model for Professional Development for UAE Higher Education Institutions. *Psychology and Education Journal, 58*(2), 3755–3763.

Embassy of the United Arab Emirates Cultural Division. (2011). *Education in the United Arab Emirates.* Retrieved from http://www.uaecd.org/education-introduction

Forawi, S. (2015). Science Teacher Professional Development Needs in the United Arab Emirates. In Science Education in the Arab Gulf States (pp. 49-68). Rotterdam: Sense. doi:10.1007/978-94-6300-049-9_3

Ghany, S. A., & Alzouebi, K. (2019). Exploring Teacher Perceptions of Using E-portfolios in Public Schools in the United Arab Emirates. *International Journal of Education and Literacy Studies, 7*(4), 180–191. doi:10.7575/aiac.ijels.v.7n.4p.180

Government of Abu Dhabi. (2008). *The Abu Dhabi economic vision 2030.* https://u.ae/en/about-the-uae/strategies-initiatives-and-awards/local-governments-strategies-and-plans/abu-dhabi-economic-vision-2030

Hamdan Bin Mohammed Smart University. (2020a). *UAE equips teachers from around the world with distance learning skills.* https://www.hbmsu.ac.ae/news/uae-equips-teachers-around-world-distance-learning-skills

Hamdan Bin Mohammed Smart University. (2020b). *Strategic partnership between HBMSU and UNESCO IITE to launch 'Be an Online Tutor in 24 Hours' course in five global languages.* https://www.hbmsu.ac.ae/news/strategic-partnership-between-hbmsu-and-unesco-iite-launch-%E2%80%98be-online-tutor-24-hours%E2%80%99-course

Hamdan Bin Mohammed Smart University. (2021a). *Be an Online Tutor in 24 hours.* https://cloudcampus.hbmsu.ac.ae/enrol/index.php?id=4

Hamdan Bin Mohammed Smart University. (2021b). *Design an online course in 24 hours.* https://cloudcampus.hbmsu.ac.ae/enrol/index.php?id=6

Hamdan Bin Mohammed Smart University. (2021c). *Here's what our learners have to say about HBMSU and its offerings.* https://www.hbmsu.ac.ae/testimonials

UAE Vision. (2018a). *Home.* https://www.vision2021.ae/en

Jung, I. (2005). ICT-pedagogy integration in teacher training: Application cases worldwide. *Journal of Educational Technology & Society, 8*(2), 94–101. https://www.jstor.org/stable/jeductechsoci.8.2.94

Koukis, N., & Jimoyiannis, A. (2019). MOOCS for teacher professional development: Exploring teachers' perceptions and achievements. *Interactive Technology and Smart Education, 16*(1), 74–91. Advance online publication. doi:10.1108/ITSE-10-2018-0081

Kozma, R. B. (2002). *ICT and educational reform in developed and developing countries. Center for Technology in Learning.* SRI International.

Laurillard, D. (2016). The educational problem that MOOCs could solve: Professional development for teachers of disadvantaged students. *Research in Learning Technology, 24*(1), 29369. Advance online publication. doi:10.3402/rlt.v24.29369

MOE Training. (n.d.). *YouTube.* Retrieved January,08, 2020 from https://www.youtube.com/channel/UCxnNZ5Wxc3VuUQtTSD2Qm4Q/featured

Mwalongo, A. (2011). Teachers' perceptions about ICTs for teaching, professional development, administration and personal use. *International Journal of Education and Development Using ICT, 7*(3), 36-49.

Oh, C. H. (2003). Information Communication Technology and the New University: A View on eLearning. *The Annals of the American Academy of Political and Social Science, 585*(1), 134–153. doi:10.1177/0002716202238572

Pearson, J. (2003). Information and communications technologies and teacher education in Australia. *Technology, Pedagogy and Education, 12*(1), 39–58. doi:10.1080/14759390300200145

Prestridge, S., & Tondeur, J. (2015). Exploring elements that support teachers engagement in online professional development. *Education Sciences, 5*(3), 199–219. doi:10.3390/educsci5030199

Punie, Y., Zinnbauer, D., & Cabrera, M. (2006). *A Review of the Impact of ICT on Learning*. Working Paper prepared for DG EAC. Institute for Prospective Technological Studies, DG JRC.

Schleicher, A. (2020). *Teaching in the United Arab Emirates: 10 lessons from TALIS*. OECD. https://www.oecd.org/education/talis/Teaching_in_the_UAE-10_Lessons_from_TALIS.pdf

Spiteri, M., & Chang Rundgren, S. N. (2017). Maltese primary teachers' digital competence: Implications for continuing professional development. *European Journal of Teacher Education, 40*(4), 521–534. doi:10.1080/02619768.2017.1342242

Stephenson, L. (2010). Developing curriculum leadership in the UAE. *Education, Business and Society, 3*(2), 146–158. Advance online publication. doi:10.1108/17537981011047970

UAE Vision. (2018b). *First-Rate Education System*. https://www.vision2021.ae/en/national-agenda-2021/list/first-rate-circle

UNESCO. (2021). *Information and Communication Technologies (ICT)*. http://uis.unesco.org/en/glossary-term/information-and-communication-technologies-ict

United Arab Emirates Ministry of Education. (2017). *Ministry of Education launches a smart training platform for teachers and SIS app for students and parents*. https://www.moe.gov.ae/En/MediaCenter/News/Pages/SISApp.aspx

United Arab Emirates Ministry of Education. (2020a). *Vision and Mission*. https://www.moe.gov.ae/En/AboutTheMinistry/Pages/VisionMission.aspx

United Arab Emirates Ministry of Education. (2020b). *Live Webinars*. https://www.moe.gov.ae/en/importantlinks/tsf/pages/webinars.aspx

United Arab Emirates Ministry of Education. (2020c). *25,000 education staff to start remote specialized training through advanced technological system*. https://www.moe.gov.ae/en/mediacenter/news/pages/specialized-training.aspx

United Arab Emirates Ministry of Education. (2020d). *Educational Professions Licensure System.* https://tls.moe.gov.ae/#!/about

United Arab Emirates Ministry of Education. (2020e). *Frequently Asked Questions.* https://tls.moe.gov.ae/#!/faq

Vrasidas, C., & Glass, G. V. (2007). Teacher Professional Development and ICT: Strategies and Models. *Yearbook of the National Society for the Study of Education, 106*(2), 87–102. doi:10.1111/j.1744-7984.2007.00116.x

Wang, S. K., Hsu, H. Y., Reeves, T. C., & Coster, D. C. (2014). Professional development to enhance teachers' practices in using information and communication technologies (ICTs) as cognitive tools: Lessons learned from a design-based research study. *Computers & Education, 79,* 101–115. doi:10.1016/j.compedu.2014.07.006

Glossary

Bio-Medical Lens on Mental Health: This lens is a deficit model approach which tends to see as the only cause of mental health issue bio-medical disorders. It prioritizes clinical evaluation and treatment with drugs. It leads to a culture of referral in schools, within which teachers may feel that they are not equipped to address mental health issues in the classroom, and must instead systematically rely on clinicians to create inclusive provisions.

Cascade Model: One of the teacher professional development model used to train a large number of in-service teachers in a short span of time. In this model, a number of teachers are often trained in a particular content, and they in turn go ahead and train their colleagues on the same.

Collaboration: Means working together with one or more people to complete a project or task or develop ideas or processes. In the workplace collaboration occurs when two or more people work together towards a common goal that benefits the team or organisation like a school.

Collaborative and Participatory Teams: Functional social quality management groupings of teachers set up in schools to achieve quality education as internal efficiency.

Communication and Autism Team (CAT): A team of specialists within the United Kingdom schooling system to support learners, school staff, and families to improve the learning experience of students with autism.

Community of Practice: A group of people who work together on their own and broader group goals, usually with a shared emphasis.

Deficit Model: An approach to mental health which construes individuals with mental health issues as inherently missing essential characteristics, not fitting into mainstream expectations, and requiring 'fixing'. Deficit model approaches to mental health are often described as bio-medical, and focus mostly on clinical treatment and medication.

Early Childhood Care and Education: Care and education provided in settings where children are cared for and taught by individuals other than their parents or primary caregivers with whom they live.

Early Childhood Program Quality: The characteristics of early childhood programs that promote the physical, cognitive, emotional, and social development of children. High quality programs typically go beyond the minimum requirements, utilize Developmentally Appropriate Practice, and prioritize sufficient teacher and administrative qualifications, among others qualities.

Early Childhood Workforce: The wide range of individuals engaged in the care and education of young children including caregiving, teaching, and administrative staff, as well as consultants, learning specialists, and others.

Earth System Science: An integrated, system-based approach to teaching earth science.

Education Health and Care Plan (EHC): A document which outlines the detailed support and provision for learners with special educational needs in the United Kingdom schooling system.

Effective: Productive teaching and classroom management that results in high performance of learners.

Inclusion or Inclusive Education: Concerned with the presence, active participation, and achievement of all learners in a mainstream school.

In-Service Education: Refers to professional development activities that working educators participate to enhance their skills and remain up to date about knowledge and practices in the field.

In-Service Teacher Training: The process by which teachers engage in further education or training to refresh or upgrade their professional knowledge, skills, and practices in the course of their employment.

Integration: The physical placement of students with special educational needs from special education to mainstream education.

Lesson Study: Is a Japanese model of teacher-led research in which a group of teachers work together to target an identified area for development in their students' learning. Using existing evidence, participants collaboratively research, plan, teach and observe a series of lessons, using ongoing discussion, reflection, and expert input to track and refine their interventions.

Local Authority: The organisation responsible for a group of schools in a specific region in the United Kingdom schooling system.

Mental Health First Aid: A word commonly used to describe short, user-friendly, non-technical courses which seek to steer participants away from ready assumptions, and misconceptions about mental health. They are careful not to focus on clinical information, and instead encourage participants to develop attitudes, approaches and reflexes which increase awareness, facilitate and support the provision of services, and avoid stigma.

Ministry of Primary and Secondary Education (MoPSE): The governing Ministry for Early Childhood Development, Primary and Secondary School Education in Zimbabwe.

National Institute of Education (NIE): Is an autonomous institute of Nanyang Technological University in Singapore. The institute is the sole education institute for teachers in Singapore.

Next Generation Science Standards: The national science standards of the United States of America with an emphasis on three-dimensional learning that involves the integration of disciplinary core ideas, science and engineering practices, and crosscutting concepts.

Non-Arabic Speakers: Learners in the Bahrain public school system, who are predominantly from South Asian countries, whose first language is not Arabic.

Policymakers: A member of a government department, legislature, or other organization for making new laws or rules.

Post-Modern Approaches to Mental Health: A stance which seeks to dissect the way language and discourse perpetuate hegemonic views of mental health which

Glossary

lock the public in simplistic views which reinforce a sharp dichotomy between mental health and mental illness, instead of privileging a vision of mental health as a spectrum and a continuum.

Preservice Education: The education, training and/or professional experiences that an educator may undergo before they assume a particular role or position within an education program.

Pupil School Support (PSS): A service provided by the United Kingdom schooling system in support of learners with learning difficulties and vulnerable groups. This support can be provided to school staff through training which in turn will support this groups of learners.

School-Based Committees: Groupings of people that are established in schools to carry out quality management work.

Scientific Inquiry: Both the ways scientists work to learn about the natural world and a constructivist model of instruction that emphasizes students doing science more like scientists do, focused on meaning making over memorization.

Scientific Practices: The actions scientists and science students do to learn about science, also considered to be science discipline-specific inquiry.

Secretary's Merit Award (SMA): An annual award given by MoPSE to those schools that manage to produce the highest pass rates in public examinations that learners sit for.

Situated Learning: Learning within contexts that are relevant and meaningful for the learner.

Social Model of Disability: The social model of disability positions disability not as an inherent characteristic of individuals, but rather as a lack of fit or as a friction between individual embodiment and the design of experiences, spaces, or products. The social model of disability places back the burden on the designer of the environment, rather than focus on the individual's exceptionality.

Special Educational Needs (SEN): Includes students with emotional and behavioural difficulties, autism spectrum disorder, learning difficulties, hearing impairment and deafness, physical and health difficulties, profound and multiple learning difficulties, deaf-blindness, speech difficulties, visual impairment, non-native language speakers, and gifted learners.

Staff Development: An informal, lifelong, and socially interactive professional development programme. The term is used interchangeably with teacher professional development to refer to training of human resources in the workplace.

Subject Cluster: Involves bringing together teachers of the same subject from different schools to facilitate pedagogical activities to improve quality of teaching and learning by addressing the diverse needs of all learners.

Teacher Self-Efficacy: Refers to teacher's belief in his/her ability to successfully cope with tasks, obligations and challenges related to his/her professional role like didactical tasks or managing discipline in the classroom.

Transformation: In the context of technology-enhanced instruction, technology changes the role of teachers and students in teaching and learning, with students taking a more central role in the use of technology and related sense making.

Work Embedded: A staff development programme that is infused or is part and parcel of the work activities, duties and responsibilities of a teacher that takes place at the workplace or in the school.

Compilation of References

Abd Rahman, S., Puteh, F., Ahmad, U. K., Deris, F. D., Azizan, A. R., Busri, R. D., ... Ramli, N. S. (n.d.). *A Symbiotic UTM-UNMC Collaboration: Supporting Postgraduates of Bangladeshi College Education Development Project (BCEDP) with English Language Proficiency through MyLinE.* Academic Press.

Ahmed, M. (2016b). The education system. In A. Riaz & M.S. Rahman (Eds.), Routledge Handbook of Contemporary Bangladesh (pp. 340-351). London: Routledge.

Ahmed, J. U. (2016a). Massification to marketization of higher education: Private university education in Bangladesh. *Higher Education for the Future, 3*(1), 76–92. doi:10.1177/2347631115610222

Ahmed, R., & Hyndman-Rizk, N. (2020). The higher education paradox: Towards improving women's empowerment, agency development and labour force participation in Bangladesh. *Gender and Education, 32*(4), 447–465. doi:10.1080/09540253.2018.1471452

Ahmed, S., & McGillivray, M. (2015). Human capital, discrimination, and the gender wage gap in Bangladesh. *World Development, 67*, 506–524. doi:10.1016/j.worlddev.2014.10.017

Ainscow, M., Dyson, A., & Weiner, S. (2013). From exclusion to inclusion: A review of international literature on ways of responding to students with special educational needs in schools. En-clave pedagógica. *Revista Internacional de Investigación e Innovación Educativa, 13*, 13–30.

Ainscow, M., & Miles, S. (2008). Making education for all inclusive: Where next? *Quarterly Review of Comparative Education, 38*(1), 15–34. doi:10.100711125-008-9055-0

Åkerlind, G. S. (2005). Postdoctoral researchers: Roles, functions and career prospects. *Higher Education Research & Development, 24*(1), 21–40. doi:10.1080/0729436052000318550

Åkerlind, G. S. (2009). Postdoctoral research positions as preparation for an academic career. *International Journal for Researcher Development, 1*(1), 84–96. doi:10.1108/1759751X201100006

Al Faruki, M. J. (2020). A critical approach to active learning: A case study of two Bangladeshi colleges. *International Journal of Research in Business and Social Science, 9*(3), 165-174.

Al Faruki, M. J., Haque, M. A., & Islam, M. M. (2019). Student-Centered Learning and Current Practice in Bangladeshi College Education. *Journal of Education and Practice, 19*(13), 95–107.

Al Grug, T. (2020). *UAE education system is a role model for other countries.* Gulf News. https://gulfnews.com/opinion/op-eds/uae-education-system-is-a-role-model-for-other-countries-1.72488846

Al Hammadi, H. I. (2020). *The Futures of Education after Covid 19. Regional Dialogue.* Unesco. https://en.unesco.org/sites/default/files/synthesis_report_future_of_education_webnair_1.pdf

Al Mansoori, H. E. H. (2020) *How the UAE's robust ICT infrastructure brought over 1 million students online amid COVID-19.* MyITU. https://www.itu.int/en/myitu/News/2020/09/21/08/01/UAE-ICTs-education-1-million-students-online-COVID-19

Alam, G. M., & Khalifa, T. B. (2009). The impact of introducing a business marketing approach to education: A study on private HE in Bangladesh. *American Journal of Business, 3*(9), 463–474.

Alawani, A. S., & Singh, A. D. (2018). Exploring a New Innovative Approach for Teacher Professional Development in UAE: A Pilot Study. *Innovation Arabia, 11,* 101.

Albion, P. R., Tondeur, J., Forkosh-Baruch, A., & Peeraer, J. (2015). Teachers' professional development for ICT integration: Towards a reciprocal relationship between research and practice. *Education and Information Technologies, 20*(4), 655–673. doi:10.100710639-015-9401-9

Al-Darwish, S., & Sadeqi, A. (2016). Microteaching impact on student teachers' performance: A case study from Kuwait. *Journal of Education and Training Studies, 4*(8), 126–134. doi:10.11114/jets.v4i8.1677

Alencar, E. B. A. (2010). *Um galo sozinho não tece um (a)manhã": o papel de uma associação de professores de inglês no desenvolvimento da competência profissional de seus associados* [Unpublished master's thesis]. Universidade de Brasília, Brasília, Brazil.

Alhashmi, M., & Moussa-Inaty, J. (2021). Professional learning for Islamic education teachers in the UAE. *British Journal of Religious Education, 43*(3), 278–287. doi:10.1080/01416200.2020.1853046

Alhebsi, A., Pettaway, L., & Waller, L. (2015). A history of education in the United Arab Emirates and Trucial Shiekdoms. *The Global eLearning Journal, 4*(1), 1-6.

Ali, S., Sarker, M. F. H., Islam, M. S., Islam, M. K., & Al Mahmud, R. (2021). Pursuing higher education: Adaptation challenges and coping strategies of rural students at urban universities in Bangladesh. *Tertiary Education and Management, 27*(2), 1–16. doi:10.100711233-021-09067-3

Allan, B., & Lewis, D. (2006). The impact of membership of a virtual learning community on individual learning careers and professional identity. *British Journal of Educational Technology, 37*(6), 841–852. doi:10.1111/j.1467-8535.2006.00661.x

Allbright, T. N., Marsh, J. A., Kennedy, K. E., Hough, H. J., & McKibben, S. (2019). Social-emotional learning practices: Insights from outlier schools. *Journal of Research in Innovative Teaching & Learning, 12*(1), 35–52. doi:10.1108/JRIT-02-2019-0020

Compilation of References

ALLT. (2020, January 3rd). *Applied Linguistics & Language Teaching. Reframing Professional Development to be Effective, Efficient and Global* [Video]. YouTube. https://www.youtube.com/watch?v=yNlP0inr0iE

AlMahdi, O., & AlWadi, H. (2015). Towards a sociocultural approach on teachers' professional development in Bahrain. *Journal of Teaching and Teacher Education, 3*(1).

Al-Manabri, M., Al-Sharhan, A., Elbeheri, G., Jasem, I., & Everatt, J. (2013). Supporting teachers in inclusive practices: Collaboration between special and mainstream schools in Kuwait. *Preventing School Failure, 57*(3), 130–134. doi:10.1080/1045988X.2013.794325

Al-Nahar, T. (2001). Evaluation of the Effectiveness of the Training Programmes for the Basic Subjects (Arabic & English Languages and Science). Directorate of Training: Bahrain.

Alshourah, S. (2021). Total quality management practices and their effects on the quality performance of Jordanian private hospitals. *Management Science Letters, 11*(1), 67–76. doi:10.5267/j.msl.2020.8.029

American Association of Colleges of Teacher Education (AACTE). (2018). *A pivot toward clinical practice, its lexicon, and the renewal of educator preparation.* A report of the AACTE Clinical Practice Commission.

Amr, M. (2011). Teacher education for inclusive education in the Arab world: The case of Jordan. *Quarterly Review of Comparative Education, 41*(3), 399–413. doi:10.100711125-011-9203-9

Anderson, N., & Henderson, M. (2004). e-PD: Blended models of sustaining teacher professional development in digital literacies. *E-Learning and Digital Media, 1*(3), 383–394. doi:10.2304/elea.2004.1.3.4

Andrade, B. C. (2017). *Comunidades Virtuais Na Prática E Na Formação Continuada De Professores De Inglês - Um Estudo De Caso Sobre A Comunidade* [Unpublished master's thesis]. Universidade Federal do Rio de Janeiro, Rio de Janeiro, Brazil.

Andrew, A., Cattan, S., Costa Dias, M., Farquharson, C., Kraftman, L., Krutikova, S., Phimister, A., & Sevilla, A. (2020). Inequalities in children's experiences of home learning during the COVID-19 lockdown in England. *Fiscal Studies, 41*(3), 653–683. doi:10.1111/1475-5890.12240 PMID:33362314

Annamma, S., & Morrison, D. (2018). DisCrit classroom ecology: Using praxis to dismantle dysfunctional education ecologies. *Teaching and Teacher Education, 73*, 70–80. doi:10.1016/j.tate.2018.03.008

Anny, N. Z., Mishra, P. K., & Rahman, M. S. R. (2020). Teaching sociology in large classes: Issues and challenges in Bangladeshi colleges. *International Journal of Research in Business and Social Science, 9*(1), 46-54.

Aperribai, L., Cortabarria, L., Aguirre, T., Verche, E., & Borges, Á. (2020) Teacher's Physical Activity and Mental Health during Lockdown Due to the COVID-2019 Pandemic. *Frontiers in Psychology, 11,* 2673. doi:10.3389/fpsyg.2020.577886

Archibald, S., & Coggshall, J. G. (2011). *High Quality Professional Development for All Teachers: Effectively Allocating Resources*. National Centre for Teacher Quality.

Armstrong, A. C., Armstrong, D., & Spandagou, I. (2010). *Inclusive education: international policy & practice*. Sage Publications.

Asención Delaney, Y. (2012). Research on mentoring language teachers: Its role in language education. *Foreign Language Annals*, *45*(s1), s184–s202. doi:10.1111/j.1944-9720.2011.01185.x

Ashton, J. R., & Arlington, H. (2019). My fears were irrational: Transforming conceptions of disability in teacher education through service learning. *International Journal of Whole Schooling*, *15*(1), 50–81.

Aspin, D. N., Chapman, J. D., & Wilkinson, V. R. (1994). *Quality schooling: A pragmatic approach to some current problems, topics and issues*. Cassell.

Atkins, M. A., & Rodger, S. R. (2016). Preservice teacher education for mental health and inclusion in schools. *Exceptional Education International*, *26*(2), 93–118. doi:10.5206/eei.v26i2.7742

Avalos, B. (2011). Teacher professional development in Teaching and Teacher Education over ten years. *Teaching and Teacher Education*, *27*(1), 10–20. doi:10.1016/j.tate.2010.08.007

Avramidis, E., Bayliss, P., & Burden, R. (2000). A survey into mainstream teachers' attitudes towards the inclusion of children with special educational needs in the ordinary school in one local education authority. *Educational Psychology*, *20*(2), 191–211. doi:10.1080/713663717

Avramidis, E., Bayliss, P., & Burden, R. (2002). Inclusion in action: An in-depth case study of an effective inclusive secondary school in the south-west of England. *International Journal of Inclusive Education*, *6*(2), 143–163. doi:10.1080/13603110010017169

Avramidis, E., & Kalyva, E. (2007). The influence of teaching experience and professional development on Greek teachers' attitudes towards inclusion. *European Journal of Special Needs Education*, *22*(4), 367–389. doi:10.1080/08856250701649989

Aysan, M. F., & Özdoğru, A. A. (2015). Comparative analysis of early childhood care and education in Europe. *Turkish Journal of Sociology*, *30*, 167–194. doi:10.16917/IU/tjs.12775

Bakioğlu, A., & Yaman, E. (2004). Career developments of research assistants: Obstacles and solutions. *Marmara University Atatürk Education Faculty Journal of Educational Sciences*, *20*(20), 1-20. https://dergipark.org.tr/en/download/article-file/1715

Bala, S. S., Mansor, W. F. A. W., Stapa, M., & Zakaria, M. H. (2012). Digital portfolio and professional development of language teachers. *Procedia: Social and Behavioral Sciences*, *66*, 176–186. doi:10.1016/j.sbspro.2012.11.259

Ball, A., Iachini, A. L., Bohnenkamp, J. H., Togno, N. M., Brown, E. L., Hoffman, J. A., & George, M. W. (2016). School mental health content in state in-service K-12 teaching standards in United States. *Teaching and Teacher Education*, *60*, 312–320. doi:10.1016/j.tate.2016.08.020

Compilation of References

Ball, D. L., & Cohen, D. K. (1999). Developing practice, developing practitioners: Toward a practice based theory of professional education. In L. Darling-Hammond & G. Sykes (Eds.), *Teaching as a learning profession: Handbook for policy and practice* (pp. 3–31). Jossey-Bass.

Bamberger, A., Morris, P., & Yemini, M. (2019). Neoliberalism, internationalisation and higher education: Connections, contradictions and alternatives. *Discourse (Abingdon), 40*(2), 203–216. doi:10.1080/01596306.2019.1569879

Banilower, E., & Shimkus, E. (2004). *Professional development observation study.* Horizon Research.

Bastian, J. (2006). Gesamtschule – Umgang mit Heterogenität. *Pädagogik, 58*, 7–8.

Baumert, J., & Kunter, M. (2013). The COACTIV model of teachers' professional competence. *Online (Bergheim)*, 25–48. Advance online publication. doi:10.1007/978-1-4614-5149-5_2

Bautista, A., & Ortega-Ruiz, R. (2015). Teacher Professional Development: International Perspectives and Approaches. *Psychology. Social Education, 7*(3), 240–251.

Bautista, A., Wong, J., & Gopinathan, S. (2015). Teacher professional development in Singapore: Depicting the landscape. *Psychology. Social Education, 7*(3), 311–326. doi:10.25115/psye.v7i3.523

Bayrakdar, S., & Guveli, A. (2020) *Inequalities in home learning and schools' provision of distance teaching during school closure of COVID-19 lockdown in the UK.* https://www.iser.essex.ac.uk/research/publications/working-papers/iser/2020-09.pdf

Becher, A., & Lefstein, A. (2021). Teaching as a Clinical Profession: Adapting the Medical Model. *Journal of Teacher Education, 72*(4), 477–488. doi:10.1177/0022487120972633

Bennell, P. (2019). The financial returns to onshore and offshore overseas students at British Universities. *International Journal of Educational Development, 70*, 102097. doi:10.1016/j.ijedudev.2019.102097

Bennell, P. (2020). The internationalisation of higher education provision in the United Kingdom: Patterns and relationships between onshore and offshore overseas student enrolment. *International Journal of Educational Development, 74*, 102162. doi:10.1016/j.ijedudev.2020.102162

Bennison, A., & Goos, M. (2010). Learning to teach mathematics with technology: A survey of professional development needs, experiences and impacts. *Mathematics Education Research Journal, 22*(1), 31–56. doi:10.1007/BF03217558

Berkovich, I., & Eyal, O. (2015). Educational leaders and emotions: An international review of empirical evidence, 1992–2012. *Review of Educational Research, 85*(1), 129–167. doi:10.3102/0034654314550046

Berner, H., Isler, R. & Weidinger, W. (2019). *Simply good teaching.* Bern: hep.

Bessa, Y., Brown, A., & Hicks, J. (2013). Postmodernity and Mental Illness: A Comparative Analysis of Selected Theorists. *American International Journal of Contemporary Research, 3*(4), 64.

Bett, H. K. (2016). The cascade model of teachers' CPD in Kenya: A time for change? *Cogent Education, 3*, 1–9. doi:10.1080/2331186X.2016.1139439

Bhattacharya, D., & Borgatti, L. (2012). An Atypical Approach to Graduation from the LDC Category: The Case of Bangladesh. *South Asia Economic Journal, 13*(1), 1–25. doi:10.1177/139156141101300101

Bildungsdirektion Kanton Zürich. (2021). https://www.zh.ch/de/bildungsdirektion.html

Blanchard, M. R., LePrevost, C. E., Tolin, A. D., & Gutierrez, K. S. (2016). Investigating technology-enhanced teacher professional development in rural, high-poverty middle schools. *Educational Researcher, 45*(3), 207–220. doi:10.3102/0013189X16644602

Bogdan, R. C., & Biklen, S. K. (1992). *Qualitative research for education: An introduction to theory and methods.* Allyn and Bacon.

Boice, R. (1991). New faculty as teachers. *The Journal of Higher Education, 62*(2), 150–173. doi:10.2307/1982143

Bonner, S. M., Diehl, K., & Trachtman, R. (2020). Teacher belief and agency development in bringing change to scale. *Journal of Educational Change, 21*(2), 363–384. doi:10.100710833-019-09360-4

Booth, T., Nes, K., & Strømstad, M. (Eds.). (2003). *Developing inclusive teacher education.* Routledge Falmer. doi:10.4324/9780203465233

Bordoloi, R., Das, P., & Das, K. (2021). Perception towards online/blended learning at the time of Covid-19 pandemic: An academic analytics in the Indian context. *Asian Association of Open Universities Journal, 16*(1), 41–60. doi:10.1108/AAOUJ-09-2020-0079

Borko, H. (2004). Professional development and teacher learning: Mapping the terrain. *Educational Researcher, 33*(8), 3–15. doi:10.3102/0013189X033008003

Borko, H., Jacobs, J., Eiteljorg, E., & Pittman, M. E. (2008). Video as a tool for fostering productive discussions in mathematics professional development. *Teaching and Teacher Education, 24*(2), 417–436. doi:10.1016/j.tate.2006.11.012

Borko, H., Jacobs, J., & Koellner, K. (2010). Contemporary approaches to teacher professional development. In E. Baker, B. McGaw, & P. Peterson (Eds.), *International encyclopedia of education* (3rd ed.). Elsevier. doi:10.1016/B978-0-08-044894-7.00654-0

Bowen, G. A. (2009). Document Analysis as a Qualitative Research Method. *Qualitative Research Journal, 9*(2), 27–40. doi:10.3316/QRJ0902027

Bradley, L. H. (1993). *Total quality management for schools.* Technomic Pub.

Compilation of References

BRASIL. (1998). *Secretaria de Educação Fundamental. Parâmetros curriculares nacionais: terceiro e quarto ciclos do ensino fundamental: língua estrangeira/ Secretaria de Educação Fundamental.* Brasília: MEC/SEF. Accessed at: http://portal.mec.gov.br/seb/arquivos/pdf/pcn_estrangeira.pdf

Braude, S., & Dwarika, V. (2020). Teachers' experiences of supporting learners with attention-deficit hyperactivity disorder: Lessons for professional development of teachers. *South African Journal of Childhood Education, 10*(1), 1–10. doi:10.4102ajce.v10i1.843

BRAZ-TESOL. (2021). Accessed at https://braztesol.org.br/site/view.asp?p=1

Breux, P., & Boccio, D. E. (2019). Improving Schools' Readiness for Involvement in Suicide Prevention: An Evaluation of the Creating Suicide Safety in Schools (CSSS) Workshop. *International Journal of Environmental Research and Public Health, 16*(12), 2165. doi:10.3390/ijerph16122165 PMID:31248082

British Council. (2014). *Learning English in Brazil 2014: Understanding the aims and expectations of the Brazilian emerging middle classes.* Author.

British Council. (2015). *O Ensino de Inglês na Educação Pública Brasileira.* Author.

Britto, P. R., Lye, S. J., Proulx, K., Yousafzai, A. K., Matthews, S. G., Vaivada, T., Perez-Escamilla, R., Rao, N., Ip, P., Fernald, L. C. H., MacMillan, H., Hanson, M., Wachs, T. D., Yao, H., Yoshikawa, H., Cerezo, A., Leckman, J. F., & Bhutta, Z. A.Lancet Early Childhood Development Series Steering Committee. (2017). Nurturing care: Promoting early childhood development. *Lancet, 389*(10064), 91–102. doi:10.1016/S0140-6736(16)31390-3 PMID:27717615

Brown, E. L., Phillippo, K. L., Weston, K., & Rodger, S. (2019). United States and Canada pre-service teacher certification standards for student mental health: A comparative case study. *Teaching and Teacher Education: An International Journal of Research and Studies, 80*(1), 71-82. https://www.learntechlib.org/p/202092/

BTC. (2021). *Academic Programs.* Retrieved from http://www.btc.uob.edu.bh/post-graduate-diploma-in-education

Buczynski, S., & Hansen, C. B. (2010). Impact of professional development on teacher practice: Uncovering connections. *Teaching and Teacher Education, 26*(3), 599-607. doi:10.1016/j.tate.2009.09.006

Buffington-Adams, J., & Vaughan, K. P. (2019). The Curriculum of Disability Studies: Multiple Perspectives on Dis/Ability. Introduction: An Invitation to Complicated Conversations. *Journal of Curriculum Theorizing, 34*(1). https://journal.jctonline.org/index.php/jct/issue/viewFile/35/2019JCTVol34Iss1

Bukamal, H. (2018). *The influence of teacher preparation programmes on Bahraini teacher attitudes and challenges with inclusive education.* Paper presented at the Sustainability and Resilience Conference: Mitigating Risks and Emergency Planning, Bahrain. 10.18502/kss.v3i10.3107

Burkhauser, S. (2017). How much do school principals matter when it comes to teacher working conditions? *Educational Evaluation and Policy Analysis*, *39*(1), 126–145. doi:10.3102/0162373716668028

Burns, M., Lawrie, J., & Inter-agency Network for Education in Emergencies Secretariat. (2016, October 5). *Education for All. Global Partnership for Education Blog*. http://www.inee.org/en/blog/new-publication-where-its-needed-most-quality-professional-development-for

Cajkler, W., & Wood, P. (2016a). Adapting lesson study to investigate classroom pedagogy in initial teacher education: What student-teachers think. *Cambridge Journal of Education*, *46*(1), 1–18. doi:10.1080/0305764X.2015.1009363

Cajkler, W., & Wood, P. (2016b). Mentors and student-teachers "lesson studying" in initial teacher education. *International Journal for Lesson and Learning Studies*, *5*(2), 84–98. doi:10.1108/IJLLS-04-2015-0015

Caldwell, N. (2019) *Teachers' Perception of Mental Health in the School System* (Master's thesis). Eastern Illinois University. https://thekeep.eiu.edu/theses/4581

Campbell, T., Zuwallack, R., Longhurst, M., Shelton, B. E., & Wolf, P. G. (2014). An examination of the changes in science teaching orientations and technology-enhanced tools for student learning in the context of professional development. *International Journal of Science Education*, *36*(11), 1–34. doi:10.1080/09500693.2013.879622

Capps, D. K., & Crawford, B. A. (2013). Inquiry-based instruction and teaching about nature of science: Are they happening? *Journal of Science Teacher Education*, *24*(3), 497–526. doi:10.100710972-012-9314-z

Carlson, S., & Gadio, C. T. (2002). Teacher professional development in the use of technology. *Technologies for Education*, 118-132.

Cassidy, D. J., Hestenes, L. L., Hansen, J. K., Hegde, A., Shim, J., & Hestenes, S. (2005). Revisiting the two faces of child care quality: Structure and process. *Early Education and Development*, *16*(4), 505–520. doi:10.120715566935eed1604_10

Cavioni, V., Grazzani, I., & Ornaghi, V. (2020). Mental health promotion in schools: A comprehensive theoretical framework. *The International Journal of Emotional Education*, *12*(1), 65–82. https://files.eric.ed.gov/fulltext/EJ1251771.pdf

Cawyer, C. S., Simonds, C., & Davis, S. (2002). Mentoring to facilitate socialization: The case of the new faculty member. *International Journal of Qualitative Studies in Education*, *15*(2), 225–242. doi:10.1080/09518390110111938

CBC. (2018, November 23). *UPEI 1-year bachelor of education program attracting more students*. CBC News. https://www.cbc.ca/news/canada/prince-edward-island/pei-upei-bachelor-of-education-one-year-program-update-1.4918105

Central Intelligence Agency. (2021). Bangladesh. In *The World Factbook*. Available at: https://www.cia.gov/the-world-factbook/countries/bangladesh/#economy

Compilation of References

Chen, J. Q., & McCray, J. (2012). A Conceptual framework for Teacher Professional Development: The Whole Teacher Approach, NHSA Dialog. *A Research-to-Practice Journal for the Early Childhood Field, 15*(1), 8-23.

Chidakwa, C. (2017a). *Quality management practices in rural primary schools in the Mashonaland provinces of Zimbabwe: Implications for policy* [Unpublished doctoral thesis]. University of Zimbabwe, Harare.

Chidakwa, C. (2017b). *Leadership practices for quality management in three rural primary schools awarded the Secretary's Merit Award in Mashonaland provinces of Zimbabwe*. HRRC.

Chikoko, V. (2006). *Negotiating roles and responsibilities in the context of decentralized school governance: A case study of one cluster of schools in Zimbabwe* [Unpublished doctoral dissertation]. University of KwaZulu-Natal, Durban, South Africa.

Chikoko, V. (2007). The cluster system as an innovation: Perceptions of Zimbabwean teachers and school heads. *African Education Review, 4*(1), 42–57. doi:10.1080/18146620701412142

Child Care Services Association. (2021, June). *Retaining educated early childhood educators* [Policy Brief]. https://www.childcareservices.org/wp-content/uploads/Policy-Brief-Retaining-Educated-Early-Childhood-Educators.pdf

Chiparausha, B., & Chigwada, J. P. (2021). *Promoting library services in a digital environment in Zimbabwe*. Retrieved from https://www.igi-global.com/chapter/promoting- library-services-in-a-digital environment-in-zimbabwe/274763

Chisaka, B. C. (2006). *Ability streaming: A stumbling block to teaching and learning*. University of Zimbabwe Publications.

Chou, C. C., Chuang, H.-H., & Wharton-Beck, A. N. (2019). Fostering the Development of Social Capital to Enrich Student Experiences Through After-School Digital Tutoring Programs. *Journal of Educational Technology Development and Exchange, 12*(1), 1. Advance online publication. doi:10.18785/jetde.1201.01

Chrysostomou, M., & Symeonidou, S. (2017). Education for disability equality through disabled people's life stories and narratives: Working and learning together in a school-based professional development programme for inclusion. *European Journal of Special Needs Education, 32*(4), 572–585. doi:10.1080/08856257.2017.1297574

Conderman, G., & Johnston-Rodriguez, S. (2009). Beginning teachers' views of their collaborative roles. *Preventing School Failure, 53*(4), 235–244. doi:10.3200/PSFL.53.4.235-244

Connor, D., & Olander, L. (2019) Influence of Medical and Social Perspectives of Disability on Models of Inclusive Education in the United States. *Oxford Research Encyclopedia of Education*. https://oxfordre.com/education/view/10.1093/acrefore/9780190264093.001.0001/acrefore-9780190264093-e-1244

Council of Higher Education (CoHE). (2018). *Okul Öncesi Öğretmenliği Lisans Programı.* https://www.yok.gov.tr/Documents/Kurumsal/egitim_ogretim_dairesi/Yeni-Ogretmen-Yetistirme-Lisans-Programlari/Okul_Oncesi_Ogretmenligi_Lisans_Programi.pdf

Cozza, B. (2010). Transforming teaching into a collaborative culture: An attempt to create a professional development school-university partnership. *The Educational Forum, 74*(3), 227–241. doi:10.1080/00131725.2010.483906

Curtis, M. D. (2019). Professional technologies in schools: The role of pedagogical knowledge in teaching with geospatial technologies. *The Journal of Geography, 118*(3), 130–142. doi:10.1080/00221341.2018.1544267

Dalby, D. (2021). Professional learning through collaborative research in mathematics. *Professional Development in Education, 47*(4), 710–724. doi:10.1080/19415257.2019.1665571

Dammerer, J. (2020). Mentoring für beginnende Lehrpersonen – ein Instrument der Personalentwicklung. In Mentoring im pädagogischen Kontext. Professionalisierung. Pädagogik für Niederösterreich, Band 10. Studienverlag.

Dammerer, J., Ziegler, V., & Bartonek, S. (2019). Tutoring and Coaching as Special Forms of Mentoring for Young Eachers Starting Their Careers. *Yaroslavl Pedagogical Bulletin.* Advance online publication. doi:10.24411/1813-145X-2019-10278

Darling-Hammond, L., Hyler, M. E., & Gardiner, M. (2017). *Effective teacher professional development.* Retrieved from: https://learningpolicyinstitute.org

Darling-Hammond, L. (2017). Teacher education around the world: What can we learn from international practice? *European Journal of Teacher Education, 40*(3), 291–309. doi:10.1080/02619768.2017.1315399

Darling-Hammond, L., Heyler, M. E., & Gardener, M. (2017). *Effective Teacher Professional Development.* Learning Policy Institute. doi:10.54300/122.311

Davis, P., & Florian, L. (2004). Teaching strategies and approaches for pupils with special educational needs: A scoping study. *Research in Reproduction, RR516,* 1–90.

de Jong, E., & Harper, C. A. (2005). Preparing mainstream teachers for English-language learners: Is being a good teacher good enough? *Teacher Education Quarterly, 32,* 101–124.

De Vries, S., Jansen, E. P. W. A., & Van de Grift, W. J. C. M. (2013). Profiling teachers' continuous professional development and the relation with their beliefs about learning and teaching. *Teaching and Teacher Education, 33*(1), 78–89. doi:10.1016/j.tate.2013.02.006

Deacon, B. (2013). The biomedical model of mental disorder: A critical analysis of its validity, utility, and effects on psychotherapy research. *Clinical Psychology Review, 33*(7), 846–861. doi:10.1016/j.cpr.2012.09.007 PMID:23664634

Compilation of References

Del Franco, N. (2010). Aspirations and self-hood: Exploring the meaning of higher secondary education for girl college students in rural Bangladesh. *Compare: A Journal of Comparative Education*, *40*(2), 147–165. doi:10.1080/03057920903546005

Delport, A., & Makaye, J. (2009). Clustering schools to improve teacher professional development: Lessons learnt from a Zimbabwean case study. *Africa Education Review*, *6*(1), 96–105. doi:10.1080/18146620902857608

Department of Basic Education. (2018). Teacher Professional Development Master Plan 2017-2022. Republic of South Africa.

Department of Education. (2007). National Policy Framework for Teacher Education and Development in South Africa. Government Gazette 29832.

Desimone, L. M. (2009). Improving impact studies of teachers' professional development: Toward better conceptualisations and measures. *Educational Researcher*, *38*(3), 181–199. doi:10.3102/0013189X08331140

Desimone, L. M., & Garet, M. (2015). Best practices in Teachers' Professional Development in the United States. *Psychology. Social Education*, *7*(3), 252–263.

DfE. (2015). *Special educational needs and disability code of practice: 0 to 25*. Retrieved from https://assets.publishing.service.gov.uk/government/uploads/system/uploads/attachment_data/file/398815/SEND_Code_of_Practice_January_2015.pdf

Diken, I. H., Rakap, S., Diken, O., Tomris, G., & Celik, S. (2016). Early Childhood Inclusion in Turkey. *Infants and Young Children*, *29*(3), 231–238. doi:10.1097/IYC.0000000000000065

Doğan, B., & Tatık, R. Ş. (2014). Okul öncesi öğretmenlerinin hizmet içi eğitim ihtiyaçlarının belirlenmesi. *The Journal of Academic Social Science Studies*, *27*(27), 521–539. doi:10.9761/JASSS2418

Doğaroğlu, T., & Bapoğlu Dümenci, S. (2015). Sınıflarında kaynaştırma öğrencisi bulunan okul öncesi öğretmenlerin kaynaştırma eğitimi ve erken müdahale hakkındaki görüşlerinin incelenmesi. *Hacettepe University Faculty of Health Sciences Journal*, *1*(Supp. 2), 460-473. https://dergipark.org.tr/en/pub/husbfd/issue/7893/103909

Doherty, G. D. (Ed.). (1994). *Developing quality systems in education*. Routledge and Kegan Paul.

Donnelly, J. H., Gibson, J. L., & Ivancevich, J. M. (1992). *Fundamentals of management* (8th ed.). Irwin.

Dorn, E., Hancock, B., Sarakatsannis, J., & Viruleg, E. (2020). *COVID-19 and learning loss— disparities grow and students need help*. McKinsey & Company. https://www.mckinsey.com/industries/public-and-social-sector/our-insights/covid-19-and-learning-loss-disparities-grow-and-students-need-help

Dotger, S. (2015). Methodological understandings from elementary science lesson study facilitation and research. *Journal of Science Teacher Education*, *26*(4), 49–369. doi:10.100710972-015-9427-2

Dudley-Marling, C. (2015). The resilience of deficit thinking. *Journal of Teaching and Learning*, *10*(1). Advance online publication. doi:10.22329/jtl.v10i1.4171

Dudley, P. (2013). Teacher learning in lesson study: What interaction level discourse analysis revealed about how teachers utilized imagination, tacit knowledge of teaching and fresh evidence of pupils learning, to develop practice knowledge and so enhance their pupils' learning. *Teaching and Teacher Education*, *34*, 107–121. doi:10.1016/j.tate.2013.04.006

Dudley, P. (2014). *Lesson study: Professional learning for our time*. Routledge. doi:10.4324/9780203795538

Eby, L., Rhodes, J., & Allen, T. (2007). Definition and Evolution of Mentoring. In T. Allen & L. Eby (Eds.), *The Blackwell Handbook of Mentoring*. Blackwell. doi:10.1002/9780470691960.ch2

EDIFY. (2021). Accessed at https://www.edifyeducation.com.br/

EF EPI. (2020). *EF English proficiency index*. EF Education First.

Eğitimde Birlikteyiz. (2021). *Eğitimde Birlikteyiz: Engeli Olan Çocuklar İçin Kapsayıcı Erken Çocukluk Eğitimi Projesi*. http://www.egitimdebirlikteyiz.org

Elatawneh, H. A. A., & Sidek, S. B. (2021). Formulation of Theoretical Framework of Teaching Quality Factors Model for Professional Development for UAE Higher Education Institutions. *Psychology and Education Journal*, *58*(2), 3755–3763.

Elder, B. C., Givens, L., LoCastro, A., & Rencher, L. (2021). Using Disability Studies in Education (dse) and Professional Development Schools (pds) to Implement Inclusive Practices. *Journal of Disability Studies in Education*. doi:10.1163/25888803-bja10010

Elliot, D. L., & Kobayashi, S. (2019). How can PhD supervisors play a role in bridging academic cultures? *Teaching in Higher Education*, *24*(8), 911–929. doi:10.1080/13562517.2018.1517305

Embassy of the United Arab Emirates Cultural Division. (2011). *Education in the United Arab Emirates*. Retrieved from http://www.uaecd.org/education-introduction

Emiliussen, J., Engelsen, S., Christiansen, R., & Klausen, S. H. (2021). We are all in it! Phenomenological Qualitative Research and Embeddedness. *International Journal of Qualitative Methods*, *20*. Advance online publication. doi:10.1177/1609406921995304

Emstad, A. B., & Sandvik, L. V. (2020). School–university collaboration for facilitating in-service teacher training as a part of school-based professional development. *Acta Didactica Norden*, *14*(2), 1–20. doi:10.5617/adno.7934

Epstein, J. L. (2005). Links in a professional development chain: Preservice and inservice education for effective programs of school, family, and community partnerships. *New Educator*, *1*(2), 125–141. doi:10.1080/15476880590932201

Compilation of References

Esau, H., & Mpofu, J. (2017). The preparedness of primary schools to implement the grade 3 new curriculum in Zimbabwe: A Case study of Bulawayo metropolitan primary schools. *European Journal of Social Sciences Studies*, 2(4), 104–116.

European Commission/Eurydice. (2020). *Switzerland. National reforms in school education.* https://eacea.ec.europa.eu/national-policies/eurydice/content/national-reforms-school-education-89_en

European Commission/Eurydice. (2021). *Switzerland. Teachers and education staff.* https://eacea.ec.europa.eu/national-policies/eurydice/content/teachers-and-education-staff-106_en

Fairman, J., Smith, D., Pullen, P., & Lebel, S. (2020). The challenge of keeping teacher professional development relevant. *Professional Development in Education*, 1–13. Advance online publication. doi:10.1080/19415257.2020.1827010

Falcão, A. (2004). *A Brazilian teacher association for teachers of English: organisational improvement through an international and comparative educational perspective* [Unpublished master's thesis]. University of Leeds, Leeds, UK.

Fantilli, R. D., & McDougall, D. E. (2009). A study of novice teachers: Challenges and supports in the first years. *Teaching and Teacher Education*, 25(6), 814–825. doi:10.1016/j.tate.2009.02.021

Farrell, P., Hick, P., & Kershner, R. (Eds.). (2008). *Psychology for inclusive education: new directions in theory and practice.* Routledge.

Fennig, M., & Denov, M. (2019). Regime of Truth: Rethinking the Dominance of the Bio-Medical Model in Mental Health Social Work with Refugee Youth. *British Journal of Social Work*, 49(2), 300–317. doi:10.1093/bjsw/bcy036

Filler, J., & Xu, Y. (2006). Including children with disabilities in early childhood education programs: Individualizing developmentally appropriate practices. *Childhood Education*, 83(2), 92–98. doi:10.1080/00094056.2007.10522887

Finn, R. (1993). Mentoring – the effective route to school development. In H. Green (Ed.), The School Management Handbook (pp. 62–88). Academic Press.

Fischer, D. (2008). Mentorieren. Zwischen kollegialer Begleitung, professionellem Anspruch und persönlichem Zuspruch. *Schulverwaltung Spezial, 1.*

Fischer, D., van Andel, L., Cain, T., Žarkovič-Adlešič, B., & van Lakerveld. (Eds.). (2008). *Improving school-based mentoring. A Handbook for Mentor Trainers.* Münster.

Fitzgerald, M., Danaia, L., & McKinnon, D. H. (2019). Barrers inhibiting inquiry-based science teaching and potential solutions: Perceptions of positively inclined early adopters. *Research in Science Education*, 49(2), 543–566. doi:10.100711165-017-9623-5

Florian, L., & Black-Hawkins, K. (2011). Exploring inclusive pedagogy. *British Educational Research Journal*, 37(5), 813–828. doi:10.1080/01411926.2010.501096

Forawi, S. (2015). Science Teacher Professional Development Needs in the United Arab Emirates. In Science Education in the Arab Gulf States (pp. 49-68). Rotterdam: Sense. doi:10.1007/978-94-6300-049-9_3

Forlin, C. (Ed.). (2010). *Teacher education for inclusion: changing paradigms and innovative approaches.* Routledge. doi:10.4324/9780203850879

Fovet, F. (2014). Social model as catalyst for innovation in design and pedagogical change. *Widening Participation through Curriculum Open University 2014 Conference Proceedings*, 135-139.

Fovet, F. (2020). Exploring the Potential of Universal Design for Learning with Regards to Mental Health Issues in Higher Education. In *Pacific Rim International Conference on Disability and Diversity. Conference Proceedings.* Center on Disability Studies, University of Hawai'i at Mānoa.

Fraefel, U., Bernhardsson-Laros, N., & Bäuerlein, K. (2017). Partnerschaftliches Lehren und Lernen im Schulfeld – Aufbau von Professionswissen mittels Peer-to-Peer Mentoring in lokalen Arbeits- und Lerngemeinschaften. In *Lehrerbildung auf dem Prüfstand 2017* (pp. 30–49). Sonderheft.

Freedman, J., Applebaum, A., Woodfield, C., & Ashby, C. (2019) Integrating Disability Studies Pedagogy in Teacher Education. *Journal of Teaching Disability Studies*. https://jtds.commons.gc.cuny.edu/integrating-disability-studies-pedagogy-in-teacher-education/

Freeman, D. (2004). Teaching in the context of English language learners. In M. Sadowski (Ed.), Teaching immigrant and second-language students: Strategies for success. Cambridge, MA: Harvard Education Press.

Frohn, J. (2021). Troubled schools in troubled times: How COVID-19 affects educational inequalities and what measures can be taken. *European Educational Research Journal*, *20*(5), 667–683. doi:10.1177/14749041211020974

Funk, C. M. (2016). *Kollegiales Feedback aus der Perspektive von Lehrpersonen.* Springer VS. doi:10.1007/978-3-658-13062-6

Furtak, E. M., Seidel, T., Iverson, H., & Briggs, D. C. (2012). Experimental and quasi-experimental studies of inquiry-based science teaching: A meta-analysis. *Review of Educational Research*, *82*(3), 300–329. doi:10.3102/0034654312457206

Gadermann, A. M., Warren, M. T., Gagné, M., Thomson, K. C., Schonert-Reichl, K. A., Guhn, M., Molyneux, T. M., & Oberle, E. (2021). *The impact of the COVID-19 pandemic on teacher well-being in British Columbia.* Human Early Learning Partnership. http://earlylearning.ubc.ca/

Gaible, E., & Burns, M. (2005). *Using Technology to Train Teachers.* http://www.infodev.org/en/Publication.13.html

Galaczi, E., Nye, A., Poulter, M., & Allen, H. (2018). *Teacher Professional Development: Cambridge Assessment English Perspectives.* University of Cambridge.

Galderisi, S., Heinz, A., Kastrup, M., Beezhold, J., & Sartorius, N. (2015). Toward a new definition of mental health. *World Psychiatry; Official Journal of the World Psychiatric Association (WPA)*, *14*(2), 231–233. doi:10.1002/wps.20231 PMID:26043341

Gallacher, K. K. (1997). Supervision, mentoring and coaching: Methods for supporting personnel development. In P. Winton, McCollum, J.A. & Catlett, C. (Eds.), Reforming personnel development in early intervention: Issues, models, and practical strategies (pp. 173 – 191). Paul Brookes.

Gandara, P., Rumberger, R., Maxwell-Jolly, J., & Callahan, R. (2003). English language learners in California schools: Unequal resources, unequal outcomes. *Education Policy Analysis Archives*, *11*(36), 1–52.

García-Carrión, R., Villarejo-Carballido, B., & Villardón-Gallego, L. (2019) Children and Adolescents Mental Health: A Systematic Review of Interaction-Based Interventions in Schools and Communities. *Frontiers in Psychology, 10*, 918. doi:10.3389/fpsyg.2019.00918

Garet, M. S., Porter, A. C., Desimone, L., Birman, B. F., & Yoon, K. S. (2001). What makes professional development effective? Results from a national sample of teachers. *American Educational Research Journal*, *38*(4), 915–945. doi:10.3102/00028312038004915

Garrison, D. R. (1993). Quality and access in Distance Education: Theoretical Considerations. In D. Keegan (Ed.), *Theoretical principles of distance education* (pp. 9–21). Routledge.

Gates, H. A. (2008). *Middle school science teachers' perspectives and practices of teaching through inquiry* (Unpublished doctoral dissertation). University of South Carolina, Columbia, SC.

Gatta, M., Miscioscia, M., Svanellini, L., Spoto, A., Difronzo, M., de Sauma, M., & Ferruzza, E. (2019) Effectiveness of Brief Psychodynamic Therapy with Children and Adolescents: An Outcome Study. *Frontiers in Pediatrics, 7*. doi:10.3389/fped.2019.00501

Gerard, L. F., Varma, K., Corliss, S. B., & Linn, M. C. (2011). Professional development for technologically enhanced inquiry science. *Review of Educational Research*, *81*(3), 408–448. doi:10.3102/0034654311415121

Ghany, S. A., & Alzouebi, K. (2019). Exploring Teacher Perceptions of Using E-portfolios in Public Schools in the United Arab Emirates. *International Journal of Education and Literacy Studies*, *7*(4), 180–191. doi:10.7575/aiac.ijels.v.7n.4p.180

Gibson, M. T. (2020). Student intimidation, no pay and hunger strikes: The challenges facing Heads of Department in Bangladesh colleges. *Journal of Higher Education Policy and Management*, *42*(3), 365–379. doi:10.1080/1360080X.2020.1733735

Gilroy, P. (2005). The commercialisation of teacher education: Teacher education in the marketplace. *Journal of Education for Teaching*, *31*(4), 275–277. doi:10.1080/02607470500280076

Goldhaber, D., Krieg, J., Theobald, R., & Goggins, M. (2021). Front End to Back End: Teacher Preparation, Workforce Entry, and Attrition. *Journal of Teacher Education*. Advance online publication. doi:10.1177/00224871211030303

Gol-Guven, M. (2017). Ensuring quality in early childhood education and care: The case of Turkey. *Early Child Development and Care, 188*(3), 1–14. doi:10.1080/03004430.2017.1412957

Gomba, G. K. B. (2019). Challenges faced by Educators in Implementation of Continuous Professional Teacher Development in South Africa. *Teacher Education in the 21st Century.* . doi:10.5772/intechopen.84836

Gomez, S.A., & McKee, A. (2020) When Special Education and Disability Studies Intertwine: Addressing Educational Inequities through Processes and Programming. *Frontiers in Education, 5*, 202. doi:10.3389/feduc.2020.587045

Gomez, R. E., Kagan, S. L., & Fox, E. A. (2015). Professional development of the early childhood education teaching workforce in the United States: An overview. *Professional Development in Education, 41*(2), 169–186. doi:10.1080/19415257.2014.986820

Gomo, E. (2003). *Zimbabwe human development report*. United Nations Development Program.

Goodyear, V. A., & Armour, K. M. (2021). Young People's health-related learning through social media: What do teachers need to know? *Teaching and Teacher Education, 102*, 103340. Advance online publication. doi:10.1016/j.tate.2021.103340 PMID:34083866

Gore, J. M., & Gitlin, A. D. (2004). [RE]Visioning the academic–teacher divide: Power and knowledge in the educational community. *Teachers and Teaching, 10*(1), 35–58. doi:10.1080/1354060320000170918

Goudeau, S., Sanrey, C., Stanczak, A., Manstead, A., & Darnon, C. (2021). Why lockdown and distance learning during the COVID-19 pandemic are likely to increase the social class achievement gap. *Nature Human Behaviour, 5*(10), 1273–1281. doi:10.103841562-021-01212-7 PMID:34580440

Gourneau, B. (2014). Challenges in the first year of teaching: Lessons learned in an elementary education resident teacher program. *Contemporary Issues in Education Research, 7*(4), 299–318. doi:10.19030/cier.v7i4.8844

Government of Abu Dhabi. (2008). *The Abu Dhabi economic vision 2030*. https://u.ae/en/about-the-uae/strategies-initiatives-and-awards/local-governments-strategies-and-plans/abu-dhabi-economic-vision-2030

Graham, L. J., Tancredi, H., Willis, J., & McGraw, K. (2018). Designing out barriers to student access and participation in secondary school assessment. *Australian Educational Researcher, 45*(1), 103–124. doi:10.100713384-018-0266-y

Granlund, M., Imms, C., King, G., Andersson, A. K., Augustine, L., Brooks, R., Danielsson, H., Gothilander, J., Ivarsson, M., Lundqvist, L.-O., Lygnegård, F., & Almqvist, L. (2021). Definitions and Operationalization of Mental Health Problems, Wellbeing and Participation Constructs in Children with NDD: Distinctions and Clarifications. *International Journal of Environmental Research and Public Health, 18*(4), 1656. doi:10.3390/ijerph18041656 PMID:33572339

Compilation of References

Gräsel, C., Fussangel, K., & Pröbstel, C. (2006). Lehrkräfte zur Kooperation anregen – eine Aufgabe für Sisyphos? *Zeitschrift für Pädagogik*, *52*(2), 205–219.

Guldenhuys, J. L., & Oosthuizen, L. C. (2015). Challenges influencing teachers' involvement in Continuous Professional Development: A South African Perspective. *Teaching and Teacher Education*, *51*, 203–212. doi:10.1016/j.tate.2015.06.010

Guskey, T. R. (2005). Five key concepts kick off the process: Professional provides the power to implement standards. *Journal of Staff Development*, *26*(1), 36–40.

Hairon, S., & Dimmock, C. (2011). Singapore schools and professional learning communities: Teacher professional development and school leadership in an Asian hierarchical system. *Educational Review*, *64*(4), 405–424. doi:10.1080/00131911.2011.625111

Halai, A. (2006). Mentoring in-service teachers: Issues of role diversity. *Teaching and Teacher Education*, *22*(6), 700–710. doi:10.1016/j.tate.2006.03.007

Hamdan Bin Mohammed Smart University. (2020a). *UAE equips teachers from around the world with distance learning skills*. https://www.hbmsu.ac.ae/news/uae-equips-teachers-around-world-distance-learning-skills

Hamdan Bin Mohammed Smart University. (2020b). *Strategic partnership between HBMSU and UNESCO IITE to launch 'Be an Online Tutor in 24 Hours' course in five global languages*. https://www.hbmsu.ac.ae/news/strategic-partnership-between-hbmsu-and-unesco-iite-launch-%E2%80%98be-online-tutor-24-hours%E2%80%99-course

Hamdan Bin Mohammed Smart University. (2021a). *Be an Online Tutor in 24 hours*. https://cloudcampus.hbmsu.ac.ae/enrol/index.php?id=4

Hamdan Bin Mohammed Smart University. (2021b). *Design an online course in 24 hours*. https://cloudcampus.hbmsu.ac.ae/enrol/index.php?id=6

Hamdan Bin Mohammed Smart University. (2021c). *Here's what our learners have to say about HBMSU and its offerings*. https://www.hbmsu.ac.ae/testimonials

Hammond, T. C., Bodzin, A., Anastasio, D., Holland, B., Popejoy, K., Sahagian, D., Rutzmoser, S., Carrigan, J., & Farina, W. (2018). "You know you can do this, right?": Developing geospatial technological pedagogical content knowledge and enhancing teachers' cartographic practices with socio-environmental science investigations. *Cartography and Geographic Information Science*, *45*(4), 305–318. doi:10.1080/15230406.2017.1419440

Handerer, F., Kinderman, P., Timmermann, C., & Tai, S. J. (2021). How did mental health become so biomedical? The progressive erosion of social determinants in historical psychiatric admission registers. *History of Psychiatry*, *32*(1), 37–51. doi:10.1177/0957154X20968522 PMID:33143472

Harris, F., McCaffer, R., Baldwin, A., & Edwin-Fotwe, F. (2021). *Modern construction management* (8th ed.). Wiley Blackwell.

Harris, S. P., Davies, R. S., Christensen, S. S., Hanks, J., & Bowles, B. (2019). Teacher Attrition: Differences in Stakeholder Perceptions of Teacher Work Condition. *Education in Science*, *9*(4), 300. doi:10.3390/educsci9040300

Hart, L. M., Bond, K. S., Morgan, A. J., Rossetto, A., Cottrill, F. A., Kelly, C. M., & Jorm, A. F. (2019). Teen Mental Health First Aid for years 7–9: A description of the program and an initial evaluation. *International Journal of Mental Health Systems*, *13*(1), 71. doi:10.118613033-019-0325-4 PMID:31788023

Hattie, J. (2012). *Visible Learning for Teachers. Maximizing Impact on Learning*. Taylor and Francis. doi:10.4324/9780203181522

Hattie, J. (2013). *Visible Learning. A Synthesis of Over 8¢000 Meta-analyses Relating to Achievement*. Taylor and Francis.

Hawrilenko, M., Kroshus, E., Tandon, P., & Christakis, D. (2021). The Association Between School Closures and Child Mental Health During COVID-19. *JAMA Network Open*, *4*(9), e2124092. doi:10.1001/jamanetworkopen.2021.24092 PMID:34477850

Hayes, D. (2000). Cascade training and teachers' professional development. *ELT Journal*, *54*(2), 135–145. doi:10.1093/elt/54.2.135

Hellblom-Thibblin, T., & Sandberg, G. (2020). A dynamic ecological approach to categorisation at school, past and present. *European Journal of Special Needs Education*. Advance online publication. doi:10.1080/08856257.2020.1790883

Helmke, A. (2012). Unterrichtsqualität und Lehrerprofessionalität. In Diagnose, Evaluation und Verbesserung des Unterrichts (4th ed.). Seelze: Klett-Kallmeyer.

Herner-Patnode, L. (2009). Educator study groups: A professional development tool to enhance inclusion. *Intervention in School and Clinic*, *45*(1), 24–30. doi:10.1177/1053451209338397

Herrera, C. (1999). *School-based mentoring: A first look into its potential*.

Hidalgo-Andrade, P., Hermosa-Bosano, C., & Paz, C. (2021). Teachers' Mental Health and Self-Reported Coping Strategies During the COVID-19 Pandemic in Ecuador: A Mixed-Methods Study. *Psychology Research and Behavior Management*, *14*, 933–944. doi:10.2147/PRBM.S314844 PMID:34239334

Hıdıroğlu, S., Önsüz, M. F., Topuzoğlu, A., & Karavuş, M. (2010). Evaluation of the perspectives of the academic medical staff and residents concerning continuing professional development in a medical faculty. *Marmara Medical Journal*, *23*(3), 360-369. http://hdl.handle.net/11424/1919

Higgen, S., & Mösko, M. (2020). Mental health and cultural and linguistic diversity as challenges in school? An interview study on the implications for students and teachers. *PLoS One*, *15*(7), e0236160. doi:10.1371/journal.pone.0236160 PMID:32687515

Compilation of References

Hill, H. C., Beisiegel, M., & Jacob, R. (2013). Professional development research: Consensus, crossroads, and challenges. *Educational Researcher*, *42*(9), 476–487. doi:10.3102/0013189X13512674

Hobson, A., Ashby, P., Malderez, A., & Tomlinson, P. (2009). Mentoring beginning teachers: What we know and what we don't. *Teaching and Teacher Education*, *25*(1), 207–216. doi:10.1016/j.tate.2008.09.001

Hoffmann, D. S., Kearns, K., Bovenmyer, K. M., Cumming, W. P., Drane, L. E., Gonin, M., Kelly, L., Rohde, L., Tabassum, S., & Blay, R. (2021). Benefits of a multi-institutional, hybrid approach to teaching course design for graduate students, postdoctoral scholars, and leaders. *Teaching & Learning Inquiry*, *9*(1), 218–240. doi:10.20343/teachlearninqu.9.1.15

Hogan A. J. (2019). Social and medical models of disability and mental health: evolution and renewal. *CMAJ: Canadian Medical Association journal/ journal de l'Association medicale canadienne*, *191*(1), E16–E18. doi:10.1503/cmaj.181008

Hogan, D., & Gopinathan, S. (2008). Knowledge management, sustainable innovation, and pre-service teacher education in Singapore. *Teachers and Teaching*, *14*(4), 369–384. doi:10.1080/13540600802037793

Holmes, A., Signer, B., & MacLeod, A. (2010). Professional development at a distance: A mixed-method study exploring inservice teachers' views on presence online. *Journal of Digital Learning in Teacher Education*, *27*(2), 76–85. doi:10.1080/21532974.2010.10784660

Hossain, M. M., & Khan, A. M. (2015). Higher education reform in Bangladesh: An analysis. *Workplace: A Journal for Academic Labor*, *25*, 64-68.

Hossain, M. A., & Jahan, S. (2000). *Bangladesh. Globalization and living together: The challenges for educational content in Asia*. United Nations Educational, Scientific and Cultural Organization.

Howes, A., Frankham, J., Ainscow, M., & Farrell, P. (2004). The action in action research: Mediating and developing inclusive intentions. *Educational Action Research*, *12*(2), 239–258. doi:10.1080/09650790400200247

Hsu, P. C., Chang, I. H., & Chen, R. S. (2019). Online Learning Communities and Mental Health Literacy for Preschool Teachers: The Moderating Role of Enthusiasm for Engagement. *International Journal of Environmental Research and Public Health*, *16*(22), 4448. doi:10.3390/ijerph16224448 PMID:31766127

Humphrey, N., & Symes, W. (2013). Inclusive education for pupils with autistic spectrum disorders in secondary mainstream schools: Teacher attitudes, experience and knowledge. *International Journal of Inclusive Education*, *17*(1), 32–46. doi:10.1080/13603116.2011.580462

Hunter, J., & Back, J. (2011). Facilitating sustainable professional development through lesson study. *Mathematics Teacher Education and Development Journal*, *13*(1), 94–114.

IFES/IPES. (2021). *Peers*. https://www.ifes-ipes.ch/ueber-das-ifes-ipes/peers

Inclusive School Communities. (2019). *Exploring Disability and Inclusion Tool 2: The Models of Disability. Toolkit.* https://inclusiveschoolcommunities.org.au/resources/toolkit/exploring-disability-and-inclusion-tool-2-models-disability

Inoue, N., & Stracke, E. (2013). Non-native English speaking postgraduate TESOL students in Australia: Why did they come here? *University of Sydney Papers in TESOL, 8*, 29–56.

Institute of Medicine and National Research Council. (2012). *The early childhood care and education workforce: Challenges and opportunities: A workshop report.* The National Academies Press., doi:10.17226/13238

International Society for Technology in Education. (2008). *National education technology standards.* Retrieved from: www.iste.org/standards.aspx

Iorfino, F., Cross, S. P., Davenport, T., Carpenter, J. S., Scott E., Shiran, S., & Hickie, I. B. (2019). A Digital Platform Designed for Youth Mental Health Services to Deliver Personalized and Measurement-Based Care. *Frontiers in Psychiatry, 10*, 595. DOI= doi:10.3389/fpsyt.2019.00595

Jenkins, J. M. (2014). Early childhood development as economic development: Considerations for state-level policy innovation and experimentation. *Economic Development Quarterly, 28*(2), 147–165. doi:10.1177/0891242413513791

Jeon, S., Jeon, L., Lang, S., & Newell, K. (2021). Teacher depressive symptoms and child math achievement in Head Start: The roles of family–teacher relationships and approaches to learning. *Child Development, 92*(6), 2478–2495. Advance online publication. doi:10.1111/cdev.13601 PMID:34131906

Johns, L. A., & Sosibo, Z. C. (2019). Constraints in the implementation of continuing professional teacher development policy in the Western Cape, South Africa. *The Journal of Higher Education, 33*(5), 130–145.

Joseph, D. (2014). Interpretative phenomenological analysis. In K. A. Hartwig (Ed.), *Research Methodologies in Music Education* (pp. 145–166). Cambridge Scholars Publishing.

Jumady, E., Suglarto, S., & Latief, F. (2021). Management Performance Analysis Based on Total Quality Management Principles. *Point of View Research Management, 2*(1). Retrieved from: journal.accountingpointofview.id/index.php/POVREMA/article/view/112

Jung, I. (2005). ICT-pedagogy integration in teacher training: Application cases worldwide. *Journal of Educational Technology & Society, 8*(2), 94–101. https://www.jstor.org/stable/jeductechsoci.8.2.94

Kangai, C., & Bukaliya, R. (2011). Teacher Development through open distance learning: The case for Zimbabwe. *International Journal on New Trends in Education and Their Implications, 2*(13), 124–141.

Kantonsrat Kanton Zürich. (2005). *Volksschulgesetz.* http://www2.zhlex.zh.ch/appl/zhlex_r.nsf/WebView/E797088926DBBD28C125864500284C64/$File/412.100_7.2.05_111.pdf

Compilation of References

Kanyongo, G. Y. (2005). Zimbabwe's public education system reforms: Successes and challenges. *International Education Journal, 6*(1), 65–74.

Kasap, S. (2020, March 4). 'Eğitimde Birlikteyiz' hareketiyle 32 bin çocuk kapsayıcı eğitime katıldı. *Anadolu Ajansı*. https://www.aa.com.tr/tr/egitim/egitimde-birlikteyiz-hareketiyle-32-bin-cocuk-kapsayici-egitime-katildi/1754490

Kazantzis, N., & Stuckey, M. E. (2018). Inception of a discovery: Re-defining the use of Socratic dialogue in cognitive behavioral therapy. *International Journal of Cognitive Therapy, 11*(2), 117–123. doi:10.100741811-018-0015-z

Keller, C., Al-Hendawi, M., & Abuelhassan, H. (2016). Special education teacher preparation in the Gulf Cooperation Council countries. *Teacher Education and Special Education, 39*(3), 194–208. doi:10.1177/0888406416631125

Kennedy, M. (2016). How does professional development improve teaching? *Review of Educational Research, 86*(4), 945–980. Advance online publication. doi:10.3102/0034654315626800

Khanlou, N. (2019). Post-Secondary Student Mental Health and Well-being: A Systems and Intersectionality-Informed Approach. *International Journal of Mental Health and Addiction, 17*(3), 415–417. doi:10.100711469-019-00105-1

Kilbourne, A. M., Smith, S. N., Choi, S. Y. E., Liebrecht, C., Rusch, A., Abelson, J. L., Eisenberg, D., Himle, J. A., Fitzgerald, K., & Almirall, D. (2018). Adaptive School-based Implementation of CBT (ASIC): clustered-SMART for building an optimized adaptive implementation intervention to improve uptake of mental health interventions in schools. *Implementation Science; IS, 13*(1), 119. doi:10.118613012-018-0808-8 PMID:30185192

Kim, L. E., & Asbury, K. (2020). 'Like a rug had been pulled from under you': The impact of COVID-19 on teachers in England during the first six weeks of UK lockdown. *The British Journal of Educational Psychology, 90*(4), 1062–1083. doi:10.1111/bjep.12381 PMID:32975830

Kingdon, G. (1996). The quality and efficiency of private and public education: A case study of urban India. *Oxford Bulletin of Economics and Statistics, 58*(1), 57–82. doi:10.1111/j.1468-0084.1996.mp58001004.x

Klapproth, F., Federkeil, L., Heinschke, F., & Jungmann, T. (2020). Teachers' experiences of stress and their coping strategies during COVID-19 induced distance teaching. *Journal of Pedagogical Research, 4*(4), 444–452. doi:10.33902/JPR.2020062805

Konalasami, K., & Arafat, Y., & MulYadi, M. (2020). Principal's management competencies in improving the quality of education. *Journal of Social Work and Science Education, 1*(2). Advance online publication. doi:10.5290/jswe.VIi2.47

Kondakçı, Y., & Haser, Ç. (2019). Socialization at the university: A qualitative investigation on the role of contextual dynamics in the socialization of academics. *Research in Educational Administration and Leadership, 4*(2), 272–301. doi:10.30828/real/2019.2.3

Koukis, N., & Jimoyiannis, A. (2019). MOOCS for teacher professional development: Exploring teachers' perceptions and achievements. *Interactive Technology and Smart Education*, *16*(1), 74–91. Advance online publication. doi:10.1108/ITSE-10-2018-0081

Kozma, R. B. (2002). *ICT and educational reform in developed and developing countries. Center for Technology in Learning*. SRI International.

Kreis, A. & Schnebel, S. (2017). Peer Coaching in der praxissituierten Ausbildung von Lehrpersonen. *Lehrerbildung auf dem Prüfstand 2017*, 1 – 7.

Krieg, J. M., Goldhaber, D., & Theobald, R. (2020a). *Disconnected development? The importance of specific human capital in the transition from student teaching to the classroom* (CALDER working paper no. 236–0520). https://eric.ed.gov/?id=ED605737

Kriewaldt, J., & Turnidge, D. (2013). Conceptualising an approach to clinical reasoning in the education profession. *The Australian Journal of Teacher Education*, *38*(6), 103–115. doi:10.14221/ajte.2013v38n6.9

Kruse, K. (2013). *What is leadership?* Retrieved from https:www.forbes.com/sites/kevinkruse/2013/04/09

Lally, J. R. (2009). The science and psychology of infant-toddler care: How an understanding of early learning has transformed child care. *Zero to Three*, *30*(2), 47–53.

Lalvani, P., & Broderick, A. A. (2013). Institutionalized ableism and the misguided "Disability Awareness Day". *Transformative Pedagogies for Teacher Education in Equity and Excellence in Education*, *46*(4), 468–483. doi:10.1080/10665684.2013.838484

Lam, B. H. (2015). Teacher Professional Development in Hong Kong Compared to Anglosphere: The Role of Confucian Philosophy. *Psychology. Social Education*, *7*(3), 295–310. doi:10.25115/psye.v7i3.521

Lamb, P., & Aldous, D. (2016). Exploring the relationship between reflexivity and reflective practice through lesson study within initial teacher education. *International Journal for Lesson and Learning Studies*, *5*(2), 99–115. doi:10.1108/IJLLS-11-2015-0040

Laurillard, D. (2016). The educational problem that MOOCs could solve: Professional development for teachers of disadvantaged students. *Research in Learning Technology*, *24*(1), 29369. Advance online publication. doi:10.3402/rlt.v24.29369

Lave, J., & Wenger, E. (1991). *Situated learning: Legitimate peripheral participation*. University of Cambridge Press. doi:10.1017/CBO9780511815355

Lawrence, C. A., & Chong, W. H. (2010). Teacher collaborative learning through the lesson study: Identifying pathways for instructional success in a Singapore high school. *Asia Pacific Education Review*, *11*(4), 565–572. doi:10.100712564-010-9103-3

Compilation of References

Lee, M. Y., & Choy, B. H. (2017). Mathematical teacher noticing: The key to learning from lesson study. In E.O. Shack, M.H. Fisher & J.A. Wilhelm (Eds.), Teacher noticing: Bridging and broadening perspectives, contexts, and frameworks. Springer.

Lee, H., Linn, M. C., Varma, K., & Liu, O. L. (2010). How do technology-enhanced inquiry science units impact classroom learning? *Journal of Research in Science Teaching, 47*(1), 71–90. doi:10.1002/tea.20304

Lever, N., Mathis, E., & Mayworm, A. (2017). School Mental Health Is Not Just for Students: Why Teacher and School Staff Wellness Matters. *Report on Emotional & Behavioral Disorders in Youth, 17*(1), 6–12. PMID:30705611

Lewis, C. (2000). Lesson study: The core of Japanese professional development. *The Annual Meeting of the American Educational Research Association – Conference Proceedings*.

Lewis, C. (2004). Does lesson study have a future in the united states? *Journal of Social Science Education, 3*(1), 115–137. doi:10.4119/jsse-321

Linden, B., Boyes, R., & Stuart, H. (2021). Cross-sectional trend analysis of the NCHA II survey data on Canadian post-secondary student mental health and wellbeing from 2013 to 2019. *BMC Public Health, 21*(1), 590. doi:10.118612889-021-10622-1 PMID:33765965

Lindqvist, G., & Nilholm, C. (2013). Making schools inclusive? Educational leaders' views on how to work with children in need of special support. *International Journal of Inclusive Education, 17*(1), 95–110. doi:10.1080/13603116.2011.580466

Lindqvist, G., & Nilholm, C. (2014). Promoting inclusion? "Inclusive" and effective head teachers' descriptions of their work. *European Journal of Special Needs Education, 29*(1), 74–90. doi:10.1080/08856257.2013.849845

Lindqvist, G., Nilholm, C., Almqvist, L., & Wetso, G. M. (2011). Different agendas? The views of different occupational groups on special needs education. *European Journal of Special Needs Education, 26*(2), 143–157. doi:10.1080/08856257.2011.563604

Lister, K., Seale, J., & Douce, C. (2021). Mental health in distance learning: A taxonomy of barriers and enablers to student mental wellbeing. *Open Learning*, 1–15. Advance online publication. doi:10.1080/02680513.2021.1899907

Little, J. W. (1990). The persistence of privacy: Autonomy and initiative in teachers' professional relations. *Teachers College Record, 91*(4), 509–536.

Little, J. W. (2012). Professional community and professional development in the learning-centred school. In M. Kooy & K. van Veen (Eds.), *Teacher learning that matters: International perspectives*. Routledge.

Liu, S., & Phelps, G. (2020). Does Teacher Learning Last? Understanding How Much Teachers Retain Their Knowledge After Professional Development. *Journal of Teacher Education, 71*(5), 537–550. doi:10.1177/0022487119886290

Lockheed, M. E., & Verspoor, A. M. (1991). *Improving primary education in developing countries.* Oxford University Press.

Lombardi, J. (2016) The Deficit Model Is Harming Your Students. *Edutopia.* https://www.edutopia.org/blog/deficit-model-is-harming-students-janice-lombardi

Lopriore, L. (2020). EFL awareness in ELT: Emerging challenges & new paradigms in teacher education. *Lingue e Linguaggi, 38,* 259–275.

Machingura, V., Magudu, S., Maravanyika, O. E., Moyo, P. V., & Musengi, M. (2012). Quality of education in independent primary schools in Zimbabwe: A national survey. *International Journal of Academic Research in Progressive Education and Development, 1*(4), 64–73.

Maeng, J. L., Mulvey, B. K., Smetana, L. K., & Bell, R. L. (2013). Preservice teachers' TPACK: Using technology to support inquiry instruction. *Journal of Science Education and Technology, 22*(6), 838–857. doi:10.100710956-013-9434-z

Mahere, S. M. (2010). *Speech read on the occasion of awarding the Secretary's Merit Award to a primary school* [Unpublished speech]. Ministry of Primary and Secondary Education.

Mahere, S. M. (2018). Clinical Supervision Model: Its role in the Professional Development of Teachers in Zimbabwe. *Zimbabwe Journal of Education, 30*(3).

Mangwaya, E., Blignaut, S., & Pillay, S. K. (2016). The readiness of schools in Zimbabwe for the implementation of early childhood education. *South African Journal of Education, 36*(1), 792. doi:10.15700aje.v36n1a792

Mantzios, M., Cook, A., & Egan, H. (2019). Mental health first aid embedment within undergraduate psychology curriculums: An opportunity of applied experience for psychology students and for enhancing mental health care in higher education institutions. *Higher Education Pedagogies, 4*(1), 307–310. doi:10.1080/23752696.2019.1640631

Maphosa, A., & Chisango, F. F. T. (2016). Why Educational Practitioners Resist Staff Development Programmes: Evidence from Binga and Hwange Districts, Zimbabwe. *Greener Journal of Educational Research, 6*(2), 44-51.

Maravanyika, O. E. (1990). Implementing Educational Policies in Zimbabwe: *World Bank Discussion Paper No. 91, Africa Technical Department Series.* World Bank.

Marcelo, C. (2009). Professional development of teachers: Past and Future. *Educational Sciences Journal, 8,* 2–20.

Marco-Bujosa, L. M., McNeill, K. L., Gonzalez-Howard, M., & Loper, S. (2017). An exploration of teacher learning from an educative reform-oriented science curriculum: Case studies of teacher curriculum use. *Journal of Research in Science Teaching, 54*(2), 141-168.

Martin, J., Elg, M. Gremyr, I., & Wallo, A. (2021). *Towards a quality management competence framework: exploring needed competencies in quality management.* Retrieved from: doi:10.1080/14783363.2019.1576516

Compilation of References

Marti, S. (2019). *Toolbox Führung. Kompendium zeitgemässer Führung*. Eigenverlag.

Mazzer, K. R., & Rickwood, D. (2015). Teachers' role breadth and perceived efficacy in supporting school mental health. *Advances in School Mental Health Promotion, 8*(1), 29–41. doi:10.1080/1754730X.2014.978119

McGugan, S. A. (2013). *Academic Development Through Teaching: A Study into the experiences of Postgraduate and Postdoctoral Researchers* [Unpublished doctoral dissertation]. The Open University.

McLean Davies, L., Anderson, M., Deans, J., Dinham, S., Griffin, P., Kameniar, B., Page, J., Reid, C., Rickards, F., Tayler, C., & Tyler, D. (2013). Masterly preparation: Embedding clinical practice in a graduate pre-service teacher education programme. *Journal of Education for Teaching, 39*(1), 93–106. doi:10.1080/02607476.2012.733193

McLean, L., Abry, T., Taylor, M., Jimenez, M., & Granger, K. (2017). Teachers' mental health and perceptions of school climate across the transition from training to teaching. *Teaching and Teacher Education, 65*, 230–240. doi:10.1016/j.tate.2017.03.018

Megale, A. (2019). *Educação bilíngue no Brasil*. Fundação Santillana.

Meissel, K., Parr, J. M., & Timperley, H. S. (2016). Can professional development of teachers reduce disparity in student achievement? *Teaching and Teacher Education, 58*, 163-173. doi:10.1016/j.tate.2016.05.01

Mercer, S. (2018). Psychology for language learning: Spare a thought for the teacher. *Language Teaching, 51*(4), 504–525. doi:10.1017/S0261444817000258

Mergler, A. G., & Spooner-Lane, R. (2012). What Pre-service Teachers need to know to be Effective at Values-based Education. *The Australian Journal of Teacher Education, 37*(8), 5. https://ro.ecu.edu.au/ajte/vol37/iss8/5. doi:10.14221/ajte.2012v37n8.5

Metin, N. (2018). Okul öncesi kaynaştırma sınıfında öğretmen. *Erken Çocukluk Çalışmaları Dergisi, 2*(2), 428–439. doi:10.24130/eccd-jecs.196720182279

Meyers, C. V., Molefe, A., Brandt, W. C., Zhu, B., & Dhillon, S. (2016). Impact results of the eMINTS professional development validation study. *Educational Evaluation and Policy Analysis, 38*(3), 455–476. doi:10.3102/0162373716638446

Mhakure, D. (2019). School-based mathematics teacher professional learning: A theoretical position on the lesson study approach. *South African Journal of Education, 39*(Supplement 1), S1–S8. doi:10.15700aje.v39ns1a1754

Mhumure, G. (2017). *Zimbabwean teachers' perspective on the History Subject Panels as an Innovation for professional development* [Unpublished PhD Thesis]. University of Free State.

Milne, A., & Mhlolo, M. (2021). Lessons for South Africa from Singapore's gifted education – A comparative study. *South African Journal of Education, 41*(1), 1–8. doi:10.15700aje.v41n1a1839

Ministry of Education (MOE). (2010). *Schools as professional learning communities*. MOE.

Ministry of Education. (2004). *Curriculum Document for English language curriculum for secondary education*. Kingdom of Bahrain: Directorate of Curricula – Secondary Education.

Ministry of Education. (2005). *Curriculum Document for English language curriculum for basic education*. Kingdom of Bahrain: Directorate of Curricula – Basic Education.

Ministry of Family and Social Services (MoFSS). (2021). *Engelli ve yaşlı istatistik bülteni Mayıs 2021*. https://www.aile.gov.tr/media/81779/eyhgm_istatistik_bulteni_mayis_2021.pdf

Ministry of National Education (MoNE). (2018). *Engeli Olan Çocuklar İçin Kapsayıcı Erken Çocukluk Eğitimi Projesi*. https://tegm.meb.gov.tr/www/engeli-olan-cocuklar-icin-kapsayici-erken-cocukluk-egitimi-projesi/icerik/537

Ministry of National Education (MoNE). (2020). *National education statistics: Formal education 2019/'20*. https://sgb.meb.gov.tr/meb_iys_dosyalar/2020_09/04144812_meb_istatistikleri_orgun_egitim_2019_2020.pdf

Ministry of Primary and Secondary Education (MoPSE). (2014). *Curriculum Framework for Primary and Secondary Education 2015-2022*. Curriculum Development Unit.

Ministry of Primary and Secondary Education. (2005). *The Director's Circular Minute Number 4 of 2005: The Secretary's Merit Award*. The Ministry of Primary and Secondary Education.

Ministry of Primary and Secondary Education. (2007). *The Director's Circular Minute Number 11 of 2007: The Secretary's Merit Award*. The Ministry of Primary and Secondary Education.

Ministry of Primary and Secondary Education. (2020). *2019 Primary and Secondary Education Statistics Report*. Retrieved from: http://mopse.co.zw/sites/default/files/public/downloads/2019%20Annual%20Education%20Statistics%20Report%20pdf%20for%20UPLOADING.pdf

MOE Training. (n.d.). *YouTube*. Retrieved January,08, 2020 from https://www.youtube.com/channel/UCxnNZ5Wxc3VuUQtTSD2Qm4Q/featured

Mónico, P., Mensah, A., Grünke, M., Garcia, T., Fernández, E., & Rodríguez, C. (2018). Teacher knowledge and attitudes towards inclusion: A cross-cultural study in Ghana, Germany and Spain. *International Journal of Inclusive Education*, 24(5), 527–543. doi:10.1080/13603116.2018.1471526

Morgan, A. J., Fischer, J. A., Hart, L. M., Kelly, C., Kitchener, B., Reavley, N., Yap, M., Cvetkovski, S., & Jorm, A. (2019). Does Mental Health First Aid training improve the mental health of aid recipients? The training for parents of teenagers randomised controlled trial. *BMC Psychiatry*, 19(1), 99. doi:10.118612888-019-2085-8 PMID:30917811

Morgan, H. (2021). Neoliberalism's influence on American universities: How the business model harms students and society. *Policy Futures in Education*. Advance online publication. doi:10.1177/14782103211006655

Compilation of References

Morton, B. M., & Berardi, A. A. (2017). Trauma-informed school programming: Applications for mental health professionals and educator partnerships. *Journal of Child & Adolescent Trauma.* PMID:32318170

Mtetwa, D., Chabongora, B., Ndemo, Z., & Maturure, E. (2015). Features of Continuous Professional Development (CPD) of School Mathematics Teachers in Zimbabwe. *International Journal of Educational Sciences*, 8(1), 135–147. doi:10.1080/09751122.2015.11917599

Mueller, C. O. (2021). "I Didn't Know People With Disabilities Could Grow Up to Be Adults": Disability History, Curriculum, and Identity in Special Education. *Teacher Education and Special Education*, 44(3), 189–205. doi:10.1177/0888406421996069

Mukeredzi, T. G. (2016). Teacher professional development outside the lecture room: Voices of professionally unqualified practicing teachers in rural Zimbabwe secondary schools. *Global Education Review*, 3(4), 84–106.

Mukeredzi, T. G. (2016). Teacher Professional Development outside the lecture room: Voices of Professionally Unqualified Practicing Teachers in Rural Zimbabwe Secondary Schools. *Global Education Review*, 3(4), 84–106.

Mullis, I. V. S., Martin, M. O., Goh, S., & Cotter, K. (2016). *Teachers, Teacher Education and Professional Development in South Africa. TIMSS 2015 Encyclopedia: Educational Policy and Curriculum in Mathematics and Science.* TIMSS & PIRLS International Study Centre.

Munawaru, I. (2010). *An assessment of the internal efficiency of basic education in the Wa Municipality of the Upper West Region: Master's Thesis:* Retrieved from https://www.grin.com/document/461294

Murano, D., Way, J. D., Martin, J. E., Walton, K. E., Anguiano-Carrasco, C., & Burrus, J. (2019). The need for high-quality pre-service and in-service teacher training in social and emotional learning. *Journal of Research in Innovative Teaching & Learning*, 12(2), 111–113. doi:10.1108/JRIT-02-2019-0028

Murphy, J. W., & Perez, F. D. (2002). A Postmodern Analysis of Disabilities. *Journal of Social Work in Disability & Rehabilitation*, 1(3), 61–72. doi:10.1300/J198v01n03_06

Murray, B., Domina, T., Petts, A., Renzulli, L., & Boylan, R. (2020). "We're in This Together": Bridging and Bonding Social Capital in Elementary School PTOs. *American Educational Research Journal*, 57(5), 2210–2244. doi:10.3102/0002831220908848

Mwalongo, A. (2011). Teachers' perceptions about ICTs for teaching, professional development, administration and personal use. *International Journal of Education and Development Using ICT*, 7(3), 36-49.

Nagashima, Y., Rahman, M., Al-Zayed Josh, S. R., Dhar, S. S., Nomura, S., Rahman, M. A., & Mukherjee, H. (2014). *A Study on National University and Affiliated Colleges in Bangladesh* (Vol. 65). International Bank for Reconstruction and Development/The World Bank.

Nakabugo, M. G., Bisaso, R., & Masembe, C. S. (2011). *The continuum of teacher professional development: Towards a coherent approach to the development of secondary school teachers in Uganda.* Retrieved from http://homehiroshima-u.ac.jp/cice/publications/sosho42-14pdf

National Institute of Education (NIE). (2009). A Teacher Education Model for the 21st Century. NIE.

National Research Council. (2000). How people learn: Brain, mind, experience, and school (Expanded Edition). Washington, DC: The National Academies Press. doi:10.17226/9853

National Science Teaching Association. (2021). *About the Next Generation Science Standards.* Retrieved from https://ngss.nsta.org/about.aspx

Ndlovu-Gatsheni, S. J. (2021). Internationalisation of higher education for pluriversity: A decolonial reflection. *Journal of the British Academy, 9*(s1), 77–98. doi:10.5871/jba/009s1.077

Nerad, M. (2012). Conceptual approaches to doctoral education: A community of practice. *Alternation (Durban), 19*(2), 57–72. https://www.ufs.ac.za/templates/journals.aspx?article=1264

Neuman, M. J. (2005). Governance of early childhood education and care: Recent developments in OECD countries. *Early Years, 25*(2), 129–141. doi:10.1080/09575140500130992

New, R. S., & Cochran, M. (Eds.). (2007). *Early childhood education: An international encyclopedia* (Vol. 1). Praeger.

Niesz, T., & Ryan, K. (2018). Teacher ownership versus scaling up system-wide educational change: The case of Activity Based Learning in South India. *Educational Research for Policy and Practice, 17*(3), 209–222. doi:10.100710671-018-9232-8

Nowell, L., Grant, K. A., Berenson, C., Dyjur, P., Jeffs, C., Kelly, P., Kenny, N., & Mikita, K. (2020b). Innovative certificate programs in university teaching and learning: Experiential learning for graduate students and postdoctoral scholars. *Papers on Postsecondary Learning and Teaching, 4*, 85–95.

Nowell, L., Ovie, G., Kenny, N., Hayden, K. A., & Jacobsen, M. (2019). Professional learning and development initiatives for postdoctoral scholars. *Studies in Graduate and Postdoctoral Education, 11*(1), 35–55. doi:10.1108/SGPE-03-2019-0032

Nowell, L., Ovie, G., Kenny, N., & Jacobsen, M. (2020a). Postdoctoral scholars' perspectives about professional learning and development: A concurrent mixed-methods study. *Palgrave Communications, 6*(1), 1–11. doi:10.105741599-020-0469-5

O'Dowd, R., & Dooly, M. (2021). Exploring teachers' professional development through participation in virtual exchange. *ReCALL*, 1–16. doi:10.1017/S0958344021000215

O'Gorman, E., & Drudy, S. (2010). Addressing the professional development needs of teachers working in the area of special education/inclusion in mainstream schools in Ireland. *Journal of Research in Special Educational Needs, 10*(1), 157–167. doi:10.1111/j.1471-3802.2010.01161.x

Oakland, J. S. (1995). *Total quality management: Test with cases.* Butterworth-Heinemann.

Compilation of References

Oberle, E., & Schonert-Reichl, K. (2016). Stress contagion in the classroom? The link between classroom teacher burnout and morning cortisol in elementary school students. *Social Science & Medicine, 159*, 30-37. doi:10.1016/j.socscimed.2016.04.031

OECD. (2009). *Creating effective teaching and learning environments: First results from TALIS.* Retrieved from https://www.oecd.org/education/school/43023606.pdf

OECD. (2019). TALIS 2018 Results (Volume 1): Teachers and School Leaders as Lifelong Learners. TALIS, OECD Publishing. doi:10.1787/1d0bc92a-en

OECD. (2020). Strengthening online learning when schools are closed: The role of families and teachers in supporting students during the COVID-19 crisis. *OECD Policy Responses to Coronavirus (COVID-19).* https://www.oecd.org/coronavirus/policy-responses/strengthening-online-learning-when-schools-are-closed-the-role-of-families-and-teachers-in-supporting-students-during-the-covid-19-crisis-c4ecba6c/

Ogegbo, A. A., Gaigher, E., & Salagram, T. (2019). Benefits and challenges of lesson study: A case of teaching Physical Science in South Africa. *South African Journal of Education, 39*(1), 1–9. Advance online publication. doi:10.15700aje.v39n1a1680

Oh, C. H. (2003). Information Communication Technology and the New University: A View on eLearning. *The Annals of the American Academy of Political and Social Science, 585*(1), 134–153. doi:10.1177/0002716202238572

Olteanu, C. (2016). Reflection and the object of learning. *International Journal for Lesson and Learning Studies, 5*(1), 60–75. doi:10.1108/IJLLS-08-2015-0026

Ono, Y., & Ferreira, J. (2010). A case study of continuing teacher professional development through lesson study in South Africa. *South African Journal of Education, 30*(1), 59–74. doi:10.15700aje.v30n1a320

Organisation for Economic Co-operation and Development (OECD). (2014). *A Teachers' Guide to TALIS 2013: Teaching and Learning International Survey.* Paris: TALIS, OECD Publishing.

Organisation for Economic Cooperation and Development (OECD). (2020a). *Education policy outlook: Turkey.* https://www.oecd.org/education/policy-outlook/country-profile-Turkey-2020.pdf

Organisation for Economic Cooperation and Development (OECD). (2020b). Turkey. In *Education at a Glance 2020: OECD Indicators.* OECD Publishing. doi:10.1787/1701b91e-

Orion, N., & Libarkin, J. (2014). Earth systems science education. In N. G. Lederman & S. K. Abell (Eds.), *Handbook of research on science education* (Vol. 2, pp. 481–496). Routledge.

Orland, L. (2001). Reading a mentoring situation: One aspect of learning to mentor. *Teaching and Teacher Education, 17*(1), 75–88. doi:10.1016/S0742-051X(00)00039-1

Osborne, D. (2021). *Professional development and growth: Instruction and pedagogy for youth in public libraries.* Retrieved from https: //publiclibraryinstruction.web.unc.edu/chapter-11-professional-development-and-growth/

Osborne, J. F., Borko, H., Fishman, E., Gomez Zaccarelli, F., Berson, E., Busch, K. C., & Tseng, A. (2019). Impacts of a practice-based professional development programme on elementary teachers' facilitation of and student engagement with scientific argumentation. *American Educational Research Journal, 56*(4), 1067-1112. doi:10.3102/0002831218812059

Ozamiz-Etxebarria, N., Santxo, N. B., Mondragon, N. I., & Santamaria, M. D. (2021). The psychological state of teachers during the COVID-19 crisis: The challenge of returning to face-to-face teaching. *Frontiers in Psychology, 11*, 620718. Advance online publication. doi:10.3389/fpsyg.2020.620718 PMID:33510694

Özaydın, L., & Çolak, A. (2011). Okul öncesi öğretmenlerinin kaynaştırma eğitimine ve okul öncesi eğitimde kaynaştırma eğitimi hizmet içi eğitim programına ilişkin görüşleri. *Kalem Eğitim ve İnsan Bilimleri Dergisi, 1*(1), 189–226.

Özdemir, S. M. (2016, October 27-30). *Temel eğitim öğretmenlerinin mesleki gelişim etkinliklerine katılım durumları ve öğrenme-öğretme sürecine etkisi* [Conference paper]. IV. Uluslararası Eğitim Programları ve Öğretim Kongresi, Antalya, Turkey.

Ozdemir, N. O. (2014). The role of English as a lingua franca in academia: The case of Turkish postgraduate students in an Anglophone-centre context. *Procedia: Social and Behavioral Sciences, 141*, 74–78. doi:10.1016/j.sbspro.2014.05.014

Özdoğru, A. A. (2018). Program development, assessment, and evaluation in early childhood care and education. In V. C. X. Wang (Ed.), *Handbook of research on program development and assessment methodologies in K-20 education* (pp. 109–127). IGI Global. doi:10.4018/978-1-5225-3132-6.ch006

Özdoğru, A. A., & Widrick, R. (2011). *New York State Infant and Toddler Resource Network 2011 evaluation report.* Early Care & Learning Council.

Özdoğru, A. A., & Wulfsohn, S. (2011). *Social-Emotional Consultation in Infant and Toddler Child Care Programs: Final evaluation report.* Early Care & Learning Council.

Özdoğru, M. (2021). Özel gereksinimli çocukların okul öncesi eğitiminde karşılaşılan sorunlar. *Temel Eğitim, 11*(11), 6–16. doi:10.52105/temelegitim.11.1

Öztürk, T., Zayimoğlu Öztürk, F., & Kaya, N. (2016). Okul öncesi öğretmenlerinin hizmet öncesi eğitimlerine ilişkin görüşleri ve hizmet içi eğitim durumlari. *Erzincan Üniversitesi Eğitim Fakültesi Dergisi, 18*(1), 92–114. doi:10.17556/jef.67571

Pandori-Chuckal, J. K. (2020). *Mental Health Literacy and Initial Teacher Education: A Program Evaluation* [PhD Thesis]. Western University. Electronic Thesis and Dissertation Repository, 6834. https://ir.lib.uwo.ca/etd/6834

Pascoe, M., Hetrick, S. E., & Parker, A. G. (2020). The impact of stress on students in secondary school and higher education. *International Journal of Adolescence and Youth, 25*(1), 104–112. doi:10.1080/02673843.2019.1596823

Peacock, M. (2009). Th evaluation of foreign-language-teacher education programmes. *English Language Teaching Research, 13*(3), 259–278.

Pearson, J. (2003). Information and communications technologies and teacher education in Australia. *Technology, Pedagogy and Education, 12*(1), 39–58. doi:10.1080/14759390300200145

PH Zürich. (2021a). *Übersicht Weiterbildung*. https://phzh.ch/de/Weiterbildung/

PH Zürich. (2021b). *Good Practice von Zürcher Schulen*. https://phzh.ch/de/Weiterbildung/volksschule/veranstaltungen/Themenreihen/good-practice/

Philipsen, B., Tondeur, J., Roblin, N. P., Vanslambrouck, S., & Zhu, C. (2019). Improving teacher professional development for online and blended learning: A systematic meta-aggregative review. *Educational Technology Research and Development, 67*(5), 1145–1174. doi:10.100711423-019-09645-8

Phillippo, K., & Kelly, M. (2014). On the fault line: A qualitative exploration of high school teachers' involvement with student mental health issues. *School Mental Health, 6*(3), 184–200. doi:10.100712310-013-9113-5

Phillips, D., & Ochs, K. (2003). Processes of policy borrowing in education: Some explanatory and analytical devices. *Comparative Education, 39*(4), 451–461. doi:10.1080/0305006032000162020

Pickering, L. E., & Walsh, E. J. (2011). Using videoconferencing technology to enhance classroom observation methodology for the instruction of preservice early childhood professionals. *Journal of Digital Learning in Teacher Education, 27*(3), 99–108. doi:10.1080/21532974.2011.10784664

Pollit, C. (Ed.). (1992). *Considering quality: An analytic guide to the literature on quality and standards in The Public Service*. Centre for the Evaluation of Public Policy and Practice, Brunel University.

Popova, A., Evans, D., Breeding, M. E., & Arancibia, V. (2018). *Teacher professional development around the world: The gap between evidence and practice*. World Bank Policy Research Working Paper (8572).

Postholm, M. B. (2012). Teachers' professional development: A theoretical review. *Educational Research, 54*(4), 405–429. doi:10.1080/00131881.2012.734725

Postholm, M. B. (2012). Teachers' Professional Development: A Theoretical. *Review of Educational Research, 54*(4), 405–429.

Prestridge, S., & Tondeur, J. (2015). Exploring elements that support teachers engagement in online professional development. *Education Sciences, 5*(3), 199–219. doi:10.3390/educsci5030199

Pretorius, C., Chambers, D., Cowan, B., & Coyle, D. (2019). Young People Seeking Help Online for Mental Health: Cross-Sectional Survey Study. *JMIR Mental Health, 6*(8), e13524. doi:10.2196/13524 PMID:31452519

Pungello, E. P., Kainz, K., Burchinal, M., Wasik, B. H., Sparling, J. J., Ramey, C. T., & Campbell, F. A. (2010). Early educational intervention, early cumulative risk, and the early home environment as predictors of young adult outcomes within a high-risk sample. *Child Development, 81*(1), 410–426. doi:10.1111/j.1467-8624.2009.01403.x PMID:20331676

Punie, Y., Zinnbauer, D., & Cabrera, M. (2006). *A Review of the Impact of ICT on Learning.* Working Paper prepared for DG EAC. Institute for Prospective Technological Studies, DG JRC.

Purinton, T. & Skaggs, J. (in press). *Knowledge mobility is the new internationalization: Guiding educational globalization one educator at a time.* Lanham, MD: Lexington/Rowman & Littlefield.

Putnam, R., & Borko, H. (2000). What do new views of knowledge and thinking have to say about research on teacher learning? *Educational Researcher, 29*(1), 4–15. doi:10.3102/0013189X029001004

Rahman, S. (2018). Globalisation, Migration and Knowledge Generation: A Study on Higher Education Institutions in Bangladesh. In *Engaging in Educational Research* (pp. 263–278). Springer. doi:10.1007/978-981-13-0708-9_14

Rahman, T., Nakata, S., Nagashima, Y., Rahman, M., Sharma, U., & Rahman, M. A. (2019). *Bangladesh tertiary education sector review: Skills and innovation for growth.* World Bank. doi:10.1596/31526

Ramsden, P. (1991). Evaluating and Improving Teaching in Higher Education. Legal Education Review, 149. doi:10.53300/001c.6008

Randall, D., Rouncefield, M., & Tolmie, P. (2021). Ethnograpy, CSCW and Ethnomethodology. *Computer Supported Cooperative Work, 30,* 189-214. Retrieved on: https://link.springer.com/article/10.1007/s10606-020-09388-8

Raufelder, D., & Ittel, A. (2012). Mentoring in der Schule: Ein Überblick. Theoretische und praktische Implikationen für Lehrer/-innen und Schüler/-innen im internationalen Vergleich. *Diskurs Kindheits- und Jugendforschung, 2,* 147 – 160. https://elibrary.utb.de/doi/epdf/10.3224/diskurs.v7i2.04

Rauf, P. A., Ali, S. K. S., & Noor, N. A. M. (2017). The Relationship Between Models Of Teachers Professional Development And Teachers Instructional Practices In The Classrooms In The Primary Schools In The State Of Selangor, Malaysia. *International Journal of Education, Psychology and Counseling, 2*(5), 120–132.

Reinke, W. M., Stormont, M., Herman, K. C., Puri, R., & Goel, N. (2011). Supporting children's mental health in schools: Teachers perceptions of needs, roles, and barriers. *School Psychology Quarterly, 26*(1), 1–13. doi:10.1037/a0022714

Renkly, S., & Bertolini, K. (2018) Shifting the Paradigm from Deficit Oriented Schools to Asset Based Models: Why Leaders Need to Promote an Asset Orientation in our Schools. *Empowering Research for Educators, 2*(1), Article 4. https://openprairie.sdstate.edu/ere/vol2/iss1/4

Compilation of References

Reynolds, D., & Neeleman, A. (2021). School improvement capacity: A review and a reconceptualisation from the perspectives of educational effectiveness and educational policy. In A. O. G. Beverborg, T. Feldhoff, K. M. Merki, & F. Radisch (Eds.), *Concepts and design developments in school improvement research: Longitudinal, multilevel and mixed methods and their relevance for educational accountability* (pp. 27–40). Zurich Rostock Springer Pub. doi:10.1007/978-3-030-69345-9_3

Richter, D., & Dixon, J. (2020). Models of Mental Health Problems: A Quasi-Systematic Review of Theoretical Approaches. PsyArXiv. doi:10.31234/osf.io/s6hg5osf.io/s6hg5

Riddel, A. R. (1998). Reforms of educational efficiency and equity in developing countries: An overview. *Compare: A Journal of Comparative Education*, *28*(3), 227–292.

Ridout, B., & Campbell, A. (2018). The use of social networking sites in mental health interventions for young people: Systematic review. *Journal of Medical Internet Research*, *20*(12), e12244. doi:10.2196/12244 PMID:30563811

Roberts, J. (1998). *Language teacher education*. Arnold.

Roman, T. (2020). Supporting the Mental Health of Preservice Teachers in COVID-19 through Trauma-Informed Educational Practices and Adaptive Formative Assessment Tools. *Journal of Technology and Teacher Education*, *28*(2), 473–481. https://www.learntechlib.org/primary/p/216363/

Ronfeldt, M., Matsko, K. K., Greene Nolan, H., & Reininger, M. (2021). Three Different Measures of Graduates' Instructional Readiness and the Features of Preservice Preparation That Predict Them. *Journal of Teacher Education*, *72*(1), 56–71. doi:10.1177/0022487120919753

Roth, K., & Garnier, H. (2007). What science teaching looks like: An international perspective. *Educational Leadership*, *64*(4), 16–23.

Rusch, A., Rodriguez-Quintana, N., Choi, S.Y., Lane, A., Smith, M., Koschmann, E., & Smith, S.N. (2021). School Professional Needs to Support Student Mental Health During the COVID-19 Pandemic. *Frontiers in Education, 6,* 193. doi:10.3389/feduc.2021.663871

Rusch, D., Walden, A. L., Gustafson, E., Lakind, D., & Atkins, M. C. (2018). A qualitative study to explore paraprofessionals' role in school-based prevention and early intervention mental health services. *Journal of Community Psychology*, *47*(2), 272–290. doi:10.1002/jcop.22120 PMID:30161268

Rust, V., & Kim, S. (2012). The Global Competition in Higher Education. *World Studies in Education*, *13*(1), 5–20. Advance online publication. doi:10.7459/wse/13.1.02

Saewyc, D. M., Konishi, C., Rose, H. A., & Homma, Y. (2014). School-based strategies to reduce suicidal ideation, suicide attempts, and discrimination among sexual minority and heterosexual adolescents in Western Canada. *Infant Journal Child Youth Family Studies*, *5*(1), 89–112. doi:10.18357/ijcyfs.saewyce.512014 PMID:26793284

Saito, E., Murase, M., Tsukui, A., & Yeo, L. (2014). *Lesson study for learning community: A guide to sustainable school reform*. Routledge. doi:10.4324/9781315814209

Sancar, R., Atal, D. & Deryakulu, D. (2021). A new framework for teachers' professional development. *Teaching and Teacher Education, 101*. doi:10.1016/j_tate.2021.103305

Sarker, M. F. H., Al Mahmud, R., Islam, M. S., & Islam, M. K. (2019). Use of e-learning at higher educational institutions in Bangladesh: Opportunities and challenges. *Journal of Applied Research in Higher Education, 11*(2), 210–223. doi:10.1108/JARHE-06-2018-0099

Sart, Z. H., Barış, S., Sarışık, Y., & Düşkün, Y. (2016). *The right of children with disabilities to education: Situation analysis and recommendations for turkey*. Education Reform Initiative. http://en.egitimreformugirisimi.org/wp-content/uploads/2017/03/UnicefOzelGereksinimliRaporENG.08.06.16.web_.pdf

Sato, M., & Loewen, S. (2019). Do teachers care about research? The research-pedagogy dialogue. *ELT Journal, 73*(1), 1–10. doi:10.1093/elt/ccy048

Saunders, M., Alcantara, V., Cervantes, L., Del Razo, J., Lopez, R., & Perez, W. (2017). *Getting to Teacher Ownership: How Schools Are Creating Meaningful Change*. Annenberg Institute for School Reform at Brown University.

Scheerens, J., & Bosker, R. (1997). *The foundation of educational effectiveness*. Elsevier Science Ltd.

Schleicher, A. (2020). *Teaching in the United Arab Emirates: 10 lessons from TALIS*. OECD. https://www.oecd.org/education/talis/Teaching_in_the_UAE-10_Lessons_from_TALIS.pdf

Schwartz, K. D., Exner-Cortens, D., McMorris, C. A., Makarenko, E., Arnold, P., Van Bavel, M., Williams, S., & Canfield, R. (2021). COVID-19 and Student Well-Being: Stress and Mental Health during Return-to-School. *Canadian Journal of School Psychology, 36*(2), 166–185. doi:10.1177/08295735211001653 PMID:34040284

Schwartz, T., Dinnen, H., Smith-Millman, M. K., Dixon, M., & Flaspohler, P. D. (2017). The urban teaching cohort: Pre-service training to support mental health in urban schools. *Advances in School Mental Health Promotion, 10*(1), 26–48. doi:10.1080/1754730X.2016.1246195

Segall, M. J., & Campbell, J. M. (2012). Factors relating to education professionals' classroom practices for the inclusion of students with autism spectrum disorders. *Research in Autism Spectrum Disorders, 6*(3), 1156–1167. doi:10.1016/j.rasd.2012.02.007

Şen, Ö., & Kızılcalıoğlu, G. (2020). Covid-19 pandemi sürecinde üniversite öğrencilerinin ve akademisyenlerin uzaktan öğretime yönelik görüşlerinin belirlenmesi [Determining the views of university students and academicians on distance education during the Covid-19 pandemic process]. *International Journal of 3D Printing Technologies and Digital Industry, 4*(3), 239-252. . doi:10.46519/ij3dptdi.830913

Sharmini, S., & Spronken-Smith, R. (2020). The PhD–is it out of alignment? *Higher Education Research & Development, 39*(4), 821–833. doi:10.1080/07294360.2019.1693514

Compilation of References

Sharon, G. B., Ball, S. J., & Bowe, R. (1995). *Markets, choice and equity in education*. Open University Press.

Shelemy, L., Harvey, K., & Waite, P. (2019). Supporting students' mental health in schools: What do teachers want and need? *Emotional & Behavioural Difficulties, 24*(1), 100–116. doi:10.1080/13632752.2019.1582742

Shiddike, M. O., & Rahman, A. A. (2019). Engaging faculty in professional development: Lessons from Bangladesh. *Journal of Educational and Developmental Psychology, 9*(2), 124–137. doi:10.5539/jedp.v9n2p124

Skaalvik, E. M., & Skaalvik, S. (2014). Teacher self-efficacy and perceived autonomy: Relations with teacher engagement, job satisfaction, and emotional exhaustion. *Psychological Reports, 114*(1), 68–77. doi:10.2466/14.02.PR0.114k14w0 PMID:24765710

Slee, R. (2013). How do we make inclusive education happen when exclusion is a political predisposition? *International Journal of Inclusive Education, 17*(8), 895–907. doi:10.1080/13603116.2011.602534

Snongtaweeporn, T., Siribensanont, C., Kongsang, W., & Channuwong, S. (2020). Total Quality Management in Modern Organisations by Using Participation and Teamwork. *Journal of Arts Management, 4*(3). https://so02tci-thaijo.org/index.php/jam/article/view/243921

Sokal, L., Trudel, L. E., & Babb, J. (2020). Canadian teachers' attitudes towards change, efficacy, and burnout during the COVID-19 pandemic. *International Journal of Educational Research Open, 1*, 100016. Advance online publication. doi:10.1016/j.ijedro.2020.100016

Sönmez, N., Alptekin, S., & Bıçak, B. (2018). Okul öncesi eğitim öğretmenlerinin kaynaştırma eğitiminde öz-yeterlik algıları ve hizmetiçi eğitim gereksinimleri: Bir karma yöntem çalışması. *Abant İzzet Baysal Üniversitesi Eğitim Fakültesi Dergisi, 18*(4), 2270–2297. doi:10.17240/aibuefd.2018.18.41844-444422

South African Council for Educators (SACE). (2011). *Redefining the role and functions of South African Council for Educators*. South African Council for Educators.

South African Council for Educators. (2013). *CPTD Management Handbook*. South African Council for Educators.

Spiteri, M., & Chang Rundgren, S. N. (2017). Maltese primary teachers' digital competence: Implications for continuing professional development. *European Journal of Teacher Education, 40*(4), 521–534. doi:10.1080/02619768.2017.1342242

Spratt, J., & Florian, L. (2015). Inclusive pedagogy: From learning to action. Supporting each individual in the context of 'everybody'. *Teaching and Teacher Education, 49*, 89–96. doi:10.1016/j.tate.2015.03.006

Stanulis, R. N., Fallona, C. A., & Pearson, C. A. (2002). Am I doing what I am supposed to be doing?: Mentoring novice teachers through the uncertainties and challenges of their first year of teaching. *Mentoring & Tutoring, 10*(1), 71–81. doi:10.1080/13611260220133162

Steinert, B., Klieme, E., Maag-Merki, K., Döbrich, P., Halbheer, U., & Kunz, A. (2006). Lehrerkooperation in der Schule: Konzeption, Erfassung, Ergebnisse. *Zeitschrift für Pädagogik*, *52*(2), 185–204.

Stephenson, L. (2010). Developing curriculum leadership in the UAE. *Education, Business and Society*, *3*(2), 146–158. Advance online publication. doi:10.1108/17537981011047970

Steyn, G. M. (2008). Continuing professional development for teachers in South Africa and social learning systems: Conflicting conceptual frameworks of learning. *Koers*, *73*(1), 15–31. doi:10.4102/koers.v73i1.151

Stigler, J. W., & Hiebert, J. (1999). *The teaching gap: Best ideas from the world's teachers for improving education in the classroom.* The Free Press.

Strauß, S., & Rohr, D. (2019). Peer-Learning in der Lehrer*innenbildung. *Journal für lehrerInnenbildung*, *10*(3), 106–116. Advance online publication. doi:10.35468/jlb-03-2019_11

Strogilos, V. (2012). The cultural understanding of inclusion and its development within a centralised system. *International Journal of Inclusive Education*, *16*(12), 1241–1285. doi:10.1080/13603116.2011.557447

Strogilos, V., & Tragoulia, E. (2013). Inclusive and collaborative practices in co-taught classrooms: Roles and responsibilities for teachers and parents. *Teaching and Teacher Education*, *35*, 81–91. doi:10.1016/j.tate.2013.06.001

Strogilos, V., Tragoulia, E., Avramidis, E., Voulagka, A., & Papanikolaou, V. (2017). Understanding the development of differentiated instruction for students with and without disabilities in co-taught classrooms. *Disability & Society*, *32*(8), 1216–1238. doi:10.1080/09687599.2017.1352488

Sucuoğlu, B., Bakkaloğlu, H., İşcen Karasu, F., Demir, Ş., & Akalın, S. (2014). Okul öncesi öğretmenlerinin kaynaştırmaya ilişkin bilgi düzeyleri. *Kuram ve Uygulamada Eğitim Bilimleri*, *14*(4), 1467–1485. doi:10.12738/estp.2014.4.2078

Sullivan, F. R. (2021). Critical pedagogy and teacher professional development for online and blended learning: The equity imperative in the shift to digital. *Educational Technology Research and Development*, *69*(1), 21–24. doi:10.100711423-020-09864-4 PMID:33192035

Sultana, M., & Shahabul, H. M. (2018). The cause of low implementation of ICT in education sector considering higher education: A study on Bangladesh. *Canadian Social Science*, *14*(12), 67–73.

Svendsen, B. (2020). Inquiries into teacher professional development—What really matters? *Education*, *140*(3), 111–130.

Swissuniversities. (2021). *Swiss Education System*. https://www.swissuniversities.ch/en/topics/studying/swiss-education-system

Tahar, A., Sofyani, H., Arisanti, E. N., & Amalia, F. A. (2022). Maintaining Higher Education Institution Performance Amid the Covid-19 Pandemic: The Role of IT Governance, IT Capability and Process Agility. *Malaysian Online Journal of Educational Management*, *10*(1), 45–61.

Compilation of References

Tan, C. Y., & Dimmock, C. (2014). How 'top-performing' Asian School system formulates and implements policy: The case of Singapore. *Educational Management Administration & Leadership, 17*(4), 114–123. doi:10.1177/1741143213510507

Tarusikirwa, M. C. (2016). Modeling Teacher Development through Open and Distance Learning: A Zimbabwean Experience. *Universal Journal of Educational Research, 4*(12), 2706–2715. doi:10.13189/ujer.2016.041203

Tasker, T. (2011). Teacher learning through LS: An activity theoretical approach toward professional development in the Czech Republic. In K. E. Johnson & P. R. Golombek (Eds.), *Research on second language teacher education: A sociocultural perspective on professional development*. Routledge.

Taylor, N. (2008). *What's wrong with South African Schools?* Paper presented at what's working in School Development Conference, Boksburg, South Africa.

Teaching Certification. (2021) *Alternative Teaching Certification*. https://www.teaching-certification.com/alternative-teaching-certification.html

Teese, R., & Polesol, J. (2003). *Undemocratic schooling: Equity and equality in mass secondary education in Australia*. Melbourne University Publishing.

Tican-Başaran, S., & Aykaç, N. (2020). Evaluation of 2018 Turkish early childhood teacher education curriculum. *Pegem Journal of Education and Instruction, 10*(3), 889–928. doi:10.14527/pegegog.2020.028

Trautmann, N. M., & MaKinster, J. G. (2014). Meeting teachers where they are and helping them achieve their geospatial goals. In J. MaKinster, N. Trautmann, & M. Barnett (Eds.), *Teaching science and investigating environmental issues with geospatial technology* (pp. 51–64). Academic Press.

Treleaven. (2020, October 8). Inside the mental health crisis at Canadian universities. *Maclean's*. https://www.macleans.ca/education/inside-the-mental-health-crisis-at-canadian-universities/

Tülübaş, T. (2017). *Orta kariyer evresinde bulunan akademisyenlerin mesleki kimlik algıları: Kolektif araçsal durum çalışması* [Professional identity of mid-career academics: A collective instrumental case study] [Unpublished doctoral thesis]. Kocaeli Üniversitesi Eğitim Bilimleri Enstitüsü.

Turkish Statistical Institute (TÜİK). (2021). *İstatistiklerle çocuk, 2020*. https://data.tuik.gov.tr/Bulten/Index?p=Istatistiklerle-Cocuk-2020-37228

Türkoğlu, B. (2020, September 16-19). *Review of the eligibility of the activity books in the Inclusive Early Childhood Education for Children with Disabilities Project to the acquisitions of the preschool education program of the Ministry of National Education* [Conference presentation]. International Pegem Conference on Education. https://2020.ipcedu.org/dosyalar/files/ipcedu_ozetlerv2.pdf.pdf

Turner, F., Brownhill, S., & Wilson, E. (2017). The transfer of content knowledge in a cascade model of professional development. *Teacher Development, 21*(2), 175–191. doi:10.1080/13664530.2016.1205508

Tyler-Wood, T. L., Cockerham, D., & Johnson, K. R. (2018). Implementing new technologies in a middle school curriculum: A rural perspective. *Smart Learning Environments*, 5(1), 22. doi:10.118640561-018-0073-y

UAE Vision. (2018a). *Home*. https://www.vision2021.ae/en

UAE Vision. (2018b). *First-Rate Education System*. https://www.vision2021.ae/en/national-agenda-2021/list/first-rate-circle

UNESCO. (1994). *The Salamanca Statement and framework for action on special needs education*. Retrieved from Paris: https://www.right-to-education.org/resource/salamanca-statement-and-framework-action-special-needs-education

UNESCO. (2021). *Information and Communication Technologies (ICT)*. http://uis.unesco.org/en/glossary-term/information-and-communication-technologies-ict

UNESCO. (2021). *Right to pre-primary education: A global study*. https://unesdoc.unesco.org/ark:/48223/pf0000375332

United Arab Emirates Ministry of Education. (2017). *Ministry of Education launches a smart training platform for teachers and SIS app for students and parents*. https://www.moe.gov.ae/En/MediaCenter/News/Pages/SISApp.aspx

United Arab Emirates Ministry of Education. (2020a). *Vision and Mission*. https://www.moe.gov.ae/En/AboutTheMinistry/Pages/VisionMission.aspx

United Arab Emirates Ministry of Education. (2020b). *Live Webinars*. https://www.moe.gov.ae/en/importantlinks/tsf/pages/webinars.aspx

United Arab Emirates Ministry of Education. (2020c). *25,000 education staff to start remote specialized training through advanced technological system*. https://www.moe.gov.ae/en/mediacenter/news/pages/specialized-training.aspx

United Arab Emirates Ministry of Education. (2020d). *Educational Professions Licensure System*. https://tls.moe.gov.ae/#!/about

United Arab Emirates Ministry of Education. (2020e). *Frequently Asked Questions*. https://tls.moe.gov.ae/#!/faq

Ustuk, O. & Comoglu, I. (2019). Lesson study for professional development of English language teachers: Key takeaways from international practices. *Journal on Efficiency and Responsibility in Education and Science*, 12(2), 41-50. doi:10.7160/eriesj.2019.120202

Vagi, R., Pivovarova, M., & Miedel Barnard, W. (2019). Keeping Our Best? A Survival Analysis Examining a Measure of Preservice Teacher Quality and Teacher Attrition. *Journal of Teacher Education*, 70(2), 115–127. doi:10.1177/0022487117725025

Compilation of References

Vaillancourt, T., Szatmari, P., Georgiades, K., & Krygsman, A. (2021). The impact of COVID-19 on the mental health of Canadian children and youth. *Facets*, *6*(1), 1628–1648. doi:10.1139/facets-2021-0078

Vaillant, G. (2012). Positive mental health: Is there a cross-cultural definition? *World Psychiatry; Official Journal of the World Psychiatric Association (WPA)*, *11*(2), 93–99. doi:10.1016/j.wpsyc.2012.05.006 PMID:22654934

van Manen, M. (2014). *Phenomenology of Practice: Meaning-giving Methods in Phenomenological Research and Writing*. Left Coast Press.

Villegas-Reimers, E. (2003). *Teacher professional development: An international review of the literature*. UNESCO International Institute for Educational Planning.

Villegas-Remers, E. (2003). *Teacher professional development: An international view of the literature*. Retrieved from UNESCO website: https://unesdoc.unesco.org/images/0013/001330/133010e.pdf

Viner, R., Russell, S., Croker, H., Packer, J., Ward, J., Stansfield, C., Mytton, O., Bonell, C., & Booy, R. (2020). School closure and management practices during coronavirus outbreaks including COVID-19: A rapid systematic review. *The Lancet. Child & Adolescent Health*, *4*(5), 397–404. doi:10.1016/S2352-4642(20)30095-X PMID:32272089

Vitalis Akuma, F., & Callaghan, R. (2019). Teaching practices linked to the implementation of inquiry-based practical work in certain science classrooms. *Journal of Research in Science Teaching*, *56*(1), 64–90. doi:10.1002/tea.21469

Von der Embse, N., Pendergast, L. L., Segool, N., Saeki, E., & Ryan, S. (2016). The influence of test-based accountability policies on school climate and teacher stress across four states. *Teaching and Teacher Education*, *59*, 492–502. doi:10.1016/j.tate.2016.07.013

Von der Groeben, A. (2003). Lernen in heterogenen Gruppen. Chance und Herausforderung. *Pädagogik*, *55*(9), 6–9.

Von Esch, K. S., & Kavanagh, S. S. (2018). Preparing mainstream classroom teachers of English learner students: Grounding practice-based designs for teacher learning in theories of adaptive expertise development. *Journal of Teacher Education*, *69*(3), 239–251. doi:10.1177/0022487117717467

Vrasidas, C., & Glass, G. V. (2007). Teacher Professional Development and ICT: Strategies and Models. *Yearbook of the National Society for the Study of Education*, *106*(2), 87–102. doi:10.1111/j.1744-7984.2007.00116.x

Waldron, S. M., Stallard, P., Grist, R., & Hamilton-Giachritsis, C. (2018). The 'long-term' effects of universal school-based anxiety prevention trials: A systematic review. *Mental Health & Prevention*, *11*, 8–15. doi:10.1016/j.mhp.2018.04.003

Wang, J., & Odell, S. (2002). Mentored learning to teach according to standards-based reform: A critical review. *Review of Educational Research*, *72*(3), 481–546. doi:10.3102/00346543072003481

Wang, J., & Odell, S. J. (2007). An alternative conception of mentor-novice relationships: Learning to teach in reform-minded ways as a context. *Teaching and Teacher Education*, *23*(4), 473–489. doi:10.1016/j.tate.2006.12.010

Wang, S. K., Hsu, H. Y., Reeves, T. C., & Coster, D. C. (2014). Professional development to enhance teachers' practices in using information and communication technologies (ICTs) as cognitive tools: Lessons learned from a design-based research study. *Computers & Education*, *79*, 101–115. doi:10.1016/j.compedu.2014.07.006

Wang, X., Kim, B., Lee, J. W. Y., & Kim, M. S. (2014). Encouraging and being encouraged: Development of an epistemic community and teacher professional growth in a Singapore classroom. *Teaching and Teacher Education*, *44*, 12–24. doi:10.1016/j.tate.2014.07.009

Watkins, A. L. (2019). *Facilitating Sustainable Professional Development Programs: A Phenomenological Study of the Use of Online Professional Development* [EdD. Thesis]. School of Education, Manhattanville College. ProQuest Dissertations Publishing, 2019. 13865370. https://www.proquest.com/openview/dbcfdf768e1c2a19e0acece9899b7908/1?pq-origsite=gscholar&cbl=18750&diss=y

Webb, A. S., & Welsh, A. J. (2019). Phenomenology As a Methodology for Scholarship of Teaching and Learning Research. *Teaching & Learning Inquiry*, *7*(1), 168–181. doi:10.20343/teachlearninqu.7.1.11

Wei, R. C., Darling-Hammond, L., & Adamson, F. (2010). *Professional development in the United States: Trends and challenges*. National Staff Development Council.

Weissberg, R. P. (2019). Promoting the Social and Emotional Learning of Millions of School Children. *Perspectives on Psychological Science*, *14*(1), 65–69. doi:10.1177/1745691618817756 PMID:30799753

Wei, Y., Baxter, A., & Kutcher, S. (2019). Establishment and validation of a mental health literacy measurement in Canadian educators. *Psychiatry Research*, *279*, 231–236. doi:10.1016/j.psychres.2019.03.009 PMID:30890275

Whitley, R. (2008). Postmodernity and mental health. *Harvard Review of Psychiatry*, *16*(6), 352–364. doi:10.1080/10673220802564186 PMID:19085389

Wiles, R., Bengry-Howell, A., Crow, G., & Nind, M. (2013). But is it Innovation? The development of novel methodological approaches in qualitative research. *Methodological Innovations*, *8*(1), 18–33. doi:10.4256/mio.2013.002

Wilkins, S., & Juusola, K. (2018). The benefits and drawbacks of transnational higher education: Myths and realities. *Australian Universities' Review*, *60*(2), 68–76.

Wilson, A. (2015). A guide to phenomenological research. *Nursing Standard*, *29*(34), 38–43. doi:10.7748/ns.29.34.38.e8821 PMID:25902251

Compilation of References

Wilson, S. M., & Berne, J. (1999). Teacher learning and the acquisition of professional knowledge: An examination of research on contemporary professional development. *Review of Research in Education*, *24*, 173–209. doi:10.2307/1167270

Wisker, G., & Robinson, G. (2014). Examiner practices and culturally inflected doctoral theses. *Discourse (Abingdon)*, *35*(2), 190–205. doi:10.1080/01596306.2012.745730

Wong, V. W., Ruble, L. A., Yu, Y., & McGrew, J. H. (2017). Too stressed to teach? Teaching quality, student engagement, and IEP outcomes. *Exceptional Children*, *83*(4), 412–427. doi:10.1177/0014402917690729 PMID:30555178

Woodcock, S., & Hardy, I. (2017). Probing and problematizing teacher professional development for inclusion. *International Journal of Educational Research*, *83*, 43–54. doi:10.1016/j.ijer.2017.02.008

World Bank. (1992). *A review of primary and secondary education for successful expansion to equity of learning achievements: Report Number 8976-ZIM*. Retrieved from: https:/document1.worldbank.org/ curated/en/474521468167384035/pdf/multi-page.pdf

World Bank. (2013). *Bangladesh Education Sector Review (Report 80613-BD)*. Available at: https://openknowledge.worldbank.org/handle/10986/17853

World Bank. (2014). *A Study on National and Affiliated Colleges in Bangladesh. Discussion Paper.* South Asia Human Development Sector, Report No. 65. Available at: https://openknowledge.worldbank.org/bitstream/handle/10986/17743/844280NWP0BD0U00Box382120B00PUBLIC0.pdf?sequence=1&isAllowed=y

Wyatt, M., & Ončevska-Ager, E. (2016). Teachers' cognitions regarding continuing professional development. *ELT Journal*, *71*(2), 171–185. doi:10.1093/elt/ccw059

Yalçinkaya, M., Koşar, D., & Altunay, E. (2014). Araştırma görevlilerinin bilim insanı yetiştirme sürecine ilişkin görüşleri [Research assistants' views on the training process of scholars]. *Kastamonu Eğitim Dergisi*, *22*(3), 1009–1034.

Yastibas, A. E. (2021). Preparing Preservice English Language Teachers to Teach at Unprecedented Times: The Case of Turkey. *Journal of English Teaching*, *7*(1). Advance online publication. doi:10.33541/jet.v7i1.2284

Yıldırım, A., & Şimşek, H. (2013). *Sosyal bilimlerde nitel araştırma yöntemleri* [Qualitative research methods in social sciences]. Seçkin yayıncılık.

Yılmaz, G. (2014). *Turkish middle income trap and less skilled human capital*. Working paper no: 14/30. Central Bank of the Republic of Turkey. https://www.tcmb.gov.tr/wps/wcm/connect/c56c98ef-1c49-4324-94af-f88191f00906/WP1430.pdf?MOD=AJPERES&CACHEID=ROOTWORKSPACE-c56c98ef-1c49-4324-94af-f88191f00906-m3fw68n

YÖK. (2017). *YÖK'te "Araştırma ve aday araştırma üniversiteleri" ile toplantı* [Meeting with "Research and candidate research universities"]. https://www. yok. gov.tr/Sayfalar/Haberler/yok-te-aday-ve-aday-arastirma-universiteleri-ile-toplanti.Aspx

Yoon, K. S., Duncan, T., Lee, S. W. Y., Scarloss, B., & Shapley, K. L. (2007). *Reviewing the evidence on how teacher professional development affects student achievement.* U.S. Department of Education, Institute of Education Sciences, National Center for Education Evaluation and Regional Assistance, Regional Educational Laboratory Southwest.

Ziyadin, S., Shash, N., Kenzhebekova, D., Yessenova, G., & Tlemissov, U. (2018). Data on the role of leadership in developing expertise in teaching in developing country. *Data in Brief, 18,* 1127–1133. doi:10.1016/j.dib.2018.03.137 PMID:29900285

About the Contributors

Osama Al Mahdi is an assistant professor in Bahrain Teachers College [BTC] at the University of Bahrain. He is a Fellow of the Higher Education Academy [FHEA] in the United Kingdom, upon completing the Postgraduate Certificate in Academic Practice [PCAP] Program in York St. John University in 2012. Dr Al Mahdi received his master's degree in Primary Education from the University of Bahrain in 2001, and his Ph.D. in Education from the University of Bristol, UK in 2009. His areas of expertise include, primary education, teacher training and professional development, educational leadership, home-school relationships, social foundations of education, sociocultural theory, and research methodologies.

Ted Purinton is Senior Education Advisor for the Economic Development Board of Bahrain with special secondment as the Dean of the Bahrain Teachers College (BTC). Previously, he served as Dean of the Graduate School of Education at the American University in Cairo (AUC), as well as Associate Provost for the University (AUC's senior internationalization officer, also responsible for academic administration and strategic initiatives). Prior, he served as Chair of the Department of Educational Administration at National Louis University in Chicago; Associate at the Center for Literacy, North Central Regional Educational Laboratory; programs administrator at the Paramount Unified School District in Los Angeles; and a high school/intermediate school English teacher in Los Angeles. He holds a doctorate in educational policy, planning, and administration from the University of Southern California. Purinton has served on multiple boards for various schools and other educational institutions and has consulted for a wide range of educational organizations and governments on issues ranging from organizational restructuring to teacher professional development, university budget allocation to tertiary system redesign, and more.

***

About the Contributors

Lucy Bailey is Associate Professor and Head of Education Studies at the Bahrain Teachers College in the University of Bahrain. She was previously an Associate Professor at the University of Nottingham Malaysia, where she was programme coordinator for the MA Education. She has written extensively about the internationalisation of education, including studies of various aspects of international schooling, the internationalisation of higher education, and the schooling of students who are refugees or asylum seekers. Her research interests also include parental involvement in education, and cultural constructions of gender.

Hanin Bukamal is a doctoral researcher at the University of Birmingham, and a lecturer at Bahrain Teachers College at the University of Bahrain. Hanin received her Master, Bachelor Honours, and Bachelor of Education from the University of Auckland. Hanin has been researching and teaching in higher education since 2011. She is a validator for qualification placement, and an evaluator for institutional listing for the Bahrain Qualifications Authority since 2016. Hanin is a Fellow of the Higher Education Academy since 2018. Her research interests are in inclusive education, special education, quality assurance in education, research methodology in education, inclusive pedagogy, and student centred learning.

Cleophas Peter Chidakwa is a former Primary School Teacher and School Head. Currently, he is a Senior Lecturer with the University of Zimbabwe where he lectures in Quality Management in Education, Educational Planning and Policy Studies, Educational leadership, Administration, and Management. He holds a Doctor of Philosophy (PhDEd), with special emphasis on Quality Management in Education, a Master of Education in Educational Administration (MEA) and a Bachelor of Education in Educational Administration, Planning and Policy Studies (BEdEAPPS) degrees awarded by the University of Zimbabwe. Doctor Chidakwa has published research papers in peer reviewed journals on Quality Management, Planning, Policy Studies and Leadership in education.

Tawanda Chinengundu, D.Ed., earned his Doctorate in Curriculum Studies with emphasis in Technical Vocational Education and Training (TVET) from the University of South Africa (UNISA), a Masters in Technical Vocational Education (Technical Graphics and Design) from the University of Zimbabwe (UZ), and a B.Ed. in Technical Graphics and Design from the UZ. Dr. Chinengundu has taught for more than 24 years. He has taught Engineering Graphics and Design and Civil Technology at High schools in Zimbabwe and South Africa. He was also a lecturer at Belvedere Technical Teachers' college in Zimbabwe for 8 years. He has also served as the National Chief Examiner for Advanced Level Geometrical and Mechanical Drawing for Zimbabwe School Examinations Council. He was a part-time lecturer in

About the Contributors

the department of Technical and Vocational Education at the UZ. Dr. Chinengundu has been a part-time and e-tutor in Civil and Engineering Drawing at UNISA. He has reviewed 5 IGI book chapters. Dr. Chinengundu has authored book chapters and articles in peer reviewed journals focusing TVET issues. His research interests are in Curriculum design and Instruction, Trends in pedagogies of Technical and Vocational subjects, infusion of technology in teaching Engineering Graphics and Design, integration of Fourth Industrial Revolution technologies in teaching and learning of TVET courses and Teacher Education dynamics in pandemic times.

Nihan Demirkasımoğlu is working for Hacettepe University, at the Department of Educational Administration. Her research interests include ethics in education, abusive supervision, public service motivation, emotional labor, and organizational principles. She teaches Turkish Education System and School Management, Organization Theories, Introduction to Management and Academic Writing Styles courses at the undergraduate and graduate levels.

Frederic Fovet is an Associate Professor within the School of Education and Technology at Royal Roads University. He is Program Head for the MA in Educational Leadership and Management. His research portfolio includes projects related to disability studies in the educational landscape, inclusion, Universal Design for Learning, social justice in the classroom, the integration of Critical Pedagogy into classroom practices, and leadership for inclusion. Frederic was Director of the Office for Students with Disabilities at McGill University for four years over the period of his PhD. He was responsible there for the campus wide development of UDL practices. He acts as a consultant on UDL, both domestically and internationally, with K-12 schools and post-secondary institutions.

Rolf Gollob, Prof. Dr. h.c. (*1955), was a primary school teacher before studying ethnology and journalism at Zurich University. After obtaining his Master's degree he concentrated on ethnological research and later went on to become a lecturer at Zurich University of Teacher Education. He has worked there as a lecturer for more than twenty years now, focusing his efforts on civic education and intercultural pedagogy. Since 1996 he has traveled frequently to South-East Europe as an expert in human rights and civic education for the Council of Europe. Rolf Gollob is the author of various textbooks on democracy education and teaching and learning.

André Hedlund is a Chevening Alumnus, MSc Psychology of Education - University of Bristol, Educational Consultant, Speaker, and Guest Lecturer on Bilingualism and Cognition in Postgraduate courses. He currently works as an Edify Bilingual Program Mentor and as a member of BRAZ-TESOL's Mind, Brain, and Education SIG. He blogs at edcrocks.com.

About the Contributors

Jerald Hondonga is a TVET practitioner with a lot of interest in Technical Teacher Education and Development, skills training and curriculum development issues.

Saadet Kuru-Çetin is a trained Educational Management with a focus on educational management, teacher education, and ethics. She completed her undergraduate degree at Gazi University in 1998, and completed her doctoral degree in educational management and Policy at Ankara University in 2013. Her currently working on the field of educational management and Ethic at Mugla Sıtkı Kocman University.

Rumbidzayi Masina (PhD, Fort Hare University, SA) is a senior lecturer at the University of Zimbabwe in the Art Design and Technology Education Department, Faculty of Education. An expert in Textile Science, Apparel, Design and Design. Conducted several researches in assessment and evaluation of programs, projects, methods and processes. Involved in research and designing of new programs, modules and materials. Possesses excellent administrative and communication skills along with constructive and effective teaching methodologies and ICT pedagogy that promote a stimulating learning environment.

Abigirl Mawonedzo (PhD Fort Hare University, South Africa) Senior Lecturer at the University of Zimbabwe, Specialist in Textile Science, Apparel, Design and Technology. Vast experience in module writing and designing of new programmes.

Ghadah Al Murshidi, is Associate Professor in language and literacy at the College of Education, UAE University. She has published extensively in the area of language and literacy. Dr Al Murshidi received award for her book "The Guide of Creativity and Innovation in the UAE", by His Highness Sheikh Hamad bin Mohammed Al Sharqi, the Ruler of the emirate Fujairah and a member of the Supreme Council in the UAE. She led a national, multidisciplinary research project "A Comparative Study of Emirati students' Academic Experiences at UAE University, Zayed University and Higher College of Technology" which was funded by United Arab Emirates University - National Research Foundation. She was the Emirati expert in international research project "A Comparative Study of global citizenship in Arabic Countries Education" which was funded by Regional Centre of Quality and Excellence in Education, KSA. She received the Young Emirati Researcher Prize and the best Young researcher award. For her community service, she received Emirati women award.

Bridget K. Mulvey received her MS in geological sciences from Indiana University in 2003. She taught science in a K-12 setting for five years before returning to school for a Ph.D. in education from the University of Virginia. She is currently

About the Contributors

an associate professor of science education at Kent State University in Ohio, USA. She teaches and researches teaching and learning related to technology, inquiry/scientific practices, nature of science/scientific inquiry, and equity.

Asil Özdoğru is an associate professor in the Department of Psychology at Üsküdar University in İstanbul, Turkey. Dr. Özdoğru completed his undergraduate degree in Guidance and Psychological Counseling and Psychology double major program at Boğaziçi University. He received his master's, certificate of advanced study, and doctorate degrees in educational psychology from the University at Albany, State University of New York. His areas of research interest include child development, adult learning, applied psychology, and team science.

Hasan Al-Wadi is an associate professor of language education in the Department of English Language Education – Bahrain Teachers College. He teaches research methods in education, principles and pratices of ELT, Best Practices in ELT, language testing and English for educational leaders. He published in several international and indexed referred journals and his research interest is teacher education, curriculum development, critical pedagogy in ESL/EFL, CPD in education, and professional knowledge of ELT. Dr. Hasan is a senior fellow of the Advance Higher Education in UK and a member of several professional networks and associations.

Wiltrud Weidinger, Prof. Dr.Phil., works as a professor for international education and transversal competencies in the management, project design, and planning as well as implementation, evaluation, and counseling at the Department for International Projects in Education, Centre for Teaching and Transcultural Learning of the Zurich University of Teacher Education, Switzerland. Her qualifications include a doctorate in Education and a Master's degree in Education/Psychology from the University of Vienna, a Master of Science in Education (School Psychology) from the City University of New York. As a project leader for various international projects in different contexts, she is familiar with the Southeastern/Eastern European and the African educational systems and project implementation mechanisms. Her research expertise includes self-competences and life skills of adolescents and children, focusing on vulnerable groups and implementation mechanisms and standards for study programmes in teacher pre- and in-service education.

Elaine Wright works to support educational research in the United Arab Emirates. She has a history of working within the field of education internationally and has an emerging interest in research topics such as international and comparative education and contextualisation of education, specifically within the Arabian Peninsula, where she has been living since 2011.

Index

B

Bahrain 39-41, 49-50, 73, 91-96, 98-103, 106
Bangladesh 73-75, 77-90
bilingual programs 108-109, 111, 115, 119, 121
Bio-Medical Lens on Mental Health 175
BRAZ-TESOL 108-109, 111, 113-114, 118-119, 121-122
BrELT 108-109, 111-113, 117-118, 121

C

cascade model 31, 36, 215, 224, 230
collaboration 7, 16, 33, 40, 66, 86, 94, 100, 102, 111, 204, 207, 209, 215, 218, 220-221, 223, 230, 237-238, 241-242
Collaborative and Participatory Teams 178, 203
college education 73-77, 82, 84, 86-87
Communication and Autism Team (CAT) 96, 100, 106
community of practice 1-2, 4, 6-7, 14-15, 17-18, 22, 71, 214
Comparative Education 88, 102, 202
Continuous Professional Development 41, 53, 101, 225, 228

D

deficit model 152, 158-159, 169, 175
digital tools 232-233, 235, 239, 241, 243

E

early childhood 23-38, 183, 203, 217, 224, 227, 230
early childhood care and education 23-26, 31-33, 35, 37-38
Early Childhood Program Quality 38
Early Childhood Workforce 38
earth science 1, 21-22
Earth System Science 2-4, 7, 10-11, 16-17, 22
Education Health and Care Plan (EHC) 94, 106
effective 3, 7, 10, 16, 18-19, 23, 31-33, 41, 47-48, 62, 73, 79, 84-86, 98-102, 104, 111-112, 119, 130, 138, 142, 146, 149, 151, 160-161, 170, 177, 179-181, 186-187, 193-194, 199, 201, 203, 206-207, 215-216, 219, 221, 223-224, 232-233, 238-239, 242, 244

G

GPS 6, 11-13, 15

I

ICT 76, 89, 125, 183, 193, 210, 232-243, 245-247
inclusion 32, 37, 91-97, 99-106, 110, 149, 151, 155, 158, 160, 162-163, 168
inclusive education 29, 31, 91-96, 99-106, 164
inclusive practice 92, 100
inclusive school 93-94, 96, 101, 158, 168

Index

inquiry 1-4, 6, 8-18, 20, 22, 71, 174
in-service education 24, 27-31, 38
in-service EFL/ESL teachers 39
in-service teacher training 33, 96, 101, 123-125, 171, 231
in-service teachers 95, 143, 152, 209, 230
in-service training 23, 25, 28, 30-31, 40, 91, 94-95, 101, 108-109, 124-127, 129, 134-136, 142, 146, 160
integration 1-2, 10, 18, 22, 91, 100, 106, 133, 135, 162, 216, 218, 242-243, 245

K

K-12 sector 149, 151-152, 155, 159, 161

L

learning 1-4, 6-8, 14-15, 17-23, 27-29, 31, 33-35, 38, 40-42, 44-57, 59-60, 62, 64, 66-69, 71, 76, 80, 82, 85, 87-89, 94, 97-98, 100, 103, 105-109, 111-113, 116, 118, 121-127, 129-146, 148, 151, 153, 157, 160, 162-169, 171, 173-175, 179-181, 190, 192-199, 201, 203-219, 221-235, 237-239, 241-246
lesson study 39, 43-51, 204, 210-213, 217-219, 226-228, 231
Local Authority 97, 106

M

maps 3, 8-9, 12-14, 17
mental health 149-150, 154, 156, 158, 163-176
Mental Health First Aid 167, 170, 175
mentoring 53-54, 70, 72, 80, 100, 108-109, 115-116, 119-122, 126-131, 134-137, 139-145, 207
Ministry of Primary and Secondary Education (MoPSE) 178, 197, 203, 215, 227
model lessons 1, 6, 14-15, 17-18, 141, 147

N

National Institute of Education (NIE) 40, 209, 228, 231
Next Generation Science Standards 4, 20, 22
non-Arabic speakers 98, 101, 106

P

peer mentoring 129, 131, 139-140
peer-to-peer learning 123, 126, 131-134, 137
policymakers 41, 205, 231
postdoctoral scholars 52-54, 56, 59-60, 63-69, 71
Post-Modern Approaches to Mental Health 176
Preschool Teachers 23, 27-28, 168
preservice education 23, 25, 27-28, 30, 38
pre-service teacher training 149-150, 152, 154-155, 157-162
process 23-25, 27, 32, 42, 44, 48, 57, 59, 62-64, 66-67, 69, 71-73, 79, 126-127, 129, 134-141, 154, 161-162, 177-178, 180, 186-189, 193-195, 199, 202, 206-208, 214, 222, 225, 231, 239
professional development 1-8, 10, 13, 16-21, 23, 28, 30-33, 36, 38-44, 46, 48, 50-51, 53, 55, 64, 66, 68-70, 73, 75-76, 79, 82-84, 86, 89, 91-93, 95-96, 98, 101-105, 108, 115, 127-129, 150, 152, 165, 169, 171, 173-174, 177-178, 180, 183, 185-187, 190, 197-199, 201-220, 222-230, 232-247
Pupil School Support (PSS) 96, 106

S

scalability 86
school development 123, 125-127, 135, 139-142, 179, 185, 229
school embedded 178
school-based committees 177-178, 187, 189, 193-195, 203
scientific inquiry 3, 6, 8-9, 13-14, 22
Scientific Practices 1, 22
Secretary's Merit Award (SMA) 183-184, 197-198, 203
Situated Learning 7, 20, 22
social model of disability 150, 155, 158-

301

160, 162, 176
Special Educational Needs (SEN) 91, 106
staff development 129, 131, 141, 180-182, 186-187, 189-192, 198, 203, 215, 225, 227, 229
Subject Cluster 231

T

teacher attitudes 91, 93, 96, 98-99, 103-104
Teacher Education 19, 21, 27-31, 33, 35-36, 40, 49-51, 70, 81, 91-93, 95, 102-106, 110, 120, 122-124, 126, 128, 143-144, 147, 162-166, 169-172, 174, 182, 202, 205-206, 209, 212-215, 218, 222, 224-230, 246
teacher ownership 73, 81-83, 86, 88-89
teacher professional development 2-4, 6, 18-20, 30-31, 40, 89, 91, 93, 105, 127, 165, 173, 177-178, 180, 183, 185-187, 190, 197-199, 201, 203-207, 209-212, 214-215, 217, 220, 222-226, 228, 230, 232-245, 247
Teacher Self-Efficacy 173, 211, 231
teacher training 28, 33, 55, 76, 94-96, 98, 101, 115, 123-125, 128, 138, 140, 149-150, 152, 154-155, 157-162, 171, 182, 209, 217, 222-223, 231, 235, 245
teaching associations 118
teaching experiences 43, 52-54, 59-60, 62-63, 67, 69, 196
technology 1-4, 6-18, 20-22, 31, 35, 59-61, 80, 89, 113-114, 120-121, 157, 164, 172-173, 183, 193, 211, 214, 216, 219-220, 225, 232-233, 235, 237-238, 240, 244-246
technology-enhanced instruction 10, 13-14, 22
TESOL 88, 113, 120-121
transformation 22, 75, 127, 149, 240

U

UAE 232-236, 238-246

V

Virtual Online Community 108

W

work embedded 177, 180, 203
World Bank 73-79, 86, 88-90, 182, 201, 203

Recommended Reference Books

IGI Global's reference books can now be purchased from three unique pricing formats:
Print Only, E-Book Only, or Print + E-Book.
Shipping fees may apply.

www.igi-global.com

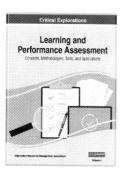

Learning and Performance Assessment

ISBN: 978-1-7998-0420-8
EISBN: 978-1-7998-0421-5
© 2020; 1,757 pp.
List Price: US$ 1,975

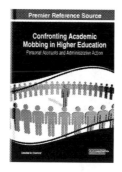

Confronting Academic Mobbing in Higher Education

ISBN: 978-1-5225-9485-7
EISBN: 978-1-5225-9487-1
© 2020; 301 pp.
List Price: US$ 195

Cases on Models and Methods for STEAM Education

ISBN: 978-1-5225-9631-8
EISBN: 978-1-5225-9637-0
© 2020; 379 pp.
List Price: US$ 195

Teaching, Learning, and Leading With Computer Simulations

ISBN: 978-1-7998-0004-0
EISBN: 978-1-7998-0006-4
© 2020; 337 pp.
List Price: US$ 195

Form, Function, and Style in Instructional Design

ISBN: 978-1-5225-9833-6
EISBN: 978-1-5225-9835-0
© 2020; 203 pp.
List Price: US$ 155

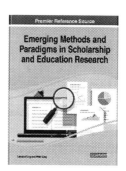

Emerging Methods and Paradigms in Scholarship and Education Research

ISBN: 978-1-7998-1001-8
EISBN: 978-1-7998-1003-2
© 2020; 330 pp.
List Price: US$ 195

Do you want to stay current on the latest research trends, product announcements, news, and special offers?
Join IGI Global's mailing list to receive customized recommendations, exclusive discounts, and more.
Sign up at: **www.igi-global.com/newsletters**

Publisher of Peer-Reviewed, Timely, and Innovative Academic Research   **IGI Global**
PUBLISHER OF TIMELY KNOWLEDGE

www.igi-global.com   Sign up at www.igi-global.com/newsletters   facebook.com/igiglobal   twitter.com/igiglobal

Ensure Quality Research is Introduced to the Academic Community

Become an Evaluator for IGI Global Authored Book Projects

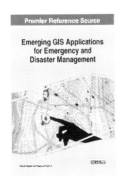

The overall success of an authored book project is dependent on quality and timely manuscript evaluations.

Applications and Inquiries may be sent to:
development@igi-global.com

Applicants must have a doctorate (or equivalent degree) as well as publishing, research, and reviewing experience. Authored Book Evaluators are appointed for one-year terms and are expected to complete at least three evaluations per term. Upon successful completion of this term, evaluators can be considered for an additional term.

If you have a colleague that may be interested in this opportunity, we encourage you to share this information with them.

IGI Global Author Services

Providing a high-quality, affordable, and expeditious service, IGI Global's Author Services enable authors to streamline their publishing process, increase chance of acceptance, and adhere to IGI Global's publication standards.

Benefits of Author Services:

- **Professional Service:** All our editors, designers, and translators are experts in their field with years of experience and professional certifications.
- **Quality Guarantee & Certificate:** Each order is returned with a quality guarantee and certificate of professional completion.
- **Timeliness:** All editorial orders have a guaranteed return timeframe of 3-5 business days and translation orders are guaranteed in 7-10 business days.
- **Affordable Pricing:** IGI Global Author Services are competitively priced compared to other industry service providers.
- **APC Reimbursement:** IGI Global authors publishing Open Access (OA) will be able to deduct the cost of editing and other IGI Global author services from their OA APC publishing fee.

Author Services Offered:

English Language Copy Editing
Professional, native English language copy editors improve your manuscript's grammar, spelling, punctuation, terminology, semantics, consistency, flow, formatting, and more.

Scientific & Scholarly Editing
A Ph.D. level review for qualities such as originality and significance, interest to researchers, level of methodology and analysis, coverage of literature, organization, quality of writing, and strengths and weaknesses.

Figure, Table, Chart & Equation Conversions
Work with IGI Global's graphic designers before submission to enhance and design all figures and charts to IGI Global's specific standards for clarity.

Translation
Providing 70 language options, including Simplified and Traditional Chinese, Spanish, Arabic, German, French, and more.

Hear What the Experts Are Saying About IGI Global's Author Services

"Publishing with IGI Global has been *an amazing experience* for me for sharing my research. The *strong academic production* support ensures quality and timely completion." – Prof. Margaret Niess, Oregon State University, USA

"The service was *very fast, very thorough, and very helpful* in ensuring our chapter meets the criteria and requirements of the book's editors. I was *quite impressed and happy* with your service." – Prof. Tom Brinthaupt, Middle Tennessee State University, USA

Learn More or Get Started Here: For Questions, Contact IGI Global's Customer Service Team at cust@igi-global.com or 717-533-8845

Celebrating Over 30 Years of Scholarly Knowledge Creation & Dissemination

www.igi-global.com

InfoSci®-Books

A Database of Nearly 6,000 Reference Books Containing Over 105,000+ Chapters Focusing on Emerging Research

GAIN ACCESS TO **THOUSANDS** OF REFERENCE BOOKS AT **A FRACTION** OF THEIR INDIVIDUAL LIST **PRICE**.

InfoSci®-Books Database

The **InfoSci®-Books** is a database of nearly 6,000 IGI Global single and multi-volume reference books, handbooks of research, and encyclopedias, encompassing groundbreaking research from prominent experts worldwide that spans over 350+ topics in 11 core subject areas including business, computer science, education, science and engineering, social sciences, and more.

Open Access Fee Waiver (Read & Publish) Initiative

For any library that invests in IGI Global's InfoSci-Books and/or InfoSci-Journals (175+ scholarly journals) databases, IGI Global will match the library's investment with a fund of equal value to go toward **subsidizing the OA article processing charges (APCs) for their students, faculty, and staff** at that institution when their work is submitted and accepted under OA into an IGI Global journal.*

INFOSCI® PLATFORM FEATURES

- Unlimited Simultaneous Access
- No DRM
- No Set-Up or Maintenance Fees
- A Guarantee of No More Than a 5% Annual Increase for Subscriptions
- Full-Text HTML and PDF Viewing Options
- Downloadable MARC Records
- COUNTER 5 Compliant Reports
- Formatted Citations With Ability to Export to RefWorks and EasyBib
- No Embargo of Content (Research is Available Months in Advance of the Print Release)

*The fund will be offered on an annual basis and expire at the end of the subscription period. The fund would renew as the subscription is renewed for each year thereafter. The open access fees will be waived after the student, faculty, or staff's paper has been vetted and accepted into an IGI Global journal and the fund can only be used toward publishing OA in an IGI Global journal. Libraries in developing countries will have the match on their investment doubled.

To Recommend or Request a Free Trial:
www.igi-global.com/infosci-books

eresources@igi-global.com • Toll Free: 1-866-342-6657 ext. 100 • Phone: 717-533-8845 x100

Publisher of Peer-Reviewed, Timely, and
Innovative Academic Research Since 1988

IGI Global's Transformative Open Access (OA) Model:
How to Turn Your University Library's Database Acquisitions Into a Source of OA Funding

Well in advance of Plan S, IGI Global unveiled their OA Fee Waiver (Read & Publish) Initiative. Under this initiative, librarians who invest in IGI Global's InfoSci-Books and/or InfoSci-Journals databases will be able to subsidize their patrons' OA article processing charges (APCs) when their work is submitted and accepted (after the peer review process) into an IGI Global journal.

How Does it Work?

Step 1: Library Invests in the InfoSci-Databases: A library perpetually purchases or subscribes to the InfoSci-Books, InfoSci-Journals, or discipline/subject databases.

Step 2: IGI Global Matches the Library Investment with OA Subsidies Fund: IGI Global provides a fund to go towards subsidizing the OA APCs for the library's patrons.

Step 3: Patron of the Library is Accepted into IGI Global Journal (After Peer Review): When a patron's paper is accepted into an IGI Global journal, they option to have their paper published under a traditional publishing model or as OA.

Step 4: IGI Global Will Deduct APC Cost from OA Subsidies Fund: If the author decides to publish under OA, the OA APC fee will be deducted from the OA subsidies fund.

Step 5: Author's Work Becomes Freely Available: The patron's work will be freely available under CC BY copyright license, enabling them to share it freely with the academic community.

Note: This fund will be offered on an annual basis and will renew as the subscription is renewed for each year thereafter. IGI Global will manage the fund and award the APC waivers unless the librarian has a preference as to how the funds should be managed.

Hear From the Experts on This Initiative:

"I'm very happy to have been able to make one of my recent research contributions *freely available* along with having access to the *valuable resources* found within IGI Global's InfoSci-Journals database."

– **Prof. Stuart Palmer**,
Deakin University, Australia

"Receiving the support from IGI Global's OA Fee Waiver Initiative *encourages me to continue my research work without any hesitation.*"

– **Prof. Wenlong Liu**, College of Economics and Management at Nanjing University of Aeronautics & Astronautics, China

For More Information, Scan the QR Code or Contact:
IGI Global's Digital Resources Team at eresources@igi-global.com.

Printed in the United States
by Baker & Taylor Publisher Services